Decline to Fall

THE TREASURY TEAM—1976

From the left—Derek Mitchell, Alan Lord, Denis Healey, the Author, Bryan Hopkin, Leo Pliatzky, Joel Barnett

Decline To Fall

The Making of British Macro-Economic Policy and the 1976 IMF Crisis

Douglas Wass

OXFORD
UNIVERSITY PRESS

OXFORD

UNIVERSITY PRESS

Great Clarendon Street, Oxford OX2 6DP

Oxford University Press is a department of the University of Oxford.
It furthers the University's objective of excellence in research, scholarship,
and education by publishing worldwide in

Oxford New York

Auckland Cape Town Dar es Salaam Hong Kong Karachi
Kuala Lumpur Madrid Melbourne Mexico City Nairobi
New Delhi Shanghai Taipei Toronto

With offices in

Argentina Austria Brazil Chile Czech Republic France Greece
Guatemala Hungary Italy Japan Poland Portugal Singapore
South Korea Switzerland Thailand Turkey Ukraine Vietnam

Oxford is a registered trade mark of Oxford University Press
in the UK and in certain other countries

Published in the United States
by Oxford University Press Inc., New York

© Douglas Wass 2008

The moral rights of the author have been asserted
Database right Oxford University Press (maker)

First published 2008

All rights reserved. No part of this publication may be reproduced,
stored in a retrieval system, or transmitted, in any form or by any means,
without the prior permission in writing of Oxford University Press,
or as expressly permitted by law, or under terms agreed with the appropriate
reprographics rights organization. Enquiries concerning reproduction
outside the scope of the above should be sent to the Rights Department,
Oxford University Press, at the address above

You must not circulate this book in any other binding or cover
and you must impose the same condition on any acquirer

British Library Cataloguing in Publication Data
Data available

Library of Congress Cataloging in Publication Data
Data available

Typeset by SPI Publisher Services, Pondicherry, India
Printed in Great Britain
on acid-free paper by
Biddles Ltd., King's Lynn, Norfolk

ISBN 978-0-19-953474-6

1 3 5 7 9 10 8 6 4 2

Dedication

This book is dedicated to the memory of the Treasury Historical Section which produced a series of histories of various strands of Treasury policy from the late 1950s until it was closed down, as one of the economy measures of 1976.

Contents

Acknowledgements

I owe a debt of gratitude to many people for the help they gave me in the preparation of this book, and it would be invidious to list them in any order of my appreciation of the magnitude of their help. But first and foremost I must thank Her Majesty's Treasury for the permission they gave me to embark on the work involved before the release of the relevant documents to the National Archives and for the help they gave me in tracking them down in the various Treasury Registries and then making them available to me. Principal among the officials involved is Irene Ripley, an old colleague from the days when I was myself in the department. Her skill, professionalism and willingness to go far beyond the call of duty in searching for the documents I wanted—and indeed in identifying documents I would otherwise have overlooked—has made this whole undertaking, for me, worthwhile and rewarding. To her also I am indebted for the patient instruction she gave me how to navigate the website of the National Archives. I also single out for thanks Gus O'Donnell who spontaneously offered the services of the department when I broached the idea of making a study of the 1976 crisis and Nick Macpherson, his successor as Permanent Secretary, who read the finished manuscript and gave me encouragement to proceed with publication.

To the other institutions involved in the history, the Bank of England and the International Monetary Fund, I am also indebted, particularly to their archivists, Sarah Millard and Michelle Dolbec respectively. They both provided invaluable help in the tracking down of relevant papers which were lodged in their registries. I am grateful to them also for their ready willingness to grant permission for me to quote from the papers of which they were the custodians. I also received useful help in the form of comment and suggestion at various stages of the work from the Bank's professional historians, Forrest Capie and Michael Anson. I would also like to thank the Bank's librarian for granting me liberal access to the Bank's excellent collection of relevant journals, periodicals, and statistical material.

Two other public bodies helped greatly with the study—the National Archives and the British Library. To the former I am indebted for their ready consent to my quoting from documents which are Crown Copyright. More particularly I wish to express my appreciation for the comprehensiveness of their cataloguing system and for its accessibility to laymen such as myself. Their use of advanced information technology has made the job of the researcher of public records so much easier than it must have been a generation ago. Their staff too showed a willingness to help to solve those more abstruse problems which were not amenable to electronic treatment and this made the visits to Kew such a pleasure. Much the same is true of the British Library, whose staff, particularly those in the Social Sciences Reading Room, went out of their way to help me to search the complex catalogues of Parliamentary publications and to suggest avenues which I would not, without their help, have identified.

Among those who read the manuscript at its various stages of evolution and offered comment and criticism, I salute with grateful thanks Bryan Hopkin, Hans Liesner, Fred Atkinson, Alan Bailey, and John Grieve Smith—all old comrades from my days in the Civil Service. I also acknowledge the helpful comments of one outside expert on the 1976 crisis—Michael Oliver. I profited greatly from what they all had to say, though I did not always accept their suggestions. Consequently they must be acquitted of any charge of conspiracy in the perpetration of those errors, either of fact or judgement, which lie embodied in the text. The shortcomings of the book in this respect are the result of my own doing or not doing, and mine alone.

Finally I acknowledge with gratitude the constructive and supportive part in the whole venture played by my publishers Oxford University Press and in particular by the Economics and Finance Editor, Sarah Caro. They have given me the sort of help and encouragement of which every writer must feel in need as he nears the completion of his work and wonders, doubtingly perhaps, whether he has really succeeded in the task he set himself. I am indeed grateful to them for the reassurance they gave me and for the confidence they have shown throughout in the value of this work.

Douglas Wass
June 2007

Preface

This book began life as a review of the events which led to the UK requesting a standby from the International Monetary Fund (IMF) in December 1976. Public interest in this episode has manifested itself on and off without much respite over the thirty years since it took place, and there have been many accounts of it from people who participated in it, as well as from academic historians. It could reasonably be argued that enough is known about its origins, how it developed and how it was resolved for it to be plausibly held that any further examination is unnecessary. I believe this to be wrong, mainly, though no means only, because most of the accounts which have appeared have not been based on all the official documents created at the time, and, apart from public statements and published papers, have relied very largely on the recollections of those who were at close quarters with the main events. Most of these recorded recollections have a substantial element of verisimilitude to them, and they certainly form a valuable corpus of information for the historian. But the fact that even those who have written at first hand have not had access to all the relevant documents means that they form an incomplete account of the events of that year. It is also the case that many of the memoirs and diaries which constitute some of the accounts have an element of self-justification to them and are selective in what they reveal. Moreover a certain amount of the evidence quoted is either hearsay or consists of non-attributable comment, and cannot be verified independently. The principal memorialists have been Denis Healey, James Callaghan, Edmund Dell, and Joel Barnett and, at the adviser level, Bernard Donoughue. Their contributions have been supplemented by the published diaries of other former Ministers, notably Tony Benn. All these contribute to an understanding of the economic problems faced by the Government in 1976—and what is more to an understanding of the dilemmas it had to resolve. They also provide a valuable perspective on the purely political aspects of the crisis. But they have been written, usually as part of a wider memoir, and largely on the basis of memory supplemented by personal notes. They fall well short of an objective account of what happened and indeed many of them contain notable errors of fact. Sometimes the memorialists offer differing and conflicting accounts of the same events. The diarists too offer interesting insights into the events, by providing, in a way that a formal, written record cannot, a sense of the atmosphere and indeed drama of what was happening. Benn likens the attitude of the Treasury and the Ministers who went along with the Treasury to the *Pétainistes* of 1940—defeatists at heart. Others have also drawn a parallel with 1940 but they have presented the government in the opposite sense—as an embattled Britain, fighting against overwhelming odds against attacks from abroad. This is interesting colour and it makes for a lively account, but it is only colour, hardly fact. And the fact that the memoirs are all the work of politicians means that they dwell on the political aspect of the crisis and give little weight to the technical and economic aspects. None of this detracts from the value of their accounts, but the final arbiter of what actually happened must be the contemporaneous written record. Moreover, at the end of the day, although political factors did play an immensely important part in contributing to the successful outcome, it was the technical analysis and the technical negotiations between officials, of both the Treasury and the Fund, which produced the essence of what was finally agreed and accepted. None of the memorialists give any weight to this. The historians who have so far written about this episode have, for their part, drawn on these memoirs and have supplemented their evidence by oral interviews with some of the participants. But they too have been hampered by not having access to the full written record and have relied, perhaps a little too readily, on what—years after the events—the participants consulted have been able to recall. Some of this is inaccurate. One of them for instance (Bernstein) describes the emergence of a two-year programme with the Fund (rather than one for a single year) as a breakthrough in the negotiations at a late stage and this statement is repeated in subsequent histories. In fact, although the acceptance of a two-year programme was important to the Fund, the Treasury never resisted the idea—it had formed an important part of the requirements they set out in Manila at the Annual Meeting of the Fund in early October. The important breakthrough occurred when Ministers allowed the Treasury to discuss possible packages of measures, one of which was known to be close to what the Fund wanted. The objective historian therefore must always wait for the release of classified official records before he[1] makes his considered judgements, for only then will he get something approximating to the full and accurate picture. This means that it is only now, thirty or more years after the events described, that anything like a full account can be given. If I have, perhaps arrogantly, given myself the task of doing this, I have to confess that I have been handicapped by the fact that I was myself a participant in the events of

---

[1] I have taken the liberty throughout this work of using the pronoun 'he' for any indeterminate person. I hope that my female readers will pardon the presumption, which I make solely in the interest of economy.

that year, having been the Permanent Secretary to the Treasury before, during and after the crisis. I do not believe that anyone as closely involved as I was can be wholly objective, and I confess to a lurking desire now that the records are on public display not to be found wanting in what I did—and what I did not do—that eventful year. My motive in attempting this account however is not apologetic but is to ensure that those who are interested in this episode have all the relevant material. I have therefore tried to detach myself from events and to record facts, minutes, and memoranda irrespective of whether I do or do not emerge with a great deal of credit. I leave it to others to decide whether I have made a reasonable stab at such an objective aim.

But if there are intrinsic reasons why a participant cannot write with complete objectivity—and certainly should not lay claim to do so—there are good reasons why he should at least make a contribution to historical knowledge. He after all knows where the relevant papers are and is less likely than an outsider to overlook, by accident, some vital piece of information which has got onto the wrong file. But even he, as I found in my research, may not see all the files, since some have been destroyed—not out of mischief, but usually because a decision was taken sometime in the past, in good faith, to destroy papers that were thought to have no enduring value. I myself failed to find some documents which I knew existed at one time and which I believed were relevant to the history. I have been very cautious in inserting any unsubstantiated recollection I might have of particular events, although my recollection has perhaps enabled me to give a particular and possibly personal emphasis on what the written records reveal.

There is, I think, another reason why an account by a participant may have some value over and above an 'independent' narration of the events. 'History' said C. V. Wedgwood, 'is lived forwards but is written in retrospect. We know the end before we consider the beginning and we can never wholly recapture what it was to know the beginning only'.[2] That is true, but a participant *can* recall what it was like to have to deal with a situation where the end was not known. I have tried to write this account capturing, if only by selective quotation, what it was like at the time not to know the end.

As I conducted my research and contemplated presenting its findings, it became increasingly evident to me that a proper understanding of the motives and the behaviour of those who participated in the events of 1976 required an appreciation of how they had come about and what influenced them. This in a sense is true of any history. But a line has to be drawn somewhere—an effort has to be made by the historian to determine where to begin and what in effect constitute the boundaries of his research. It seemed to me as I reflected on this that the events of 1976 had their origins essentially in what the Labour Government had committed itself to when it took office in March 1974, and

---

[2] 'William the Silent', 1943.

what it had done in the field of macro-economic policy in office in the two and a half years prior to the onset of the crisis. Of course events prior to that date were important too—notably the quintupling of oil prices in the autumn of 1973 and the upsurge in inflation even earlier. But these can be thought of as, so to speak, 'given' conditions. I believe that it was what the Government of the time did, or did not do, in the three years up to the IMF drawing that were the prime determinants of what happened in the autumn of 1976. I hope that my account will justify that belief.

So I decided to broaden the study and look at the immediate antecedents of the crisis. But although I did this, I also limited the extension very precisely. I decided that I would concentrate on those events which were relevant to the making of UK macro-economic policy and would eschew those activities in government—and outside—which were not strictly relevant to the making of that policy. It was after all the failure, or the perceived failure, of macro-economic policy which led to the crisis, and it was solely in the field of macro-economic policy that the remedy for it was found. These considerations led me to define the ambit—and make the subtitle—of this book 'The Making of British Macro-Economic Policy and the 1976 IMF Crisis'. It is not therefore an account of the development of the British economy over the period leading up to the crisis, although of course I have referred to economic events, of both a macro- and a micro- kind where they had to be taken into account by the policy makers. Nor does it deal, except parenthetically, to the making of *micro-economic* policy. It does not for instance give much space to the policy of the government to take significant parts of the private sector into public owner-ship, for example the shipbuilding and aircraft industries, or by enabling the new National Enterprise Board to acquire industrial assets, or to use the powers of the Industry Act to encourage the private sector to enter into so-called Planning Agreements with the Government. Nor does it deal, except ob-liquely, with the government's approach to the development of an Industrial Strategy in the autumn of 1975 by engaging the two sides of industry with the relevant government department under the auspices of the National Eco-nomic Development Council in an attempt to remove obstacles to growth and promote efficiency at the industrial sector level. My neglect of these issues is not out of disdain for their relevance to economic performance. It is solely due to my classifying them as outside the area of macro-economic policy, and therefore largely irrelevant to the emergence of the 1976 crisis and to its resolution.

In another important respect my study is somewhat circumscribed. It is an account essentially of how the Treasury, and to some extent the Bank of England, formulated their ideas about macro-policy, what conclusions they came to, and how they sought to persuade Ministers—first the Chancellor and thereafter when necessary the Cabinet—to their way of thinking. My justification is that it was Treasury analysis, and Treasury thinking that for the most part formed the basis of Ministerial decisions and hence for the making of macro-economic policy. No doubt many will say that therein lay our problem and that it would have been better for all concerned if there had been other sources of advice to challenge the officials in the Treasury. To some extent of course there were such sources. At various times the Central Policy Review Staff (CPRS), based in the Cabinet Office, presented ministers with their views on macro-economic policy. But these were usually at a high degree of generality, and in any case scarcely differed from what the Treasury were saying—hardly surprising as there was a great deal of collaboration and consultation between the CPRS and the Treasury at the working level. There was also advice coming to the Chancellor from his special adviser, for most of this period Lord Kaldor. Although located in the Treasury and a recipient of all the main Treasury papers, Kaldor did not accept by any means all that the Treasury were saying. He had strong and idiosyncratic views on a great deal of macro-economic policy and did not hesitate to express them both to officials and to the Chancellor. But the record shows that, except for one or two instances, his advice and prescription were not accepted either by officials or by Ministers, and I have not included in my account all those occasions where he differed from the Treasury and offered his own remedy for the ills the economy endured. He was a stimulant to the Treasury, but his influence on policy was minimal.

But if Ministers collectively did not have anything like the access to information and technical advice that was available to the Chancellor and his Treasury colleagues, many of them had strong opinions about the direction of policy and they did not shrink from expressing them in Cabinet and Cabinet Committee discussions. They also raised powerful objections to the Chancellor's arguments when these appeared to them to be unconvincing. The narrative gives full weight to those opinions and those objections—every Cabinet and Cabinet Committee meeting on macro-economic policy is documented in these pages—but what emerges is how little these opinions were backed by rigorous appraisal and material evidence and how little they affected the ultimate outcome of the collective consideration of economic policy. For this reason I have not taken the reader through every nuance of argument that took place in the prolonged Cabinet discussions of macro-economic policy.

I give little prominence to the role of the Chancellor's ministerial colleagues in the Treasury apart from Harold Lever who, as Chancellor of the Duchy of Lancaster, was not formally in the Treasury but received most of the relevant Treasury papers and participated in many of the meetings on policy the Chancellor had with his official advisers. The other Treasury ministers were Edmund Dell, the Paymaster-General, Joel Barnett, the Chief Secretary, and Robert Sheldon, the Financial Secretary. Dell and Barnet have written their own memoirs, which give their accounts of some of the events which I describe. The official documents suggest, and this is my own recollection, that none of them made a significant impact on the business of macro-economic policy making—indeed Dell openly admits this as far as he was concerned. Barnet, although not at the time a member of the Cabinet, had a considerable role in the deliberations about the public expenditure survey and he was undoubtedly the 'work-horse' who had to carry out most of the bilateral discussions with the spending ministers and press the Treasury case. But when it came to specific decisions about the aggregate level of spending to aim at, it was the official Treasury who carried out the analysis and made the recommendations and the Chancellor, not his colleagues, who took the decisions. The other two Ministers in the Treasury (Dell and Sheldon) played an important role in relation to the detailed operations of the Customs and Excise, the Inland Revenue, the Royal Mint, the National Debt Office, and the other 'Treasury' Departments, but they too made only a marginal contribution to the evolution of macro-economic policy. In his own account Dell describes his position on some of the macro-economic issues but in fact he wrote very little[3] at the time and his contribution consisted largely of oral comments in the course of the Chancellor's meetings, many of which were of a lapidary character and did not get recorded. He was in the Treasury from March 1974 until April 1976 and did not therefore participate in the Treasury discussions during the financial crisis, although by this time he was in the Cabinet and proved to be one of the Chancellor's few outright supporters. In the earlier period he clearly favoured a very restrictive approach to fiscal policy, but the Chancellor did not seem disposed to follow his advice (as he himself notes), which was not backed up by any analysis. He shared the Treasury's concern about the exchange rate, but again did not press his views. I have brought his comments into the narrative where they were relevant, but they do not occupy a great deal of space.

There were of course important exceptions to the general description I have given of the way policy was made. The whole thrust of macro-economic policy in 1974 for instance was determined by the commitments the Labour Party had entered into with the TUC before the election in February that year; and the mini-Budget of July 1974, which probably had as its inspiration the need to prepare for a second General Election within a short space of time, was in effect the brain-child of Ministers, not their advisers. Even the taking of the Central Bank credit in June 1976 was based on an idea of one Minister, not the official Treasury. But these were exceptions and as exceptions I have given full weight to the thinking of the relevant Ministers behind these initiatives. I hope therefore that I shall be acquitted of the charge of having arrogantly put the

---

[3] In this respect he was not perhaps much different from most ministers, who wrote very little themselves and relied on the spoken word to convey their views. Nearly all the written ministerial material, including the papers they put to Cabinet, were drafted by their officials.

Treasury into an excessively prominent position in the determination of economic policy.

Because it was the Treasury which played such a crucial part in the evolution of policy my main sources, apart from Cabinet papers, have been Treasury files. But I have also used a certain amount of material which reposes in the Bank of England. I have not however drawn on such possibly relevant sources as the TUC archives or, with one or two exceptions, those of the IMF. In the former case I decided that what the TUC said or did not say to government ministers and officials and what they did publicly was what was relevant: and though it might be interesting to know for instance how far or near they were at particular times to breaking with the government on policy, what really mattered was what they eventually decided to do and on this the official files provided ample evidence. The same is true of the International Monetary Fund, whose archives I have not consulted in any detail. A great many of the Fund's documents on policy and practice were provided to the UK Economic Director in the ordinary course of business on a day-to-day basis and as such found their way to Treasury files which I have studied. Many others have been published as part of the Fund's programme of openness. The Fund has throughout its history published very full accounts of its activities. As for the Fund's papers during the vital negotiations in 1976 (and to some extent in 1975), the Fund set out their views and their position in documents which they presented to their British counterparts and these I have consulted. It might have been interesting to see what the Fund staff were saying privately to each other during the negotiations, but this would be of little relevance to the main issue of macro-economic policy. So the book is essentially about the Treasury and the Bank and the Ministers they served and is not an exhaustive account of what all the players—in private institutions and in foreign governments—were up to.

In constructing my account I became conscious that I could not avoid going into a certain amount of technical detail much of which the general reader would be bound to find dull, if not incomprehensible. I decided that the history could not avoid such detail without corrupting the story, so I have included it. But in doing so I felt that I owed it to the reader to explain these dimensions, even though the effect was to hold up the narrative and detract from the drama. The way that the annual public expenditure survey was (and so far as I know in its guise as the Comprehensive Spending Review still is) carried out and the time constraints it was subjected to played quite an important part in consideration of the substantive issue whether expenditure programmes could be adjusted in the way that people not familiar with the methodology demanded. Of course bureaucrats can always find reasons why political aims can be frustrated. But sometimes these reasons are compelling and the least that the disinterested observer needs to know is what these reasons are. So I have devoted a good deal of the first chapter of the book to explaining, for the non-technical reader, how the Treasury, functionally and intellectually, addressed itself in the 1970s to the business of economic forecasting, how monetary policy making adapted itself—or did not adapt itself—to the prevailing nostrums of the monetarists, how the problem of inflation was regarded and why such (to a present-day reader) antiquated ideas as incomes policy were thought to be the remedy for inflation, how the relationship of the Government to the Trade Union Movement complicated—although not always unhelpfully—the business of 'objective' policy making, how the mechanics of intervention in the foreign exchange markets took place and who the operators in those markets were. Much of this makes rather difficult reading and I have to ask the reader to bear with me if I appear excessively didactic and keep him waiting for the exciting bits. A. J. P. Taylor once said[4] that the beginnings of the First World War were imposed on the statesmen of Europe by railway timetables, and while he may have gone a little far in assigning to bureaucratic necessities such a determinant role, it is often the case—and it certainly was in 1976—that procedural issues impose constraints on choices which materially affect the outcome of events. I have therefore spent some time in the preliminary narrative dealing with 'timetables', for some of the decisions and events I have described were, in fact, greatly conditioned by them.

Writing this book has posed one problem which most writers of history—as opposed to memorialists—do not experience. I have wherever relevant—and that was quite frequently—referred to or quoted *ipsissima verba* from specific minutes or memoranda and I have given the names of the authors where these were necessary, although in general I have tried to depersonalise the narrative as much as possible by referring to the Treasury Division which produced the note rather than the individual. One reason for doing this is that the opinions and advice expressed, although usually signed by one individual, were really those of the Sector of the Treasury he worked in. A personalized account would, in my view, have given the impression of personal differences, whereas the differences, when they occurred, were usually of a functional kind. I have also referred to Ministers usually by the office they held, rather than by name, for what they said and did was, as was the case with officials, usually—though again not always—determined by the portfolio they held rather than out of personal opinion. For my own minutes I have in general referred to the author as the Treasury for I felt that I was really expressing a departmental view. Occasionally I have had to refer to myself and where I have done so I have used the third person singular (though I hope without sounding too much like General de Gaulle or Julius Caesar). All this means that there is a certain lack of consistency in the style and treatment of the subject. An outside

---

[4] 'The First World War', 1963.

historian would not have had this problem, but as I said earlier he might have had other problems.

This book claims to be a narrative of the making of macro-economic policy between the beginning of 1974 and the end of 1976. That is true, but I have also heeded the advice of E. L. Woodward[5]:

The writing of history is of its nature something more than the collection of historical material. It is idle to pretend that the foreground to the present can be forgotten. The great historians have had a sense of the value of civil society which has impelled them to pass judgments as well as to narrate what has happened; the very selection of their material from the mass of data implies these judgments.

I am conscious that I have made selections of what I have referred to or quoted from and have—albeit unconsciously—betrayed my prejudices. I cannot help that. But I have sought to be objective and to record evidence even where it now shows the Treasury in poor light. In the final chapter I have gone further and have attempted to make some deliberate judgements about matters where the Treasury's reputation is at issue. It is right to do this, because, as I have said the Treasury were responsible for most of the input to the making of macro-economic policy. But my judgements are bound to be subjective too, though not, I hope, unreasonably so. The most difficult matter that I had to address, and have reserved for the final chapter, is whether, in spite of (or perhaps because of) what had happened in the previous two years, the whole episode of the Fund standby in 1976 was unnecessary and whether it could have been avoided by more prudent management by officials, particularly Treasury officials—whether in fact, objectively, in the autumn of 1976 the UK's macro-economic policy was fundamentally flawed and needed to be corrected or whether in reality the whole episode was, as Denis Healey implies in his memoirs, a charade in which nothing really happened, but everyone thought it was *grand'chose*. That is the issue about which I hope this book will help the reader to make up his own mind.

The structure of the book is chronological, in that I have devoted one chapter to the events of 1974, one to those of 1975, and two to 1976. The reason for this is that, partly because of the nature of 'the timetables', a great deal of policy advice was structured round a calendar (though, more often than not, the Government's financial calendar which was not quite the same as the Gregorian calendar) and the beginning of each year did in some sense mark a renewal of policy. Breaking up the narrative into annual instalments did therefore make quite a lot of sense, although of course the end of each year was not quite the sharp break with the past that I have perhaps implied.

[5] 'Three Studies in European Conservatism' Constable 1927.

The exercise on which I have been engaged has in one sense been an exploration, but an exploration of territory which I thought I knew, but found when I read the papers that I knew less than I thought. Perhaps this is true of every exploration. As T. S. Eliot said:

> We shall not cease from exploration
> And the end of all our exploring
> Will be to arrive where we started
> And know the place for the first time

Douglas Wass
March 2007

Glossary

BEQB	Bank of England Quarterly Bulletin
BIS	The Bank for International Settlements—a Basel based institution of Central Banks, set up in 1930 to handle the reparation payments levied on Germany following the First World War, but subsequently developed as the institution for overseeing the central bank aspects of the international monetary system
Budget Committee	A Committee of senior Treasury and Revenue Department officials whose remit was to advise the Chancellor on the content of his Budget. Abolished in 1974 and replaced by STEP
Competition and Credit Control	A system introduced in 1971 of regulating the growth in the size of commercial banks' lending, based on general rules for the placing by the banks of deposits with the Bank of England in relation to the expansion of their individual liabilities
CBI	The Confederation of British Industry—the main employers' representative body
CDL	The Chancellor of the Duchy of Lancaster—a ministerial office, normally involving membership of the Cabinet, which was occupied in the Labour government by Harold Lever. He was treated *de facto* as a member of the Treasury team and had access to Treasury officials
Corset (The Supplementary Special Deposits Scheme)	A regulation laid down by the Bank of England intended to control the growth of the interest-bearing liabilities of the commercial banks. It operated only for specific periods and was sus-

	pended or re-instated as and when conditions required
CPRS	The Central Policy Review Staff—a small body established in the Cabinet Office in 1970 with a general remit to examine any area of government policy or practice and to present its findings directly to the Cabinet
EY	The term applied to the Ministerial Committee on Economic Strategy from April 1976
Financial Year	The standard period for the government's accounts, running from 1 April to 31 March the following calendar year
FSBR	Financial Statement and Budget Report—'The Red Book'—the publication at the time of each Budget of a summary of the economic outlook, of the state of the public finances and the details of the taxation changes proposed by the Budget
GAB	General Arrangements to Borrow—an agreement by the Group of Ten (q.v.) countries to lend a specific amount of their own currencies to the IMF to enable the latter to permit drawings from member countries which could not easily be accommodated within its own resources
G10	The Group of Ten industrialized countries, notably the USA, Japan, Germany, France, Canada, Italy, Holland, Belgium, Sweden, and the UK. Switzerland was associated with but not a member of the G10
HF	The Home Finance Divisions of the Treasury, responsible for government borrowing, interest rates, debt management, and monetary policy
IMF	International Monetary Fund—the international institution established in 1946 with responsibility for the regulation of the international monetary system. The UK was a founder member, and at the time of the events described was, in shareholding terms, the

	second largest member. It had the right to nominate its own Executive Director, who received all important Fund documents which he relayed to London as a matter of course
J-curve Effect	The phenomenon of the balance of payments for a time actually worsening in financial terms when a devaluation takes place and for the benefits only to come through after a delay—typically of the order of one year
£M3	The preferred measure of the money supply—roughly the aggregate of bank demand deposits in sterling, including interest bearing deposits, plus notes and coin in circulation
MES	The Ministerial Committee on Economic Strategy from March 1974 to April 1976
MISC	The label given to *ad hoc* Ministerial Committees serviced by the Cabinet Office from March 1974 till April 1976
MLR	Minimum Lending Rate—the annualized rate of interest at which the Bank of England would normally discount Treasury bills presented to it by the Discount Market. Introduced in October 1972 to replace Bank Rate, it was the main determining factor for short-term interest rates, though very short-term rates, e.g. for overnight money could, and often did, differ markedly from MLR. Now called Base Rate
MTA	Medium Term Assessment—a somewhat formal appraisal made by the Treasury of the medium-term outlook for the growth in resources to be available to be devoted to the main beneficiaries assuming trend growth and incorporating known commitments and requirements. Used as a basis for drawing up public expenditure plans
NEDC Six	The six members of the National Economic Development Council who were nominated by the TUC. They were the 'heavyweights' of the TUC General Council and had substantial authority with the whole trade union movement

NIESR	National Institute for Economic and Social Research—an independent research body which conducted its own short-term economic forecasts and published them in its quarterly review. There was a good deal of collaboration between the Institute and the Treasury, in which several of the Fellows had served
NIF	National Income Forecast—a short-term (18 month) economic forecast prepared by the Treasury three times each year
OECD	The Organisation for Economic Cooperation and Development, an international body set up in 1948 as a specific European body to administer the distribution and allocation of Marshall Aid, but later developed into a body for international cooperation in the area of finance and economics and for the coordination of Development Assistance. Its members eventually were all the countries of the industrial and developed world excluding the Soviet bloc
OF	The Overseas Finance Group of Divisions of the Treasury—responsible for international financial issues including foreign borrowing, the exchange rate and financial relations with other countries
OPEC	The Oil Producing and Exporting Countries. This was mainly the group of Middle Eastern producers and those in Africa and Latin America as well as Indonesia. Soviet bloc countries were not members
PCC	Policy Co-ordinating Committee—the committee of senior Treasury officials set up in December 1974 with an ongoing remit to draw together the threads of policies involving different instruments and to put its conclusions to the Chancellor
PE	The Public Sector Group of Divisions of the Treasury—responsible for the control and allocation of public expenditure

PEWP

The annual Public Expenditure White Paper, published early each year giving the government's plans for the growth in public spending over the ensuing four financial years. The PEWP for 1975 would therefore give the plans for each of the financial years 1975/76, 1976/77, 1977/78, and 1978/79

PSBR

Public Sector Borrowing Requirement—broadly the aggregate of central and local government and certain nationalized industry borrowing in a particular period. Now called the Public Sector Net Cash Requirement

RPE

The relative price effect—the effect on the level and growth of total public expenditure of allowing for the fact that the average price paid by the public sector for all its goods and services tended to increase, whatever the average rate of inflation, faster than the general level of prices, whether measured by the RPI or the GDP deflator

RPI

The retail price index—the price index most frequently referred to when questions of inflation and pay bargaining were concerned. It covered the main items of daily expenditure by relatively low-paid members of the community and covered only about one half of all consumers' expenditure. It was published monthly

SCE

Steering Committee on Economic Policy—a committee of senior officials from the main economic departments whose principal remit was to pull together all the factors governing the outcome of the annual Public Expenditure Survey and present Ministers with a set of policy choices. It performed this function only once—in 1975—in later years the pressure of events did not permit this intermediate step to take place

SDR

Special Drawing Rights—the unit of account of the IMF. SDRs were created in 1969 as a supplement to international liquidity, each member of the Fund being allocated, without charge, an amount proportional to its quota.[1] At the outset one SDR was defined in terms of gold but was equivalent to $1. After the devaluation of the dollar in February 1973, the SDR was redefined in terms of a basket of major currencies, and at the time covered by this book it was equivalent to about $1.20. SDRs were hardly used as a unit of account in commercial transactions and there was never a market in them

Second Secretary · The most senior Treasury grade. Each of the three (or later four) Second Secretaries commanded a block of work and reported directly to the Chancellor on matters specific to that block. On issues involving more than one Second Secretary the submission was made by the Permanent Secretary. The Second Secretaries and the Permanent Secretary had an informal meeting at least once each week to review 'the state of play'

STEP · The Short-Term Economic Policy Committee—a committee of the Permanent Secretaries of the main economic departments plus the Governor of the Bank of England. Established in 1974 as a replacement of the Budget Committee and with the purpose of broadening the basis of advice on macro-economic policy generally

[1] There have in fact been only two allocations of SDRs, the most recent of which was in 1979–81.

1

The Anatomy of Economic Policy Making in the 1970s: 'The Railway Timetables'

The economic forecasting and the budgetary process

In the 1970s, when the events described in this book took place, economic policy making by the government was still firmly cast in the Keynesian mould. Emerging from the school of Keynes in the 1930s, the idea that the central government, principally through the instruments of fiscal and monetary policy, could determine the level of activity of the whole economy had been broadly accepted by British governments as early as 1941. By 1970 this idea constituted the foundation of macro-economic policy not only in the UK but in most of the developed world as well. It was the intellectual creed of such international bodies as the Organisation for Economic Cooperation and Development (OECD) and the European Economic Community (EEC), and debates in those bodies about the ideal stance of policy in the member countries took place essentially in Keynesian terms.

The essence of this Keynesian idea was that fiscal and monetary policy should be drawn up and executed so as to realize an ideal outcome for the disposition of the national resources. The aggregate of future national economic activity based on current policies was assessed and compared with the potential of that activity. If that likely activity fell below potential, then some adjustment of government budgetary policy or of central bank monetary policy was called for to make good the deficiency. Whether the budget was in balance or had a surplus or deficit was a secondary consideration (indeed for some policy makers it was of virtually no importance). Interest rate decisions were less relevant to the issue of aggregate economic activity, although they could play a supporting role, either in the direction of promoting activity or restraining it, particularly in the field of investment and stockbuilding in the private sector. They could also play an important part in promoting or discouraging financial flows into or out of sterling, so affecting its exchange rate.

By the 1970s in the UK, as elsewhere in the industrialized world, the collection of statistics from the various components of the economy was highly developed and the government statisticians were able to build up a comprehensive system of national accounts. Although drawn up in financial terms, these accounts were analysed more in resource terms, and broadly showed the composition of national output (income) and the composition of national demand (expenditure). In simple terms they analysed demand into private consumption (what consumers generally were spending on day-to-day goods and services), private investment (what individuals and businesses were spending on capital goods such as industrial plant, housing, etc.), public consumption (military expenditure, the payment of public employees salaries), public investment (the building of schools, hospitals, etc.) and net exports (the excess of exports of current goods and services over imports). To these elements of the measurement of demand had to be added the net accumulation by businesses of stock in trade. The analysis of these elements of aggregate demand was complemented by the collection of data on the supply of goods and services by UK producers. In this way a system of national accounts was produced, with the two sides of the accounts being represented by demand and output (not as in ordinary accounts by expenditure and income) although in many ways the national accounts could be seen in such terms and were often referred to as such.

The collection of national data of these elements of economic activity was gradually complemented, from the late 1940s, by a system of economic forecasts for all the elements which constituted the two sides of the national accounts. By 1970 the techniques of economic forecasting had essentially become econometric, that is to say they were based on mathematical relationships which were derived in part from economic theory and in part from statistical observation—that is the collection of data over a long period in which relationships could be derived even when the theoretical justification for those supposed relationships was not fully understood. The relationships were expressed in money terms, but the equations used and the techniques of forecasting were essentially in resource terms, that is to say an item of expenditure on a single unvarying product was treated in identical terms from one year to the next even if the cost of that item might be increasing due to the existence of inflation in the system. Of course the existence of inflation was brought into the national accounts in certain important areas of forecasting, for example the balance of payments, which has to be treated as a financial variable, and in price forecasting generally: and by the 1970s the Treasury had developed a financial model of the economy, which was expressed in money terms, took account of inflation and attempted to forecast the surpluses and deficits of each of the main sectors of the economy (the public sector, the personal sector, the company sector, and the overseas sector) and, on a more problematical basis, how those deficits and surpluses would be financed, in particular how much of each deficit would require bank, as opposed to non-bank, credit. In this way forecasts of the growth of the money supply were derived.

The development of a comprehensive economic and to some extent financial model enabled policy makers in government to assess the effects of a fiscal or monetary policy change. The usual forecast made by the Treasury economists was based in some sense on 'unchanged policies', a rather loose term implying that, for instance, existing tax rates continued to apply and existing government spending plans were implemented. A forecast, or, in the jargon of the time, a simulation, could then be made of the likely consequences of some explicit change in those policies. The users of the forecast could then see what the effect of such a policy change would mean both for the pattern of national resource use and the totality of activity. Techniques were thus developed for assessing the effect of a tax change on the growth rate of the whole economy, on the output of particular industries, on unemployment, on the level of consumer spending, on the balance of payments, and indeed on the monetary variables as well.

It was this system of forecasting and of policy simulation which formed the background of economic policy making, in particular of framing the budget, from the late 1940s until the 1970s. The government of the day would formulate its macro-economic objectives—for example a reduction in the level of unemployment or an improvement in the balance of payments—and would then look at various policy instruments the use of which, on the basis of the economic model, would deliver those objectives over some time period. The model would of course also indicate what the consequences for other economic variables would be. Thus a tax reduction to stimulate personal consumption would be shown to have adverse effects on the current balance of payments (crudely through the increase generated in the import of consumer goods). The model would also show the deterioration in the government accounts and the increase in its borrowing requirement caused by the loss of revenue generated by the tax cut.

This system of analysis of forecasting and of simulation was more reliable in some areas than others and the degree of confidence which users might have in what was predicted varied considerably. For small changes in fiscal policy the assessment of their effect was quite good over a short time horizon (i.e. twelve to eighteen months) for some elements of the analysis (e.g. consumer spending). But their effect on some other elements (e.g. inflation) was never very reliably determined. And when substantial changes in policy were under consideration (e.g. when a big fiscal adjustment was being contemplated) the effect of all those changes taken together was difficult to assess. In part this was because the empirical evidence for the effects of such changes was lacking. In part it was because it was inherently difficult to forecast the behaviour of economic agents (consumers, producers, trade unions) in the face of what was a shock to the system.

The forecast was also unreliable in the financial field, in part because the financial model was inherently more difficult to construct, and in part because so many of the financial variables were themselves differences between two large magnitudes. A good example of this is the forecast of the Public Sector Borrowing Requirement (PSBR), that is the amount which in any specified period the Government, as to some extent the financier of the whole public sector, has to borrow to meet the spending plans of that sector. This variable is simply the difference between total tax and other government receipts and total public sector outlays—spending plus lending. This difference is a difference between two very large variables each of which is subject to many uncertainties. Small changes in economic activity, for example a fall in the rate of growth of output, involving a rise of 0.1 per cent in unemployment can lead to significant changes in the Government's borrowing requirement. Similarly bank lending may be very markedly affected by a small increase in business spending, and a big change in the monetary variables (broadly the aggregate of the banking system's deposit liabilities) may ensue.

The rather patchy reliability of the forecasts and the simulations modelled was something the economic policy makers increasingly had to come to terms with, particularly as in the 1970s the financial markets, whose significance in policy making is described later, became increasingly monetarist in their appraisal of the economic and financial outlook. Though users of the forecast might have doubts about the reliability of what was predicted—Ministers in particular—they in fact had nothing better on which to base policy decisions and they sometimes overlooked the amount of uncertainty which was inherent in what the Treasury statements about the outlook for the economy contained. This was particularly true of the forecasts of the financial variables. In the 1950s and to some extent the 1960s, the volatility of some of these, like the growth of the money stock, was not something that greatly affected either markets or policy makers. The level of government borrowing—provided it was not excessive—did not get much attention apart from special interests like gilt-edged market makers; and the rate of increase of bank lending and hence of the money stock was not thought by most to be relevant to economic decision taking. The government rarely had difficulty in financing its deficit, in part it is true because the Bank of England was always at hand to supply credit but mainly because the sale of Treasury Bills on any reasonable scale to the money market could always be achieved by the Bank. This state of affairs was reviewed by the Radcliffe Committee[1] in the late 1950s, which broadly endorsed the *status quo*. It certainly gave little support for any role for money

---

[1] Cmnd 827.

in the sense in which, later on, the monetarist school argued was vital. But all this was to change, and the significance of the financial forecast, as we shall see in the narrative history, assumed huge proportions, mainly without those who attached significance to it realizing how hugely uncertain it was.

A word must be said about the details of the forecasting system to appreciate its role in the momentous events of the 1970s. The Treasury produced three forecasts a year and each forecast took something like two months to construct from start to finish. A lengthy period of consultation took place between the forecasters and the relevant policy experts within the government apparatus on the likely outlook of what were essentially non-forecastable variables. For instance, in the field of wage negotiations, the Treasury would be advised by the Department of Employment on the likely outcome of the next wage round. In the field of private investment it would seek help from the Department of Industry from surveys of business investment intentions. At the end of the exercise the Treasury forecasters would present their results to the policy makers—senior officials whose job it was to use the forecast to give advice to Ministers on what, if anything, ought to be done in the light of the forecast. The most important forecast was therefore the one which immediately preceded the annual budget. This forecast was embarked upon around the end of the previous calendar year and was completed in late February—a timing which gave policy makers a matter of weeks in which to contemplate and evaluate a policy response. A second forecast was begun in May of each year following the Budget in which all the changes made by the Budget and all the other changes in the world economy since the February forecast could be taken into account. This produced a forecast in June or July. As a rule this forecast did not lead to any policy action unless it revealed some significant changes to the economic outlook or there had been some important change in the whole economic climate. A third, and final round was embarked on after the summer and led to the production of a forecast in late October. This forecast was able to take account of the outcome of the annual Public Expenditure Survey (about which more will be said later). As a rule, the autumn forecast was only used for policy purposes if it revealed some big changes from the previous forecast. It had a usefulness, however, in that it gave the policy makers some indication of what issues the following Budget would have to address.

The time horizon of the forecast, known in the Treasury as the NIF (National Income Forecast), was about eighteen months—this being about the limit for the reliability of the forecast as a short-term macro-economic tool. Its value lay in the use to which it was put in the formulation of fiscal (chiefly tax) policy over that time scale.

Another and somewhat different system of forecasts was in operation in the 1970s, and although it had some affinities with the NIF, its purpose and hence its design was quite different. This system was known as the Medium Term Assessment (MTA) and it had first been developed in the Department of Economic

5

Affairs (DEA) during the Labour Government of 1964–70. The time horizon set for the MTA was five years, and the purpose of the exercise was broadly to assess whether *on the basis of existing policies* (however defined) the economic outlook over that time scale was credible—or at any rate plausible. These terms are themselves somewhat question-begging, but they had a certain operational value, as we shall see when we look at the actual course of events in the mid-1970s. The model[2] used for this assessment was not unlike that used for the NIF, although it was simpler and more formal. It was also constructed almost entirely in resource, as opposed to money, terms, the justification being that it was simply impossible to allow for price variations over a five-year period. For many of the variables used in the MTA it was impossible to make reliable forecasts, and the model therefore fell back on the use of formal projections of some important economic factors. For instance the growth of world trade was taken on a long-term trend basis, as was the growth of labour productivity. Moreover the assessment made no allowance for the economic cycle; if at its starting point the economy was in recession, the assessment assumed that policy would be set so as to recover the shortfall in demand and thereafter that the economy would grow in line with productive potential.

Such a process had only limited usefulness to policy makers. Indeed policy in most areas was not set on a five-year basis. Decisions, for example in the field of tax policy or interest rates, were set with much shorter time horizons, and in such fields it was accepted that the decisions taken would have to be reviewed as the economy developed—for instance if it began to over-heat or as the balance of payments deteriorated. Whether in those fields the decisions were too short-term and generated uncertainty in the minds of those affected (e.g. business managers) is something that can be debated, but that there was a lack of permanence to those decisions was not—and probably still is not—questioned.

In one very important field, however, the taking of decisions which had some element of durability to them was considered—and again still is considered—to be of great importance, that is the field of public expenditure. Indeed it was as an aid to the construction of medium-term public expenditure plans that the MTA was generally regarded and it is to this aspect of economic policy making that we now turn.

The public expenditure survey

The definition of what is public expenditure has changed over time and the changes have not always met with universal approval. Some of the definitional

[2] The two models were in fact unified in 1974 so that the equations covering the same relationships in the two models became identical. But they continued to have very different time horizons.

changes took place in the 1970s and they form part of the story of that period and indeed of the history of the financial crisis of 1976. These changes will be looked at in their proper context. But leaving this issue aside for the moment, public expenditure can be classified broadly as all expenditure by the Central Government on goods, services and financial transfers (like social security payments), all similar expenditure by local authorities and some element of the expenditure of the nationalized trading corporations. The term 'some element' has to be used since there was a good deal of debate in the 1970s as to whether that element should consist of the capital spending of the industries or only that part of it for the financing of which they had to call on the central government or the market. (It was always accepted both within and without government that the trading outlays of the industries in no sense constituted public expenditure since, for the most part if not the whole, they were recovered from their customers. Indeed charges for Government services generally were netted off public expenditure, leaving totals to be funded by taxation or borrowing.)

During the mid-1970s the level of public spending was of the order of £50 billion and constituted about 42 per cent of GDP. Although expenditure was classified into fourteen different programmes, 80 per cent of all public spending went on only five programmes: Defence, Social Security, Education, Health, and Housing. This has to be borne in mind when the question of making significant cuts in expenditure is being discussed. These programmes were inevitably the main focus for discussion whenever some major adjustment of the level, or growth, of public expenditure was at issue.

The way that public expenditure was (and for that matter to some extent still is) controlled is a legacy of reforms made in the early 1960s following the publication of the report of the Plowden Committee.[3] This body had been set up by the Macmillan Government following widespread disquiet about the problems faced by managers of public programmes by the short-term nature of decisions affecting those programmes. Prior to 1960, authority to incur expenditure was given to the managers (broadly the Departments responsible for the programmes) in the main for one year only. When the Treasury approved the Parliamentary Estimates (usually in the late winter of each year) the approval given was for the twelve months beginning 1 April. No formal authority was given for expenditure beyond that period, and departments had to argue their case afresh each year. This was a good discipline for programmes that did not involve long-term commitments, but made little sense for those which, like the purchase of complex weapons systems or the building of hospitals, had to be settled on a multi-year basis. Of course in practice the Treasury recognized that when it approved a multi-year project it was implicitly committing itself to finance it over its lifetime. But there was always an

---

[3] Cmnd 1432.

element of uncertainty in the one-year approval system and Plowden sought to address this question. The solution recommended was that the single year system should be replaced by a four-year planning cycle, in which departments would submit for Treasury approval each year a spending plan running from the year immediately ahead for four years. The system recommended would also apply to *all* public expenditure, not just that part which formed part of the annual Estimates. Thus it would include local authority spending—capital and current—and some element of spending by public corporations, including the nationalized industries. The degree of 'definiteness' in the programme would decline from a very high level in the year ahead to relative sketchiness five years ahead. But, once approved, the four-year programmes would give managers a reasonably firm basis on which to make specific policy decisions and enter into specific financial commitments for a number of years ahead. The approved programmes became, in the following year, the 'base' from which discussion of them in the new quadrennium would start. It was recognized, however, that the programmes, even if approved, were not sacrosanct. Governments of a different political complexion with different priorities might replace the government which approved the particular four-year plan, and managers would have to be prepared for this. So the plans were not set in concrete: and indeed it was part of the whole system that Departments had to resubmit even the approved programmes each year so as to provide a basis for the annual review which the system envisaged. But the starting point of each annual review, or Survey as it was known, was the previously approved programme. The onus was then on the Treasury to show cause why the approved programme should be reduced and on the spending Department to show why it should be increased. The system was therefore in a sense an incremental one. It did not involve, unless this was specifically provided for, a fundamental review of whole programmes (something termed 'zero-based' budgeting, in which every programme would be reviewed afresh at the start of the annual Survey).

A further element in the new system recommended by Plowden was that since, in the 1950s and 1960s when the system was being considered, the element of price inflation was very uncertain—and particularly uncertain in the field of public expenditure—the plans should be drawn up in constant price (or resource) terms. Programmes would be prepared in terms of the prices ruling for the items to be purchased at the time of the annual survey and would be approved in precisely those terms. The finance that in due course would be provided to the spending departments would, however, be whatever was required to purchase the volume of spending approved. The Treasury was asked, in effect, to underwrite the inflationary element in departmental spending. This was to become a serious issue in the 1970s when inflation reached heights hitherto unknown in the UK and when the price increase differential between different elements of public spending became very large indeed.

Another issue which was to cause confusion and difficulty was that over the time horizon of the spending plan the prices paid for public services and investment would change in different, and often unpredictable, ways. Thus spending on wages and salaries would tend to rise in line with average earnings in the economy generally, but spending on consumable goods would rise at a different rate, which in turn would be different from the rise in the price of investment goods, such as buildings or roads. This proved to be a very vexatious issue in the 1970s when policy makers began to be concerned with the financial consequences of public spending and not only with the resource consequences.

One of the consequences of the Plowden system was that the final say as to what the approved programmes should amount to was put firmly into commission. In the nineteenth century and under the influence of Gladstone it was the Treasury which had the last word on what Departments could spend (or more precisely put to Parliament for annual approval). It was the Treasury which had responsibility for raising the finance for the expenditure, whether through taxation or borrowing, and it was accepted that the Treasury should therefore decide what expenditure should be. Of course even in the nineteenth century the system never worked quite like that. The doctrine of collective responsibility gave the Cabinet a large voice in the determination of public policy generally, and if the Cabinet decided on a particular course of action, like declaring war, the Treasury had to find the funds to finance it. But the predominance of the Treasury in expenditure decision taking was largely unquestioned. In the twentieth century things began to change, in part because the experience of two world wars showed the politicians that the Treasury could not have the last word on everything and that if the Cabinet as a whole were to be in the driving seat on policy the Treasury's writ had to be circumscribed. This issue came to a critical head in January 1958 when the attempt of Treasury Ministers to cut programmes to a level they deemed to be financially justifiable was rejected by the Cabinet and led to their collective resignation from the Government. From that moment on, it was recognized in Whitehall that, although the Treasury remained the central department for the control of expenditure, the final word on the level and content of public spending was for Ministers collectively.

Following the report of the Plowden Committee, a regular annual drill was established in Whitehall for the execution of expenditure planning and control. An interdepartmental committee—the Public Expenditure Survey Committee (PESC)—was set up consisting of the Finance Directors of the main spending departments with the Treasury providing the chairman and secretariat. This committee was charged with responsibility for producing the draft annual White Paper on Public Expenditure setting out, in schematic terms, a possible plan for the Government's spending over the following quadrennium with options for possible reductions and options for increases.[4] It began its annual programme in the early summer of each year by inviting departments to update the programmes contained in the previous year's White Paper. Any increase in the previously authorized programme had to be bid for, either on the grounds that the increase had already been specifically approved by Ministers collectively or that it was a 'necessary' increase, for example on the grounds that unemployment had increased more than expected and that the social security programme had to be revised or that some new defence commitment had been accepted. These variations were scrutinized by the Treasury and by the PESC and were incorporated in the first report to Ministers, who could thus see the extent to which departments were seeking to increase aggregate expenditure during the planning period. The PESC report was, in terms of policy and value judgement, quite neutral. It made no recommendations to speak of, but contented itself with displaying the bids that departments were making for spending above the level for the relevant period in the previous White Paper and the possible options for reducing expenditure, either to bring spending back to its previous level, or indeed to reduce it if that was what Ministers wished. Ministers were also presented, when they came to look at the Survey report, with a summary of the MTA, which gave them an idea of what, for any given profile of public spending, was the proportion of the annual accretion of resources which would (in some cases should) be devoted to public programmes and what therefore was available for other uses (e.g. the balance of payments, privately-financed consumption, private investment etc.). Not unexpectedly it almost always proved to be the case that the bids of departments, if approved, would lead to an excess of aggregate demand on the national capacity or the squeezing of resources for the private sector. The Cabinet were presented with this picture usually by way of a paper submitted by the Chancellor of the Exchequer and were invited, usually in the late summer, to agree that not all the bids could be accepted without compromising the claims of other users of national resources and that some limit had to be put on the bids. If Ministers agreed with this assessment, the Treasury at Ministerial level thereafter held a series of bilateral meetings with each spending department to examine what exactly would be involved if the bid put in by the department were not allowed or were not allowed in full. At the end of this process the Treasury drew up a paper outlining the options open to Ministers with suggestions as to what changes in the previously approved programmes were consistent with good economic management and could be incorporated in the revised four-year plan. Almost inevitably this process was a difficult and prolonged one, both for the Treasury Ministers

[4] The Plowden system of expenditure planning was developed further in April 1969 with the publication of a White Paper (Cmnd 4017) laying down a programme involving the publication each year at the conclusion of the Survey of an annual Public Expenditure White Paper.

and for spending departments. The bridging of the gap which usually existed between the two positions was both time-consuming and, in political terms, often quite painful. Sometimes a change in policy was required which the spending minister might be most reluctant to accept. At the conclusion of the process, usually about the end of the calendar year, an agreement was reached—at Cabinet level—and the decisions would be incorporated in the White Paper usually published early in the following year.[5]

Whatever the merits of this system in giving spending departments the assurance they needed to plan and execute their programmes, it placed the Treasury in a very difficult and defensive position when the macro-economic question arose, as it did in the 1970s, whether these programmes in aggregate were, in the event, consistent with the emerging national economic situation as the Treasury saw it. There was a strong inbuilt bias towards the regarding of the programmes in the last White Paper as sacrosanct and incapable of downward adjustment. But it was reasonably self-evident to the Treasury that the basis on which the programmes had been approved, that is the Medium Term Assessment, might very well change over the period of the expenditure cycle and that what might have seemed an acceptable level of public spending at the outset of the process was no longer sustainable. This fact became starkly clear in the course of the 1970s and became a central issue in the events of 1976.

The role of taxation

The other side of the Governmental accounts—the proceeds of taxation—were treated quite differently. The structure of the tax system does not usually vary from year to year, although of course structural changes are made from time to time. But the rates at which taxes were levied were, and still are, usually fixed on an annual basis in the Chancellor's budget in the spring of each year.[6] They applied solely for the following financial year, with no commitment to their continuance at those levels thereafter. As mentioned above, these decisions were taken by the Chancellor on the basis of the short-term economic and financial forecasts presented to him by his Treasury advisers and were in no sense a collective Cabinet matter. Consequently convention gave the Treasury a much freer hand in determining tax rates—and hence the revenue side of the

[5] A very full account of the 'nuts and bolts' of the PESC process is given in chapter 4 of the unpublished Treasury 'Manual on Public Expenditure', August 1983. A briefer account is given in the Treasury evidence to the House of Commons Select Committee on Expenditure Thirteenth Report in the Session 1975/76, Parliamentary Papers Vol xxxi. The Prime Minister outlined the timetable and process of consideration of public expendure in his 1975 paper to Cabinet C(75)60—CAB 129/183/10. See also the booklet written by Sir Samuel Goldman 'The Developing System of Public Expenditure Management and Control', T 331/947.

[6] At the time of writing, 2007, the rates of tax are also disclosed in outline form in the Pre-Budget Report, usually presented in November of the year prior to the relevant financial year.

government accounts—than in determining spending levels. This imbalance of authority itself had an effect on Treasury choices when economic adjustments had to be made. It was a much easier matter for the Chancellor to raise taxes than to get his colleagues to agree to spending cuts. This fact too had its effect in the course of 1976 when adjustments had to be made.

But if the ease with which decisions could be taken in the field of taxation was much greater than in the field of expenditure, the impact of taxation, or changes thereto, was very different in micro-economic terms from that of expenditure. For the most part public expenditure gives a benefit to society which the beneficiaries do not pay for when they receive it, or do not pay for it in proportion to their benefit. By contrast taxation levies a charge on the taxpayer for which he sees no direct personal benefit and the incidence of taxation deprives him of a part of his ability to dispose of his income as he wishes. At the margin a rise in tax rates (some would say even the existence of different tax rates for different categories of income or expenditure) causes economic agents to be less incentivized to offer their services to the economy. *Per contra* a fall in public benefits generally has no direct effect on work incentives. On the other hand some public expenditure does contribute to the more efficient working of markets, although this cannot be said of the totality of public spending. The imbalance between the incidence and perception of taxation on the one hand and public benefits on the other leads classical economists to argue that, faced with a choice whether to remedy a fiscal gap by increased taxation or reduced expenditure, there are advantages in terms of economic efficiency in reducing expenditure.

This issue is a good deal more complicated than is suggested above, but the difference in economic effect at the micro-economic level did form a large element in the thinking of some of those involved in the 1976 crisis. By and large those whose help was needed (the markets, the IMF, etc.) were strongly of the view that if an adjustment had to be made to the government's fiscal deficit there were powerful arguments for making that adjustment to the expenditure side of the accounts. (Many trade union leaders, conscious of their members' aversion to paying taxes shared this view.) *Per contra*, Ministers, most of whom had spending programmes to safeguard, usually had a preference for making the adjustment on the income side. However, in 1976 the levels of taxation in the UK, certainly the level of income tax as a proportion of income, was so high that the option of raising taxes to meet a large deficit was recognized by most of those involved in decision taking as very limited.

Sterling and the balance of payments

An endemic problem facing the British economy from the end of the Second World War in 1945, certainly until the 1980s, was the balance of payments and the vulnerability of sterling to speculative attacks. The loss of most of the country's financial assets during the war and with them the substantial income derived from them, meant that the UK had to undergo a large structural adjustment to its economy in order to give a prominence to exports that had not been necessary before 1939. A good deal of progress was made in this direction in the post-war years, but because of the high propensity to import which British consumers and businesses displayed there was a constant need to promote exports beyond the level that, without encouragement, they would achieve. This took the form of special attempts by the Government to encourage exports with financial and other incentives. It also caused the Treasury to be particularly concerned about the level of the exchange rate especially, though by no means wholly, when the UK's unit costs of production were rising faster than those of its main competitors. The concern of the Treasury about the external value of sterling was not, however, matched during most of the post-war period by any desire to 'manipulate' that value. Indeed, under the Bretton Woods system of international finance, such manipulation was expressly prohibited, and changes in exchange rates were under the supervision of the International Monetary Fund (IMF), who had to be convinced that there was a 'fundamental disequilibrium' in the member's payments accounts before it would authorize a revaluation of the currency.

But there was another reason why the Treasury (and even more strongly the Bank of England) were opposed to the idea of using the exchange rate as a tool of policy. Sterling was the currency in which a large number of countries—former colonies and dependencies in particular—kept their foreign exchange reserves and indeed conducted their trade. This was certainly the case with the members of the Sterling area (roughly the Commonwealth less Canada), but it was true also of a number of countries which had traditional economic and political ties with the UK. Among the latter were the independent countries of the Middle East, notably the Gulf Sheikhdoms and Saudi Arabia, which became very rich with the rapid expansion of oil use in Western economies and even more so with the sharp rise in crude oil prices in the early 1970s. Both the Treasury and the Bank felt that the UK had a fiduciary duty to members of the Sterling area and the independent countries that kept their reserves in sterling to protect its value, in terms of its rate against gold and other currencies, notably the dollar. But quite apart from this fiduciary duty there was a more hard-headed reason to keep the parity if at all possible. This was because the overseas central banks and monetary authorities which held their reserves in sterling would, it was thought, be quick to sell their sterling holdings for dollars if they thought that the currency was likely to be devalued other than very infrequently and under pressure. Such selling would put immense pressure on the exchange rate—or, if the rate was fixed, on the level of officially-held foreign exchange reserves—and could put the Treasury and the Bank in a difficult position. The foreign exchange reserves were not of sufficient magnitude to meet the selling pressure which might develop—the volume of externally held sterling was usually much greater than the volume of foreign currency assets. In short, a suspicion that the UK authorities could use the exchange value of sterling to support macro-economic objectives could have had disastrous consequences. No other country, apart from the United States had such a relatively large level of overseas liabilities in its currency as the UK, and the USA was much less concerned about the overseas value of the dollar, not least because overseas trade was relatively unimportant to its economy and because so many commodities had their international prices denominated and quoted in dollars. The system of fixed but adjustable exchange rates administered by the IMF received a severe blow in 1971 when the USA ceased to offer overseas central banks the right of converting their dollar holdings for gold at the fixed price of $35 per ounce, which had been the practice for nearly forty years and a firm element in the whole IMF structure. The system had to be recreated—in terms of the dollar rather than gold. At the international meeting at the Smithsonian Institution in Washington later that year a new system based on the old cross-rates rather than gold was agreed, but it was evident that after the American action it would be a much less hallowed one than what had gone before, and it was not long before it too was destroyed. The UK left the fixed-rate system in June 1972 when the government announced that it would no longer be bound to intervene in the currency markets to keep sterling at a prescribed level in terms of gold or the dollar, and the United States had little hesitation in devaluing the dollar against other currencies some months later in order to improve its competitiveness. Sterling—as well as many other currencies—became freely floating, with, in principle, its international value determined by the market. It is important to note that this state of affairs was quite unlike anything that the UK authorities were familiar with. Since the Tripartite Agreement[7] of September 1936 made jointly by the British, US, and French Governments to promote currency stability following the end of the gold standard in 1931, sterling had had a *de facto* fixed value against most of the important international currencies and the UK authorities had a policy of intervening in the foreign exchange markets to keep that value. No one in the Treasury or the Bank had therefore had any experience before 1972 of managing the exchange rate in a system where there were no formal obligations to maintain a parity and the markets were unsure of what the pattern of rates and cross-rates might become. This unfamiliarity with the new system and how it would work in practice was another important element in the situation which developed from 1974 when currency cross-rates became very erratic.

The mechanics by which the British authorities operated and still operate in the foreign exchange markets are fairly straightforward. The foreign exchange

---

[7] Sayers Appendix 28.

reserves are held in a Treasury account, the Exchange Equalisation Account (EEA), which is managed by the Bank of England. The account consists of gold, foreign currency, and sterling and the management of it involves changing the composition, but not the total, in line with a general policy understanding agreed with the Treasury. The aim of that policy is usually to support the established rate of sterling in a fixed exchange rate system and smooth fluctuations of the rate in a floating rate system. Occasionally, in a floating system the authorities might attempt to defy market tendencies by aggressively buying or selling sterling and accepting that the composition of the reserves might change substantially as a result. This activity became particularly marked in 1976, as we shall see, when the Bank were selling large amounts of foreign currency in an attempt to stem what would otherwise have been a substantial fall in the external value of sterling. It became marked in a quite different sense the following year when the Bank sold large amounts of sterling in an attempt to prevent the market from causing the exchange rate to appreciate.

Most of the Bank's activity was in the spot market, but it also operated in the forward market, that is the market in which a firm commitment to purchase or sell is made for some foreign currency for delivery at some future date, usually three months hence. Currency arbitrage normally leads the forward rate of sterling against, for instance, the dollar, to be at a discount or premium to it of an amount which is simply equal to the differential between short-term interest rates in London and those in other financial centres like New York. When, through market imperfections or because of speculation about the sustainability of the existing exchange rate, this does not happen, the Bank may operate in the forward market to restore equilibrium, but the net effect on the reserves is much the same as operations in the spot market. Because of the phenomenon of arbitrage, the Bank could manipulate the spot rate by operating in the forward market alone. This technique was adopted occasionally when it was desired to influence the spot rate without spending dollars immediately for 'window dressing' purposes, for example to enable the Treasury to publish figures for the level of the reserves which did not in fact fully reflect the state of 'the book'.

Another feature of the Bank's foreign exchange operations which was important in 1976 was its agency work on behalf of central banks in the Sterling area. If such a central bank wished to acquire dollars by selling some of its sterling holdings it could either do so by simply entering the foreign exchange market on its own account or it could ask the Bank of England to obtain the required foreign currency by either buying it in the market as agent or by supplying it from the UK's reserves. The Bank could then replenish the reserves subsequently by buying the currency concerned in the open market. With large orders from an overseas central bank, the latter process enabled such orders in effect to be spread over a period and so avoid a possible distortion of the market caused by a 'lumpy' transaction. The Bank therefore saw its usual role as that of smoothing the movements of the sterling rate. Only rarely, however, did it attempt to 'manipulate' the rate in any substantive sense.

The balance of payments, a factor which dominated much of the thinking of the Treasury in the 1970s consisted essentially of two parts—the current and the capital account. The current account balance was simply the net of all receipts (in whatever currency) from the export of goods and services minus corresponding imports. This included both visible trade, that is trade in tangible goods, and invisibles, which constituted services and net investment income. The capital account consisted broadly of the balance of the movement of long-term capital—that is to say direct and portfolio investment—and this could be assumed to be reasonably stable and secure. It did not include short-term movements of capital, for example sales of sterling by foreign holders nor instant purchases or sales of currency by the Bank of England—these conventionally were treated as 'financing items'. The 'overall' account was simply the net sum of the current and long-term capital account and constituted the amount of short-term foreign borrowing (or reduction in net liquid assets) which the authorities had to achieve to secure an overall balance. This was referred to at the time as the External Financing Requirement, and it assumed an importance in official thinking and official calculations on a par with such economic variables as unemployment and inflation.

The External Financing Requirement played an important part in the consideration of macro-economic policy, for the financing of the overall capital and current account proved to be a serious problem throughout the period covered and much of the narrative is inevitably concerned with how this was assessed and how the forecast impinged on policy making.

Inflation

This brings us to the vitally important issue of the inflation of wages and prices, which after the oil crisis of 1973, reached levels which were unprecedented in the UK and indeed in much of the developed world. Although there were very occasional periods of high inflation, for example in the aftermath of the outbreak of the Korean War in 1950, inflation of a relatively modest kind—that is to say an annual rate rarely exceeding 5 per cent and often below 2 per cent—had become endemic in the period following the Second World War. In the fifteen years from 1945 to 1960 it had not been so high as to pose serious threats to economic management, but it was nevertheless a significant complication to the decision taking in both the public and the private sector—and it had an adverse effect on foreign holders of sterling who, insofar as British inflation was higher than that of the UK's competitors, saw the relative international value of their financial assets decline.[8] The causes of this infla-tion, indeed of inflation generally, and the best means of countering it, were in the 1970s (by which time it was showing a secular increase) matters of dispute among economists, with the monetarist school holding that it was due to lax control of the money supply, and with more conventional economists believ-ing that, to some extent at least, it was due to excessive pressure of demand in both the product and labour markets. That there had been a consistently fairly high pressure of demand in the two decades following the war cannot be questioned. This was due to the commitment accepted by all the main polit-ical parties to operate macro-economic policy so as to secure full employment, the latter being generally regarded as involving less than 3 per cent unemploy-ment of the labour force, with the average level significantly below this level. The commitment more or less assured the various economic agents, the labour force and employers, that there was little or no risk to their security in infla-tion. Provided producers raised their prices in line with each other they suffered no penalty (apart that is from some loss of competitiveness with overseas producers) from conceding price increases to their suppliers or to their workforce; and the trade unions and their members suffered no disad-vantage from pursuing wage increases, again provided these increases were general to the workforce as a whole or to the particular sector involved. In the Government statement on post-war Employment Policy in 1944[9] it had been emphasized that the objective of full employment required stability of wages and prices. But although in the period immediately following the war neither producers nor the workforce exploited the situation described *à outrance*, that the system was prone to inflation was clearly evident. The response of Gov-ernments to this state of affairs was to seek to obtain moderation in wage and price increases by exhortation. This technique was first adopted in 1948 by the Chancellor of the day—Sir Stafford Cripps, and was followed at various times thereafter until 1960. The appeals for moderation may have had some success each time for a limited period but it was difficult to measure it and the outcome was not lasting. Government ministers found the process of deciding whether and in what degree a particular pay claim for exceptional treatment could be allowed a very tiresome and time-consuming one, and the unions became restive at having to sacrifice one of their cherished freedoms. The efficacy of incomes and prices policies at containing inflation often dimin-ished as time wore on, and at the conclusion of each period of 'control' there was general relief at its demise. At other times the Government had adopted for a brief period a measure of deflation, causing unemployment to rise briefly

---

[8] For a comprehensive account of the Treasury's early attitude to wage inflation see Treasury Historical Memorandum 'The Government and Wages 1945–60' T267/8,9 and 10.
[9] Cmd 6527.

but only to levels of 2 per cent or even less: and the deflation was soon reversed by stimulating measures to restore the level of employment.

International opinion about the causes and remedies for inflation was authoritatively set out in the publication in 1960 of a work by a group of internationally renowned economists appointed by the Organisation for Economic Cooperation and Development (OECD, at that time it was known as the OEEC, the Organisation for European Economic Cooperation).[10] This asserted that the cause of inflation in all the industrialized countries was not primarily a demand-pull matter (which could therefore be countered by appropriate demand reducing measures), but was essentially a cost-push process and that the remedy was to act directly on costs, in particular the cost of labour. In technical terms the view was taken that the Phillips curve, which seeks to plot the rate of inflation (as measured by the rate of increase of money wages) in an economy against the level of unemployment, was a straight horizontal, or near-horizontal line. The implication, which was firmly embraced by the authors, was that the only way to reduce and control inflation was to 'administer' a limit on the increases which labour and capital could secure for their products, that is to have a system whereby wages and prices would be directly acted on, either by an understanding with all the economic agents, or somehow legally enforced. The government of all countries experiencing inflation (and this was most of the developed world) should assert their authority by 'requiring' economic agents to limit the annual price increase of their products to some small percentage. How this should be done was left rather vague, but the implication was that governments should, if necessary, take legislative powers to enforce their will.[11]

The UK embraced this nostrum in 1961 when, following a period of excessive growth and rising inflation, the government of the day introduced some demand-reducing measures and at the same time called for a wage and price freeze for a limited period. Although the government had no power to enforce this appeal except in an area such as the public sector where it had a measure of direct control, the appeal did have some force and the success achieved in the six months in which it applied led to it laying down thereafter a percentage increase to wages and prices which it deemed 'acceptable'. This second phase of Incomes Policy had some success, but it proved very unpopular with both the trade unions and employers and a number of blatant breaches of the guidelines led the government to abandon the policy altogether just over a year after its introduction. In the ten years between 1964 and 1974 an incomes and prices policy either on a voluntary or a statutory basis was tried on a number of occasions, in each case with limited success for a period after

[10] 'The Problem of Rising Prices' OECD 1961.
[11] Not all the economists involved in the study subscribed to the view that the policy should be enforced by a system of legal penalties.

which the agents affected rebelled against their loss of freedom. In 1974, where our story really begins, there occurred one of the periodic breakdowns of the existing policy, and with it a return to complete freedom for unions and employers to extract whatever pay and price increases they felt able to extract from those to whom they sold their products. But in 1974, as we shall see, the ending of Incomes Policy did not take place in a situation of declining inflation (as had been the case with the ending of previous incomes policies) but with rising inflation. The augurs for the future, as regards inflation, therefore, were not good and indeed for a significant period got worse.

Monetary policy

The instruments of monetary policy changed a good deal in the 1970s. In the twenty-five years following the war the main tools had been short-term interest rates and direct controls over the granting of credit by credit-creating institutions (principally the banks and other credit providing institutions such as hire purchase firms). Short-term interest rates in the market were determined by the actions of the Bank of England in supplying or withdrawing credit to or from the discount market or fixing the price at which they would discount the bills in which that market dealt. Thanks to the fact that the Bank was the principal dealer in Treasury bills it had considerable market power and had little difficulty (except perhaps on special occasions when the state of the market proved difficult to control) in asserting its market strength. By custom the discount market usually took good notice of the Bank's views on the appropriate level of short-term interest rates and placed its bids for Treasury bills accordingly. The system was a very effective means of setting short-term rates for the whole economy and determined indirectly the charges the clearing banks made for credit to their customers. Insofar as businesses (or for that matter consumers) were price sensitive about the credit they obtained, for instance to finance the holding of stocks or the buying of houses, the regulation of short-term interest rates was a useful supplementary instrument for regulating demand. Bank Rate, or Minimum Lending Rate (MLR) as it was subsequently termed, was used frequently in the post-war period to reinforce fiscal measures designed to promote the government's economic objectives. But short-term interest rates had little effect on consumer demand, mainly because the ordinary consumer was thought to be insensitive to the cost of the credit he obtained. The only exception was the class of mortgage owners, but in the immediate post-war years this class was not a large one by the standards of the end of the century and in any case the mortgage system allowed mortgagors to restructure the pattern of their payments when interest rates changed so that the latter had little impact on net personal income. As for other consumer-debtors the interest rate he paid on, for instance hire purchase loans, was so much higher than the bank rate set by the Bank of England that small changes in the latter, even if passed on to the consumer by the hire purchase firms, had little effect on personal consumption.

Monetary policy, that is to say the level of short-term interest rates, also had, or was thought to have an effect on the exchange rate for sterling. A change in the differential interest rate in New York and London certainly affected the forward rate but the effect on the spot rate was erratic and unpredictable. A great deal depended on the response of overseas holders of sterling to their perceptions of the risks and advantages of that currency as compared with other currencies. Nevertheless monetary policy was generally used in the sense described when a package of economic measures was introduced by the government designed to reassure the currency markets and to regulate demand.

The government's debt-management programme, that is to say the rate and price at which it issued medium- and long-term debt (gilt-edged securities) was not, except marginally, seen as an instrument of monetary policy—at any rate in the twenty-five years following the Second World War. It was certainly a useful way of absorbing excessive liquidity in the economy, an issue on which the Radcliffe Committee on Monetary Policy[12] had focused in its report in 1960 as the main issue to be addressed by the monetary authorities. For its part, the Bank of England, as the government's agent in the gilt-edged market, was anxious to see that market operating in a stable fashion and its advice on the government's long-term borrowing programme was influenced primarily by this factor. It therefore functioned to supply the market with what it seemed to want, but not to flood it with stock, the price of which would fall with consequential losses to holders of gilts. But the idea that the sale of gilt-edged stock could have a valuable effect on the level and growth of the money supply did not greatly occupy the thoughts of policy makers in Whitehall and Threadneedle Street—at any rate until the mid- to late-1970s. It is probably fair to say that in the twenty-five years following the end of the war the main monetary instruments used for regulating the economy were direct controls over the volume and terms of bank and other credit institutions' lending. Although there was no legal control over the banks, they were very responsive to requests by the Bank of England to limit their lending, both qualitatively and quantitatively. The specifically consumer credit institutions were subject to control orders made by the Treasury and the Board of Trade under subordinate legislation.

The machinery for the implementation of monetary policy—the fixing of short-term interest rates and the selling of government debt—was extremely informal. There was, in the 1970s, a joint Treasury–Bank Group on Monetary Policy (MPG) but it did not function as a mechanism for taking day-to-day decisions. It was more concerned with such matters as examining the

---

[12] Cmnd 827.

implications of the financial forecast for the growth of bank credit and the money supply and testing its findings for internal consistency. Proposals to change MLR always emanated from the Bank, usually at gubernatorial level, but the Bank never made a move without first establishing that the Treasury were content, and this usually meant that the Chancellor, sometimes the Prime Minister, were involved. The Governor's recommendations were, as often as not, based on technical considerations (e.g. the state of liquidity in the discount market) although the Bank could and would, if necessary, resist market pressures if it thought that they would lead to interest rate levels which were not justified on other grounds (e.g. to maintain an appropriate relationship to dollar rates or to protect the market value of sterling). And of course the Bank would take deliberate action on interest rates to support other objectives of policy (e.g. to maintain a healthy banking system). By no means all of the technical activities of the Bank involved the Treasury, who were content to give the Bank a free hand in this area. It was only when the Bank wanted to make a move on interest rates which the Treasury thought inappropriate on wider macro-economic grounds that the two institutions had to get together to resolve their differences. But the Treasury never took the initiative in this area.

Much the same was true of debt-management, where the Bank operated largely to maintain an orderly market in gilt-edged securities and sought, over time, to ensure that a sizeable proportion of the Government's funding requirements were met by the issue of medium- to long-dated securities. The terms and maturity of new debt issues were very much left to the Bank, although invariably these matters would be cleared with the Treasury, whose credit and liabilities were involved. But the clearance with the Treasury that took place was usually at a low level, and reference was made to higher authority only if on those rare occasions when some important external consideration arose. This state of affairs was justified on the grounds that only the Bank could know what the state of the market was and that it was better to leave that institution to form its own judgement. It was almost unknown for the Treasury to find fault with the Bank's tactics. But these tactics took little account in those days of what was happening to the growth of the monetary aggregates, mainly because the movement of those variables was not in any sense a prime consideration of policy.

Monetary policy, though not its handling in Whitehall, underwent a significant change in 1971, when the Bank issued a policy document 'Competition and Credit Control'[13] (CCC), which argued that the system of direct controls over the growth of credit was breaking down as the credit supplying industry expanded with the evolution of banks outside the Clearing System and found means of evading those controls. At the same time borrowers found

[13] BEQB May 1971.

alternative sources of credit which were outside the banking area. CCC stated that the policy would henceforth rely primarily on the price mechanism for the containment of credit and that physical controls on the supply of consumer credit (i.e. the cost and repayment period of that credit and the amount of spending which could be financed on credit) would be relied on to a much lesser extent than hitherto. There was no indication in the Bank document that the new system would have any regard to the money supply. It did not involve any change in the basic belief of the monetary authorities that it was the cost and availability of credit which was important in the exercise of monetary policy. The change in the method of implementing monetary policy did however contribute substantially to the explosion of (inadequately secured) secondary bank credit to the property market in 1972 and 1973 and contributed to the crisis in both markets which emerged at the end of 1973.

'Competition and Credit Control' built on the existing mechanisms for influencing the growth of the banks' balance sheets and applied such concepts as 'reserve assets' and 'special deposits' to the whole banking system and not only to the London and Scottish Clearing Banks. It did, however, pay little attention to the role of *monetary growth* as an object of policy attention. Its intellectual foundations still rested on the arguments of the Radcliffe Committee that it was overall liquidity which was the variable which needed to be watched and, to some extent, controlled. The money supply was simply not a target variable. This might be thought with hindsight to be surprising given the emergence of the monetarist school at the time and to the gradual acceptance of its arguments by central banks generally. The doctrine of monetarism, that is that the growth of the money supply in an economy had, with something of a lag, a determining effect on the growth of prices generally, can be said to have been launched (or perhaps more precisely relaunched) by Milton Friedman in his presidential address to the American Economic Association in December 1967.[14] To a world which by then had become weary of inflation and impatient with the measures governments adopted to deal with it, this was a very seductive suggestion, and it was embraced quite widely, in particular by parts of the financial press, and hence by financial markets, and in the UK by some politicians. The intellectual foundations of monetarism consisted mainly of some statistical research by Friedman and his associates covering nearly a century of experience in the United States together with a theoretical model of how the principle functioned.[15] Although the validity of the empirical research was challenged, and the model was questioned by other economists, the enthusiasm of the adherents was not noticeably diminished and it was not until the 1980s, after experimentation in some countries, including the UK with policies designed to control the money supply growth which had

[14] Friedman 'The Role of Monetary Policy'.
[15] Friedman 'A Monetary History of the United States 1867–1960'.

dubious results, that the belief in the direct relation of the growth of the money supply to the increase in the general price level began to erode. However, during the 1970s, the period covered by this study, monetarism held great sway in financial markets and the routine publication of the monetary variables in all countries became the subject of intense interest. Some central banks began to set their policy objectives in terms of the growth of some particular measure of the money supply and adjusted their short-term interest rates with a view to achieving the desired outcome.

The Treasury and the Bank of England did not accept the precepts of the monetarist school, at any rate until 1979 when, with the advent of a government committed to its ideas, it became the foundation of economic policy.[16] Although, in the 1970s these institutions were sceptical about the strict nostrums of the monetarists they accepted that the growth of the money supply, like the temperature of a sick person, did convey some information about the state of the economy, and figures relating to it were studied with care in order to see whether they indicated anything unusual about, for instance, the liquidity of the economy and the possibility that future demand might depart from its expected path. Neither institution believed that the money supply figures had a *determining* effect on future inflation, and policy was certainly not framed with a single-minded wish to secure some desired outcome for the monetary variables. (This issue did assume some importance in 1976, as the narrative reveals, and in that year a shift was made in the stance of the authorities towards monetary expansion, but not nearly to the extent of accepting the precepts of the monetarists.)

In one very important respect, however, the two institutions did accept that the monetary variables were important and that was their effect on financial markets. If as a result of some outcome—or forecast—of the growth of the money supply financial markets reacted by, for instance, selling sterling in large quantities or refusing to buy government securities, the effect on some key financial variables could be serious. At its most extreme, this could take the form of a decline in the exchange rate or an inability of the government to fund its Budget deficit except by the issue of short-term instruments which greatly added to the liquidity of the financial system. From the early 1970s this factor played a significant part in policy making and, perhaps sometimes slightly disingenuously, in what was said about the aims of policy.

Another factor greatly affecting the authorities' attitude to the money supply at this time were the two facts that no one knew which particular measure of it was what the monetarists thought important and secondly that there was no known mechanism for determining *a priori* what the movement of the

---

[16] The Bank Governor described himself as a 'practical monetarist' in a lecture in 1978 but this hardly qualified as a commitment to an attempt to secure the rigid control of the money supply, Mais Lecture 1978.

money supply would be over any time period. The money supply could be measured in many different ways depending on whether it should include elements like highly liquid bank term deposits which were 'virtual' money, and the movements of different measures were found to differ significantly. But perhaps more importantly the monetary authorities knew that there was no means of guaranteeing any particular outcome of a money supply variable by the means of some policy instrument. The Bank of England had no means of establishing in advance what the growth of any measure should be. It could fix the level of short-term interest rates, which indirectly and rather uncertainly affected the public's appetite for money, and it could give guidance to the deposit-taking institutions about the aggressiveness with which they should bid for deposits in the money markets. It could also, with greater or less vigour, attempt to sell gilt-edged securities to the non-bank sector so as to absorb liquidity in the banking system. But there was simply no way that the authorities could lay down a target for some particular measure of the money supply and confidently expect to achieve it.[17] It was this awareness of its inability to secure a specified outcome that led the authorities to devise schemes like the 'Corset', which is described later, which had the effect of constraining certain measures of the money supply by heavily penalizing banks which disregarded the target, but without regard to what that constraint might have for other measures or for liquidity generally. Such measures are a good indication of the extent to which the authorities bowed to the wishes of financial markets without accepting that those markets had any justification for their beliefs and expectations.

Industrial policy

In the 1960s the Treasury began to take a direct interest in the performance of British industry, notably the manufacturing sector. It had become apparent that the rate of growth of productivity in this sector was significantly less than that in most of continental Western Europe. This meant that unless the UK were able to engineer a fall in real wages compared with those abroad, the country would steadily lose market share in tradeable goods both abroad and at home and the balance of payments would deteriorate. The balance of payments—and in particular the balance of trade—was, throughout the

[17] In March 1980 the Treasury issued a report (Cmnd 7858) under the authority of the new Chancellor shortly after the change in government in 1979 which examined the various possible methods of controlling the growth of the money supply including control of the monetary base and concluded that fiscal policy and interest rates had to be the principal mechanisms—there was no 'tap' called the money supply which could be adjusted at will. Moreover the response of the money supply to changes in fiscal policy and interest rates was a medium-term matter and in effect a 'trial and error' business.

immediate post-war years as we have mentioned, a source of concern to all policy makers and indeed to financial markets, mainly because the war had led to a huge fall in invisible income, which meant that the current account deficit which the country was habituated to in pre-war years had to be closed if external viability was to be secured. The first deliberate attempts at dealing with this situation were focused on the National Economic Development Office (NEDO) and the Council (NEDC) which oversaw its activities, institutions which had been established in 1962 with a view to a tripartite (government, business, and trade unions) approach to determining what needed to be done to improve productivity and industrial performance generally. In the early 1960s Neddy (as it was familiarly termed) produced a number of general works dealing with the causes of slow economic growth and poor productivity in the UK, but the analysis was at a high level of generality. It was not until the work of the Office and the organization started to look at particular industrial sectors through the tripartite Economic Development Committees that were set up, that the serious business of identifying specific reasons why some areas of British industry performed relatively so poorly began. The area examined in each industry included labour practices, the extent of research and development in particular industries, the harmonization of industrial standards and so on. This was painstaking work and although the fruits it bore were not easy to identify and were certainly not visible at the macro-economic level, the general feeling in government (whatever the political party in office) and indeed by both sides of industry was that it should be persevered with.

In 1964 the work was raised to a higher level of importance by the new Labour Government and a new department, the Department of Economic Affairs (DEA), was created to devise a National Plan for economic growth which it was supposed would lead to greater confidence and to the likelihood of faster growth. The National Plan proved to be a pipe-dream and the harsh realities of the economic and financial crises of 1966 and 1967 led to its abandonment and to the demise of the DEA. But the work of Neddy and its committees did not come to an end and the failure of a grandiose national economic plan did not diminish the enthusiasm of Whitehall to persevere with the micro-economic work of the sectoral committees of NEDC with the participation of both sides of industry. By the mid-1970s responsibility for this work in government was shared between the Department of Industry and the Treasury. In November 1975 a White Paper[18] was published outlining what it described as an 'Approach to an Industrial Policy'. The narrative we set out in the following paragraphs gives little space to these 'micro' measures to promote an increase essentially in national productive potential, partly as said earlier because they were not of a 'macro' character but partly because their perceived effect on overall performance was too small to be measured. In any

---

[18] Cmnd 6315.

case they were largely abandoned after 1979 and their life-span was too short to determine whether they would have had any effect if persevered with. It was the case, however, that the Government put considerable emphasis on the Industrial Strategy and indeed persuaded the IMF, when they reviewed the UK economy, to take it as a serious contribution to the improvement of macro-economic performance.

The International Monetary Fund

We turn now to some of the institutions which played an important part in the events described in the following chapters. Of these the main one outside the UK was the International Monetary Fund (IMF) which played a crucial role in the resolution of the 1976 crisis (and indeed had figured in the drama of the previous year). The Fund had been founded in 1946 following the Bretton Woods conference two years earlier and by the early 1970s its membership comprised most of the independent countries of the world outside the Soviet bloc. It had been set up essentially by the USA and the UK as a mechanism to prevent the destabilizing features of the financial system (if it can be so described) which obtained before the Second World War when countries indulged freely in such practices as competitive depreciation of their currencies, exchange controls on current payments (which acted as a form of trade discrimination) and multiple exchange rates (which also had a distorting effect on the pattern of trade).

The essence of the new financial world order created by the IMF and its Articles of Agreement were that members should abide by a fixed exchange rate system and should abolish all restrictions on current (though explicitly not capital) payments. The former was secured by the establishment of a system of par values for each currency in terms of gold-equivalent and the latter by the oversight by the Fund of the system of restrictions, if any, which member countries applied in contravention of the Fund's Articles. But the founders of the system recognized that adherence to the rules prescribed could involve members in temporary foreign exchange difficulties pending the adoption of policies which would restore equilibrium. The Fund was therefore endowed with a substantial capital, subscribed to by all members, which could be drawn upon by members on a medium-term basis to finance temporary disequilibria.[19] Access to this capital, apart from that part which the member had subscribed in gold in the first place, was not automatic.

---

[19] This was for 'normal' drawings. The Fund also had supplementary facilities which were introduced from time to time to provide credit for members in special difficulties. One of these in being during the period covered by this narrative was the Oil Facility, described later in the book.

The conditions governing access were fairly permissive for the first slice (or tranche[20]) of the member's quota and gradually became more demanding as the amount of capital assistance sought rose. The conditions applied were that the member should be pursuing economic policies which the Fund judged to be 'appropriate' for the restoration of payments equilibrium and that it should not be resorting to 'anti-social' practices like trade and/or exchange restrictions. Access to the Fund's resources could therefore involve an examination whether the (fixed) exchange rate needed to be changed (as it could be with the Fund's approval) and whether domestic policies, notably fiscal and monetary policy, were conducive to equilibrium, and what impediments the applicant was putting in the way of 'free trade'.

Besides being the authority which alone could permit exchange rate changes and which had control of the supply of its capital to members needing access to it, the Fund had the legal right to conduct annual 'consultations' with all members to ensure that, irrespective of whether the member was seeking access to the Fund's resources, the policies being pursued in both the domestic and external field were acceptable to the Fund. The consultations were clearly necessary in the period from 1946 to 1958 when most members were only partly accepting the obligation to free all current payments from restrictions and to allow full convertibility to their currencies. But after 1958 the Fund continued with annual consultations even with members who had at the end of that year lifted most, if not quite all, restrictions. This they were entitled to do under the Articles and most members would have agreed that the annual consultation was a useful exercise in giving the Fund staff opportunities to comment on minor derogations from the full rigour of the Fund's rules and indeed to make suggestions about the conduct of economic policy generally against the possibility that the member might at some stage be obliged to seek access to the Fund's capital.

The Fund's approach to the question of a member's exchange rate was largely pragmatic. If there was a 'fundamental disequilibrium' in the member's payments, that is if the member had a serious and persistent payments deficit (or, in theory but practically never in practice, payments surplus) and that deficit could not be corrected by changes in domestic policy designed to secure internal and external equilibrium, the Fund actively encouraged an exchange rate change and sometimes insisted on one. The Fund was also reasonably pragmatic about the existence of payments restrictions which were in contravention of its Articles, taking the line with most members that encouragement to obey the rules was preferable to heavy-handed threats to withdraw access to its resources for minor infringements. The Fund's chief problems in this area lay with developing countries which were subject to greater payments

---

[20] Each tranche was equal to 25% of the member's quota, which was made up as to the 'gold' tranche and three equal credit tranches.

fluctuations because of their dependence on trade in primary products whose prices could vary significantly from year to year and whose crops were also likely to rise and fall with climatic conditions. The Fund accordingly developed a number of policies and facilities designed to meet these exceptional conditions without the fullest application of the original rules.

It was, however, in the field of a member's domestic economic policies that the Fund developed policies which were more contentious. Many of the members who sought access to the Fund's capital in the early years of its existence were developing countries which did not have sophisticated systems of national accounts or in some cases did not have the data at an aggregate level which would have permitted the sort of appraisal of the appropriateness of policy in an advanced country like the UK. The Fund had to rely, therefore, on such data as it could obtain and make a judgement based on that partial data. The area where data were reasonably easily obtainable was the banking system and the Fund sought to develop techniques which, relying on figures for the public finances and the evolution of the member's banks collective balance sheets, gave an indication whether the trends were consistent with balance of payments equilibrium. Over time this approach led the Fund to give high prominence in its examination of domestic policies to the fiscal balance (i.e. the need of the government to borrow to finance its programmes) and to the supply of bank credit to the private sector. The measure favoured by the Fund was labelled Domestic Credit Expansion (DCE) and consisted of the rate of increase in the supply of bank credit to both the government and the domestic private sector. The rationale for this approach to the balance of payments problems of a developed country with sophisticated financial markets is examined in the final chapter of this book.

The organization of the Treasury

Some understanding of how the Treasury in the 1970s was organized to handle economic policy making in general and negotiations with the Fund in particular is essential to any appreciation of how views were formed and recommendations made to ministers. There were four main blocks of work—not by any means separated by water-tight bulkheads. Each was overseen by a Second Secretary.[21] The first, headed by Derek Mitchell, was the Overseas Finance Group referred to in the narrative as OF whose remit comprised all international financial and monetary questions including of course relations with

---

[21] This was only the case from October 1975, when the Industrial Sector was created. Prior to that a miscellaneous group of divisions, mainly home finance, counter-inflation and 'general economic policy' reported to Deputy Secretaries who in turn reported to the Permanent Secretary.

the IMF. It had responsibility for the exchange rate of sterling, for the management of the foreign currency reserves, for exchange control and for relations with overseas governments including, critically, those of the sterling area. It worked closely with the overseas sector of the Bank of England. The second group was the Public Expenditure Group (PE). Its head during the period covered by this review was Douglas Henley (until late 1975) and thereafter Leo Pliatzky. Its role was to exercise control over the level, growth, and distribution of public expenditure both in total and at the detailed departmental programme level. A central division of this group was concerned with general questions and totals, but there were several specialist divisions whose remit was to oversee the expenditure of particular programmes, like health, defence, etc. One important element of public expenditure—that on industry—was, from the autumn of 1975, excluded from the departmental remit of the PE Group and given to the third group, the National Economy Group (NE). The latter had a miscellany of functions, ranging from domestic monetary policy, tax, counter-inflation, and the nationalized industries. The head of this group from the end of 1975 was Alan Lord. The fourth and last group was the Economists Group, which consisted of all the economists concerned with the macro-economy, that is the forecasters and model-builders as well as the analysts. It was headed from December 1974 to 1976 by Bryan Hopkin and for the early part of 1974 by Kenneth Berrill. In the 1960s all the Treasury economists had been housed in this group, but as the Department became aware that economists could make a contribution to policy making at the micro-economic level, in particular in the appraisal and analysis of public expenditure programmes, specialist economists were 'bedded out' in the division where they could help policy to be formulated. As a result of this move the Treasury incorporated micro-economic techniques and 'cost–benefit analysis' into the process of evaluating expenditure proposals. Monetary economists were also bedded out in the Home Finance division (HF and a part of NE) and they contributed to the development of a financial model of the economy and to the analysis of the impact of monetary factors on the real economy.

With such a spread of functions and activities the Treasury had always had a need to find ways of systematically coordinating the various strands of policy, many of which could impinge on areas which lay outside the responsibility of the sector concerned. It was, in short, necessary to ensure that policy as a whole had an internal consistency and that conflicts of objectives were properly identified and resolved. Such a consistency was not always possible. Sometimes government objectives themselves lacked consistency or at the very least impinged on each other. Highlighting inconsistencies and making recommendations on the optimum way of resolving them was the function of a piece of machinery which was set up at the end of 1974 to remedy deficiencies in this area. This was the Policy Coordinating Committee (PCC), and consisted of those Treasury officials of the rank of Deputy Secretary and above[22] (about a dozen). Its membership ensured that no part of the Department was not represented and the inclusion of Deputy Secretaries ensured that the level of expertise was sufficient for a thorough-going discussion of any issue to be conducted. The PCC was served by a small unit, the Central Unit, whose responsibilities included the identification of issues to be brought to the Committee, the flow of papers and the writing of minutes and the drafting of briefs. The Committee met every Thursday as a routine; but it also met whenever occasion required it, for instance in the preparation of a Budget. All the main issues of policy from the end of 1974 were processed through the PCC and the upshot of consideration by the Committee was frequently a submission to the Chancellor inviting him to consider the issue involved, identifying the policy options for dealing with it and recommending to him a particular course of action. Because the issues often involved conflicting interests the discussion at PCC was frequently animated. Sometimes a unity of view was not achieved and it fell to the Chairman, the Permanent Secretary, to present the Chancellor with a summary of the conflicts of view and a personal recommendation as to the course of action.[23] There was in fact during the period covered by this history a division of opinion within the PCC on whether the Chancellor was best served by being told that his advisers were not at one. But the Chancellor had made it plain that he wanted to know when there were differences of view among his advisers, and the Permanent Secretary favoured this course as well. Not all the issues presented to the Chancellor were however processed through the PCC. It was a feature of the delegation which took place within the Treasury that issues involving only one Division were submitted by that Division—usually, though by no means always, through the Second Secretary, although of course copies of the submission were copied to all senior officials if the gravity of the issue merited it. This system combined a reasonable amount of delegation with a reasonable amount of coordination. But the blend of the two elements was often a matter of judgement and no hard-and-fast rules existed to define how they should be applied in practice.

The Bank of England

The Bank played an important part in the shaping and development of macroeconomic policy, although somewhat different from the part it played twenty years later after the reforms of 1997. It had three main executive functions in this area: the management of short-term interest rates through its operations in the money market and its relations with the discount houses; the

[22] The working methods of the PCC are set out in PCC (75) 113, T277/3059.
[23] See for instance the discussion of the Second Secretaries on 19 October 1976, DW014 (T364/15).

management of the gilt-edged market, that is the market in government securities; and the management of the foreign exchange market. All three were free markets,[24] and accordingly were subject to 'management' in only a limited sense, although the Bank's ability to determine the market rate of interest on short-term debt was considerable as we described in the section on Monetary Policy. In the gilt-edged market the Bank was the source of advice to the Treasury on the timing and the terms of new issues and it exercised this authority so as to be conducive to an orderly market. With the same end in view, the Bank supported the jobbers (the somewhat undercapitalized professional traders in gilts) when necessary by taking surplus stock off their hands. In the foreign exchange market the Bank had much less market power as there were very many operators and the market was an international one, with sterling traded on many overseas exchanges. It did, however, have available to it for market purposes the whole of the UK's foreign exchange reserves as was described in the section on Sterling.

The Bank also had an important non-market macro-economic function—one derived from its role as prudential supervisor of the banking system, or at any rate the clearing banking system. It laid down the proportion of the clearing banks' deposit liabilities which had to be held as reserves at the Bank itself, special deposits as they were called. Although this originated as a prudential measure, it became, in the whole post-war era, a powerful tool for reining in the banking system's proclivities to lend to its customers and therefore as a means of controlling the expansion of credit. The Bank could call for extra special deposits at will and it could also build on this system, as it did with the Corset to limit the growth of particular categories of the banking system's liabilities.

In the exercise of all these functions the Bank operated with a good deal of contact with the Treasury, although the precise way that it exercised its management functions in these areas was often determined on an *ad hoc* basis, that is to say the Bank would consult whenever there was an important issue at stake, such as that of a change in MLR and it would certainly seek Treasury authority for a new issue of gilt-edged stock and for the precise terms it should have. It was also customary for the Bank to consult the Treasury if it judged that market conditions required substantial intervention in the foreign exchange market to deal with turbulence or instability. In all three areas there was an implicit understanding of what the objectives of macro-economic policy were and the Bank's operations had these objectives in mind in exercising its market power.

The Bank was closely involved in the formulation of macro-economic policy, particularly those areas which impinged on its market functions, but increasingly during the 1970s in all areas. The three areas where the Bank

[24] The London foreign exchange market was not open to UK residents (at any rate for capital transactions) but the banks and businesses had a great deal of freedom to operate in this market. The market was made entirely free when exchange control was abolished in late 1979.

was least involved were the control of public expenditure, policy on taxation, and the weapons then conventionally used to combat inflation.[25] But in all other areas, monetary and exchange rate policy in particular, it had an important, indeed vital, contribution to make and it did not hesitate to do so at whatever level of authority that was appropriate. The Chancellor expressed a view early in his period of office that the Bank should be more involved in policy making than had hitherto been the case and to some extent he realized this wish.

The Bank had one other important function in the realm of macro-economic policy and that was to advise the Treasury on the opportunities for public sector borrowing in foreign currency—a function it was able to exercise with considerable authority because of its network of overseas contacts with market operators and with overseas Central Banks—and indeed because of its operations in the foreign exchange market. The Bank also, as effectively the sterling banker of many overseas, and especially sterling area, central banks, had considerable inside knowledge of the activities of those operators; and although as their banker the Bank did not feel able to disclose to the Treasury the details of those activities, the insight that this privileged position gave the Bank made its advice to the Treasury on such matters as market sentiment very valuable indeed.

In the area we are dealing with the Bank was organized functionally, with operations in the domestic markets largely in the hands of the Chief Cashier and those in the foreign exchange markets and overseas handled by the Overseas Sector. The Governor and his Deputy together with the Executive Directors were in control and command of all the Bank's market and advisory functions. Any issue of more than day-to-day business was usually handled at this level—the Bank was a much more centrally controlled institution than the Treasury. In financial terms the Bank had broadly two accounts, which it designated as the Issue Department and the Banking Department. The former was in effect the account which managed the note issue and consisted, on the assets side, mainly of government securities and, on the liabilities side, of the aggregate of the note issue. The profits deriving from this activity accrued to the Treasury—there being no reason why the 'seigniorage'—the privilege of issuing fiduciary currency—should accrue to the Bank, and the Treasury were in effect, if not in name, the beneficial owner of the Department. The Banking Department, much smaller in financial terms, consisted of the Bank's own capital which it was independently responsible for managing and which it used, without Treasury guarantee, for specifically banking purposes such as the operation of the 'Lifeboat'—a fund to which the Bank contributed together with the Clearing Banks to rescue secondary banks in financial difficulties.

---

[25] The Bank did not in the early part of the period of this study place much reliance on monetary targeting as a counter-inflation weapon, but it gradually shifted its stance on this issue as the decade progressed.

At the time of the events described in this book the post of Governor was occupied by Gordon Richardson, who had been appointed in 1973 having previously been a merchant banker and before that a barrister. All the other senior posts—the Deputy Governor (Jasper Hollom) and the three Executive Directors (Kit McMahon on the overseas, John Fforde on the domestic and Christopher Dow on the economic analysis side) were filled by career public servants—people who had worked variously in the Bank itself, in other parts of the public sector or academia or in international economic organizations.

The organization of ministerial discussions

The principal forum for collective ministerial discussions of economic policy in the 1970s was, of course, the Cabinet, which met regularly each Thursday but which also held meetings at other times when the need arose. Much of the narrative in the account presented in this book of policy making relates to how the Cabinet addressed itself to the issues of macro-economic policy which were presented to it, as a rule by the Chancellor of the Exchequer, but on some few occasions by other ministers who either wished to offer a departmental view of the matter under consideration or who had a different view of the course of policy generally and wished to present that view in writing. The usual course was for those ministers who differed from the Chancellor to do so orally in the course of the discussion, but this was not invariably the case. The procedural rules usually required a minister who wished to present in writing a different view from that of the Chancellor to seek the approval of the Prime Minister before doing so. In the period covered by this account it was customary for both Harold Wilson and James Callaghan to give that approval. There was therefore little to inhibit free and open discussion of the merits of policy. Indeed as the account of the Cabinet consideration of the IMF negotiations in 1976 shows the discussions covered all aspects at issue. The Cabinet was given a full account of the position of the Fund and of the options open to the Government, as the Chancellor saw them, for reacting to it.

The Treasury's privileged position as the presenter (through the Chancellor) to the Cabinet of the policy choices was not unique. There had been established in the early 1970s an independent body charged with the review of any element of government policy that it thought merited investigation—the Central Policy Review Staff (CPRS), located in the Cabinet Office. This body exercised its right to conduct reviews of economic policy in the period covered by this account on a small number of occasions, most notably in the examination of policy priorities in the field of public expenditure in 1975 and of the case for and against a system of import controls. But for the most part, the CPRS did not offer noticeably different advice from that of the Treasury and the Chancellor, perhaps because there was a good deal of prior discussion between CPRS staff and the Treasury before matters went to Cabinet which meant that any differences of view between these bodies tended to be ironed out before they came to Ministers. The narrative does not therefore give much of a role to the CPRS in the evolution of macro-economic policy in the 1970s. But this does not mean that its influence was negligible. It is rather that its influence was more indirect than perhaps its authors intended.

Although the Cabinet was the main ministerial body which reviewed and authorized the execution of macro-economic policy, one or two subordinate bodies also came into the picture. The main such body was the Ministerial Committee on Economic Strategy, which was known by the acronym MES during the Wilson administration and by EY when Callaghan succeeded him in April 1976.[26] This Committee, comprising a relatively small number of senior ministers, not all with departmental responsibilities for economic policy, met whenever the Prime Minister thought that an issue, which would come to the Cabinet for final decision, would benefit from prior debate in a smaller forum. One advantage of this course, from the point of view of the Chancellor and indeed the Prime Minister, was that the two-stage process enabled the proponent of policy, usually the Chancellor, to secure the support of some senior members of the Cabinet before the Cabinet as a whole addressed itself to the issue. For crucially important issues however, like the settling of the details of public expenditure in the medium term or the acceptance of the IMF's proposals in 1976, the technique of using MES was of limited use. The Cabinet as a whole had to be in the driving seat.

Of less relevance were a number of other Cabinet Committees, such as the Ministerial Committee on Economic Policy,[27] which devoted itself to matters not of a macro-economic kind, like the handling of an industrial relations dispute or the closure of nationalized industry plant. These issues were not of more than incidental relevance to the formulation of macro-policy and are not dealt with other than tangentially in the narrative. From time to time the Prime Minister would establish an *ad hoc* Ministerial Committee to deal with a matter which had by its nature a limited life expectancy. These were referred to in Cabinet Office terminology as GEN or MISC Committees. Only one such committee makes an appearance in our narrative—MISC 91,[28] which was set up in June 1975 to settle the terms of the Incomes Policy which the Government had then decided it had to introduce. It was, however, as were the other ministerial committees, subordinate to the Cabinet, which always had the last word on any aspect of policy.

[26] It was the practice of the Cabinet Office to redesignate Ministerial Committees with a new acronym whenever there was a change of Prime Minister or *a fortiori* when there was a change of government.

[27] CAB 134/3891 and 3892.   [28] CAB 130/819.

2

1974—Marking Time

The Labour Government's inheritance

On 4 March 1974 Harold Wilson formed his second ministry. The General Election which had taken place on 28 February had produced a murky result. The outgoing Conservative Government had failed to get the Parliamentary majority it had sought to enforce its existing policies, notably on incomes restraint, but the main opposition party, Labour, had fared little better and did not secure an overall majority, although it did capture more seats than the Conservatives. Edward Heath attempted to form a coalition government with the Liberal Party, but the negotiations broke down and Heath tendered his resignation, advising the sovereign to invite Wilson, whose party had secured the most seats, to form a government.

The circumstances and result of the Election of February 1974 exercised a dominant influence on the policies and events which followed over the next three years. Heath had called the election in response to the outright challenge to his government's authority which had come from the miners' overtime ban that had begun three months earlier. That challenge, in turn, had stemmed from the response of the government to an inflationary situation which developed from 1972 onwards. It is necessary, therefore, to look at how that situation had emerged and why Heath responded to it as he did.

The Heath government had been formed in June 1970 following what was a surprise victory at the General Election which the ruling Labour Party had called after some six years in office. The economic and political situation in 1970 was by no means unfavourable to the party in power. The financial crisis of 1967 had been resolved thanks largely to a devaluation of sterling and the introduction of an economic programme of retrenchment involving substantial cuts in public expenditure and increases in taxation. Within eighteen months of the introduction of this programme the balance of payments had begun to show signs of improvement and as we now know had moved into surplus. The economy was operating with a substantial margin of surplus capacity, and inflation, which had risen quite sharply in the late 1960s, seemed to be under control despite the absence at the time of any explicit policy on wages and prices. The popular expectation was that the Labour Party would be returned to office. This was not, however, to be the case and the Conservatives gained power with a working overall Parliamentary majority.

The Heath government's economic policy was significantly different from that of its predecessor and indeed from that of previous Conservative governments. It involved a good deal of economic liberalism in its attitude to business, it forswore resort to wage and price controls, support for failing industries, and it favoured cuts in public expenditure and reductions in taxation. It also involved the abolition of the Selective Employment Tax, which the Labour Government had introduced three years earlier as a manipulative attempt to divert manpower from the service industries to manufacturing. And it proposed the replacement of the classical system of Corporation Tax (introduced like the Selective Employment Tax by the preceding government) with one designed to promote the distribution of company profits and give financial markets a bigger role in the allocation of capital. Finally it stated that it was going to introduce a major reform of Industrial Relations by reducing the power of the trade unions and subjecting them to statutory provisions from which they had been significantly exempted since the legislation of the 1870s. This was in many ways a programme of drastic reform and might, had it been persevered with, have led to fundamental changes in the way that the British economy functioned. But although some elements of the programme were retained, and subsequently became accepted by all the political parties, its core element was abandoned within two years.

The main reason for the policy change was the intensity of the economic recession which emerged early in 1971 and the sharp rise in unemployment and business failures which were its manifestation. The earliest sign of policy change occurred with the possible failure of an important Scottish shipbuilder and shortly thereafter the imminent collapse of Rolls-Royce, until then a successful developer and manufacturer of aero-engines with a world market. The government shrank from the logic of its declared policy and was instrumental, through the provision of public funds in one case and partial nationalization in the other, in saving both companies from the failure that would undoubtedly have occurred. These events were followed in the spring of 1972 by a strongly reflationary budgetary package which was designed to pull the economy out of the recession and was strongly reminiscent of the sort of action which all post-war governments had taken when faced with an economic slump. The sum total of these actions was to cast doubt on the viability and credibility of economic liberalism in the prevailing political climate.

This retreat, and the effect it had on opinion, was compounded later in 1972 when, as wage and price inflation began to increase, the government resorted to a statutory prices and Incomes Policy which involved its (at least tacit) acceptance by the trade unions and by employers and therefore implied that these elements would have a greater say in the formulation of economic policy than had been envisaged at the outset of the Heath government. The inflation of 1972 was by no means solely due to the reflationary package embodied in the Budget of that year. There had been a sharp rise in commodity prices worldwide, caused in part by harvest failures particularly of the wheat crop. There was also a renewed outburst of industrial discontent in the UK, mainly over wages. In May of that year following a threatened strike by railwaymen, a body of public sector workers for whom the government was effectively the employer, a large pay increase was conceded. By the late summer of 1972 it was clear that the inflationary outlook was dangerous. Moderation in wage settlement was unlikely to be achieved in the face of rapid economic growth and falling unemployment.

With more than a little reluctance, the government decided that it had no alternative but to resort to a Prices and Incomes Policy along the lines of those of the 1960s. This decision was the final nail in the programme of economic liberalism, for it involved the participation of employers and trade unions, both of whom were prepared to collaborate only if some at least of what they wanted in the way of economic concessions were granted. The main price sought by the unions was, not unnaturally, the repeal of the industrial relations legislation enacted earlier in the Parliament. The government resisted this pressure but looked at other concessions which the TUC sought—principally the provision within the new policy of special treatment for the low paid, and some subsidization of prices in the field of necessities, notably food. The government at first sought to have the policy they proposed an agreed one and therefore one not requiring legislation and the introduction of statutory penalties for non-observance—an approach that has always been recognized in the discussion of incomes policies as fraught with political danger. But, as it became clear that the government was not prepared to concede the main demands of the TUC, the need for the policy to have statutory backing was inevitable.

The new policy was accordingly launched on a statutory basis on 6 November 1972. It involved initially three stages. The first was an outright freeze on pay, prices, rents, and dividends for a 90-day period with the possibility of extension for a further 60 days. This was followed by Stage 2, which was to run effectively from April to November 1973. It was enacted that in this period pay increases should be limited by a formula equivalent to about £2 per week— effectively about 7.5 per cent of weekly earnings. The terms of Stage 3 were left till nearer the time of its coming into operation. The structure of the allowable increases in Stage 2 conceded something to the unions by prescribing a flat-rate element in the formula and hence involved a proportionately higher percentage pay increase for the low paid: and it also met the unions' concern with prices generally by prescribing a strict regime for price increases.

It established new organizations: the Pay Board and the Price Commission which were charged with examination of claims for exemption from the full rigours of the policy.

The policy worked reasonably well in the first year and the Pay Board claimed that approved settlements led to increases in earnings of 7.66 per cent. It was accepted by most of those involved and the number of breaches was few. However, actual earnings increased in 1972–73 by something like 13.5 per cent, the discrepancy with the formula being largely due to the delayed implementation of pay increases that had been agreed before the freeze and implemented at its expiry. Price inflation therefore continued to increase and this was reinforced by strongly rising food prices. However by mid-1973, when the formula for the wage round beginning in the autumn of that year was being formulated, the mood in Government circles was cautiously optimistic. The statutory policy seemed to be succeeding and it was judged appropriate that, while some flexibility could be permitted, the pay increases which could be prescribed for that round should be ambitious—7 per cent or £2.25 per week. This would have involved a small cut in real wages; in order to make the policy palatable to the unions and their members, the government returned to the question of subsidizing the costs of certain 'necessities' in everyday life—in particular food. But this still proved to be a sticking point for Ministers and they declined the gambit. What they offered instead was an escape clause from the full rigours of the policy of fixed pay increases under which the prescribed and allowable pay increase could be further increased if the rate of increase of prices exceeded some 'threshold' amount. When and if the retail price index (RPI) rose by 7 per cent above the figure for October 1973, a pay increase of 40p a week could be given, and the same increase for every further 1 per cent in the index until October 1974. At the time that this proposal was launched the likelihood of the threshold being breached was judged to be small—in fact it was fixed at a level which it was thought allowed for a significant margin of error. In due course the policy for the wage round of 1973–74 was announced together with the threshold provision.

It was precisely at this point that things began to go seriously wrong. On 6 October 1973 a group of Arab countries launched a war against Israel and immediately afterwards, in a move that was seen as consequential, the Arab oil-producing countries took a succession of steps both to reduce oil production and to increase posted prices. Later on they went further and imposed a ban on oil sales to some of the developed world and followed this from 1 January 1974 by further doubling the price increase—a step which was endorsed by the non-Arab members of the cartel known as the Organisation of Petroleum Exporting Countries (OPEC). The effect of these successive measures was to increase the posted price by four-fold over a period of three months. The extent to which this action was directly connected with the Arab-Israeli War need not concern us. What must, however, is that the strength of the oil cartel virtually ensured that worldwide oil prices rose rapidly and strongly. The immediate impact on retail prices in the developed world was probably of the order of 3 per cent[1]—and this could of course increase as other price makers, notably the labour unions, raised their prices. Equally importantly it was seen that the action of OPEC would have the effect of transfering a substantial element of the national income of the oil users— again principally the developed world—to the oil producers. Only if the producers were prepared to lend their new surpluses back to the oil consuming countries could the latter sustain their existing levels of expenditure, although this would involve taking large amounts of international credit. This idea became a large element in the thinking of the UK in the following months, but it was not on the whole shared by other developed countries.

In the main the developed countries responded to these events by seeing the inflationary consequences as the more serious, with the income effect a poor second. Several of them introduced measures which restricted domestic demand as the means of countering the inflationary pressures. By reducing demand such measures would also reduce the size of the oil import bill and hence the balance of payments effect of the increase in oil prices, although this was not the primary aim. The UK sought in international discussion of the appropriate response to the oil price development to encourage the developed world not to compound the problem by deflating further. But this argument largely fell on deaf ears. Of the developed world, only Italy followed the UK line of seeking to maintain income and demand. Significantly the UK and Italy were the two countries which subsequently had to seek assistance from the IMF in the following two years.

The inflationary effects of the oil price increase were to have a most serious consequence for the success of Stage 3 of the Incomes Policy. The outlook for the retail price index was such that the small allowable pay increase would lead to a fall in real wages. This was of course inevitable from the actions of OPEC which had the direct effect of transferring real income from oil importers to oil exporters. But to the ordinary trade union member and officials it seemed that it was the Incomes Policy that was causing the income loss. The second effect of the oil price increase and the embargo which preceded it was to make alternative sources of energy very attractive, both to government policy makers and energy users. The message was not lost on the National Union of Mineworkers (NUM) who clearly saw that the developments following the price increase were bound to strengthen their negotiating position *vis-à-vis* the government (effectively the miners' employers) and energy users (notably the electricity supply industry). The normal timing of the miners' wage round was early in the winter of each year but the NUM had passed a resolution at

---

[1] Author's estimate based on the general level of imported energy input in the economies of the industrialized world.

their annual conference in July demanding pay increases ranging from 22 to 46 per cent.[2] The government's response to this challenge was to seek to head it off by incorporating into the terms for Stage 3 provisions allowing special increases for efficiency and productivity gains; in behind-the-scenes discussions between the NUM and Ministers the latter formed the impression that these would satisfy the miners' demands.[3]

Stage 3 began shakily but there was no direct challenge to its terms at first, as there had been no challenge to Stage 2. The National Coal Board, the miners' employer, took full advantage of the flexibility of the terms of the Pay Code and made a pay offer worth about 13 per cent. But the miners were in no mood to carry on with their acquiescence into the new round, no doubt fortified by the power which the oil crisis gave them. The precise course of the dispute between the government and the NUM need not concern us here. It suffices to say that the miners made little effort to compromise and the government for their part dug their toes in. A number of efforts were made to secure a compromise settlement including a reference to the Pay Board. No solution was found and the government prepared itself for a struggle. The miners began an overtime ban on 12 November, joining a similar step taken by the workers in the electrical supply industry. The impact on industry was more or less immediate and the government introduced measures greatly restricting the use of energy. They also introduced on 17 December a mini-Budget—designed primarily to deal with the immediate effects of the oil crisis rather than with the miners' dispute—which made significant cuts in public expenditure, mostly in construction projects. In the financial year beginning 1 April 1974 these amounted to £1,200 million. The mini-Budget also increased the higher rates of income tax (then called surtax). These measures were justified by the then Chancellor (Anthony Barber) on the grounds that it was necessary to curtail the private and public consumption of energy, which at the margin was a charge on the balance of payments and which, in turn, had deteriorated with the rise in oil prices. The Chancellor explained that although it would be wrong to respond to the situation created by the oil crisis and the miners' action simply by deflating the economy, 'in our case some policy action needs to be taken to keep the prospective total deficit within limits'.[4] The Bank of England introduced the Corset for the first time (see Chapter 1). It so happened that the Public Expenditure White Paper for 1974 had been timed for publication on the same day as the mini-Budget and the Government was in the embarrassing position of having to state that the plans incorporated in it would have to be changed to take account of the announced cuts. What the Chancellor said was:

[2] *Blackaby.*   [3] Ibid.   [4] *Hansard* 17 December 1973.

The White Paper which was to be published this week was prepared before the developments which have caused this statement. Although it does not take account of these decisions it will still be published as a baseline for the reductions I have announced.

The effect of the announcement was that, whereas the White Paper envisaged that expenditure in 1974–75 would be some 1.8 per cent higher than a year before, it would now fall by about 2 per cent. It is important to bear this in mind for, as we shall see, one of the first acts of the new Labour Government was radically to change this pattern and budget for a sharp *increase* in expenditure that year.

The mini-Budget was not, of course, sufficiently strong to deal with the drop in energy supplies caused by the miners' industrial action and on 1 January 1974 regulations were put in place to oblige businesses to restrict their working to three days per week in an attempt to conserve energy (and particularly coal) stocks. The hope of the government was clearly that the NUM would climb down, but they had no strategy to secure that aim. Consideration was given to the removal of social security benefits from strikers' families, but this would have required legislation which would have been highly controversial. It would also have imposed hardship on women and children not party to the dispute and this was judged to be unacceptable.[5] The government fell back on the step of calling a General Election, in the hope that winning an appeal to the country would put the NUM into an untenable position. Whether this would have happened and whether the NUM would have deferred to a democratic verdict cannot be known, for the government did not obtain the mandate it sought, and, as we have seen, resigned from office and left the field to the Labour Party.

The position of the opposition Labour Party during the currency of the Incomes Policy had been to oppose it. In February 1973 they had negotiated an understanding with the TUC entitled 'Economic Policy and the Cost of Living'[6] which committed the Party, if returned to office, to allowing a resumption of normal wage bargaining in return for the Government taking action on the prices of goods which were important for low-paid employees and expanding certain socially important public programmes, notably social security and housing benefits. It also involved the repeal of the Industrial Relations legislation of the Heath Government. The commitments contained in this understanding, which came to be known as the Social Contract, were embodied in the Labour Party manifesto published on 8 February 1974. In the field of wage negotiations the TUC undertook to advise unions to limit wage increases broadly to the price increases which had occurred since their previous wage settlement. The aim was to preserve the real value of wages. The theory behind this deal was that wage increases strictly confined to price

---

[5] T 357/334.   [6] LAB 77/47.

increases would lead to a gradual decline in inflation, as the growth in labour productivity would enable producers to lower their prices in relation to the wages they paid. What the theory did not take into account was the element of 'drift' which occurs in wage settlements, that is the tendency for unions to squeeze some extra element of remuneration and the tendency for increases in overtime to lead to higher 'take home' pay with little effect on extra output.

The March Budget

This, therefore, was the inheritance of the new administration. The new Chancellor, Denis Healey, was confronted with an economy that was experiencing a significant loss of national income and had a serious inflation problem and he was saddled with policies which, so far from resolving its problems, were likely to exacerbate them. For inflation, for the balance of payments, for economic growth and employment, for business profitability and investment and for the public finances the outlook was worse than it had been for a very long time: and for most of these issues the commitments of the Party made in opposition were likely to make them worse.

On inflation the retail price index was over 12 per cent higher than a year earlier. Wage settlements which had been within the limits prescribed for Phase 3 until the end of 1973 were likely to be affected both by the possible settlement of the miners' dispute and by the freedom of negotiators to settle on the basis of 'maintaining living standards', which would, as a minimum, lead to pay increases in double figures as opposed to the modest increases prescribed for Stage 3. There was also in the background the inflationary effect of the thresholds—likely to be triggered as a result of the revised outlook for retail prices.

On the balance of payments the monthly trade deficit which had been running at an average of £150 million per month in the first three-quarters of 1973 was averaging £400 million in the first quarter of 1974. Economic growth which had been strong in 1972 under the impulse of the Budget of that year had run out of steam—the economy actually declined in the fourth quarter of 1973. Unemployment which had fallen steadily in 1973 had begun to rise again, though it was difficult to be sure, because of the distortion caused by the three-day week, how great the reversal was. The most recent CBI quarterly survey of business intentions published in February was, in the words of *The Times*, 'the most pessimistic survey it [the CBI] has ever produced'. Seventy-eight per cent of respondents stated that they were now more pessimistic about the outlook than in the previous survey.[7]

---

[7] *The Times* 8 February 1974.

The public finances too showed a marked deterioration during the latter half of 1973 and as the Treasury were to inform the new Chancellor, on existing policies, let alone policies which provided for a significant increase in some public programmes, the Public Sector Borrowing Requirement for the year beginning 1 April 1974 was likely to be some £4 billion (about 4 per cent of GDP).[8]

The new Chancellor decided to open his first Budget on 26 March—only three weeks after taking office. There was not a great deal of time for him to take new decisions and his task was mainly to implement the immediate fiscal commitments made by the Labour Party in opposition and to ensure that these were financed appropriately. He decided, therefore, to leave until a later time (implicitly the autumn) those fiscal measures of a structural kind such as the introduction of a Lifetime Gift Tax which were in the Party's programme but would require a great deal of administrative and legal preparation. He took a meeting with senior Treasury officials on 7 March to hear their views on the economic outlook. The Permanent Secretary said that he thought the Budget should be 'mildly deflationary' taking out about £500 million of demand. He was supported by the heads of both the Overseas and the Home Side of the Treasury. Harold Lever, who had been appointed to the office of Chancellor of the Duchy of Lancaster (and in that capacity was treated *de facto* as a member of Healey's ministerial team) argued for a neutral budget.[9]

The following day the Chancellor was given a considered Budget judgement[10] and it was a cautious one. It conceded that the economy was in the doldrums, although it was less pessimistic than the National Institute of Economic and Social Research which was predicting a very weak economic outlook.[11] 'The reasons for not concluding...that the Budget should be mildly reflationary', said the Treasury, 'are basically the position of the external balance. We do face a deficit of £4 billion; we shall find difficulties in borrowing to this extent unless we maintain confidence; we must show that we are improving our balance of payments at the fastest rate compatible with reasonable levels of unemployment'. In this situation the Budget judgement given to the incoming Chancellor was that 'the choice lay between a neutral Budget or a mildly deflationary [one].... Now that it has been decided to have two Budgets the arguments for having a mildly deflationary intention in the first Budget have strengthened'.

---

[8] This figure has to be inferred from the fact that the Chancellor presented his Budget as reducing the PSBR he had inherited by £1.5 billion to produce a deficit of £2.7 billion. GDP was running at about £100 billion at current prices.

[9] T 171/1166.

[10] T 171/1067.

[11] The NIESR Review of February painted the state of the economy with bleak pessimism: 'It is not often that a government finds itself confronted with the possibility of a simultaneous failure to achieve any of the four main policy objectives—of adequate growth, full employment, a satisfactory balance of payments and reasonably stable prices.'

In the event the Chancellor sided with Lever and decided on a Budget whose overall effect was judged to be neutral. In his Budget Statement he gave as his economic and social objectives the achievement of full employment, a satisfactory balance of payments, the containment of inflation and 'the achievement of social unity'. The first three of these were in the nature of a ritual restatement of conventional economic objectives given by successive Chancellors over the years, but the fourth was a clear indication that the new government would not adopt measures which were likely to be socially divisive—or to put the matter somewhat cynically—would not create problems with the new government's supporters. The Speech said very little about employment or inflation, but did deal at length with the balance of payments. Here the theme was that the UK should borrow as much as was feasible. 'Borrowing', said the Chancellor, 'is more sensible, in economic and human terms, than trying to cut imports by massive deflation'—a clear dig at those developed countries which were adopting strong measures to counter inflation.

The Budget then went on to outline the public expenditure increases which the Labour Party had committed itself to in its manifesto and were to be implemented without delay: pension increases amounting to £1,240 million, food subsidies of £500 million and expenditure on housing (mainly through the subsidization of rents of local authority accommodation) of £350 million. These increases were to be financed in part by increases in employers' national insurance contributions and by increases in taxation, notably the basic rate of income tax which went up by 3 per cent and the higher rates by even more. It had been evident to the Chancellor in formulating his Budget proposals that the upshot of these proposals would leave him with a borrowing requirement which would make him vulnerable to criticism from the markets. His objective was to show some reduction in this, an aim he achieved by raising a forced loan on corporate business through the imposition of a surcharge on the payment of Advance Corporation Tax. This measure would have a once-and-for-all effect of reducing the government's need to borrow on the markets by about £1 billion.[12]

The Chancellor was therefore able to present his Budget as leading to a reduction in the PSBR for 1974–75 of £1.5 billion compared with the previous year. The Financial Statement optimistically predicted that GDP would grow at 2.5 per cent between the second half of 1973 and the corresponding period in 1974, but of course the forecast was based on relationships that were untested in the environment in which the economy was now operating. The Budget did nothing for the balance of payments, which the Chancellor acknowledged was a serious problem—the trade deficit for the months of January and February amounted to £800 million, a figure which would have caused consternation to

[12] FSBR March 1974.

policy makers of an earlier generation. The Chancellor simply focused on his ability to finance it.

The Chancellor had prepared his Budget in accordance with the usual conventions, that is to say that it was carried out within the Treasury and collective discussion was confined to the usual Cabinet meeting on the eve of Budget Day. But it was evident that in future decisions on economic policy would generally be taken more collectively than had conventionally been the case. The documentary evidence for this is hard to find, although subsequent events, including the extensive use of the Ministerial Committee on Economic Strategy (MES), amply confirm it. The Secretary of the Cabinet informed his official colleagues at the outset of the administration that 'there is evidence of a general desire among Ministers for thorough collective discussion of the main aspects of economic policy'.[13] Collective discussion—and decision— did in fact become the norm in the Wilson administration and indeed its successor under Callaghan, although two areas of economic policy remained under the sole jurisdiction of the Chancellor who consulted the Prime Minister as appropriate: taxation policy and monetary policy (both domestic and external).

The Budget may have been the immediate preoccupation of the Treasury and the Chancellor, but there were more strategic and indeed more complex problems that had to be tackled: the medium-term profile of public expenditure now that the figures in the published White Paper of December had been abandoned; the balance of payments and its financing; and, what was perhaps the most intractable of all, inflation. The first two of these were to take up a great deal of ministerial and official time in the course of 1974, and we deal with them below in some detail. The third, although of great concern, had somehow been quarantined by the Social Contract. However, as it became clear that this was not, in its original form, an effective answer, it too became a major issue.

Public expenditure I

The question of the level—and rate of growth—of public expenditure in the medium-term was one which the exigencies of the Parliamentary and financial timetable made of immediate concern. The PESC cycle began in the spring and officials had to complete their report by early summer in order to give Ministers sufficient time for consideration of what should go into the annual White Paper (which had to be presented to and debated by Parliament before the beginning of the following financial year). Within the Treasury public expenditure issues were largely handled by the PE Group reporting on detailed

---

[13] CAB 134/3838.

matters to the Chief Secretary. An important feature of the new Government was that the latter was not given a seat in the Cabinet (contrary to the practice of previous administrations). This meant that a heavier load was borne by the Chancellor, particularly when issues came to the Cabinet.

The Chancellor had cleared in mid-March with his Ministerial colleagues in MES[14]—the collective body which was to play a key role in the oversight of economic strategy—the implementation of the expensive manifesto commitments for spending on social programmes and subsidies in 1974–75, but had warned them on Treasury advice that thereafter the scope for increases would be severely limited. The Treasury put forward its own ideas for the future in two papers presented to the Chancellor: first an assessment of how the economy might fare over the next four years and secondly an outline basis for the survey with suggestions how programmes might be structured in order to take account of the likely economic constraints. The Treasury's assessment of the economic background was a sombre one and emphasized the need to make a substantial shift of resources into the balance of payments to correct the large deficit which the oil price rise had brought about as well as to give high priority to productive investment, both in the public and private sectors. But in one respect it was almost wildly optimistic. On the empirical basis that the annual rise in productive potential was 3 per cent the paper said that 'one might for planning purposes put the average rise in gross domestic product (GDP) 1973–78 also at 3% per annum', an assumption which implied that the economy would be working at full capacity. In judging whether this was a pessimistic or optimistic assumption it noted that in only eight of the past twenty years had GDP grown at more than 3 per cent and that the average had been only 2.75 per cent. Perhaps in March 1974 it was not possible to foresee the depth and length of the economic recession which would afflict not only the United Kingdom, but the entire developed world in the following three years; but it certainly seems that the planning assumption did not, as might have reasonably have been supposed, err on the side of caution. As to how the annual accretion of resources should be distributed, the Treasury argued that just over half should be applied to productive investment and to the balance of trade— the former to improve productive potential and the latter to removing the deficit. These pre-emptive claims would leave the residual element, personal consumption and public spending, room to grow at an annual rate of 1.5 per cent. On this basis the Treasury proposed first that, since 1975–76 was likely to be a difficult year because of the incipient recession, spending in that year should be held to the new and higher level established by the Budget for the current year (1974–75); and second that public expenditure on goods and services should thereafter grow 'at a modest pace', which for planning purposes should be treated as the growth rate posited for those years by the

---

[14] CAB 134/3838.

outgoing Conservative government in its final White Paper of December 1973—about 2 per cent per annum. Transfer payments coming from the public sector (mainly social security benefits) would be treated differently since their level was determined by policy decisions (embodied in legislation) on entitlement, and by uncontrollable factors such as the level of unemployment, sickness, etc. The Treasury proposed that to achieve something like this outcome it would be necessary to plan for very significant reductions in the levels of spending on certain programmes envisaged in the previous Expenditure White Paper: reductions of some 12.5 per cent for goods and services in 1975–76 and 25 per cent for capital items. This was, on the face of it, an ambitious target, although some progress towards this end had been made by the spending cuts announced by the Conservative government in December 1973. The ambition of the aim was diminished somewhat by the number of exceptions: Defence, the investment programmes of the nationalized industries, infrastructure spending on North Sea Oil projects, housing and 'Northern Ireland', the last being a clear recognition of the need not to compromise an already difficult political situation by reducing public spending there.[15]

These proposals were put first to MES on 3 April and then a week later to Cabinet, who approved them, although not without some 'teeth-sucking' at the degree of restraint proposed, and at the balance involved in the relative claims of the public and private sector. There was talk, which was to resonate in the Cabinet room over the next two years, of 'alternative strategies' to improve the balance of payments and encourage productive investment—these involving some form of direct controls over imports, and the Prime Minister only secured the approval of Cabinet to the course proposed by the Chancellor on the basis of there being further discussion of the general direction and balance of the Government's economic strategy before considering the outcome of the Survey. This, however, was to be some months in the future, for the Survey occupied the Treasury and departments for little short of four months, and in the meantime a good deal was happening on other fronts. We deal with these before returning the question of how Ministers dealt with the highly political and sensitive issues which the PESC report, in due course, threw up.[16]

The balance of payments deficit Part 1—its financing

The second area which preoccupied the Treasury in the summer of 1974 was the balance of payments, and in particular how it could be improved and how the large deficit which followed the oil price rise could be financed. These were, of course, not problems confined to the UK, and the international

[15] CAB 134/3789 (MES (74)2).   [16] CAB 128/54/10.

community had been addressing itself to them almost from the onset of the crises. The feared repercussions were that the impact of the oil price increase might lead to widespread trade and payments restrictions (most of which had been steadily dismantled in the course of the evolution of the General Agreement on Tariffs and Trade (GATT)) and the acceptance of the developed countries of the full obligations of the IMF Articles of Agreement. To this end, in 1974, the UK participated in two international 'declarations'. The first was made by the members of the IMF Committee of Twenty, a body set up in September 1972 to examine ways in which the Fund's constitution and rules might be adapted to promote the use of the SDR in the wake of the dollar crisis of August 1971 and to accommodate a regime of flexible rates of exchange. At its meeting in Rome on 17 and 18 January 1974 the Committee put out a communiqué which stated that 'countries must not adopt policies which would merely aggravate the problem of other countries'.[17] Accordingly they stressed the importance of avoiding competitive depreciation and the escalation of restrictions on trade and payments. They further resolved 'to pursue policies that would sustain appropriate levels of economic activity and employment while minimising inflation'. The last sentence is particularly interesting as it was warmly embraced by the UK in the immediate aftermath of the oil price increase but was largely ignored by other countries. The second affirmation of the need to avoid restrictions was made in a 'Trade Pledge' made by all the members of the OECD at its meeting on 30 May 1974.[18] The collective declaration stated the intention of members 'to avoid having recourse to unilateral measures, of either a general or a specific nature, to restrict imports or having recourse to similar measures on other current account transactions which would be contrary to the object of the present declaration'. Neither of these statements added to the formal and legal obligations most developed countries had assumed by joining the IMF or subscribing to the GATT or, in the case of European countries, by their membership of the EEC. But they did something to counter any move towards the sort of restrictions which were a consequence of the Great Depression in the early 1930s.

Though trade and payments restrictions were addressed in these moves, the question of handling the large payments deficit generated by the oil price increase remained the problem each country had to solve itself. For the UK, the immediate external issue was to *finance* the enlarged deficit. This was something the Treasury had addressed as soon as the oil crisis broke. Indeed, in one sense, it had been considering the implications of what was happening in the oil market from the beginning of 1973, as it became clear that that market had, from about 1970, moved significantly from being in the buyer's favour to one in which sellers had the dominant market power. For over a year a Working Party consisting of Treasury, Bank and Foreign Office officials

---

[17] T 277/2920.   [18] T 354/439.

(VSOP) had been examining what might need to be done to address this situation.[19] It did not, however, envisage anything as drastic as the five-fold increase in prices in the space of two months that occurred in the autumn of 1973, and the focus of its attention was on how to persuade the new surplus countries, most of whom did not have great absorptive capacity, to recycle their new financial balances to the rest of the world. This looked at ways to encourage them to hold their surplus in sterling, but without any sense of urgency.

The implications of the new situation for the UK were examined in a series of memoranda the Treasury had put to the Chancellor in the Heath administration just before Christmas 1973. These took as given that the current account would be in severe deficit throughout 1974 and that existing methods of financing it as well as the structural capital account deficit would not be sufficient to close it. They looked at ways to make the holding of sterling more attractive to the surplus countries, but concluded that some additional new source of finance would be necessary. The preferred route was that of a large drawing from the IMF, mainly on the grounds that this was the cheapest source. The main alternative, that of a syndicated bank medium-term credit in eurodollars, was judged to be too costly. A meeting took place between the Chancellor and the Managing Director of the Fund on 15 January 1974 but it was inconclusive, with the latter expressing some misgivings about the adequacy of the measures announced on 17 December as a basis for a standby. A subsequent meeting between the head of the Treasury OF Group and the head of the European Department of the Fund two days later drew the comment from the latter that 'there could be no guarantee that an application by the UK for a standby would get approval other than on terms which HMG might find unacceptable'. By this time the UK was in the middle of the three-day week crisis, and a General Election was being mooted. The idea of a drawing from the Fund as a central plank in the financing structure was allowed to lapse.[20]

One of the first submissions made to the new Chancellor in March 1974, following a meeting between the Treasury and the Bank, was to apprise him of the size of the financing problem and the various sources of funds which were available. The Bank had been aware of the possibility of a syndicated eurodollar credit of $2.5 billion from a number of commercial banks on a medium-term basis and the Chancellor was asked to agree that this credit should be taken. The more general question of how the overall balance of payments deficit should be financed was dealt with in a joint Treasury/Bank paper dated 30 May. This addressed itself to the question of the size of the problem in the period to the end of 1975 and the means that were available to resolve it. It was a very thorough piece of analysis but its findings can be summarized as follows. The overall financing need was likely to be of the order of £4.5 billion. About

---

[19] T 277/2866.   [20] T 171/1181, T 338/296, T 358/129.

half of this could be expected to come from inflows of sterling, mainly from the oil-producing, low-absorbing, countries and the other half from foreign currency borrowing on the financial markets by the public sector. We now have to look at how these mechanisms worked and what the opportunities for employing them were[21]—in addition to the risks of doing so.

Sterling inflows from the oil-producing countries were to some extent a phenomenon that occurred without especial effort. Several of the larger oil producers simply did not have the ability to spend their new surpluses on goods and services and had, perforce, to save them in the form of additions to the foreign currency reserves of their central banks or monetary authorities. This was particularly true of Saudi Arabia and the Gulf Sheikhdoms, but it was also the case to some extent of Iran and Nigeria, although for these countries, having large populations and a growing propensity to import manufactured goods, the problem of absorbing the new surplus was largely a transitory one. The Treasury/Bank memorandum of 30 May asked the question whether the scale of sterling financing posited in the assessment was satisfactory and concluded that it was 'acceptable and desirable if induced by a relatively small uncovered differential [i.e. a margin of short-term interest rates in London over those in New York]. But given the potential instability of sterling holdings, the balance of advantage switches in favour of foreign currency borrowing if the uncovered differential necessary to sustain net inflows were to widen appreciably'. Subject to this *caveat*, the Treasury saw it as an import-ant objective of policy that these oil-rich countries should think of holding as much as possible of their new financial wealth in sterling assets—this indeed had been one of the suggestions of the VSOP. There were reasonable grounds for assuming that this would be the case anyway. The small Persian Gulf Sheikhdoms, as well as Saudi Arabia, had a tradition of looking to the UK for advice and help in financial matters and senior positions in the Saudi Arabian Monetary Authority (SAMA) were often filled by Bank of England officials on secondment. Moreover the City of London offered a unique range of financial instruments and services which foreign investors could use to deploy their surplus funds. The desirability, as it was seen at the time, of inducing the surplus countries to add to their sterling holdings caused the Treasury and Bank to consider the contribution which a form of exchange guarantee to the holders might make to the solution of the problem. Guarantees of this sort had been given to official sterling holders as part of the arrangements of a 'safety net' set up in 1968.[22] These guarantees of the maintenance of the exchange value of the official balances were given in return for the holders' agreeing to hold certain minimum levels of sterling balances. They ran initially for five

[21] T 358/105.
[22] This issue is dealt with more fully in Chapters 4 and 5 where the question of a new safety net is discussed.

years, but when they were due to come to an end in September 1973 they were unilaterally extended for six months, mainly to give the Treasury and the Bank time to consider the options in the new environment of floating exchange rates. The two institutions were not at one on this issue. The Treasury saw the guarantees as contributing little to the stability of the holdings—they now applied to only a relatively small proportion of the total liabilities—and they were complicated to administer in a floating rate environment. The Bank differed and thought that they could make a useful reinforcement of the inducements to holders to remain in sterling. In the event, the guarantees were again extended in March 1974 as a holding operation until the end of the year. But, as we shall see, the Treasury prevailed on the Chancellor in the run-up to the autumn budget to let the guarantees lapse altogether.[23]

The second major source of funds identified by the Treasury and Bank was that of public sector borrowing in foreign currency. There were two strands to this. The first was to give every encouragement to public sector bodies to make use of what was known as the Exchange Cover Borrowing scheme. This was a measure which had been in operation in the 1960s but had lapsed in early 1971 when the balance of payments was strong. It was reintroduced in March 1973 as the external situation deteriorated. Under this measure certain nationalized industries and local authorities were given a financial incentive (and an insurance against the exchange risk) to cover at least a portion of their capital requirements by borrowing on their own initiative in foreign currency at medium- to long-term on the international capital markets, principally the Eurocurrency markets. The bodies affected were also encouraged (as the need for external borrowing increased) to borrow directly from the monetary authorities of the oil-rich countries, and in due course Saudi Arabia proved to be a useful source of such funds.

The other strand to public sector borrowing was to be direct credit in foreign currency obtained by the British Government itself. We have seen that in February a medium-term market credit of $2.5 billion had been recommended and was subsequently obtained for the Government through the international commercial banks who were benefiting from the dollar deposits made by the surplus countries. This was unlikely to be a continuing situation however, as the latter were likely to seek longer-term, non-bank, outlets for their investments. A more appropriate approach would be to make overtures to the surplus countries themselves and persuade them to invest in the UK. This was not an issue seen as immediately available in the paper put to the Chancellor in May but it emerged as a possibility as the situation developed. The first opportunity taken was with the Government of Iran. The initiative seems to have come from the Shah himself early in the year following a meeting he had with the then Chancellor (Barber) in St Moritz in February. It led to the

---

[23] T 338/296.

despatch of a high-level mission to Teheran in early July and to a fairly rapid agreement to a government-backed medium-term credit of $1.2 billion to be drawn in three instalments by UK public sector bodies.[24] The comparative ease with which it was concluded led the Treasury to hope, if not expect, that other medium-term foreign currency credit could be obtained directly from the oil-rich countries. Saudi Arabia was certainly thought to be a possibility, and several visits were paid to Riyadh by Treasury and Bank officials (not to mention the Chancellor himself in December 1974) in the hope that something on the Iranian lines could be negotiated. However, nothing on the scale of the Iranian loan was forthcoming and indeed several attempts in the following two years to interest the Saudis in large-scale foreign currency lending to the British Government were abortive.[25]

The tapping of these sources of credit in 1974 together with the accretion of the sterling balances of the OPEC countries were more than sufficient to provide the UK with the finance it needed that year and the gold and foreign exchange reserves actually rose from $5,612 million in January to $5,711 million in December. In many ways the Treasury and the Bank could congratulate themselves on having so successfully dealt with a potentially difficult problem. But there was a cost to the countenancing of such a large build-up of the official balances and this cost was two-fold. In the first place it ran counter to an assurance the UK had given to the European Community when it was negotiating its entry in 1971. Mindful of the difficulties the UK had had with the official balances during the devaluation crisis of 1967 the members of the Community sought—and obtained—from the UK delegation a declaration that 'we are prepared to envisage an orderly and gradual run-down of official sterling balances after our accession' and this statement was reiterated in a letter from the Minister responsible for European Affairs (Geoffrey Rippon) in a letter dated 22 June 1972 which was annexed to the Treaty of Accession.[26] It is difficult to see anything in the policies followed by the Treasury and the Bank in the years following this declaration that gave effect to this statement; indeed the willing—even enthusiastic—acceptance of the increase in the official balances in 1974 ran directly counter to what had been envisaged.

But whether avoidable or not, the build-up of the official balances in 1974 did give a very large hostage to fortune as the Treasury and the Bank were to discover in the course of 1975 and 1976. Both institutions had set their face against the financing of the external deficit by short-term credit and yet the build-up of the balances involved the shortest-term credit there was—it could be called 'on demand'—and it became the single most volatile element in the whole scene when the exchange value of sterling came to be questioned by the market at various times over the following two years.

[24] T 338/189.   [25] T 338/188.   [26] T 277/2859 and 2860.

The balance of payments deficit Part 2—its correction

The external financing problem may have been the most immediate of the balance of payments issues that had to be addressed in 1974, but to many in the Treasury there was an equally important, though less immediate, issue on the external front which had to be addressed, viz the need to take positive steps greatly to improve the *current* account. The external deficit escalated sharply at the end of 1973, and during 1974, thanks to the combination of accelerating wage costs and the relative stability of the exchange rate, the UK's competitiveness in internationally traded goods declined significantly. The new Chancellor was briefed on this issue in a memorandum put to him on 26 April, but the analysis was essentially a short-term one and the focus of attention was on the appropriate management of the exchange rate for the remainder of the year. The question posed was how interest rates and exchange market intervention should be handled in the interest of maintaining competitiveness. The objective proposed was to keep the effective exchange rate at roughly the level it held at the beginning of the year 'using the proceeds of foreign borrowing for any necessary intervention. This should leave scope for further reduction in UK interest rates.' It was made clear to the Chancellor, however, that a fuller appreciation of the pace at which the balance of payments should be brought into equilibrium would be given to him when the medium-term assessment, then in preparation, was available. The first intimation of what this perspective might entail was given in a further note, dated 16 May, which spoke of what would be required 'to go from a deficit of £4,000 million in 1974 to balance by the end of the decade. Any loss of competitiveness from now on would have to be met by a depreciation of the exchange rate', which, the paper asserted 'should take the form of a gradual downward float rather than a step change (whose size would in any case be subject to wide margin of uncertainty)'. This was perhaps the first time that the Treasury had faced up to the huge problem which an acceleration in wage costs relative to those experienced by the UK's competitors was going to present.[27]

A much fuller appraisal of the need to shift resources on a massive scale from domestic use to the external sector was made at the beginning of June. This was inspired by the preliminary findings of the Medium Term Assessment (MTA), which was carried out primarily to examine the options for increasing public expenditure. It looked at the trend of likely developments on the basis of existing policies over the following five years and posited two possible paths for improving the balance of payments neither of which involved strong action to effect such a change. The issue was discussed at a meeting the Chancellor held on 7 June.[28] This revealed a number of different attitudes. The Governor and the Paymaster-General (Dell) both thought that the rate of improvement

[27] T 358/105.   [28] Ibid.

posited was too leisurely, the former being concerned at the accumulation of external debt which would be involved in either case. The Chancellor was sceptical, but in deference to the 'hawks' he asked for a new paper that would incorporate a further case involving the closing of the deficit in three years. The new analysis was set out in a Treasury minute dated 14 June in which three cases were examined (not quite options for there was no concrete proposal as to how the cases would be put into effect). Case I was intended to secure external balance by 1979 and involved the allotment of £100 million of the annual accretion of resources into the balance of payments;[29] Case II would secure balance by 1978 and would require the allotment of £400 million annually; and Case III implied balance by 1977 and would require a huge shift in resource use. The last case was recognized to be very demanding and in any case it implied a significant devaluation of sterling (in whatever manner it might be achieved) in the third quarter of 1974. Apart from the reference to devaluation in Case III the paper did not specify the means by which resources could be transferred to the external sector. At this stage the question was less about means and more about ends. As the paper put it:

The choice is quite simply whether we should aim to give a very high, if not the highest, practicable priority to the growth of exports and to the closing of the external deficit; or whether we should take a more leisurely path, insofar as our creditors will allow us, and rely more heavily on the ultimate flow of North Sea Oil to restore the balance of payments to equilibrium.

After further analysis the minute went on:

The Treasury has hitherto refrained from making a policy recommendation, but the time has perhaps now arrived when we should declare where officials stand. . . . Our collective view is that we should lean on the side of severity.

Discussing the policy means by which resources could be transferred, the note went on:

The severe course would require an early depreciation of sterling, perhaps 2% more than in the leisurely course. . . . It would involve the Chancellor taking an even firmer stand on public expenditure, but in practice it may prove impossible to get this (the annual rate of increase) below 3% p.a., which we reckon is the slowest rate spending Ministers would accept.[30]

---

[29] In the early to mid-1970s the annual accretion of resources, based on a 2.5 per cent growth potential would have been about £1,800 million at 1974 prices, although at that time the actual accretion of resources, because of the decline in economic activity, was less than half this amount. In any year the bulk of the increase was taken by consumers. The amount left for private investment, public consumption, and investment and the balance of payments would be measured in a few hundred million pounds. The pre-emption of £400 million each year for the balance of payments was therefore a very ambitious aim.

[30] DW 015.

It is interesting that at this stage of the public expenditure round the Treasury did not expect to get the rate of increase over the Survey period below 3 per cent, whereas, as we shall see, when the round was completed at official level the projected rate of increase (in terms of resource use) was in fact about 2.75 per cent. It may be that the Treasury simply did not believe at that stage that Ministers would adopt the targets set by officials; or possibly that they thought that even with a projected increase of about 2.75 per cent, the inevitability of drift, and of new commitments being entered into, would make 3 per cent a target unlikely to be achieved. After all, public expenditure had been increasing at an annual rate of 4.2 per cent for the previous four years and a 3 per cent limit had an air of wishful thinking. In mid-1974 moreover the cash limits[31] regime had not yet been introduced and the rigour of that regime in securing tight control over a very large proportion of public spending was not appreciated.

The Bank of England differed somewhat from the Treasury, who had implicitly rejected Case III, and the Governor expressed his view on 18 June that the Bank had a preference for the most severe case. He was apprehensive about the UK's ability to continue to borrow abroad on the scale required to meet Cases I and II, and commented 'Japan and France seem likely to reduce their deficits relatively quickly'. He went on:

A policy of shifting resources into the balance of payments will require the maintenance of *a competitive exchange rate and this is likely to involve further depreciation of sterling*. The Bank is very sensitive to the danger that this could prove bad for confidence and increase the difficulties of borrowing. (Italics added.)[32]

The Chancellor had a meeting to discuss the Treasury memorandum on 21 June 1974 and said, following the line he had taken at the earlier meeting that he rejected Case III, which as noted above would involve a depreciation of 17 per cent in a matter of months. At the meeting there was a discussion about the response of exports to a change in the sterling rate and the Chancellor noted that the Treasury and the Bank took different views. This question, viz the price elasticity of demand for UK exports (and also of the elasticity of demand for imports), was to assume some importance in subsequent discussions of the amount of depreciation that might be required to restore balance. But in the middle of 1974, with the most severe case ruled out, the issue of how much depreciation was required could be put on one side. No decision was taken at the meeting—hardly surprising as no policy recommendation was made by officials.[33]

But the issue of modalities had to be addressed sometime and the question of how, in a floating rate system, a depreciation could be achieved was not one

---

[31] Cash limits were a system of expenditure control introduced in 1976—see Chapters 3 and 4.
[32] Ibid.   [33] DW 015.

which could easily be brushed aside. At official level throughout the summer the Treasury had been concerned at the stickiness of the exchange rate and at a discussion of top management on 22 July OF stated that they were looking at measures to secure depreciation, 'including announcing a rate which the UK would cap, but not support', something that only three months earlier had been rejected. The idea was that the markets would be taken by surprise by, in effect, a step-devaluation to a new exchange rate which would be a ceiling for sterling, but not a floor. Such a policy would not require the use of foreign exchange reserves, since the authorities would not be buying sterling—only selling it if the market's demands for it were not supplied by commercial transactions or by speculation. This measure was looked at more seriously in the months that followed, but no proposals were put to Ministers for the time being.

However the mid-year Medium Term Assessment, which was completed on 18 July and was designed to assist in the taking of decisions on public expenditure, had been constructed on the basis of external balance somehow being achieved by 1978–79, a not unreasonable assumption given the outcome of the meeting of 21 June. Meantime OF were becoming concerned with what they regarded as the rather bland way that a contrived depreciation was being talked about. It seemed to be assumed that once the chosen path of depreciation had been specified, managing the rate in accordance with that aim was only a technical matter. A note dated 22 July put the problem precisely: 'the forces which may now be brought to bear upon the exchange rate in the market are such that it may well prove exceedingly difficult, if not impossible, to manage it in the direction which policy may require.'[34]

On 30 August OF Division again highlighted the problem:

The successful management of a depreciation in a situation of wafer-thin confidence in the prospects for the UK and the world must be very much in doubt. If a major break in external confidence does not happen anyway, an attempt to bring the rate down—particularly in a step change—could well precipitate one. There can be no guarantee of fine-tuning.[35]

A later paper, dated 17 September, noted that the short-term economic forecast (NIF) in June had assumed a depreciation of 19 per cent in the space of two years (as the requirement to eliminate the deficit in 1978) but noted that on the markets sterling continued to be strong even though monthly trade deficits of £400 million were occurring—and could be expected to continue. The competitive price loss in the first half of 1974 was estimated to be about 6 per cent. The strength of sterling in the teeth of this performance was put down to the continued preference of overseas investors, particularly the oil-rich countries, for the New York and London markets rather than the less sophisticated

---

[34] T 358/132.   [35] DW 102.

markets of Paris and Frankfurt. Another factor was that the failure of the Herstadt Bank in Germany in early 1974 had caused foreign investors to be wary of the Deutchmark market.

The paper went on to discuss whether the rate could in any sense be managed by the Bank. On the assumption that it might be done 'through modest intervention by the authorities...or by a further easing of interest rates', it noted that such 'a managed downward float would avoid the risk [which lay in the present policy of inaction] that, once the erosion of UK competitiveness became apparent the rate could then fall very sharply.'

On the other hand the paper doubted whether fine-tuning in any sense was possible. 'An officially engineered sharp decline [in the rate] might damage confidence and cause the market to over-react, and the expectation of a further decline might start a speculative movement against sterling.' In an annex, the view was expressed that 'there is a strong case for reliance on the market's own assessment of an appropriate rate for sterling'—a view which was in fact contested in the main body of the paper as quoted above. It was clear that in OF at any rate there was a good deal of ambivalence about depreciation as an instrument of policy. The need for it was not disputed, but the possibility of achieving it through any known act of policy was regarded as very limited.

The Chief Economic Adviser set his face against this passivity. In a minute dated 17 September[36] he argued that of all the means of countering the decline in the UK's competitiveness and achieving the elimination of the deficit which the paper of 17 June had called for, that is depreciation, deflation, an Incomes Policy or import controls, depreciation was the only viable one in the present circumstances.

The two conflicting views were put to the Chancellor in a note dated 18 September which sought to resolve the issue with the recommendation that 'we should continue, through our control of domestic interest rates, to seek to move the rate down "a little and often"'.

The Chancellor held a meeting two days later to discuss this issue when agreement was reached 'that any action to depreciate the rate should be taken via domestic interest rates rather than through the EEA' (intervention in the currency markets by the Bank). The Treasury did, however, decide to look into the feasibility of a payroll subsidy as an alternative or supplement to a depreciation. The Chancellor, for his part, 'said that he was not inclined to seek to manufacture opportunities for depreciation if they did not arise in the normal course of events'. There matters were allowed to rest for the time being. On 23 October, however, the issue was raised with him again—the third time within four months—as part of a wider review of macro-economic policy.[37] The Treasury had been putting together such a review to provide the Chancellor

---

[36] Ibid.   [37] T 171/1148.

with material from which he could make choices for his Autumn Budget. The outcome of this review is dealt with below in the account of the evolution of this Budget. Here it suffices to say that the Chancellor was invited in October to see the exchange rate and the current account of the balance of payments as issues materially relevant to his fiscal policy. They could affect employment—and inflation—in ways not dissimilar to the way expenditure and tax policies could. The main paper on the exchange rate was written by the Treasury economists who had been the prime movers of the earlier initiatives. It leaned heavily in the direction of positive action to reduce the exchange value of sterling. None of the arguments differed from those canvassed in the two earlier approaches to the Chancellor. The UK was steadily losing competitiveness and the deficit on the non-oil account alone was getting worse, while of course oil imports were costing a great deal more than they had a year earlier. The accumulation of external liabilities was assuming worrying proportions. They would in due course have to be repaid or refinanced and in the meantime they had to be serviced. The paper examined the options of a 'determined push', that is some deliberate action in the exchange market to weaken sterling, and of 'a more passive approach, which could take a number of forms'. One would involve 'nudging the rate downwards by buying US dollars'. Some easing of UK interest rates could also be employed. As an alternative to depreciation the paper looked at the idea of a wage subsidy, an idea broached at the September meetings, on the grounds that it would achieve the same ends as a devaluation without putting domestic prices up. But it exploded this argument by pointing out that the financing of a wage subsidy would itself be likely to raise prices and the advantages would be largely illusory. The idea was therefore strongly opposed.

The economists' enthusiasm for a managed devaluation was, as we have seen, not shared by the Overseas Finance sector of the Treasury who were deeply worried about the impact of any foreign perception that the British Government were seeking to reduce the value of sterling. They produced an appraisal of the practical difficulties of a policy of deliberate depreciation—one they assumed would involve a shift of 5 per cent or more. Even a slowly depreciating rate 'would cast a pall of uncertainty over the market and there would be increasingly nagging fears, both at home and abroad, about where the downward drift would stop'. A crash programme of sufficient outright sales of sterling to bring the rate down by 5 per cent would be consistent with the widely accepted view that exchange rate adjustment should be small and prompt rather than delayed and big. But such a course would be likely to damage confidence severely 'by suddenly shattering illusions that have been nurtured by the recent relative stability of exchange rates, in particular of sterling'. The paper went on to argue that any action in the exchange market designed to do something more than smooth day-to-day fluctuations would call for international consultation under the IMF's guidelines for floating rates.

The rather doubtful conclusion was that while either course would have serious risks, the argument pointed towards a gradual depreciation.[38]

The two notes were considered at a large meeting the Chancellor had with Treasury officials on 25 October.[39] Also present were the Governor, the Chancellor of the Duchy of Lancaster (Lever) and the Paymaster-General (Dell), the last two being effectively in the Chancellor's close confidence. Given the size of the meeting and the uncertainty of the advice in terms of specific action, it is hardly surprising that the outcome was inconclusive. Lever spoke strongly against devaluation in principle, Dell equally strongly in favour. The Governor 'warned that an "imperceptible" fall of 7% in the exchange rate was unrealistic'. In his view the right course was for the authorities to be thought to be responding to market forces. This was not quite the view he had expressed at the meeting on 18 June. Even so there was a danger that the rate would fall a long way. Faced with such conflicting and uncertain advice, the Chancellor said that 'if a slow depreciation could be achieved without the appearance of engineering, that would probably be the best outcome ... but it would be best to wait and see how the Budget [*which was then only two weeks away*] was received'. This was hardly the description of clear policy. But at all events he did not want a wage subsidy.

There matters were allowed to rest. No real decision on policy had been decided and when sterling next came under pressure in mid-December the Bank responded aggressively—spending $1 billion of the foreign exchange reserves[40]—to defend the rate. There was little talk then of allowing events to take their course, although in spite of the Bank's support the rate did fall slightly. None of this should have caused any surprise. The Chancellor's advisers were themselves both divided and uncertain and had differing agendas. The Bank and OF in the Treasury were absorbed by the problem of attracting and retaining capital to finance the deficit. The rest of the Treasury were mesmerised by the lack of viability of existing policy in the medium-term. The Chancellor himself, at this stage, probably had more sympathy with the former than the latter, and a policy of relative inaction was not unacceptable to him. It was not until much later, when the unemployment consequences of indifference to the medium-term became clear to him, that he began to revise his views. But as we shall see, when in early 1975 the Treasury again raised the issue of the viability of existing external policy, the issue of a depreciation was still an illusive one and no firm recommendations were forthcoming. It was not to be for another twelve months, in October 1975, that the Treasury seriously raised the issue with him again as a matter which simply would not go away.

---

[38] Ibid.   [39] T 171/1166.
[40] Meeting of the Chancellor 13 December 1974—T 358/132.

The balance of payments deficit Part 3—managing the foreign exchange market

Our account of the development of Treasury thinking on the medium-term problem of correcting the large external payments imbalance has ignored the day-to-day developments during 1974, when decisions had to be taken daily on how to respond to exchange market developments. This practical issue is important to the question of strategy, for the way it was handled brings out the inescapable dilemmas which confronted the Treasury and, more especially, the Bank in their handling of both domestic monetary policy and exchange market intervention. On the one hand it was accepted in principle by all concerned that the exchange value of sterling would have to fall to compensate for the steady deterioration of the UK's competitiveness in the face of escalating wage costs. On the other the need to finance a huge overall deficit in the balance of payments as an immediate and compelling issue (and to finance it in part at least by inducing overseas investors to hold sterling as a reserve asset) meant that any overt action to cause sterling to fall would cause those investors to ponder whether sterling was a safe reserve asset. Any such doubts, leading to a drying up of sterling inflows if not the disposal of existing holdings, could create a massive financing problem and, as a consequence, a fall, which might well be considerable, in the exchange value of sterling. Such a fall would intensify the domestic inflationary problem, which in turn could intensify the confidence problem. It is small wonder, therefore, that whenever the question arose in 1974 of defending the exchange rate or of allowing some depreciation to occur those responsible for external financing and for relations with overseas official holders—mainly the Bank and OF—tended to err on the side of caution and press for action to stem the fall, while those whose concern was with the longer-term issue of regaining competitiveness preferred to allow the fall to occur without too much resistance. The Bank, at times, were even inclined to allow sterling to appreciate somewhat when market pressures developed, as they did from time to time, which strengthened sterling and this caused some misgiving among the economists in the Treasury.

It was in fact the conflict of aims between the domestic side of the Treasury and the overseas side that brought out some of the dilemmas faced when decisions had to be taken on interest rates. We deal with the general approach to monetary policy later in the narrative, but here we have to bring out some of the day-to-day dilemmas which arose when a choice had to be made between allowing interest rates to rise (or not to fall) and resisting such a development. The first occasion arose as early as the end of January when the Bank reported that a combination of factors—a large Government budgetary surplus, a substantial buying of gilt-edged and competitive bidding of the commercial banks for funds—led them to propose the release of some Special Deposits to ease the tightness so caused. But the overseas side of the Treasury were fearful of the effect on overseas confidence of such a relaxation, even though technically it was hardly an easing at all. The domestic side of the Treasury saw things differently and were concerned that the liquidity problems of business in the middle of the three-day week crisis could get out of hand. In the event, the then Chancellor (Barber) agreed with the domestic case.[41] The issue of a conflict of interest was again brought out in a memorandum produced by both sides of the Treasury at the end of March. This acknowledged that the strength of sterling inflows at the time was such that the balance of policy could properly lie with an easing of interest rates. By early May, however, some differences were beginning to surface again. The Treasury was still in favour of an easing of interest rates but the Bank was now becoming anxious:

While there had been general agreement towards the end of March that it was appropriate to narrow the uncovered differential (then about 6%) by perhaps 2%, the combination of the reduction in UK rates that has already been achieved plus the parallel hardening in US rates have meant that the uncovered differential is now down to about 2%. To narrow the differential much further would be to run a serious risk of a flip over into a situation in which funds ceased to flow into sterling and, very quickly, we could see a large outflow.

The issue went to the Chancellor on 15 May when the Governor argued strongly against a release of special deposits to ease the domestic monetary situation because of its effect on external factors and the Chancellor accepted the advice, but on the footing that the situation should be kept under review.[42] The issue was again raised at another meeting of the Chancellor and Governor on 22 May when the same outcome was reached, but not before the Chancellor had expressed a wish to see interest rates fall. The Bank duly obliged by cutting MLR by 0.25 per cent on 24 May. These events clearly brought out the Bank's acute concern about the external factors and its reluctance to see a weakening of the exchange rate, even though in principle such a weakening was something it acknowledged had to take place. A similar situation arose at the end of June when the uncovered differential between forward sterling and forward dollars fell in response to a tightening of monetary conditions abroad. This time the Bank proposed to deal with the matter by exchange market intervention which mopped up some of the liquidity in the domestic market—and again the Treasury acquiesced.[43] The fear of upheaval in the exchange markets following the failure of the Herstadt Bank in Germany was quite widespread. The issue of interest rates and the exchange rate was again discussed between the Chancellor and the Governor in mid-September when the latter reported what the Bank had done to move money-market interest rates down and that this, combined with a surplus in Exchequer transactions, had led to a fall in the exchange rate of about 1 per cent. MLR was reduced a further 0.25 per cent a week later.

[41] T 358/129.   [42] T 358/132.   [43] Ibid.

These exchanges did not reveal any very serious operational differences between the Bank and the Treasury. Indeed the latter was as concerned as the Bank not to create a situation in which sterling fell precipitately and the financing problem became potentially intractable. It was much more a question of degree than of kind. Although the Treasury had, as we have seen, brought to the Chancellor's attention the need to secure a depreciation of sterling of quite a significant amount, when the occasion arose of a possible slide, it backed away from the logic of its position. The reaction of the Bank and the Treasury to a general disturbance in the foreign exchange markets at the end of November casts some interesting light on this. The dollar had weakened against all currencies, except sterling which went down with the dollar. In the space of a few days the Bank had spent over $500 million supporting sterling even though the market's doubts were clearly about the dollar. It was not until this was appreciated by the Treasury that intervention was reduced so that 'we should go very easy on further intervention and enter the market only to stop any material change in the dollar rate.'[44] This slight difference between the two institutions was perhaps of no great significance at the time and it was only in 1975 and even more so in 1976 that operational, as opposed to theoretical, differences began to appear in the consideration of how much—and when—support should be given to sterling when it came under attack.

The IMF consultation

We now have to go back somewhat in time and look at some of the peripheral issues that arose during the course of 1974. Of some interest is the annual routine consultation with the IMF that took place at the beginning of May. Their visit was preceded by a formidable list of questions about the conduct of economic policy and was marked by a series of meetings at which the objectives of policy and the means of achieving them were examined in forensic detail. Nearly all the meetings were with the Treasury and Bank of England. At the conclusion of the visit the staff wrote a comprehensive report which was submitted to the Executive Board of the Fund and then 'noted'. As the UK had not at the time drawn upon its credit tranches and was not seeking a drawing or a stand-by, the consultations had little force in terms of requiring action. Generally speaking, however, members of the Fund liked to have its broad approval for the action they were taking.

The Fund visit gave the UK the opportunity to explore in more detail (than had been the case the previous December when a drawing from the Fund had been considered as a serious possibility) what would be the conditions laid

[44] T 358/132.

down by the Fund and what were the points of weakness, in the eyes of the Fund, in UK policy. The question of a UK drawing was not now raised as a serious issue as it had been six months earlier, but there were some very tentative probings about the use of quantitative monetary targets in any conditionality of a UK drawing. This had been a serious issue at the time of the UK's previous drawing in 1967 and there was considerable concern in Whitehall that the Fund might be equally insistent in the event of a new drawing, particularly in the higher reaches of the credit tranches. The talks with the Fund staff on this issue were cordial and understanding on both sides. When the Head of the European Department of the Fund was in London just before the formal visit he made it clear that if the UK were to seek a substantial drawing 'the IMF would want some clear understanding of the evolution of policy, particularly in the monetary field. They were not wedded, however, to any particular concept e.g. to DCE etc.'[45]

The Fund staff were of course concerned about the UK's current account deficit and focused on demand management and the exchange rate as the two issues which needed careful attention. There was no problem with their appreciation that resources should be free to move into the external sector, but on the exchange rate there was some underlying difference of view over what was possible. The Fund made no secret of their view that sterling was overvalued and that the UK seemed 'to have got into the groove of a fixed rate'. The Treasury replied that there was no commitment to a particular rate, but gave no encouragement to the implicit suggestion that we should be seeking some downward movement.

When it came down to the appraisal the Fund staff made of UK policies, the judgement was surprisingly mild. They expressed concern over the rate of inflation and had some doubts about policy, or lack of it, in this area. On credit expansion—a routine hobby-horse of the Fund—the staff noted that it was high by historical standards, but this 'seems warranted'.[46] There was very little comment about fiscal policy and virtually nothing critical about the growth of public expenditure. In the light of the strong line taken over the growth of public expenditure in the 1976 negotiations (when its growth had in fact come under serious control) this omission seems curious.

Monetary policy

The Fund's concern about monetary expansion did not come as a surprise to Treasury or to Bank officials. The Fund was, after all, a monetary institution and the rate of growth of domestic credit (DCE) had become a touchstone of the Fund's critique of members' economic policies and was seen as a

---

[45] T 354/227.   [46] T 354/223.

determining factor so far as the balance of payments was concerned. Quantitative limits to this variable were usually imposed on members' seeking to use the Fund's resources and the UK was well aware of this preoccupation from its experience during the consultations in 1967 which led to the large stand-by sought at that time. But in terms of the formulation of domestic policy, monetary matters—in 1974—hardly entered into the calculations of policy makers. Neither DCE nor the rate of growth of the money stock were target variables, although they were looked at from time to time, particularly by the joint Treasury/Bank Monetary Policy Group, rather as indicators of liquidity in the economy than as signals which should prompt action of one sort or another.[47]

Monetary measures were not therefore used as an active instrument of policy in 1974 except to moderate the interest rate increases which market conditions were creating and, as we have seen, to arrest any incipient decline in the exchange rate. The government in general, and the Treasury in particular, did not see interest rate policy other than as a supplementary tool in the management of the economy: it certainly did not regard the rate of growth of the money stock as having any determining influence on the economy as a whole, although it was prepared to acknowledge that if that growth rate were 'large' it could be an indicator that all was perhaps not quite right. That said, an important development in the evolution of monetary policy took place shortly before our narrative begins—on 17 December 1973—when Anthony Barber, the Conservative Chancellor, introduced his mini-Budget in response to the oil price explosion and the miners' industrial action in defiance of Stage 3 of the Incomes Policy at the time. Besides tightening hire purchase controls and calling on the banks to raise the rate of repayment of credit on credit cards, he referred to the introduction by the Bank of England, at the same time, of the Supplementary Special Deposits Scheme, colloquially known as the 'Corset'. Under this arrangement the Bank laid down a permitted rate of increase of a bank's interest-bearing eligible liabilities and any increase beyond that rate attracted a financial penalty. The penalty took the form of a requirement for the bank to deposit with the Bank of England a proportion of the excess in a non-interest bearing special account. The greater the excess over the specified permitted rate, the greater the penalty. The measure was intended to cause banks to limit their bidding for savings deposits from customers and so limit the growth in the money supply, the bulk of which of course consisted of bank deposits. Private savings which would have gone into bank accounts would tend to be deflected into other instruments such as National Savings, Treasury bills, short-term bonds (including local authority debt). None of these would be counted as 'money' and therefore add to the money supply.

---

[47] For a statement of the Bank's attitude to the money supply at the time, see the speech made by the Deputy Governor on 11 April 1973—*BEQB* Vol 13 No 2.

The measure was the first specific one to be introduced with the sole aim of controlling the growth of the money supply and represented perhaps the first tentative acknowledgement by a British government (and the Bank) that this was an important factor in the performance of the economy. But whether that factor was psychological, in the sense that markets would regard it as important, or real, in the sense that it determined something tangible, as the monetarists believed, was not made clear. How far the rate of increase in the money supply contributed to developments in the months that followed is difficult to determine, but it is significant that the government's preferred measure of it, £M3, rose by only 3 per cent in the six months following the introduction of the 'Corset' compared with 27 per cent in the year from the end of 1972 to the end of 1973. The comparison is not an altogether apt one, as economic and financial conditions were very different in the two time periods, but the sharp fall in the rate of growth of the money supply must have owed something to the new measure. The fact that inflation was accelerating while the growth of the money supply was shrinking did not greatly incline the policy makers to embrace the tenets of monetarism—although again, in fairness, it has to be said that the monetarists argued that inflation was heavily lagged on the rate of growth of the money supply.

The easing in the rate of growth of M3 in the early months of 1974 led the Bank to take an accommodating stance on short-term interest rates, and MLR which had been 13 per cent at the end of 1973 was reduced in stages to 11.5 per cent during the course of 1974. The one business which had difficulty as a result of the tightening of monetary policy at the end of 1973 was the Building Society sector, and this was a particularly sensitive political constituency. Building Societies—at that time the virtually only suppliers of housing finance—were, as 'Friendly Societies', averse to raising their mortgage rates to borrowers, although they had to increase the rates they paid on deposits and shares in order to attract the funds which new mortgagors were requiring; and governments had, over a long period, recognized the political significance of high mortgage rates on a large segment of the population. It was fairly commonplace for ministers to lean heavily on the Building Society movement not to hasten to raise their lending rates when interest rates generally were rising. In the early months of 1974, in the face of an MLR of 13 per cent, the Societies were holding their lending rates at 11 per cent, but were not able to meet from their own inflows the demands of their customers. On 10 April the new Government, which it will be remembered had given a high priority to housing in the Budget, introduced an arrangement whereby the Bank of England eased the position of the Societies by making advances to them of up to £100 million at MLR (then 12.5 per cent) and the Department of the Environment financed the difference between this interest cost and that involved in a rate of 10.5 per cent. Further advances up to £400 million would be made if required.

The move was a risky one. It was clearly out of the question for the government to commit itself indefinitely to the subsidization of private housing in this way, and the hope—not an unreasonable one given the way monetary policy was developing—was that short-term rates would decline and the subsidy could be terminated. This in fact proved to be the case and the Building Societies were in due course able to finance themselves in their usual way. But the development was significant in two respects. It demonstrated again the new government's willingness to use public expenditure rather freely and it indicated how difficult it could be in future to use short-term interest rates to support economic policy generally.

If short-term interest rates showed a tendency to ease during the course of 1974, the same was not true of long-term rates. Long-term interest rates are not, of course, as susceptible to government fiat as short-term rates. They are determined primarily by the bond markets' views about the relative prices of different long-term securities and their expectations about the long-term outlook for inflation. Given that equity prices were falling sharply in 1974 in the face of the financial difficulties of companies and given that the inflationary outlook was extremely uncertain, it is not surprising that bond prices fell and that the yield on undated government stock at the end of the year was 17.5 per cent compared with 14.5 per cent earlier in the year. It is interesting to note, however, that although confidence diminished during the course of the year, the Bank managed to sell some £2,267 million of stock to the non-bank sector in the financial year 1974–75 compared with only £1,473 million in the previous year. This made a significant contribution to the relatively slow growth of the money supply.

Inflation—Part 1

Our narrative has described how the Treasury was addressing itself to two of the three strategic issues it had identified—public expenditure and the balance of payments—but has been silent on the question of inflation, mainly because this issue lay at the heart of the Social Contract, which was essentially a political, as opposed to a technical, matter. By the middle of June however, after three months in office, Ministers began to consider whether an adjustment in policy under the Social Contract was required. Inflation was picking up and the economic forecast due at the end of June was expected to predict a further rise. The statutory basis for the pay policy of the previous government was brought to an end by Order in Council at the beginning of July and the Employment Secretary (Foot) had some discussions with the TUC and CBI about how pay matters should be handled thereafter. He reported the outcome to MES on 13 June.[48] The TUC planned to issue a statement to their constitu-

---

[48] CAB 134/3789.

ent unions on how they should approach pay negotiations when formal restraints had been removed. Although this was to emphasize that the objective should be to retain real wages, it provided for a number of exceptions, notably the completion of the 'equal pay' programme and any measures to increase the earnings of the low paid—the target being to aim at a minimum wage of £28 per week. There was also provision for special increases for certain public sector workers. The TUC were adamant that the statement should be unilateral on its own part and that the Government should not have a hand in it. They argued that their guidance would be more likely to be heeded by the unions if it came from within the union movement itself and was not seen as the outcome of collusion with employers and government. The Employment Secretary said that he agreed with this and, although when the Cabinet discussed the issue on 20 June there was some debate as to whether the Government should put out some form of statement by way of comment, it was subsequently decided not to do so. The TUC guidance was duly issued on 26 June and the Government did no more than welcome it.

Ministers were not, however, totally inactive on the counter-inflation front. On 26 June the head of the Treasury Prices and Incomes Division reported that 'the Chancellor had asked for an *urgent* note on steps which might be taken in the near future to moderate (price) increases',[49] and on 27 June the Chancellor of the Duchy of Lancaster put in a paper on his own initiative to the MES entitled 'The Attack on Inflation' in which he advocated 'a massive programme for holding down prices'. This set alarm bells ringing in the Treasury, who briefed the Chancellor on Lever's paper in the following terms:

The question is have we in fact sufficient capacity in terms of men and materials, at present and in prospect, to justify the stimulus to the economy which price cutting would involve without damaging our balance of payments and external financing objectives?.... We do not want to give our creditors the impression that we are managing our affairs in an irresponsible way.... Outside observers would contrast reflation in the UK with the deflationary measures abroad, notably in France and Italy.[50]

The Treasury thought that at the earliest no decision should be taken by Ministers until the mid-year NIF was available at the beginning of July.

The Chancellor put in to MES, alongside Lever's paper, one of his own as a background to a general discussion on economic strategy. This repeated much of what he had said about the policy aims he had in mind earlier in the year: the need for more and better industrial investment, an improvement in the balance of payments, more overseas borrowing and moderation in wage claims. No specific action was suggested nor would it have been appropriate in the absence of an up-dated forecast.

---

[49] T 171/1151.   [50] Ibid.

The two papers were discussed at MES on 1 July together with one by the CPRS. By this time the Chancellor had received the NIF (see below), though he declined to be drawn on it as he had not had time to study it. However, he did say that there might be some scope for reflation and he conceded that there might be some advantage in devoting any expenditure increases to measures which would reduce prices and slow down the rate of inflation. 'Such measures would have a double effect since they would reduce the impact of the threshold agreements, but in order to affect the Stage 3 threshold agreements[51] decisions would be needed in July'.

Lever, speaking to his paper, argued for a reflationary package of £2 billion to achieve a reduction in the retail price index of 4 points. 'If however it was possible to secure the effective cooperation of the TUC it would be worth stepping up the effort substantially beyond the initial £2,000 million'. The head of the CPRS agreed that there should be some reflation of demand by subsidies or reductions in VAT. The Chancellor kept his counsel.[52]

The ministerial discussion was wide-ranging and reflected differing views on the best approach to the management of the economy, some participants arguing for a more interventionist policy towards private industry and for consideration of a 'siege economy' if world trade declined further. The Prime Minister, however, confined further action to another discussion a week later when the NIF—and the scope for some reflation—would be examined. The Committee would also want to examine a programme of price subsidies designed to reduce the increase in the RPI to 10 per cent in 1975.

The Chancellor was given a brief summary of the NIF on 28 June.[53] This made fairly sombre reading. All the components of demand were forecast to be flat, or nearly flat, in 1974. Unemployment would rise to 650,000 by the year end and by a further 150,000–200,000 in 1975. The balance of payments deficit, which was now expected to be about £4.5 billion in 1974, would still lie in the range of £2,725–4.5 billion in 1975. Domestic prices would rise on a year-on-year basis to 21 per cent by year end and the following year might be anything between 13 and 21 per cent. On 4 July the Permanent Secretary gave the Chancellor the views of the Budget Committee on what the options for action, if any, were. He prefaced it by saying that the economy was now in such unchartered territory that the model might well not be a reliable guide to what was going to happen. The policy response would depend on where the main emphasis of the Government's aims lay. These could be described as:

---

[51] The thresholds were being triggered in an alarming way. The Treasury had informed the Chancellor that when he took office they had forecast that there would be nine triggers before the expiry of the agreements. Now they were forecasting thirteen or fourteen.

[52] CAB 134/3789.   [53] T 338/247.

1 an improvement in the balance of payments and a strong borrowing position;
2 full (or nearly full) employment;
3 a decline in the rate of inflation

If the primary aim were the third item above, a case could be made for a substantial fiscal package involving subsidies and reductions in indirect taxes, principally VAT. But this would have an adverse effect on overseas opinion which 'would see it as a major act of reflation, comparable perhaps to the 1972 Budget with its £1,200 million stimulus to consumer demand. We would be severely criticised for reflating at a time when other countries, with external accounts much stronger than ours, were deflating.' There were other objections, including the fact that reductions in indirect taxes would be seen as inconsistent with the Budget of three months before when they had been raised. The only case for a substantial package would lie in the Government claiming, if it could, that 'it had obtained a genuine and demonstrable *quid pro quo* from the TUC in the sense of some assurance that wage demands would fully reflect the price effects. The prospects of this, however, are not bright'.

Two other options were discussed: 'Wait and see' and a compromise approach involving modest measures to reduce prices. The former would involve postponing action until the Autumn Budget to which the Chancellor had committed himself. It would allow time for reflection on the right course of action and time to detect what the actual course of the economy was in the new environment. On the other hand, if unemployment continued to rise strongly and the Chancellor took no action to deal with it, the annual TUC conference in September could be difficult and might lead to its failure to ratify the wage guidelines. The modest package, put by the paper, of some £500–600 million, would demonstrate that the Government was taking some action. It would not attract the overseas criticism involved in a massive fiscal programme, and it would have a useful, if small, effect on prices and on employment.

The Treasury made no specific recommendation at this stage, but suggested a full discussion with the Chancellor as well as his non-Treasury advisers in the Bank and the Revenue Departments. This was held the following day, 5 July.[54] The Chancellor said at the outset that 'he was concerned *above all* to make full use of our resources. He was not prepared to accept the prospect for next year as it stood, with its terrifying under-use of resources and mounting unemployment' (italics added). The Governor counselled against a major policy change on an uncertain forecast and warned that a reflationary package could be tripped up by external factors. The Chancellor, however, was in no mood to do nothing and said that he was inclined to go for a package which would primarily be intended to break into the wages/prices spiral.

[54] Ibid.

He talked of something of the order of £1,500 million. The Permanent Secretary warned of the effects of this on the Borrowing Requirement which had already risen far above the Budget forecast to around £4,200 million. He also suggested that 'a little more slack in the economy could be desirable', presumably by helping to reduce the external deficit and curbing wage pressures. The head of Overseas Finance said that 'a package of the kind the Chancellor was considering, if presented as a set of anti-inflationary measures, would not necessarily affect the exchange rate or our ability to borrow in the short term.' The Chancellor asked for a paper for MES to be prepared, giving his colleagues the outline of the forecast and proposing substantial price cutting measures to help with both employment and inflation. This was duly submitted and circulated for the meeting on 10 July. It described the economic outlook and said that what was required was 'a set of measures which would stimulate demand and reduce the upward pressure on prices, without damaging the external balance....For this reason the required package must be seen and presented with exceptional care.' He carefully avoided giving any figures for what he had in mind and gave his colleagues only a general indication of the areas in which he might operate—at this stage a cut in VAT, a reduction in the employers' national insurance contributions and an increase in the Regional Employment Premium (REP). The ministerial meeting was also presented with a paper by the Prices Secretary (Shirley Williams) that discussed a variety of measures which could be used to reduce prices. Ministers had a balanced discussion of the situation and the appropriate policy response—recognizing the dangers both of doing nothing or very little and of doing too much. The Chancellor summed up the conclusion as being in favour of caution rather than boldness. He would reflect on the discussion and submit a package of measures to the Cabinet with a view to announcing them on 22 July. Later that day he reported to Treasury officials how the MES meeting had gone. He classified his cautious colleagues as including the Prime Minister and said that their preference was for a limit of £500 million on the total of fiscal action. A slightly smaller number, including the Employment Secretary and the Prices Secretary, wanted something like £1,500 million.

There then followed a detailed examination by Treasury and Customs officials of the measures which could usefully reduce prices and promote employment. What was decided was summarized by the Chancellor's Private Secretary on 18 July as a reduction in VAT of 2 per cent, a doubling of the Regional Employment Premium, an increase in food subsidies, and some action on domestic rates. The Chancellor had not yet, however, finally made up his mind about the total content and before he did so the Permanent Secretary reported to him a conversation he had had with the Governor:

The Governor continues to press for a small rather than a large package. On this he has my support, and for much the same reasons as he gives. I judge that his view would be that the sort of package as now constituted is disturbingly on the large side.

This plea had little effect—indeed given the nature of the Chancellor's presentation of the issues at MES on 10 July it could hardly do so—for the Chancellor finally decided to go for the package set out in the note of 18 July and he cleared this with the Cabinet on the morning of 22 July. His statement to the House of Commons in the afternoon justified the measures on the grounds that they would help with the implementation of the Social Contract and would only worsen the borrowing requirement in the current year by £340 million (he did not give a 'full year' figure). Under questioning by the Opposition he had to concede that the measures would largely cancel the effect of the indirect tax increases of the March Budget.[55]

Public expenditure II

The Public Expenditure Survey by Treasury and spending department officials was completed in June and a report was submitted to Ministers at the end of the month. It made the point that the programmes had been constructed within the growth limits laid down by Ministers in April. This meant that the figures for a number of major programmes were *not* derived from the cost of implementing existing policies—something which had been the basis for expenditure policy in previous years; it simply represented the outcome of an externally imposed constraint. On this basis the report was agreed interdepartmentally at official level, but it acknowledged that, the current year excepted, no spending Minister was committed to the policy implications of the report. It was evident that there would be some serious challenges to the proposed programmes when the consequences of the report were fully digested.

The actual profile of programme spending in the report—on the assumptions made—showed modest growth over the quadrennium. The average annual increase in programme spending, based on 1974 Survey prices, between 1974–75 and 1978–79 was just under 2.5 per cent, but if the figures were adjusted to express the claims they made on resources rather than on finance (which was the basis of the original Ministerial decision) the annual rate of growth came to about 2.75 per cent—the limit laid down by Ministers on Treasury advice. But the report made an important qualification to this simple description of the profile. This was that it was in *volume* terms and was based on the level and pattern of prices in 1974. But, based on past experience, the prices paid by the public sector for its goods, services and transfers could be

---

[55] *Hansard* 22 July 1974.

expected to rise significantly faster than prices in general—a phenomenon known as the Relative Price Effect. When allowance was made for this, the average annual rate of growth of programme spending over the four-year period was nearer 2.7 per cent than the 2.5 per cent cited in the report. This rate of increase contrasted with 2.0 per cent for the same period, which had been proposed in the last Public Expenditure White Paper—that of the outgoing Conservative Government in December 1973.[56] The difference was largely accounted for by the big increases in spending which the new Government had authorized for 1974–75 when it took office. Much of this spending became embedded in each of the relevant programmes for the whole Survey period. The modesty of the increases allowed for thereafter were going to test very severely the resolve of Ministers to abide by their decision in principle in April, and so it proved to be.[57]

The Chancellor was preoccupied with his mini-Budget when the PESC report was delivered, but with this out of the way he felt able to invite his colleagues to consider its findings. We saw earlier that the Prime Minister had promised the Cabinet a full review of economic policy before the outcome of the Survey was considered. He clearly did not regard the discussions of early July about the possible measures to stimulate the economy and reduce the rate of price inflation as meeting this promise, and the item was duly tabled for the Cabinet of 26 July. The Chancellor had other ideas, for the paper he presented to his colleagues specifically asked them to approve the main conclusions of the Survey and dealt only peripherally with the Government's economic strategy. The argument he put forward was in fact largely a repetition of the paper he had presented in April as a launching pad for the Survey. He talked of the annual accretion of resources that might be expected and how these should be distributed between the main claimants—the balance of payments, investment, personal consumption, etc.—and in effect asked the Cabinet now to agree to the broad proposals that officials had made which gave effect to the earlier decision that expenditure on goods and services should grow over the quadrennium at an annual rate of 2.75 per cent. He did however acknowledge that there were a number of areas which could not be settled at that time, such as the level of nationalized industry prices, food subsidies (both of which had been affected by the July mini-Budget), and Defence, where a new review had been embarked upon by the government earlier in the year and where the Survey report implied very substantial reductions in long-term costings. He now acknowledged that to accommodate the extra items expenditure should be held 'close to the rate in the PESC Report'—a tacit acknowledgement that there was likely to be some overrun.[58]

[56] Cmnd 5519.   [57] T 277/2949 (PESC (74)12).
[58] CAB 129/178/4 and 5—C (74) 80 and C (74) 81.

The Cabinet discussion was inconclusive, perhaps inevitably so given the many open questions the Chancellor himself pointed to, but it did bring out the fact that adhering to the 2.75 per cent growth rate implied some considerable trimming of programmes that were dear to the heart of the new Administration: notably health, education, and social provision generally. The Prime Minister, perceiving a difficult decision-making process, said that decisions on the Survey would have to wait until after the Recess, but it was agreed that the Chancellor should have bilateral discussions with the relevant spending ministers in the problematic areas.[59] These took place in August and the Chancellor reported the outcome of them to the Cabinet on 10 September.[60] Unresolved claims, that is those which could not be accommodated within the growth target (including estimating changes) amounted to over £0.75 billion in 1975–76 and about £0.5 billion in later years, involving a rise in expenditure of 3.25 per cent p.a. over the Survey period in demand terms. He proposed reductions designed to bring the annual rate of growth to just over 3 per cent and further cuts would still be needed to bring the profile of spending into line with what Ministers had agreed to, in principle, earlier in the year. Moreover the Chancellor reminded his colleagues that the government had substantial prospective commitments beyond these claims: increases in family allowances, a double uprating of social security benefits, not to mention bringing the aircraft and shipbuilding industries into public ownership, as the Election Manifesto had promised. The discussion that followed[61] reaffirmed once more the decision in principle to keep the profile of spending growth to 2.75 per cent over the four years and asked the Chancellor to suggest specific measures in each of the main programmes to secure this. He came back to his colleagues at the end of October with firm proposals for honouring the commitment. The totals for 1978–79 exceeded the limit set for that year by £300–400 million and he asked for this to be dealt with by considerable retrenchment in the field of local authority spending: education, personal social services, law and order, and local environmental services. There then followed another series of bilateral meetings with all the spending departments and two further Cabinets on 5 and 25 November[62] before the programmes were finally agreed for presentation to Parliament early in the new year in the Public Expenditure White Paper (Cmnd 5879). Although in presentational terms this document reflected much of the optimism about the potential growth rate of the economy over the following four years, it did manage to present a profile of spending from the base year which could be regarded as cautious. At 1974 Survey prices the budgeted spending pattern was as shown in Table 2.1.

---

[59] CAB 128/55.   [60] CAB 129/179/10—C (74)100 and 101.
[61] CAB 128/55/10—C (74)35th Conclusions.   [62] CAB 128/55/18 and 24.

Table 2.1 Budgeted spending pattern, 1974–79, based on 1974 Survey prices (£ million)

	1974–75	1975–76	1976–77	1977–78	1978–79
Programmes	35,164	35,465	35,865	36,281	36,967
Contingency reserve	——	300	400	550	750
Total	35,164	35,765	36,263	36,831	37,717
% increase on previous year	10.9	1.7	1.4	1.5	2.4

Between the first and the last year, the annual average increase in spending on goods and services was to be 2.4 per cent and on transfer payments it would be less than zero. The latter would be achieved by a scaling back of subsidies to the nationalized industries, on food, and on housing. For programmes as a whole, the average annual increase of spending in volume terms was only 1.76 per cent, a relatively modest figure by the standards of the past ten years. But the increase was on top of an inflated base—1974–75—and the doubts about the programme were whether in the event Ministers would hold to the profile of spending they had assented to.

The experience of the spending round in 1974 showed that the achievement of the Treasury's objectives of limiting expenditure to what they thought the economy could accommodate in the medium term was going to take a great deal of ministerial time and would be a great burden on the Chancellor. The process was essentially one of negotiation between him and the whole team of spending ministers—and it was very protracted. The survey began in April and the programmes were not finally decided until the end of November. There was not much question of a Treasury fiat, as, for instance, there was in the field of taxation and monetary policy. There was nothing new in this. But the commitment of the new government to public programmes was particularly strong—perhaps stronger than in any previous peace-time government. Secondly it was much easier to reach a desired level of spending by obtaining decisions to moderate the growth of transfer payments (which could easily be reversed when the time of implementation came) than in firm programmes involving, for instance, construction projects where a decision to reduce expenditure even at some fairly remote future date involved a decision early on to cancel or postpone specific items. The year 1974 may be counted not wholly wasted as far as the control of expenditure was concerned, for it provided the Treasury with a test-bed for what was wrong with the control system by exposing it to an unusually high rate of inflation and to a ministerial control which was not particularly sympathetic to Treasury nostrums. In the following year, as we shall see, the Treasury began to seek remedies for the weaknesses that had emerged.

What the experience of spending control also brought out in 1974 was that, however virtuous Ministers collectively were in addressing themselves to the longer-term, they found many reasons to allow *current* spending to increase, without much regard to containing the increase within the contingency reserve. In 1974–75 when they embarked on the mid-year review in July, they had already agreed significant increases in current expenditure without considering whether these could be accommodated within the totals agreed. Later in the year the Chancellor announced a programme of spending on the construction industry, which was in serious recession.[63] This admittedly did not increase expenditure in 1974–75 but it added £100 million to the programmes for the following year, and complicated the problem which he was going to have to address in his Budget the following year. In the early months of 1975, still within the current financial year, he approved the purchase of the BP shares held by the Burmah Oil Company, then in financial difficulties. This cost nearly £200 million. There was a good economic case for all these decisions, but they did complicate the job of the Expenditure Sector of the Treasury which was trying to keep spending within the totals everyone paid lip-service to. In 1974–75 the volume of spending actually incurred exceeded by about 2 per cent the forecast made at the time of the Budget—an excess of over £500 million.

The 1974 Survey and the White Paper which encapsulated its findings were significant in another respect. The exercise had been conducted in essentially Keynesian terms, with the emphasis on resource use, not finance. Indeed at times during the Cabinet discussion the Chancellor seemed relaxed about items which involved little in the way of additional demand. For instance, in his Cabinet paper of 23 July, he acknowledged that while the proposals for nationalizing certain industries and providing for the community ownership of development land would alter the type of assets held by the public, even if paid for in Government stock and have much the same monetary effects as other increases in the PSBR, he conducted the debate in essentially resource terms. In this he simply reflected the prevailing Treasury ethos. But this ethos was about to change, as we shall see, although not until the external situation had become more serious.

The state of business

In the course of 1974 the business sector of the UK was subjected to some severe financial pressures, and these came to exert a considerable influence on the formulation of macro-economic policy towards the end of the year. Gross trading profits of industrial and commercial companies (net of stock appreciation) fell by 12.5 per cent between 1973 and 1974 partly as a result of declining economic activity and partly in consequence of the 'squeeze' which the application of the Price Code involved—and tax payments actually

---

[63] Treasury Press Notice 11 September 1974.

doubled. The latter was partly due to the measure in the Chancellor's March Budget to require companies to make additional payments of Advance Corporation Tax (ACT) when this liability fell due (usually on the payment of dividends) and partly to the fact that companies were being assessed for tax on the purely paper profits they made from the financial appreciation of their trading stocks. Inspite of these financial difficulties, gross capital formation (investment in plant and equipment) held up well—mainly because the decisions had been taken sometime in the past when business conditions had been less bleak. The effect of the relatively high level of investment was, of course, to put the company sector into even more severe financial deficit. The market impact of these developments was very disturbing to business and investors' confidence and the FT Actuaries index of stock prices fell steadily during the year from 150 in January to 63 in mid-December—an almost unprecedented collapse in peace time. Confidence had already been badly affected by the secondary banking problems that emerged at the end of 1973 when a large property company (London and County Securities) experienced severe liquidity problems. It had borrowed extensively to finance property development and found itself caught by the collapse in property prices and the rise in interest rates which occurred in the second half of 1973. This development led to the creation of the 'Lifeboat' consisting of the Bank of England and the main Clearing Banks whose function was to keep the financial situation of deposit taking institutions under review and reinforce their liquidity where support was both feasible and justified.[64]

The problems of the banking sector were not diminished by the fall in asset values generally which was taking place and at one point in the autumn of 1974 the National Westminster Bank felt obliged to scotch market rumours and issue a statement to the effect that it was not in financial difficulties. The banking problem was, however, of a different kind from the liquidity problems of industrial and commercial companies generally, although the effect on confidence was similar.

The whole question of the financial problems of the company sector was raised at a meeting between the Chancellor and the Governor at the beginning of August, after which the Bank produced a considered paper—put to the Treasury in early September—analysing how the problems had arisen and examining what remedial action was possible.[65] At the same time the Deputy Governor reported that the 'entire financial system was under some degree of stress' and 'industrial and commercial companies are cutting their spending plans'. The suggestions were that action could be taken to moderate the effects of the Price Code and to give some fiscal relief to companies. Both these suggestions were accepted and, as we shall see in the following section, were incorporated in the Autumn Budget.

[64] Reid 'The Secondary Banking Crisis 1973–75'.   [65] STEP (74)3—T 277/2959.

The November Budget

The Chancellor had committed himself in his first Budget statement to a further Budget before the end of the year. This was primarily to give him time to work out with the Inland Revenue the details of the 'Gift Tax' he wanted to introduce as a supplement to the Estate Duty. He also wanted to take stock of the possibility of introducing a Wealth Tax—an annual impost on personal assets. These issues lie outside the scope of this study. But the need for a second Budget, even one primarily devoted to structural issues, gave him, and Treasury officials, an opportunity to consider whether any fiscal changes should be made for conjunctural reasons, that is to redress any short-term problem on the macro-economic front as opposed to the structural changes which were the main purpose of the Budget.

Shortly after the summer break, the Permanent Secretary undertook to give the Chancellor a paper setting out the preliminary Treasury judgement about the shape of the Budget, 'the intention being to enable the Chancellor to reflect during the next few weeks on the measures he might want to introduce' and a paper was produced on 11 September.[66] The Treasury clearly wanted to get its views in early and avoid the situation of July when Ministers, without any prompting, became carried away with the idea of a stimulatory mid-year package and officials had been left largely reacting to ideas about which they had reservations. The paper stressed that it was written ahead of the Autumn NIF and its analysis was therefore somewhat tentative, although it stated that it could be taken as a fair working assumption that unemployment would continue to rise over the course of the following year, perhaps reaching 950,000 by the beginning of 1976, and that economic growth would be significantly below productive potential. It took as given that the Government would continue to treat the Social Contract as the cornerstone of its counter-inflation policy. 'This leads us to the view that in order to secure the Contract the Government has this autumn to be seen to be taking some remedial action to deal with rising unemployment.... It seems that the Social Contract would be jeopardised if the Government were to take no stimulatory action. Wage demands might intensify, the union leaders arguing that if the Government would not reflate the economy they themselves would, and industrial relations might deteriorate.' The main economic objectives were seen to be:

1 to improve the current account of the balance of payments with the object of eliminating the deficit by 1978–79—this was the target agreed at the meeting on 21 June when it had been decided that resources should be switched into the external sector at a rate of about £400 million a year at an unemployment figure of 600,000;

[66] T 171/1148.

2 to make the fullest possible use of resources consistent with other objectives;
3 to reduce substantially the rate of inflation by the end of 1975.

The first of these presented especial difficulties, because the UK's competitiveness had continued to fall and was expected to fall further. Such improvement in the current account as would occur in 1975 would simply be as a result of the under-employment of domestic resources. However the practicability of a managed and controlled depreciation was open to question, as we saw in the section dealing with the balance of payments. In the short run, therefore, there was little likelihood of the balance of payments providing a stimulus to demand—but the constraint of having to secure overseas confidence to finance the deficit, the paper argued, 'presents a major constraint on our being able to put the thrust of policy on domestic demand'. The room for manoeuvre was therefore very limited. One area which merited attention was the business sector which was discussed in the previous section. The Treasury reported that the operation of the Price Code was under review with the aim of reducing the squeeze on profits and put forward a number of ideas for giving business some fiscal relief.

The Treasury paper also looked at a number of measures in the fiscal field which might help to moderate the increase in retail prices and provide a modest stimulus to demand as well as considering what the options were for improving the financial outlook for business. The Chancellor had a meeting with Treasury and Revenue Department officials on 19 September to discuss the paper.[67] One 'extraneous' event intervened at this point. On 18 September the Prime Minister announced his decision to ask for a dissolution of Parliament and a General Election on 10 October. This did not deter the Chancellor from formulating his own plans. He told officials that his inclination was to reflate the economy somewhat—he mentioned a figure of £1,000 million in demand terms—but the measures should be focused on investment and exports—he did not want to do much to help consumers. There matters were left for the time being, but early in October the Chancellor told the Permanent Secretary that, if he remained in office, he would like to construct the Budget so as to secure a number of objectives, chief of which were to improve the financial condition of the company sector, to promote industrial investment, to stimulate exports, and to promote energy conservation—'any increase in demand to be slanted towards the price level'.

On 23 October, the NIF having been delivered and the General Election having been won by the current administration with a working Parliamentary majority, the Treasury gave expression to its ideas on the appropriate course of action. The paper it put forward was a complete review of all aspects of macroeconomic policy and put the Budget into a context that was wider than a

[67] T 171/1166.

normal Budget submission. It was structured around the objective of doing something about inflation, about exports and about the plight of the company sector. Pointedly the Treasury stated, in contradiction to what it had said in the September paper, that it had not included general unemployment as a main problem. It had come to the conclusion that although the crude figures were alarming, the economy did not have substantial resources of labour which could easily or without much cost be brought into use. 'In the main employers still have great difficulty in recruiting skilled and semi-skilled labour and ... the duration of most of the unemployed on the unemployment register is short'. There then followed an appraisal of the scope for doing anything about inflation, for example by subsidizing prices, and the conclusion was that 'the present and prospective pay situation does not justify any action on prices comparable to that taken in July when the thresholds were current'.[68] Next came a discussion of the scope for action on the exchange rate, the substance of which was set out above. Finally the paper looked at specific ways to help companies and concluded that the most effective method would be to devise some way of relieving them of an immediate tax liability on profits which arose simply through the appreciation in value of their stock-in-trade. A figure of about £1 billion in cash flow terms was put forward as a suitable magnitude. To this was added some relaxation of the effect of the Price Code and the enlarging of the financial intermediary known as 'Finance for Industry', a financial institution owned by the Clearing Banks and the Bank of England and which provided mainly loan finance for medium- to large-sized companies which were at that time finding it difficult to obtain finance through the banks or the market themselves.

This was, therefore, a proposal for a broadly neutral Budget in demand terms, although as the Treasury admitted it would significantly worsen the public sector financial accounts (in order to benefit the company sector). The borrowing requirement would rise to about £7 billion in 1974–75 and £8 billion the following year. But, said the Treasury, 'our judgement is that it would not in fact be damaging provided the Budget measures as a whole appeared economically sensible and relevant, and in particular that it was made clear that the rate of growth of the money supply would remain under control'. However the warning was given that a Budget on the lines put forward would make it harder to keep this growth rate down later on. The Chancellor called a meeting two days later to discuss this advice. The Bank were now represented, as were the Revenue Departments and all the Treasury Ministers. After some preliminary discussion about the reliability of the

---

[68] The effect of the thresholds was to translate into wages every increase in prices, so containing prices did have an effect on wages. But the threshold agreements had expired in the summer and there was no longer an automatic case for subsidizing prices to influence wages.

economic forecasts, the meeting got down to the specifics which the Treasury had put forward. The discussion on the exchange rate has already been dealt with. For the rest, the meeting was agreed on action to assist companies on the lines previously proposed, but on the question of energy saving, an issue the Chancellor wanted to deal with in the Budget, the ideas seemed to be largely presentational and lacked substance. The only measure having immediate impact was to impose a 25 per cent VAT rate on petrol. This would hit consumers but not businesses which would, under the normal VAT rules, simply pass on the impost to their customers.

In the run-up to the Budget, OF decided that this would be a suitable occasion to announce the ending of the residual guarantees of the value of the sterling balances of the official holders.[69] The guarantees had become something of an anachronism in that, because of the nature of the agreements, they applied to only a part of the holdings and certainly did not apply to the recent large increase which had occurred in the balances of the major oil-exporting countries. They had, moreover, become somewhat complicated to operate, given that sterling was now floating and the agreements had been structured to deal with a fixed-rate system. The Chancellor had no difficulty in accepting the Treasury recommendation, and the termination of the agreements was therefore included in the Budget package.

The Chancellor duly opened his Budget on 12 November. The occasion was very much like that of a Spring Budget and was followed by the resolutions needed to give effect to its proposals and a Finance Bill. It was also accompanied by a 'Red Book'—the Financial Statement and Budget Report (FSBR)[70]—containing a fair amount of detail both about the state of the economy and the tax measures proposed. Although the rationale for an 'out of season' Budget was to enable the Chancellor to introduce the structural measures he had not had time to work up for the spring budget, these issues occupied a very small part of his speech and came at the very end. He had in fact presented a Green Paper in August as a discussion document about a possible wealth tax and a White Paper at the same time outlining his plans for incorporating life-time gifts within the ambit of the Estate Duty and renaming it the Capital Transfer Tax; so it was not unreasonable that he should spend little time on them. The speech was therefore mainly about the conjuncture and contained a wide-ranging survey of both the domestic and the world economy, very little of which was new. On inflation he warned that if wages rose beyond the limits set by the TUC 'the Government will be compelled to take offsetting steps to curtail demand'. On public finances he admitted that his spring forecast of a PSBR of £2,733 million had been revised to 'about £5.5 billion' mainly due to the effects of wage inflation being so much greater than price inflation and to the additional expenditure incurred during the year. But the money supply

[69] T 358/163.   [70] *Parliamentary Papers* 1974–75, Vol. xix, p. 551.

had been kept within strict limits and 'the inflationary impact of the enlarged borrowing requirement had been contained'. Turning to the medium term, he set as his objectives giving priority to the balance of payments and to investment, to adjust prices to reflect real costs and 'to see that inflation is not fuelled by an excessive increase in the money supply'. There was little in the speech to show how these objectives would be secured. The measures he set out were very much on the lines of those the Treasury and the Bank had been proposing. Substantial help was given to the business sector through an adjustment of Corporation Tax to relieve some of it on stock appreciation profits and to soften the impact of the Price Code on businesses. He announced the intention of the Governor to ask the banks to give high priority in their lending to businesses and the initiative to enlarge Finance for Industry in order to provide some £1 billion of extra lending to industry. On energy conservation he increased the VAT on petrol to 25 per cent. He also announced some minor measures in the field of personal taxation. The main impact of the budget was undoubtedly to give relief to the financial plight of industry, which was expected to benefit, in terms of cash flow, to the tune of about £1.5 billion in the following year. But the benefits to industry were at the cost of a further deterioration in public finances, which would now show a deficit in the current year of £6,300 million. The FSBR gave a forecast of the main elements of demand in the period up to mid-1975 but did not predict what would happen to the balance of payments, nor to the rate of increase of wages and prices. It was by the usual standards a rather slim publication.

The informed reaction to the Budget was of relief for what it did for industry. The termination of the sterling guarantees attracted little comment. The Chancellor expressed himself as pleased with the reception. The budget measures to help industry and do something to brighten the outlook for companies, although helpful, did not, however, do very much to restore the confidence of the financial markets which continued to take a gloomy view of the outlook for company profits and solvency. The *Financial Times* index of thirty leading shares continued to fall and reached 160 at the year-end (1935 = 100) from 325 at the beginning of the year.

Inflation—Part 2

The account we have given of the evolution of macro-economic policy in 1974 has said nothing about the consideration which officials were privately giving to the underlying problem of rapidly increasing inflation, except to describe their attitude to measures which helped to cement the Social Contract. In fact the need to take more decisive action was something which increasingly preoccupied Whitehall as the year progressed. The year of 1974 saw a marked acceleration in the rise of the retail price index and in the index of average earnings. The percentage increase of the former on the corresponding figure a year earlier rose from 10.3 per cent at the end of 1973 to 15.9 per cent six months later and to 18.2 per cent by the year end. The rate of increase of the earnings index rose from 13.3 per cent at the end of 1973 to 24.1 per cent a year later. This state of affairs was not a matter which the Treasury—or indeed anyone in Government—could view with equanimity. From the middle of the year when the statutory control on pay was abolished, the only restraint on pay increases, apart from the unwillingness of employers to comply with union demands, lay in the observance of the trade unions of the TUC's guidance that pay settlements should broadly maintain workers' living stand- ards. This guidance, however, made provision for a number of special in- creases, notably for the low-paid and for the implementation of the final stage of the 'equal pay' provisions.

It was clear to officials, however sceptical they might be about the adequacy of the guidelines to bring about a fall in the rate of inflation, that Ministers would not be willing—for the time being at any rate—to contemplate a de- parture from the Social Contract.[71] The options for tackling inflation were therefore limited, and amounted to a continuance of the policy of subsidizing prices (as was done in both the March Budget and the July mini-Budget) and in persuading the unions to be more disciplined than they apparently were in the application of the TUC's guidelines. A report by officials in November[72] found that, apart from one or two special cases in the public sector, like nurses who were recognized by the government as requiring special treatment, less than one-half of the settlements reached since the abolition of the statutory con- trols were within the guidelines, although the breaches tended to be for smaller groups of workers. Ministers had decided in July to continue to rely on the TUC to monitor the guidelines. When, in October, senior officials in Whitehall considered whether a departure from the voluntary approach was a possible option, the conclusion was that 'the Social Contract is so fundamen- tal that it would be fruitless to suggest to Ministers that they abandon it'. The papers prepared for the November Budget all accepted that the Social Contract was the cornerstone of Government policy and indeed the first recommenda- tions for the Budget were designed to reinforce it.

Notwithstanding this inhibition, the Treasury had put in hand in July some contingency planning against the possibility that Ministers might eventually be prepared to accept that active intervention by the Government in the wage determination process was necessary. This contained nothing that might not have been expected. It followed the pattern of previous excursions into in- comes policies. Urgent consultations with the TUC and the CBI would be followed by legislation for a short freeze on pay followed by a regime of

[71] See for instance correspondence between Permanent Secretaries in DW 085.
[72] CAB 134/3738.

controlled pay increases—a formula modelled on the policy followed by the Heath Government in 1972. Early in December the Treasury examined the options more fundamentally.[73] These were, as they put it:

1 do nothing, live with inflation and wait for it to 'burn out';
2 embark on a sharply deflationary economic strategy;
3 'another Incomes Policy'.

The first option was ruled out as inherently unstable. On the second 'the conclusion seems to be that the chances first of standing the political racket (sic) and second of achieving the objective when one has done so are slight, at any rate in UK circumstances'.[74] The paper went on to discuss a possible structure of new pay policy. It concluded that 'another attempt at direct action on pay might be the least unsatisfactory of the unattractive options open to us'. The paper did not go into the form that direct action might take but subsequent discussion within the Treasury showed an inherent disbelief that the Social Contract could become the basis of an effective Incomes Policy.

In Whitehall generally consideration of the policy options remained rooted in the belief that the Social Contract was inviolable. A group of officials from all the departments concerned began to consider whether some strengthening of the pay provisions of the Social Contract ought to be attempted and reported their findings to the Ministerial Committee on Economic Policy on 16 December. This merely amounted to an hortatory approach to the TUC and the CBI as well as to the leaders of the nationalized industries and the local authorities, as key employers in the public sector. The possibility of penalizing employers and employees who connived at settlements outside the guidelines, by imposing financial sanctions through the Price Code or Corporation Tax or by increases in personal tax, was mentioned only to be rejected on the grounds that it would involve the laying down of a 'government norm' and in any case would be very difficult to administer. The only practical recommendation was to have discussions in the National Economic Development Council. When Ministers considered this report there was an underlying anxiety about the existing policy and the Chancellor, as Chairman of the Committee, specifically invited those of his colleagues who wished to put forward a case for a radical reconsideration of policy to do so at Cabinet or MES level.[75] This, as we shall see, did in fact lead to some practical suggestions early in the New Year.

---

[73] T 357/389.

[74] This judgement may look odd in 2007, given the UK's success in virtually eliminating inflation in the 1990s as a result, in part at any rate, of a sharply deflationary policy and in circumstances where union power had been greatly reduced. But in 1974 the unions had much more industrial strength and had shown earlier in the year that they could, in effect, bring down a government whose policies they disapproved of.

[75] CAB 134/3738.

A complete overhaul of economic policy

Three developments occurred in December which were to have a profound effect on the thinking of the Treasury at the highest level. The first was the sobering report by the Chairman of the Official Committee on Pay Negotiations which highlighted the effect to which the guidance of the TUC and the exceptions to the general policy were having on pay settlements. This was not new but it had the same sort of impact on senior officials as it did on the Ministerial Committee to which it was submitted. The second was a report about the balance of payments put to the high level Committee which the Treasury had set up with participation of all the economic departments to replace the Budget Committee (STEP).[76] The third was a very sharp attack made on sterling in the exchange markets in the middle of December when the Bank spent $1 billion in defending it.[77] This came on top of another significant development—the decision of ARAMCO, the consortium which had the principal oil concessions in Saudi Arabia, to invoice its sales of oil in dollars, not sterling. In terms of actual demand for, and supply of, sterling it had little effect, but psychologically it sent a signal to the markets that all might not be well with sterling.

The mood among policy makers in Whitehall and the City as the year drew to a close darkened considerably. The November Budget was now seen to have done little to deal with the UK's basic problems. The balance of payments deficit on current account for the year as a whole was emerging at over £4 billion compared with deficits of only £70 million in 1972 and £1.77 billion in 1973. The economy which had stopped growing in mid-1973 was showing mixed signals: there was some pickup in the second and third quarters from the sharp downturn at the beginning of the year when output was affected by the three day week, but GDP at the end of the year was only 0.5 per cent higher in the fourth quarter than it had been a year earlier. Unemployment was approaching three-quarters of a million having dipped to just over half a million in 1973. Most worrying of all was that average earnings from employment were beginning to rise very fast indeed. But other indicators were worrying, not least the serious deterioration of the public sector's accounts. The financial situation of business had been improved by the measures of relief from the taxation of profits due to the appreciation of stock values caused by inflation, but the confidence of financial markets was at a very low ebb, not least as a result of the secondary banking crisis which occurred in the course of 1974.

Abroad things were not much better but the approach to the problems created by inflation and payments deficits varied considerably. All the industrialized countries experienced sharp rises in inflation of both wages and prices. Almost all the OECD countries saw a fall in output and a worsening

---

[76] STEP (74)4.   [77] This estimate appears in T 358/163.

in the balance of payments. But most countries were putting in place measures designed to bring inflation under control and reduce the balance of payments deficits that were arising.

The whole economic situation was considered by STEP on 18 December, when, after a lengthy discussion, it was concluded that Ministers had to be informed of their collective grave disquiet. The view was that a radically new approach to the UK's economic problems was now required. The Social Contract was clearly not being observed in a manner which would lead to a decline in the rate of inflation and there was little prospect of the balance of payments deficit being eliminated. The UK's ability to finance this deficit by explicit borrowing and by allowing the sterling balances to go on accumulating could not be counted upon to continue. A memorandum was therefore submitted to the Chancellor by the Treasury Permanent Secretary on 19 December[78] which explicitly claimed to represent the collective view of officials, not only in the Treasury but in all the economic departments and the Bank of England. It described the problem in the following bleak terms:

The situation is serious in three important respects:

(i) Even when some recent exaggerations are discounted, pay increases are at a level inconsistent with a reduction in the rate of inflation next year. The social contract does not prevent an increase in inflation, even if it were broadly observed, and would indeed be consistent with a further rise in pay settlements as the price index rises.

(ii) Contrary to the prospects as seen at the time of the Budget the balance of payments is worsening. The poor showing of the non-oil deficit in October and November suggests that the forecast for 1975 could well be between £500–£1000 million worse than we thought even a couple of months ago. Last week's flurry in the exchange markets clearly demonstrated how vulnerable we are. We depend critically on overseas confidence to hold sterling balances and to maintain our capacity to borrow, either in sterling or dollars, to finance our continuing deficit. Confidence is growing more fragile and could collapse at any time.

(iii) The public sector financial deficit this year and, prospectively, next year is at a level which may well prove unsustainable.

The minute went on to advocate resort to some form of Incomes Policy:

We have no alternative but to attempt once more to break into the wage/price spiral by laying down a norm for the rate of pay increases. That norm ought to be below, perhaps significantly below the going rate of increase, year on year, of the RPI and ought not to vary with it. The pay control might have to be statutory, but what really matters is that the Government should give a strong lead to public opinion, should tell the country it must accept pay restraint and should be prepared to resist breaches of it. It must also be recognised that a solution to our problems does not lie in a short sharp crunch with a

---

[78] PCC (74)4—T 277/3053.

return to old ways thereafter. What is required is a period of wage restraint in one form or another lasting perhaps three or more years.

But action should not be limited to direct intervention in the setting of wages and prices:

We must also tackle the structural imbalance in the use of resources by which [is meant] a situation in which we are consuming as a nation 6 per cent more than we are producing, resulting in an excessively large balance of payments deficit quite apart from the oil price rises. This situation has arisen very largely because our domestic consumption has been sustained partly through protective policies at a time when our real national income, after correcting for the terms of trade, has fallen. A further manifestation of structural imbalance is the massive and increasing public sector deficit.

The note went on to call for significant budgetary action both on the taxation front and on public expenditure, recognizing that the deflationary effects could well raise unemployment to between 1 and 1.5 million.

This message was inevitably strong meat for the Chancellor who had only a month previously introduced an Autumn Budget that had painted the picture in far less bleak terms. Officials recognized this. They also understood that what they were advocating was a substantial change of course, which had serious political implications. But the alternative was worse:

If....we continue with existing policy, there is a very serious—some would say over-whelming—risk that an external crisis will hit us and when it does we are likely to experience an attack on sterling which is many times the force of the one we sustained last week. In this situation we shall not have the foreign exchange reserves to defend the rate and though we could let the rate fall we are quite likely to have to produce something like the measures...outlined—though they might have to be even more severe—to rally confidence and defend the parity at any reasonable level.

This was not, in the event, such a fanciful prophecy, as the events of 1976 were subsequently to show.

In a separate move, the Governor made his personal views known to the Chancellor. At a private meeting on 17 December he described the situation as 'grave' and spoke of the 'vulnerability of sterling'. He said quite bluntly that there was 'a need for a new economic strategy'.[79]

The Chancellor's reaction to these stark messages and the influence they had on the policies and measures taken in 1975 are matters that are discussed in the next chapter. But it is significant that at a meeting of the Ministerial Committee on Economic Strategy (MES 74 12th Meeting), the day following the minute quoted, he made a statement to his colleagues which was remarkably similar in style and content to that of the minute and it led some

---

[79] DW 085 20 December.

Ministers to express, for the first time, the view that 'some move towards the establishment of a pay "norm" was perhaps necessary if the Government were not ultimately to be driven to something far more severe'.[80]

Summary

1974 was a year in which the immensity of the economic problems confronting the UK was probably greater than that of any previous post-war year. The two biggest issues were the loss of national income inflicted by the huge oil price rise of late 1973 and the rise in inflation caused in part by the same event, but compounded by the abandonment of a formal Incomes Policy designed to contain the spreading out of price rises. But there were other problems, not wholly unrelated to these two. The first was the emergence of a huge balance of payments deficit—itself a symptom of the failure to accept the national income loss imposed by the oil price rise. The second was the significant increase in public expenditure which occurred in the financial year 1974–75 largely due to the measures of the March Budget and the July mini-Budget. This by itself might not have been a major problem, but combined with others it exacerbated the difficulty of achieving effective management of the economy; for it implicitly made the share of national income which flowed to the personal and private sector much less when those sectors were already being squeezed—and would continue to be squeezed—by the consequences of external events.

The Treasury had clearly recognized these problems from the outset of the oil crisis, but, except perhaps in the field of public expenditure, it was not very successful in devising satisfactory remedies for them. The sharp increase in spending in 1974–75 was of course a political decision which the Treasury was in no position to prevent, or for that matter to oppose. However it was reasonably successful in persuading Ministers that from 1974–75 onwards the growth of expenditure should be severely contained. A rate of growth of 2.75 per cent per annum in terms of resources, and rather less in financial terms, seemed at the time to be affordable and this formed the basis of the White Paper which was to be published early in 1975. But even this was based on assumptions about the likely rate of growth of the economy which seemed at the time to be on the optimistic side and turned out to be wholly unrealistic. What was perhaps equally worrying was that the discipline of holding to the plans for expenditure was lacking. Ministers found it easy to agree to tough overall limits, but baulked at the consequences for individual programmes; and when unforeseen developments occurred, like some industrial failures and of course the rise in unemployment benefits, there was no mechanism

---

[80] CAB 134/3789.

in place to ensure that these did not lead to net additions to the total of expenditure. Another failure in 1974 was the inadequacy of financial control in public spending. The volume basis laid down by the Plowden Report was satisfactory in times of low inflation, but clearly broke down as a mechanism for both controlling and auditing expenditure when prices were accelerating and when relative prices were changing rapidly. These failures were perhaps partly due to an element of indiscipline on the part of Ministers. But the Treasury has to accept a good deal of responsibility for the failure of the system to provide adequate safeguards. It implicity recognized that responsibility in the following years by introducing systemic changes to the process of expend-iture control, and, as we shall see, these proved to be effective safeguards against the sort of excesses which occurred in 1974.

But if the Treasury can claim some limited success in containing public expenditure, it can hardly do so in respect of the question of devoting resources to the external sector (by improving the balance of payments) or of attacking inflation. On the former it brought to the attention of Ministers early in the life of the new administration the seriousness of the problem and it recommended a solution to it—depreciation of the sterling rate. But it was not successful either in persuading Ministers of the seriousness of the issue, or in having put forward a concrete and practical method of achieving it. There were, of course, good reasons for these failures. Depreciation would have compounded the problem of inflation and would have presented great problems for those whose job it was to mobilize external finance to cover the deficit. More importantly perhaps was the fact that the Treasury—and others including the IMF who saw the need for depreciation—had no credible practical policy for achieving it in the regime of floating rates which now prevailed.

The Treasury may have had more excuse for the failure to deal with inflation than it had for its shortcomings in other areas. The abolition of the statutory Incomes Policy which had been in existence since November 1972 was a political decision, as was the setting up of the Social Contract as the corner-stone of the Government's economic policy. The Treasury may have had its doubts about the viability of this approach, but it was clearly in no position in the early months to urge Ministers to abandon it. The narrative shows that the Treasury was giving thought to alternative approaches, but it was not until late in December that Ministers were formally invited to reconsider their position. It is difficult to see how the Treasury could have done otherwise than give the Social Contract a chance to prove itself. And indeed as we shall see, in 1975 it did spectacularly prove itself, in a way that the Treasury and indeed other departments could not foresee.

But whatever justification can be provided for the nature of the policy advice which the Treasury were giving, 1974 must be judged to have been a year in which things got worse, not better. They were perhaps getting worse for other countries too—inflation and the balance of payments were problems which the whole of the developed world was having to cope with—and the UK was by no means alone in failing adequately to deal with them in 1974. In the following chapter we deal with the evolution of policy in 1975 and show how the shortcomings of policy in 1974 were addressed, at least in part, if not completely.

3

1975—Policy Changes

The Budget

The Chancellor did not take kindly to the advice he received on 20 December 1974. He seemed reluctant to accept the implications for employment which the recommendations, if accepted, would entail.[1] He was also no doubt somewhat nonplussed to get proposals some of which were new and apparently at variance with previous official advice. The concern of the Treasury about the level of pay settlements and the failure of the Social Contract to lead to any fall in the rate of inflation could not have come as much of a surprise to him; nor can he have found the ideas put forward for giving priority to an improvement in the balance of payments very novel. But the fact that the Treasury now saw a pressing need to improve the state of the public finances even if action to achieve this would cause unemployment to rise was a new one. The Treasury had, after all, gone along with his November Budget Statement in the course of which he said:

If we add to the cut in demand in the (oil) consuming countries already imposed by the increase in oil prices a further cut in demand in the belief that this will somehow cure cost inflation we shall risk turning 'stagflation' already affecting so many countries into 'slumpflation'

and later in the Speech he added:

There is no real evidence that the adoption of deflationary policies will produce a worthwhile impact on the rate of inflation—at any rate within the time-scale that a democracy will tolerate.

The Financial Statement[2] issued at the time of this budget envisaged a PSBR of £6.3 billion for 1974–75 compared with £2.7 billion at the time of the March Budget. The measures of the November Budget had added nearly £800 million to the borrowing requirement. The Chancellor could be forgiven for

---

[1] T 277/3053—PCC (75)3.   [2] *Parliamentary Papers* 1974, Vol. viii, p. 1257.

seeing the position taken by the Treasury at the end of 1974 as being a distinct shift from its previous stance. Nevertheless he seems to have had little hesitation in giving, on the day following its delivery to him, much the same message to his Ministerial colleagues on the Economic Strategy Committee.

It is worth asking at this stage why the Treasury had not taken the opportunity of the November Budget to propose restrictive measures. The answer must be speculative but there are some indications from the papers. In the first place the Treasury's ideas for the Budget were formulated in September when the deterioration of the economic situation had not really become apparent and policy was firmly rooted in the Social Contract, which placed some constraints on the options open. Sterling was still fairly strong and foreign confidence had not evaporated, as it did to a considerable extent in December. Sterling inflows from official holders only started to dry up in the fourth quarter of the year—the exchange rate fell by about 4 per cent in that quarter having been fairly stable in the previous nine months. The papers do suggest that the Treasury was having some second thoughts about the nature of the Budget as it was being prepared. In the early submissions the emphasis was very much on the need to avoid any untoward increase in unemployment. As the thinking developed, the Treasury seemed to accept that labour constraints might still be stifling the export effort, and the case for avoiding anything savouring of deflation was argued with much less conviction.

But whatever weight these arguments might have had, it has to be conceded that the Chancellor would have been open to the most serious political criticism if he had taken the opportunity of the November Budget to raise taxes and/or cut social programmes. Parliament and the public would have wanted to know why he had not spelt out his ideas in the run-up to the Election a month earlier. Political memories recalled the occasion in 1955 when the then Chancellor, R. A. Butler, brought in a restrictive autumn Budget after a General Election which had in turn been preceded by a 'give-away' Budget. Sheer political realism would have inhibited the Treasury from proposing a deflationary approach at that time and indeed the Chancellor's response to the memorandum of 19 December provides adequate evidence that he would have been deeply averse in October to the sort of policy restructuring that the Treasury later on felt bound to propose. Thirdly it seems to have been judged that the most opportune moment for a policy change would be in the normal annual budget which would be presented in the Spring of 1975. This timing would give the Treasury time to work out a fully articulated new approach to policy making and allow time for them to persuade the Chancellor, and the Chancellor in turn to persuade his colleagues, of the need for a significant change of direction.

The Chancellor's only formal response to the December minute was to commission a good deal of further work of a technical nature[3]—which seemed very much like the temporary shelving of the substantive issues. Most of the questions asked by the Chancellor stemmed directly from the minute, but one piece of work did not. This was a request for 'a paper on import restrictions, including a description of the recent French measures to control oil imports and comments on the recent Italian measures'. To Treasury officials it confirmed their expectation that a good deal of spadework would have to be done to move the Chancellor to their point of view.

The spadework began very early in the New Year. In spite of the Chancellor's apparent reluctance to contemplate a shift of policy, officials began the task of putting flesh on the outline ideas of the December note. The central forum in the Treasury for the development of policy advice was now the Policy Coordinating Committee (PCC) which was established at the end of 1974, and whose composition and role was described in Chapter 1. In the run-up to the Budget, preparatory work was put in hand on four issues:

1 the state of the public finances—what might be called the stance of the Budget;
2 the financing of the balance of payments deficit in the coming year;
3 a more aggressive approach to the containment of inflation;
4 the future profile of public spending.

These proved to be, for the year as a whole, the main preoccupations of the Treasury, at any rate at the macro-economic level. The Budget was to make a substantial contribution to the first and last of these issues, and we have to examine how it came to be so structured. But the Budget left virtually untouched the other two issues, and substantial progress on them had to wait until the Budget was out of the way. We look at the four issues in turn, although inevitably there is some overlap in the treatment we give them.

The opening salvo in the discussion about the stance of the Budget was a paper presented to the PCC early in January by the Chief Economic Adviser.[4] This took it as axiomatic that there would have to be some intervention in the wage determination process and that it should be a principal aim of macro-economic policy to secure a substantial improvement in the balance of payments in the course of the following year or so—a view which commanded assent from all parts of the Treasury. What emerged in the course of the discussions of January and February was a difference of view about the pace at which the improvements should be made, and to some extent a difference of view about the analysis. The Chief Economic Adviser's appraisal took a conventionally Keynesian form and was indeed entitled 'The Background to Demand Policy'. Its analysis was essentially in resource terms and saw the objective of policy as a balanced and

---

[3] DW 015 2 January 1975.   [4] T 277/3053—PCC (75)8.

sustainable level of aggregate demand. The shift of resources from domestic consumption into the balance of payments required a two-fold approach, the first involving fiscal policy to free resources from home to overseas use and the second, given the serious loss of competitiveness which the UK had suffered in the course of 1974, involving some measure to help producers to compete more effectively with foreign suppliers, both in home and overseas markets. On the second issue the instruments looked at were, as in the exchanges the previous autumn, some form of induced fall in the sterling exchange rate and (picking up the idea thrown out by the Chancellor in his reaction to the December minute on Economic Strategy) some form of import restrictions. Neither of these were then seen to be viable options, at any rate for the moment. Import restrictions would be beset with institutional objections from the UK's trading partners in the European Economic Community (EEC) and the GATT and might meet with retaliatory action which would frustrate their purpose. But there was an even more important objection in that trade restrictions would undermine the role of international competition in promoting efficiency in UK industry. As the Chief Economic Adviser put it:

We would be removing a large part of the pressure of international competition from British industry when we want the maximum progress in efficiency and in adaptation to technical and market opportunities. There might be a case for such a policy if the competitive strength of British industry was so hopelessly low and in such decay that the alternative was a wholesale and permanent loss of markets to foreign competition at home and abroad, with resulting abandonment of production and unemployment on a colossal scale. But surely we do not think things are as bad as that.

But there was not much scope for acting purely through the market and seeking a change in the relative prices of British and foreign goods through a change in the exchange rate. The difficulties here had been examined inconclusively in the summer and autumn of 1974 and the Chief Economic Adviser now took no more sanguine a view than the one that had prevailed then. The conclusion was that exchange-rate management policy could do very little to improve competitiveness and the authorities had to leave the rate largely to market developments. This meant that, for the time being, the Government would have to rely on the reduction in domestic demand which was advocated to lead to a reduction in imports and to a consequential improvement in the balance of trade. Some, although perhaps not much, improvement would come from the removal of any capacity constraints on exporters and hence to an increase in overseas sales. But the improvement in the external balance would be slow—unless the cut in domestic demand which was under consideration was very substantial, in which case there would be a very large increase in unemployment. The paper argued that the slow pace of recovery in the external position could be accepted if the Government could put in place an effective Incomes Policy to show the UK's creditors that it was serious about tackling the principal cause of its loss of competitiveness and at the same time show them that the Government was bringing our allocation of resources into some sort of balance. If these premises could be secured, there seemed to be no reason why the UK should not be able to attract the external finance it needed to bridge the gap until the flow of North Sea oil in 1978 brought in the revenue which would balance external payments. The Chief Economic Adviser therefore advocated a mildly deflationary budget and the acceptance of a moderate pace of structural change.

The analysis was, as has been said, conducted in demand, not financial, terms and on this the memorandum was frank. It acknowledged that the PSBR was high (£6.5 billion in 1974–75) and would grow higher still on present policies. (The NIF forecast due to be completed a few weeks later would put the figure at 'about £10 billion'[5] or about 10 per cent of GDP.) 'The view adopted here,' said the note 'is that the size of the borrowing requirement does not constitute a policy objective in its own right, but rather that it should emerge from decisions about public sector taxation and expenditure determined by reference to their economic consequences in the terms already discussed.' This position, which had been almost an article of faith in the Treasury in the postwar years was elaborated in a separate annex, which stated its position categorically:

There is no way of directly assessing the acceptability of a given public sector financial deficit. There is a simple relation between the financial surpluses/deficits of the three sectors which together embrace the economy, viz (1) the private sector (2) the overseas sector and (3) the public sector. *Ex post*, these must add up to zero.... The way to judge the rightness or wrongness of Government fiscal and expenditure policies as a whole is not to look at the size of the financial deficit but to look at the situation in terms of demand pressure and the balance of payments which will result from these policies.... There is no way of evaluating the public sector deficit other than in terms of the contribution it makes to the state of the economy defined as above.

But one concession at least was made to financial orthodoxy. 'There is a quite separate argument about whether our existing methods of forecasting and policy appraisal take proper account of the monetary effects of fiscal policies. Arguably they have not done so, and attempts are being made to improve on past procedures in this regard'. The last point was to remain valid with increasing insistence over the next two years—no more so than during the negotiations with the IMF at the end of 1976. We shall say more on this later on.

The record of the collective discussion of this position paper is no longer extant, but it is clear from subsequent documents that the Chief Economic Adviser's views did not command universal assent within the Treasury. He

[5] DW 013 4 Feb and T 277/3053 26 February 1975.

himself acknowledged that there was a body of opinion that felt that the slower pace of adjustment which he advocated was not viable. The dissenters wished to see a massive reduction in the PSBR in 1975–76—the figure of £3–4,000 million was mentioned—and the acceptance of whatever would be the economic consequences. There were some informal discussions with the Chancellor which led the Permanent Secretary to report to his colleagues on 11 February that the Chancellor would not be prepared to deflate the economy unless it would improve the balance of payments.[6]

The upshot of internal official deliberations on the Budget were eventually set out in a submission which the Permanent Secretary sent to the Chancellor on 24 February.[7] This drew his attention to the Chief Economic Adviser's view, which by then had crystallized into a preference for a neutral budget, but said that all other senior advisers felt that what was required was a sizeable reduction in the PSBR. It was notable that the discussion was now not in terms of the optimum level of demand, but of the financial implications for the public accounts. This represented a significant shift in the basis of policy analysis and advice, and from that moment, although the demand effects of policy (including particularly the employment effects) continued to receive attention, they no longer held centre-stage.

The Treasury recommendation at this stage, which was ahead of the completion of the NIF and therefore somewhat provisional, was that the target of policy should be set as the reduction of the PSBR of £4 billion in 1976–77, with a reduction of about half that amount in 1975–76, that is the financial year about to start. The reason for this two-year approach will emerge later. The importance of international opinion was underlined. 'A reduction in the borrowing requirement in the coming year of less than about £2 billion would carry the risk that we should not appear to have a credible policy with our creditors'. Implicitly the Treasury was saying that the UK could no longer shape economic policy as though it was the unfettered master in its own house. On the other hand officials did not want to recommend so deflationary a package that, however desirable this might be on credit-rating and confidence grounds, 'might' as officials said to the Chancellor, 'lead to so much unemployment this year that the Government is driven by force of circumstances to reflate later in the year by stimulating domestic consumption instead of waiting for the export growth which we hope will pull us out of the recession in 1976'.

The last point is an important one. All the omens pointed to a resumption in the growth of world trade in 1976 after the massive slump in 1974 and early 1975, and it was beginning to be felt in the Treasury that the balance of payments could show a respectable, though perhaps not adequate, improvement in the eighteen months ahead. A parallel submission argued the case for a medium-term strategy.[8] 'Political and economic constraints combine to make

---

[6] DW 013.   [7] Ibid.   [8] Ibid.

it feasible to construct a plausible strategy based on a two-year profile.... It is crucially important that UK industry should be poised to take the opportunities (over this period) to UK exports and that satisfying export demand should (not) be frustrated by a wrong balance in domestic demand. A two-year strategy makes particular sense because the effects of most policy measures tend to have longish lags, and this is especially the case with measures designed to improve the balance of payments through price effects—a depreciation or an alternative scheme discussed in this note.' The first element in this two-year strategy was, as we have noted, a significant reduction in home demand through a restrictive Budget. The second element was the promotion of export demand to fill the hole so created and to close the external gap. This issue was to become one of the three main preoccupations of the Treasury through the remainder of 1975, and the discussions on this subject in the run-up to the Budget were, although inconclusive, a dress rehearsal for the debate which was to continue on and off for the remainder of the year and come to a critical head in November and December.

The Treasury paper looked at a variety of options for improving the trade balance over a period of time:

- a depreciation of sterling;
- a wage subsidy;
- import controls;
- an import surcharge and export subsidy which would be dressed up as a dual-exchange rate regime.

The first three were summarily dismissed. Despite what had been argued the previous autumn, depreciation as a policy option was, for the moment at any rate, considered impracticable. The Treasury had, as all the previous discussion amply demonstrated, no mechanism in a floating rate system to change the parity to a new, desired, level. Moreover a depreciation, if it occurred, would add to the price level and exacerbate the inflationary problem. 'Finally, yet another fall in the exchange rate, and a consequential cut in the capital value of the sterling loans we have received from the oil-producing countries, notably Nigeria, would effectively kill off any further inflow; indeed a loss of confidence could lead to a substantial withdrawal of sterling.' The alternative ideas of a wage subsidy or of generalized import controls received equally short shrift. But the possibility of some form of import surcharge and export subsidy was seen to be less objectionable. Presented as a dual-exchange rate system, it would apply one rate for current transactions and a higher one for capital transactions and for imports of raw materials and food. The scheme was an ingenious one in that it obtained most of the advantages of a depreciation from the improvement it gave to UK exports and to the discouragement of the import of finished foreign goods, but at the same time did not damage the assets of overseas holders of sterling. Moreover the effects of the scheme on the domestic price level would be less than that of a devaluation as the internal prices of food and raw materials would not be affected. In practical terms the scheme would operate not through the banking system and the foreign exchange markets, but through the payment of an export subsidy and the imposition of a surcharge on finished imports. In those terms it would closely resemble the scheme the incoming Labour Government had introduced in the autumn of 1964. That scheme had run into very strong international and institutional criticism and had had to be modified and then abandoned as unacceptable to the UK's trading partners. With this experience in mind, the scheme under consideration would be called a 'dual exchange rate' system and as such would belong to a family of schemes which had been accepted, albeit reluctantly, by the IMF and the EEC for certain countries.[9] It would however have to be cleared with external partners before it was implemented and their acquiescence could not be relied upon. At best agreement would be grudging and only if those external partners were satisfied 'that [the UK] had a satisfactory and comprehensive programme and were doing something about the borrowing requirement'. The memorandum was lukewarm in its commendation of the scheme. Indeed it hardly commended it at all, but put it forward as a *pis aller*, all other alternatives, apart from the alternative of doing nothing, being flawed in one way or another. At this stage the idea was to take the Chancellor's mind as to whether he would be prepared to take the political risks involved in such a complex scheme.

The Chancellor was not unreasonably very doubtful about the wisdom and feasibility of any of the options put to him to improve the trade balance and at a meeting with officials on 11 March[10] he expressed misgivings about whether a contrived scheme, such as the dual exchange rate proposition, would be accepted by the international community. But he did ask for more work to be done on the possibility of import restrictions which might offer the prospect of a better reception of a deflationary budget and a step devaluation of sterling. The Treasury thought that the idea of 'buying' a deflationary budget by imposing trade restrictions was not a good one and even argued in a paper put forward on 14 March[11] that it would be better to sacrifice a severe budget if that were the price of avoiding import controls. Moreover, by 18 March, officials had themselves come to the conclusion that the dual rate idea was not a viable option and the following day the Chancellor agreed.[12] The issue of what, if anything, could be done to improve the trade balance was examined at length at a meeting on 25 March,[13] when the Chancellor accepted that the international risks of a scheme of export subsidies and import surcharges were

---

[9] The French had been permitted a 'financial' franc for a year or two following their financial reforms of 1971.
[10] T 171/1237.   [11] DW 433.   [12] Ibid.   [13] T 171/1237.

too great—at any rate in the Budget—although they should be kept in reserve for possible use later in the year. The Chancellor had asked at the meeting on 11 March for work to be done on a possible step depreciation of sterling (even though the question had been fully gone into the previous autumn) and two days later OF produced an appraisal of it. The first question the paper asked was how this could be achieved. One possibility would be for the authorities to announce that they would no longer intervene in the markets to support sterling when it was above a certain rate—an idea which had been looked at in the middle of 1974 when the exchange rate change had last been considered. Again the effects on official sterling holders (who currently had £5 billion in liquid assets in London) was thought to be a big obstacle, not so much because of the possibility that they might remove their holdings as because the 'breach of faith' involved in an engineered depreciation would materially worsen our immediate problem of financing the still large trade deficit. Compensating official sterling holders and perhaps giving them some form of guarantee of sterling's future value against the dollar was a possibility, but this might well not restore confidence and in any case would sit oddly with the decision announced in the 1974 Autumn budget to end the regime of sterling guarantees which were a residue from the 1967 devaluation and the safety net which followed it. The paper also thought that a 20 per cent depreciation, in a world where there were widespread trade deficits following the oil price increase, would trigger similar action from other deficit countries. The Bank of England chimed in with a strong objection to the idea for much the same reasons. The Treasury, as a whole, accepted the OF conclusion that a 20 per cent depreciation was not a viable option, but was less certain that a smaller change—10 per cent was mentioned—should be ruled out. But in view of the uncertainties over the financing of the deficit and the need to retain international confidence, this more modest idea was not pursued. Instead the policy to be followed was simply 'to continue to accept a gradual fall in the rate over a period, thus minimising the risk of a precipitate drop'.

The decision not to include in the Budget any measure to improve the trade balance led the Chancellor to decide on 25 March that the scale of fiscal action should be smaller than he had originally had in mind. It will be recalled that the Treasury's ideas in the February memorandum were that the Budget should take out some £2 billion in 1975–76 and £4 billion the following financial year. These figures were too much for the Chancellor and most of the discussion about the Budget was focused on the question of the measures it should include rather than the precise quantum of the Budget as a whole. The range of tax increases contemplated was large. It included Vehicle Excise Duty, Value Added Tax, and the excise duties on alcohol and tobacco, three categories having a revenue effect of about £1.5 billion—but the Chancellor wanted to use some of the increased revenue to increase the personal income tax allowances. His ideas on this were evidently more political than economic, for he said that he would delay taking a decision until one week before the Budget. In the event he did increase the personal allowances more than the amount that was required to maintain their real value, and the size of the Budgetary action eventually agreed was just over £1 billion.

Perhaps the most notable feature of the 1975 Budget was that it contained very large measures to cut public expenditure, but not in the 'year of focus', that is the financial year about to begin, but in the year following—1976–77. The Treasury's decision to use the Budget process to seek large reductions in spending in 1976–77, rather than wait for the beginning of the public expenditure exercise (PESC) a month or so later, was determined by the desire to make the Budget Statement as a whole more credible and to present it as a strategy covering two years. Work to determine a feasible programme of expenditure reductions began soon after the December memorandum had been submitted in which substantial cuts in the PSBR were seen to be a high priority. The Expenditure Group addressed themselves to two issues, the need for a crash programme of cuts designed to deal with a crisis situation and the need to get a 'better' balance of resource use in the medium-term. The former need not detain us, as it was very much in the nature of a contingency plan in which the disruption to departments' spending programmes was seen as a small price to pay for the success of some hypothetical rescue operation. This plan envisaged immediate cuts, in 1975–76, and was feasible only when the economic situation was critical. A less disruptive approach was to plan to make reductions in programmes beginning in 1976–77 and these should be sought, not as a crisis measure, but in an orderly fashion and with the purpose of addressing the weakness which the Treasury now saw in the outcome of the 1974 PESC exercise. Even before the 1975 Expenditure White Paper was published, on 30 January, the Treasury was developing the case for a substantial reduction in the programmes it set out. The unfolding of economic events since the previous PESC exercise made it clear that the assumptions on which it had been based—a 3 per cent growth rate for the GDP and virtually full employment of national resources—were much too optimistic. To adhere to the plan to increase the resources claimed by the public sector by 2.75 per cent p.a. over the following four years would starve the other sectors, notably the balance of payments, industrial investment and privately-financed consumption, of anything like an acceptable allocation.

The choice the Treasury faced was whether to seek to correct this imbalance in the course of the 1975 PESC round or to make a start on the cuts immediately and in the context of the Budget. The advantage of the latter course was that Ministers collectively would see the case for an adjustment as part of the radical new approach to economic policy making and might more easily be persuaded to accept the Treasury case. They would also be faced with the rigours of the Budget timetable and not be able to string things out as they had in the previous year's PESC exercise. The disadvantage was that the more immediate course would have to concentrate on the first year of the new exercise only—it would be impossible for departmental ministers to review their whole four-year programme in the space of a few weeks. The decision was to go for the second option and to seek to persuade the Chancellor to open up with his spending colleagues the case for an immediate decision to cut the programmes for 1976–77 and to announce that decision in the Budget Speech. The Treasury put forward a paper on 7 March[14] examining in detail the problems which would have to be faced, not least with the Chancellor's spending colleagues in seeking cuts of the order of £1 billion in the year 1976–77. The aim was to spread the cuts as widely as possible—'We have tried . . . to spread the burden among the spending ministers. Unless this is done, there will be inevitable comparisons and cries of unfairness; but the Government's scope for seeking substantial savings is very severely restricted by the policies adopted since they took office.' The largest programme was social security but on political grounds this offered practically no scope for net reductions. Defence was a special problem, as a full-scale review had just been completed and the Cabinet had made it clear that the decisions on that must stand. The Chancellor therefore faced a stiff challenge to what he was going to propose. A meeting was held with him on 11 March[15] and he accepted the Treasury's advice. He put his ideas to the Cabinet in a paper addressed to his spending colleagues dated 19 March.[16] This gave a *resumé* of the economic outlook and the need for retrenchment. 'One essential element in the change of policies must be a substantial and progressive reduction in the public sector borrowing requirement. I cannot achieve all that is necessary by increases in taxation alone, for both short- and long-term reasons.' He went on 'My judgment is that we must secure a reduction in the expenditure programmes in 1976–77 of about £1,000 million at 1974 Survey prices.' The annex set out the Treasury's ideas as to how this total should be made up. As the Chancellor said it was spread as broadly as possible—with one exception, Defence from which one fifth of the total was sought.[17]

The Chancellor's proposals were discussed at two Cabinets—in the morning and the afternoon of 25 March.[18] Not surprisingly there was a good deal of questioning of the need for the public expenditure cuts. One element of the Cabinet was sceptical about the whole approach to economic policy and sought to have consideration of the cuts deferred until 'the overall strategy of which such cuts were only a part' could be discussed. (The Industry Secretary, Benn, had put a paper to MES in February raising the issue of economic strategy in its widest terms, but without eliciting much response from his colleagues.) The discussion was wide ranging and the Chancellor's proposals came in for a great deal of criticism and not only from the spending Ministers. But after an exhaustive debate, the Lord President of the Council, who presided in the absence of the Prime Minister, concluded that 'a majority of the Cabinet were

---

[14] T 171/1182.　　[15] T 171/1237.　　[16] CAB 129/182/14.
[17] CAB 129/181/39.　　[18] CAB 128/56/17 and 18.

in favour of the proposals put forward by the Chancellor' and he was invited to embark on a round of discussions with the spending Ministers on the individual proposals. These took place over the following two weeks and the Chancellor reported their outcome in a paper to Cabinet on 8 April.[19] In this he said that in three areas there was strong opposition to his proposals as they stood, and he offered a compromise, mainly on Defence (where he halved the figure he had put forward) and in transport subsidies. These would reduce the total to £870 million. The Chancellor invited his colleagues 'to consider how the gap should be closed' but the only proposal he himself put forward was to abandon the mid-term annual census that year to give a saving of £15 million. In the event when the Cabinet discussed the matter again on 10 April it was agreed to let the total stand at £870 plus £15 million.[20]

The episode of the Cabinet discussions of the public expenditure items of the Budget once again gave evidence of the considerable difficulty the Chancellor faced in controlling—and even more in reducing—public expenditure. It was the one element of macro-economic policy over which he did not have control and he was faced with his own colleagues, some of whom had reservations about the whole thrust of policy and many of whom had spending programmes about which they were highly protective.

The Chancellor opened his second 'annual' Budget on 15 April. It was inevitably a far less up-beat presentation than those of the 1974 Parliamentary statements, for in most respects the economic situation had deteriorated considerably and the Treasury's advice had changed too. Not everything was bad, however, as the Chancellor pointed out early in his speech. Exports of goods had increased by 7 per cent in the course of 1974 and the volume of imports was flat. These figures of course concealed the movement of prices of both exports and imports and it was only in the Financial Statement[21] that despite the volume improvement the money change was not great—the balance of payments deficit having increased from just over £1 billion in 1973 to nearly £4 billion in 1974. There was, therefore, a continuing need to borrow and 'if we are to go on attracting (overseas) funds their owners must believe that the value of the money they have placed with us is not threatened by the consequences of our policy actions or inactions'. This then was to be the basis of the Budget and the normal approach of Chancellors in the post-war years was to be abandoned. The Chancellor was quite scathing about the practices of the past—the 'Budget Judgment' approach in which the analysis was conducted in demand terms and the aim of the Budget to regulate aggregate demand to what the capacity of the economy could accommodate—subject only to what the balance of payments could permit. It was necessary to strike a new sort of balance and he added 'I do not believe that it would be wise to put unemployment as the central

[19] CAB 129/182/21.   [20] CAB 128/56/19.
[21] *Parliamentary papers* 1974–75, Vol. xix, p. 551.

problem'—a striking break with the past, including his own past. 'I cannot afford' he added 'to increase demand further today'.[22] The overriding need was to improve the balance of payments and attract overseas finance for the current account deficit by having a stable exchange rate. On inflation the statement acknowledged that pay increases on the scale which had been seen—the wage rate increase was 28.9 per cent at an annual rate in February—had restricted his room for manoeuvre. But no policy initiative in this area was contemplated. 'A statutory policy for incomes is unlikely to produce better results'. The policy put forward was quite simply to create sufficient spare capacity in the economy to ensure that exports were not supply-constrained and to keep the level of imports down, and the principal aim was to maintain overseas confidence so that we could continue to finance our ongoing current account deficit. 'My intention in this Budget is to establish a strategy which will enable us to achieve a very substantial improvement in our current account in the next two years'. He then spelt out his fiscal decisions, including of course those on public expenditure, which he said would lead to a reduction in the PSBR of £1 billion in the year ahead and by £3 billion in the following year. This outcome was not all that different from what the Treasury had sought in the memorandum of 24 February. What did emerge however was that even with these cuts the PSBR for 1975–76 would be £9 billion (a little under 10 per cent of GDP): and the accompanying Financial Statement showed that the PSBR for 1974–75, which the Chancellor had expected to be £2.7 billion in his first 1974 Budget statement and £6.3 billion in his second, was now likely to be £7.5 billion. For 1976–77 he added there is a 'good prospect that the borrowing requirement will be significantly lower as a proportion of GDP (than for the previous year)' but he refrained from giving a monetary forecast.

In the field of monetary policy he announced that the growth of £M3 in 1974 had been only 12.5 per cent thanks in part to the substantial sales of public sector debt outside the banking system and (although he did not mention this) to the sharp fall in bank lending to the private sector during the course of 1974. He noted that the Bank of England had, on 28 February, suspended the operation of the Corset. The implication, quite reasonably, was that all was well in the monetary sphere in spite of the escalation of inflation. It would be difficult for the monetarist school to criticize monetary policy for fuelling inflation, although the continuing high level of public borrowing would have been a source of some concern to it.

The reaction of the financial markets to the statement was on the whole moderately favourable. The sterling exchange rate dipped a little from $2.40 at the beginning of April to $2.35 at the end, but this was only back where it had

---

[22] The Chancellor could not help making his usual criticism of other oil importers whom he called on 'to recognise the need to take compensating measures to offset the demand reduction caused by the oil price increase "as I did in July and again in November"'.

been at the beginning of the year. The Chancellor and the Treasury could be reasonably satisfied that confidence was holding and that the funding of the current account deficit might not, in the immediate future, be all that difficult.

Financing the external deficit

Since the problem of financing the current account deficit in the period immediately ahead was such an important factor in the consideration of an engineered change in the sterling parity, it is worth looking in detail how the Treasury saw itself handling this issue for the remainder of 1975. At the end of January OF produced its assessment of how the UK could mobilize external funds during the remainder of the year.[23] This acknowledged that we had been quite successful in meeting our capital requirements in 1974 when we had received (net) £1.5 billion in sterling inflows, mostly from Nigeria and Saudi Arabia and had borrowed (net) about the same amount in foreign currency, mostly dollars, from the capital markets via the Exchange Guarantee Scheme and from bilateral creditors, for example Iran. The forecast for 1975 was that our capital needs would be about the same as 1974. But the situation was no longer what it had been a year previously. There was now much less confidence in sterling and in the UK, and this had manifested itself in the market pressure in December. During the last quarter of 1974 the sterling effective rate had declined by 4 per cent and the inflows from the Gulf Sheikhdoms had dried up completely. It was true that there was an uncovered interest rate differential of about 2.5 per cent between sterling and the dollar but this now scarcely compensated for the perceived risk of holding assets in sterling. This differential could be increased if the UK were prepared to increase short-term rates, though such action would conflict with domestic objectives and could endanger the solvency of British financial institutions.[24]

The range of possibilities for purely sterling inflows in 1975 was wide open, from zero to something like the level achieved in 1974 if confidence were to be fully restored. But the expectation was nearer the former than the latter. Foreign currency borrowing was slightly less uncertain, if only because the lender would not be exposed to the risk of sterling weakening. Public sector borrowers, notably the nationalized industries, had been active borrowers under the Exchange Guarantee Scheme in 1974 and had raised nearly £2 billion. The eurodollar market was a good source, with petro-dollars in plentiful supply. But lenders were now turning away from public borrowers towards the private sector and the

---

[23] T 277/3053—PCC (75)11.
[24] 1974 had seen the emergence of the property and secondary banking crisis with many well known financial institutions having to be supported by the Bank of England's Lifeboat mechanism—see Chapter 2.

judgement was made that it would be unwise to count on much from market borrowing. There was the possibility of bilateral borrowing from some of the surplus countries, for example Iran, Saudi Arabia, and Kuwait, as had been done with Iran in 1974, and it was thought that we might be able to get up to $2 billion from this source.[25] The short-term facilities available, like the swap with the New York Fed, were not really suitable for what were essentially medium- to long-term requirements. There remained the IMF where we had a substantial credit position in the General Account and could possibly get access to the new oil facility—a source which is described later in this chapter. But Fund finance ought to be regarded as a fall-back facility: to use it to meet ongoing needs was to defeat the purpose of the institution.[26] In any case we might want to use the Fund in an emergency and as part of a programme to restore confidence. The message was a gloomy one but it powerfully reinforced the case which was made for a Budget which gave some assurance to our creditors and to markets generally. Indeed it is perhaps not too much of an overstatement that the need to secure adequate funding of our deficit played the dominant role in the Chancellor's acceptance of the need for a restrictive budget.

The problem of inflation

Although, measured by the time taken up in deliberation, the problems of the fiscal imbalance, the payments deficit and its financing, and the containment of public expenditure were the main preoccupations of senior Treasury officials in the early months of 1975, that of continuing—and indeed rising—inflation was perhaps the most difficult to resolve. Ministers collectively continued to pin their faith on the TUC's observance of the terms of the Social Contract under which individual unions would be expected, in general, to make pay claims designed only to compensate their members for previous price increases. The Employment Secretary had gone out of his way in a television broadcast on 11 December 1974 to extol this approach,[27] and when Ministers raised its effectiveness with union leaders they were left in no doubt that a voluntary policy was the only option. The Chancellor, for instance, had an informal meeting with the six TUC members of the National Economic Development Council (NEDC) on 8 January and took the opportunity to warn them of the dangers of the rate of inflation then being experienced. This could kill off the programmes of overseas borrowing on which we so hugely depended to finance

---

[25] Two senior officials, from the Treasury and the Bank, paid a visit to Saudi Arabia early in the year to explore this possibility, but the reception, though polite, was not forthcoming.

[26] This argument had not however weighed heavily with the Treasury in December 1973 when it had specifically recommended the then Chancellor to use the Fund's resources to finance an ongoing need.

[27] LAB 77/49.

the payments deficit and he implied that some sort of action on wages might be necessary. The union leaders reacted coolly, if not with hostility, to this idea. The two most influential members of the TUC (Hugh Scanlon and Jack Jones) said that it was 'out of the question to persuade members to accept a reduction in their living standards' and 'any attempt to tighten the guidelines would do more harm than good'. The message was clear—any policy involving the active support of the TUC would have to be based on something like the existing arrangement.[28]

Treasury officials did not feel that this could be accepted as the final word, and work was put in hand in January which involved the examination of a statutory approach and the end of the policy of leaving the TUC in charge of pay policy. The scheme drawn up was not unlike that adopted by the Government's predecessor in November 1972. It envisaged a temporary freeze on pay followed by a norm of 10 per cent—this being the rather arbitrary assumption of the minimum that would stand any chance of acceptance—for those who had no threshold payments since their last settlement and 5 per cent for those who had. Prices would be subject to the Price Code (which had been retained by the Wilson administration) and firms which were party to breaches of the pay rules might be denied any price increase at all. A variant scheme was examined in which direct pay controls would be confined to a delaying power of the kind which had operated in 1966 when the first Wilson administration introduced a formal Prices and Incomes Policy. Although the scheme was put forward as an imposed one, Treasury officials thought that the unions in general and the TUC in particular might be persuaded to accept it since the only alternative approach to defeating inflation would have to be a massive deflation of the economy and a high level of unemployment. But the Treasury emphasized that an Incomes Policy was not a substitute for suitable macro-economic policies. 'We are still of the view', the Chancellor was told, 'that there will (as well) have to be appropriate policies affecting the level of demand involving a reduction in the pressure of domestic demand on resources'. This was of course before the Budget—indeed before the Chancellor had accepted the idea of deflationary fiscal action.[29]

The Chancellor was not much taken by this advice, which was submitted to him on 13 January—no doubt in part because of what the union leaders had told him at the meeting on 8 January. He had also expressed some scepticism about the efficacy of incomes policies in general and a note was submitted to him analysing this issue without, however, making any extravagant claims for them. Whatever doubts the Chancellor might have had about formal incomes policies, he clearly thought that the time was not then ripe for the policy put forward. In his private thinking, however, he had not ruled out some drastic action but he did not believe that the radical change suggested, even

---

[28] T 357/424.   [29] T 277/3053—PCC (75)2 and 6.

if it worked, could be introduced other than in a crisis situation. The Treasury went back to see what could be put forward which might be acceptable to Ministers and would contribute to an abatement of inflation. They came back with a note dated 7 February.[30] This time the emphasis was on building on and reinforcing the Social Contract. The key propositions were:

- The government should give more leadership in the field of pay—it could not just leave it to the TUC and their guidelines.
- There must be some readiness to resist industrial action in the public sector to prevent 'unacceptable' increases.
- The test of success would be an actual fall in the going rate of pay increases (which had been rising steadily all through 1974).

The programme of action envisaged was very qualitative. There would be a campaign of ministerial speeches in which the emphasis would be on a very strict interpretation of the guidelines. The TUC would be expected to make the same points. Any industrial group which had had special treatment in 1974 (notably the nurses and teachers) would be held to a very strict interpretation of the guidelines. One possibility canvassed was that an inflation target might be set, but there was little discussion of what the position of the government would be if that target were exceeded. The paper briefly looked at the possibility of a back-up to the policy through the tax system. Such a scheme had been suggested by a veteran labour economist—Barbara Wootton. The idea was to tax away the excess increases over the norm secured by particular groups. A more general scheme to tax earnings in the whole economy in excess of some norm as a general surcharge on income tax liabilities and recycle the proceeds in some subsidization of the price level had been put forward by a New Zealand economist (Professor Elkan) and although the Treasury were sceptical it was an idea which Ministers subsequently wanted to examine in detail. The Inland Revenue had argued strongly against the feasibility of either scheme, and they did not receive more than a token reference.

The note putting these ideas to the Chancellor was shot through with doubts about whether the approach envisaged would achieve very much, but it was clearly better than inaction in the face of a worsening situation. It was, however, suggested that the time was ripe for a Ministerial discussion of the issue and a paper was prepared for the Chancellor to put to MES.[31] This was circulated on 19 February and was largely based on the Treasury memorandum referred to above. It contained no significant policy proposals, but frankly admitted that it only asked that existing policy, which was of course largely in the hands of the TUC, should be more strictly followed. The Ministerial Committee went along with this approach, as did the Cabinet when the

---

[30] T 277/3053—PCC (75)19.   [31] CAB 134/3929—MES (75)14.

matter was reported to it on 27 February.[32] One small proposal put forward, and endorsed by the Cabinet, was that there should be a campaign of ministerial speeches on the themes of the Treasury outlined above. The Chancellor himself embarked on a series of public speeches, warning of the perils of a continuation of wage settlements at the prevailing level—by early 1975 the going rate of settlements was well over 20 per cent and indeed seemed to be heading for 30 per cent. For the moment the policy of containing and reducing inflation rested on no more robust foundations than this. A further meeting between the Chancellor and the NEDC 6 from the TUC had taken place on 12 February but it revealed no greater a disposition of the latter to countenance any interference in collective bargaining. The Chancellor begged them to take account of the benefits they had derived from the action he had taken to increase the 'social wage' and repeated his warnings of the dangers that inflation posed on the external side. The TUC were not impressed. Jack Jones said that the Government should 'leave it to the TUC' without however specifying what this would imply.[33]

While the general debate both among officials and in the relevant Ministerial Cabinet Committee was proceeding, individual Ministers outside the Treasury were themselves tackling the Chancellor on possible courses of action. As early as mid-December 1974 the Prices Secretary (Shirley Williams) had expressed her doubts at the way events were unfolding. In a paper put to the Committee on Economic Strategy (MES) she warned that 'our counter-inflation strategy is reaching a cross-roads. The acceleration of the RPI will make the Social Contract even more inflationary and a sterling crisis more likely.... If we are to avoid the inevitability of choosing between allowing a massive increase in unemployment and statutory wage controls, will we not need to rethink radically our whole counter-inflationary strategy before it is too late?.'[34] The Treasury could not have put it more starkly. At the discussion of the Committee two days later, however, the idea of such a dramatic shift in policy was not pursued. But Mrs Williams was not to be deterred from seeking some action. She decided on a less authoritative approach than a formal control of wages and suggested in a letter to the Chancellor on 5 February[35] that the Government should look at some ideas which were being put forward by academic economists for a scheme in which pay increases which exceeded some defined level would be 'clawed' back by fiscal action on the part of the Government.[36]

Coincidentally the Employment Secretary (Foot) was working on his own ideas. He had asked his officials to look at ways in which the existing policy might be reinforced—but still within the context of the Social Contract. His

---

[32] CAB 128/56/10.   [33] T 357/486.   [34] CAB 134/3790—MES (74)35.
[35] T 357/425.   [36] The Elkan scheme described in the Treasury paper of 7 February.

advisers were not encouraging. In their reply on 8 January[37] the principal official involved said that 'there is no package of voluntary measures that I can at this stage suggest as constituting an effective reinforcement of existing policy.... There seems little point in undertaking any radical change or reinforcement of policy, with all the difficulty involved, unless a really significant reduction can be made in the rate of inflation.' As for seeking some amendment to the existing guidelines, the official thought that the TUC would not do this 'until the Government has made it plain that there has been a radical deterioration in the economic situation'. The Employment Secretary was not deterred by the scepticism of his officials and wrote to the Chancellor on 28 January[38] suggesting that the best approach would be for the Government to act directly on prices in the hope that this would enable the unions to settle their pay claims at a lower level than was currently taking place; there should also be a surcharge on income tax to subsidize prices.

The three Ministers involved in these exchanges had a meeting in the Treasury on 13 February[39] but there seems to have been little meeting of minds. The Treasury had not been much impressed by Foot's ideas (which suggested a repeat of the July 1974 policy of subsidizing prices in the hope of a response from the unions). The Chancellor told his colleagues that in his view the TUC had either got to go for settlements 5 per cent or 6 per cent below the level in 1974, or accept that the Government would have to deflate the economy or accept a statutory Incomes Policy. The idea canvassed by Mrs Williams of a tax-based Incomes Policy on Elkan lines did not receive much attention, but Ministers commissioned officials to make a serious examination of what would be entailed and what might be achieved. Officials subsequently worked over a period of six weeks to appraise the administrative and economic effects of the tax-based alternative schemes and produced a report at the beginning of April.[40] This, perhaps unsurprisingly, was deeply sceptical about both the feasibility of such schemes and of the effect they would have in practice on the rate of inflation. The Inland Revenue were strongly opposed to the idea of a tax on incomes additional to income tax. In the face of the criticisms made of the ideas put forward there was no further discussion of any of the schemes examined. Ministers collectively did not return to the question of inflation and how to reduce it until well into the early summer.

Through March and early April the Chancellor was immersed in his Budget and particularly in the discussions with spending Ministers about the expenditure cuts he was seeking and discussion with him on the development of a pay policy, whatever form it might take, was for the time being shelved. But he made it clear that one of the priorities he had in mind, post-Budget, was to

[37] LAB 77/49 and T 357/431.　　[38] T 357/424.　　[39] T 357/426.　　[40] Ibid.

look at 'pay policy for the next round'. On 18 April the Treasury put forward a note[41] covering precisely this issue. The idea of continuing with the existing policy of leaving it to the TUC to issue and monitor their own guidelines was dismissed as unviable—even if the Government enforced a strict application of them in the public sector. The Government had to come out of its corner by stating what its views were about the size of pay increases that were consistent with some desired reduction in the rate of inflation, and the only question was how it should seek to bring this about. The Treasury had no illusions about the problems of a statutory policy—the memory of the collapse of the previous attempt was still fresh in its collective mind. Nevertheless its scepticism about the ability of the trade union movement voluntarily to follow government 'advice' led it inexorably to go for a statutory policy. The Chancellor was out of the country from 20 April to 5 May visiting Tehran as part of the programme of maintaining the external borrowing facilities and discussion of the options did not get under way until early May. But on his return things started to move briskly. In the Chancellor's absence abroad there had been a meeting of the TUC/Labour Party Liaison Committee at which the Prime Minister had made it plain that the Government were *not* thinking of statutory controls.[42] The TUC for their part confined their comments to the question of how to make the guidelines more effective. The Employment Secretary meanwhile had reported the outcome of discussions he had been having with TUC leaders about the developments in pay settlements in the current round. His paper to Cabinet was a bland affair.[43] The TUC undertook 'to extend their efforts to secure strict adherence to the guidelines in particular cases' but there was no prospect of a generally lower level of settlements in the rest of the round. As for the next round it 'was for the Government to create the right social and economic climate and for the TUC to recommend appropriate negotiating objectives to its membership'. The paper looked to the timetable for decisions. The key meetings of the TUC bodies which would take decisions on what to recommend to the constituent unions would be the Economic Committee in June and the General Council immediately thereafter. Any influence the Government could bring to bear should be made in the period before then.

The Chancellor returned to the subject of pay and held a meeting with his advisers on 5 May.[44] Despite what had been said by the Prime Minister to the TUC and the Employment Secretary to MES, he left the meeting in no doubt but that his mind was moving towards a statutory policy for the next pay round with a Government-determined norm for wages. He seemed then to be thinking of some sort of freeze on pay increases which would give a breathing space for the determination of the content of a more permanent policy. The discussion focused on the enforcement problem—what sanctions could be applied to those who breached the policy. The Chancellor, conscious of the

---

[41] T 357/426.   [42] Ibid.   [43] CAB 129/183/16.   [44] T 357/426 and 435.

events of 1973–74, wanted to have explored the idea of sanctions being imposed on errant *employers* rather than errant unions, and asked officials to discuss the legal issues this would raise with the Treasury Solicitor. The latter produced an opinion[45] shortly after which revealed the most serious difficulties in any such approach and the idea of penalizing employers was not thereafter pursued—although it did briefly resurface in late June when ministers collectively looked seriously at a statutory policy.

The Treasury now produced a flurry of papers[46] setting the issues and options that would be open if a Government-based policy was decided upon. The pros and cons of a statutory and a non-statutory policy were again looked at in a lengthy memorandum dated 16 May and the conclusion expressed by the head of the Prices and Incomes Division, which was accepted by the Policy Coordinating Committee, was put as follows:

> The majority of us feel—and this is also my [the Permanent Secretary's] view—that the objections to a non-statutory no-norm policy are too strong to make it acceptable. Most of us conclude, without minimising the risks, that the best available course is a plan based on an initial period of statutory control, covering as a minimum the 1975–76 pay round and designed to produce a progressive deceleration of pay and price inflation through that and the 1976–77 pay round. We see a gradual relaxation of control after the initial period, perhaps with reserve powers and with firmer financial control of nationalised industries and local government designed during the statutory control period.

It was in fact the re-entry problem—how to disengage from a strict pay policy and to allow unconstrained negotiations to resume—which began to preoccupy the Treasury. The experience of previous pay policies showed that the gains arising from a period of severe restraint could be rapidly eroded by a subsequent 'free-for-all', and given that the issue of inflation and UK price-competitiveness was seen as a long-term issue this concern about re-entry was more than justified. The Chancellor was given an idea of the options which might be open in a memorandum dated 20 May.[47]

The need to take some decisive action in the field of pay inflation was now becoming very pressing. Sterling had come under strong market pressure in the course of May when it fell by nearly 2 per cent as holders, particularly official holders became alarmed as the erosion of the real value of their sterling assets declined. The Kuwaitis delivered a stark warning to the Treasury on 16 May[48] that they were considering a diversification of their assets away from sterling. Time was running out. At his meeting with officials on 5 May (referred to above) the Chancellor had told his advisers that the Prime Minister was unwilling to act before the holding of the Referendum on the UK's continued membership of the European Community (as it was then called). This was timed for 5 June. The Chancellor said that he would talk to the TUC NEDC 6

---

[45] T 357/428.   [46] T 277/3055—PCC (75)51–56.
[47] T 357/426.   [48] T 357/435.

sometime before the next meeting of the TUC Economic Committee in the middle of June. (There was in fact a meeting between himself and the Committee on 21 May[49] but this was largely devoted to the TUC's concerns over employment and public expenditure cuts and virtually nothing was said about the problem of inflation. The only surprise occurred when one member of the TUC delegation, Frank Chapple, said that in his view the only fair way to deal with the problem of wages was a statutory policy. However the Chancellor could take little comfort from such a minority and, indeed in the eyes of many, 'maverick' opinion.)

By 19 May at a meeting between Treasury and Employment Department officials[50] the former revealed that the Chancellor had had direct talks with some Ministers in the course of which he had canvassed the idea of a statutory policy running for two years. Three days later he warned his Cabinet colleagues that they should ask themselves whether 'the Government could rely upon a further round of voluntary bargaining'.[51] The Employment Department said that in their view the TUC would only accept a reaffirmation of the Social Contract. By this time the Treasury felt confident that the Chancellor was persuaded that only a statutory policy would accomplish what the situation needed and it began work again on the 're-entry' problem, that is how the statutory policy could be ended without a new pay explosion. The Chancellor asked for contingency planning against the possibility of strike action against a new policy,[52] thinking no doubt of what had happened in early 1974 and asking about the level of coal stocks. This was covered in a note dated 28 May. By early June the Treasury was looking at the timetable which could determine the progress of action. The operative factor was that a new policy should be in place before the beginning of the next pay round—which would be after the union conferences in late summer. A meeting of the NEDC had been arranged for 17 June at which the Prime Minister was to take the chair and which he was inclined to use as an opportunity to raise the question of a national 'dividend'—that is some form of allocation of the fruits of the growth in national productivity. This was seen as a means of entry to a public discussion of the division of the national cake and thereafter as a means of arriving at a consensus on an Incomes Policy. The Treasury were not impressed and thought that ministers should not take their eye off the vital issue of giving a strong lead to the country through a statutory policy on incomes.

The Employment Secretary continued to put his faith in the Social Contract. He had a meeting with the TUC NEDC 6 on 9 June and reported the outcome in a Cabinet paper dated 12 June.[53] All that he got out of the TUC was an acknowledgement from the General Secretary that the next pay round should begin with settlements at levels less than those currently being negotiated.

---

[49] T 357/487.   [50] T 357/426.   [51] CAB 128/56/25.
[52] T 357/426.   [53] CAB 129/183/16 and T 357/487.

This was something of an advance, but there was little indication of a mechanism for securing it. Foot looked at what the Government could do to bring about a satisfactory outcome. His ideas were vague and the only concrete suggestion he made was that the Government should issue a public statement of where the pay guidelines could lead to in the next round and 'might possibly encompass an announcement of a price inflation target for the next pay round'. He addressed the obvious question 'Could we do better?' and concluded, predictably, that any alternative of a Government-led policy was likely to be disastrous. The Employment Secretary's report was considered not by the Cabinet, but by MES on 16 June[54] with the aim of briefing Ministers how they should approach the meeting of the TUC/Labour Party Liaison Committee on 23 June. This too led to a somewhat vague outcome. Ministers should welcome the general approach of the TUC set out in a draft statement which had been shown to the Employment Secretary and should exhort them to seek a low level of settlements. One of the ideas canvassed in this was that in the next pay round settlements should be based on *future* price increases, not *past* increases. But, no doubt prompted by an unscripted statement the Chancellor had made to Cabinet on 12 June about the deteriorating situation in the foreign currency markets and about 'the urgent need for an new Incomes Policy', the Prime Minister said that he would call a special meeting of Cabinet on 20 June 'for a thorough discussion of the economic situation'.

There were now clearly two schools of thought about the future direction of policy. The Employment Secretary had nailed his colours to the mast of the TUC's guidelines and the Chancellor had gone out for a full-blooded Incomes Policy. The Cabinet of 20 June—an all-day affair at Chequers—saw the two sides battle their position out. The Employment Secretary rested his case on the two papers he had prepared a week earlier and which had been briefly discussed at MES on 16 June. The Chancellor decided not to put in a paper, preferring to keep his powder dry and deliver his case orally. The Cabinet Secretary submitted a paper which had been prepared by a group of Permanent Secretaries setting out in a neutral way, with an analysis of the risks and advantages of each, the various options for dealing with pay in the coming round—options ranging from a continuation of existing policy to the introduction of a fully fledged statutory scheme.[55]

The Chancellor discussed with the Permanent Secretary on 19 June[56] how he should play his hand. He would go for an Incomes Policy of some sort, involving a norm designed to reduce inflation substantially in the year ahead. But he needed some ammunition to use if his colleagues opted for the Foot approach. The Permanent Secretary said that, on the assumption that the TUC General Council, meeting the following week, were unable to agree to anything stronger than what was contained in their draft policy statement, the

[54] CAB 134/3929.   [55] CAB 129/183/20.   [56] T 277/3056—PCC (75)67.

only alternative to an Incomes Policy with a norm was 'a stiff measure of demand deflation, based largely on a fiscal package'. Foreign opinion was not impressed by the argument that we already had sufficient deflation in the economy. Germany and America had both deflated further or sustained a deflation much greater than the UK—unemployment in these countries was respectively well over twice what it had been three years ago, whereas ours was up by about one half. The Chancellor wanted some argument other than 'confidence' to use with his colleagues.[57] The Permanent Secretary said that he now believed that some easing of domestic pressure would contribute to an easing of wage pressures and a strengthening of employer resistance to excessive wage demands. He gave the Chancellor a list of expenditure cuts which, totalling about £1 billion in the current financial year and rising to £2 billion in the following year, he thought would have to be proposed if the Cabinet baulked at an Incomes Policy. The list was a draconian one, involving an immediate moratorium in building projects, the reduction of nationalized industry price subsidies, a limitation of the forthcoming social security uprating and an increase in the price of school meals.

The Cabinet discussion the next day was very wide-ranging.[58] While the Employment Secretary repeated his case for relying on the TUC, the Chancellor weighed in with a warning that the economic situation required something drastic. His argument had to be, however, essentially one of confidence—the continuance of a high rate of inflation and no palpable means of combating it could lead to a run on the pound, which could only be countered by a massive programme of emergency measures. He said that public expenditure would have to be cut by £1 billion. It was much better to put in place a credible Incomes Policy. He did not advocate a freeze—'there was no chance that such a policy would be acceptable'. But if the aim was to halve the rate of inflation in the coming year it would be necessary to keep wage increases below 10 per cent, or a flat rate of £5 per week. (Where precisely this figure came from is not clear. It had been mentioned illustratively in the Treasury internal paper at the beginning of the year, but it was in many ways an arbitrary figure. In informal and unrecorded discussions with his advisers, the Chancellor had mooted the idea of having 10 per cent as the target rate of price increases by the middle of 1976 and the Treasury advised him that in effect this would mean limiting pay increases to about that figure.) The new policy should be in place by the end of July when the unions would be preparing for the next pay round. The Chancellor received some welcome support from the more hawkish of his colleagues who thought that he had, if anything, understated the problem and

---

[57] This was to be a recurrent theme of the Chancellor's. He instinctively distrusted the 'confidence' argument for a policy change and said that he wanted an 'objective' economic argument. This issue is discussed further in later chapters.
[58] CAB 128/56/29.

that his timetable was too relaxed. A statutory policy was thought by them to be inevitable, although if a voluntary acceptance of the need for a norm was forthcoming this would be preferable. On the other side the Employment Secretary received support from those who thought that an Incomes Policy not based on consent would be a failure. The Prime Minister summed up by siding with the Chancellor and saying that the consensus seemed to be that the Government's aim should be to secure a norm of 10 per cent (or its equivalent) for the next pay round. The TUC should be told of this and invited to go along with it on a voluntary basis; but if they did not 'the Government would have to consider unilateral action as a matter of urgency'. This was perhaps less definite than the Chancellor—and other colleagues—would have wanted, but it represented a big shift in the Government's collective position.

At some point in the days that followed the General Secretary of the TUC (Len Murray) was seen by the Chancellor and the Employment Secretary and told that the Government thought that the limit on pay increases should be 10 per cent and this information was fed into the meeting of the General Council of the TUC when it met on 25 June. On 26 June the Permanent Secretary saw the Deputy General Secretary of the TUC (David Lea) and had a frank exchange of views.[59] The latter said that senior members of the TUC 'had moved a long way in the last two or three weeks under pressure from the Chancellor and the staff at Congress House'. There was, however, a big gap between the size of pay increases which the TUC thought appropriate for the next round (£9–10 per week) and those the Government had revealed it had in mind (10 per cent or the equivalent of £5 per week).[60] There was no discussion whether the policy should be voluntary and TUC-inspired or statutory and, as it were, Government-determined.

The whole question of the future of the Incomes Policy, so far as the Government was concerned was now referred to an *ad hoc* committee of Ministers (MISC 91), the first meeting of which was arranged for the afternoon of Monday 30 June. This was to be a day in which events moved with a speed and in a manner uncharacteristic of life in Whitehall. The meeting was scheduled for 3.00 p.m., but before it could meet there was a massive bear attack on sterling in the currency markets. The Governor sought an immediate meeting with the Chancellor and this took place at 12.15 p.m.[61] Kuwait and Nigeria were selling substantial amounts of their sterling holdings. The reserves loss since Friday was of the order of £130–150 million. The Governor said that 'he feared that we might be faced with a real collapse in our position'. The idea was put forward that it might be necessary to announce an immediate freeze on all pay increases, but the Chancellor said that he was not attracted by such an

[59] T 357/487.
[60] There is a reference on file T 357/389 to a paper the TUC staff had prepared for the General Council indicating that guidelines of less than the RPI were not impossible.
[61] OF 98/33/03.

extreme idea. However, he had been given some extremely useful ammunition for the afternoon meeting, and he used it to powerful effect.

The Chancellor opened the meeting of the new Committee by giving his colleagues a sobering account of the state of the foreign exchange market.[62] Sterling had fallen 1.5 per cent since Friday to $2.1825. The Kuwait Government had already indicated that they would move their funds out of London if the rate fell below $2.20 and they were now doing so. Saudi Arabia had said that they would act similarly if the rate fell below $2.17. 'The whole of the United Kingdom's reserves could disappear within 24 hours; defence of sterling by intervention in the market was not therefore to be contemplated. It therefore became essential that the Government should take immediate decisions and make an announcement the following day on their counter-inflation policy.... In his view it must be made clear that the Government would aim to get the increase in the RPI down to 10 per cent by the third quarter of 1976, which could be demonstrated to require a maximum on pay increases from now on of 10 per cent (or its equivalent, for example a flat rate of £5–£6).... The urgency of the situation was such that Cabinet should meet the following morning to agree the content of a statement to be made in the afternoon.... Legislation, which would need to be retrospective to 1 July in order to prevent forestalling, would need to be introduced the following week... [it] should be effective for 12 months.' Enforcement of the policy would be by imposing penalties on employers (not employees) who broke the guidelines. The Chancellor had clearly forgotten the advice he had received in May about the legal difficulties of imposing penalties on employers.

Some of the committee members put up a token resistance to this proposal. A suggestion was made that the sterling rate should be allowed to fall and find its own equilibrium level, but this was recognized as being too dangerous. The Prime Minister summed up by saying the Committee agreed that a statement on the lines proposed should be made the following day, but said that the Chancellor and the Employment and Prices Secretaries should see the General Secretary of the TUC 'and consult with him on the desirability of summoning Mr Jack Jones from his union conference in Blackpool that evening in order to ensure that he was fully apprised of the likely action the following day'. This suggestion seems not to have been acted on, as in his autobiography Jones states that the first he knew about the Government's intentions was by media reports when he was still at the union conference.

The Chancellor and his colleagues saw the TUC General Secretary at 7 p.m.[63] He was told of the situation in the markets and informed that the Government would be taking action the following day by announcing a 10 per cent (or £5 per week) limit on pay increases, with sanctions on employers. It would be necessary to get the legislation on the Statute Book by the end of

---

[62] CAB 130/819.   [63] T 357/487.

July. Murray listened, but did not say much. He commented that 'the TUC were being invited to negotiate at pistol point'. He was worried about the acceptance of a 10 per cent limit and thought that the reaction would be hostile.

Overnight the Chancellor sent over to No 10 Downing Street the text of the statement he proposed to make in the afternoon. It was an announcement of the introduction of a statutory policy with a norm of £6 per week. The Cabinet was invited to approve it at its meeting at 11.00 a.m. The Chancellor introduced the item much on the lines of his statement to MISC 91 the day before, and he immediately ran into opposition. Many ministers continued to argue that a statutory policy was a recipe for political disaster. The Chancellor received some support but the strength of opposition was such that the Prime Minister summed up by saying that the statement would simply express the Government's firm intention to secure a reduction to about 10 per cent in the rate of pay increases and that urgent discussions would take place to ensure that this was accepted by both sides of industry. The statement as redrafted was very firm, even though it stopped short of either announcing a statutory policy or formally threatening one if its aims were not accepted in a suitably binding way by the TUC. What it did was express the Government's complete commitment to getting inflation down one way or another. As such it was well received by the press and public generally. But the difficult problem now was to get the TUC's acceptance that they would ensure voluntarily that the Government's pay norm was achieved. The General Council of the TUC met on 9 July, and eventually, thanks it seems to the decisive part played by Jack Jones, agreed to adopt the norm as its own. But there was a significant dissenting minority of members. However the Council felt able to make a public declaration of its policy and it was suitably definite and binding. The next day the Cabinet considered whether this would be sufficient to reassure market opinion. The Chancellor said that he thought it would, provided the Government immediately took reserve powers to introduce a statutory policy if the TUC failed to deliver on its statement. These were essentially penalties to be imposed on employers who acquiesced in settlements in excess of the norm. Even this limited and conditional commitment to a statutory policy was too much for some of the Cabinet. Given the strength of opposition which had emerged in the General Council, it was thought by some Ministers, particularly the Employment Secretary, that the immediate taking of reserve powers could endanger the whole policy. A majority of the Cabinet agreed, and it was decided that the White Paper to be published the following day would not involve the Government in the immediate taking of any powers, reserve or otherwise. But it would indicate that the Government would have to take legislative action if its objectives in the pay field were not met voluntarily. The TUC had told the Prime Minister that they could accept this.

The White Paper[64] defining the government's position drew heavily on the TUC document put out two days earlier and as if to underline that the policy was that of the TUC it annexed part of that document. It went into a fair amount of detail on how the policy would be interpreted, notably by the government as an employer, and how such issues as the implementation of the last stage of equal pay would be accommodated. It also digressed into such fields as the growth of the money supply (which it ritually stated would be kept firmly under control). These need not concern us here. The whole tone and language of the White Paper were modulated in a deliberate effort to assure market opinion that the UK was turning over a new leaf. It ended with a Churchillian flourish:

This is a plan to save our country. If we do not over the next twelve months achieve a drastic reduction in the present disastrous rate of inflation ... the British people will be engulfed in a general economic catastrophe of incalculable proportions. If we do succeed, as we are resolved to do, we can turn with fresh energy and hope to tackle the fundamental problems which will still face us in constructing an economy in which high pay is earned by high output.

The decisions and events of 30 June and of the first ten days of July constituted a watershed in the progress of inflation. Whereas prices had been rising by well over 20 per cent in the first half of the year, from mid-1975 the annualized rate of inflation fell to just over 10 per cent. Despite the reservations of some members of the General Council at the outset, the pay policy was strictly interpreted by the TUC and strictly enforced by them. There were no recorded breaches in the first year in which it operated, and no attempt by constituent unions to depart from the guidelines. Indeed even in the second year, as we shall see, there was only one challenge to the policy and that was not successful. But again, as will emerge from the narrative, there was a price to pay. The TUC's successful and compliant implementation of what was essentially the government's Incomes Policy gave it a great deal of leverage over other elements of policy, and they were by no means averse to employing it. To that extent the Government was to find itself constrained in the next two years, perhaps even more than ever, to pay heed to what the TUC thought about policy. The new policy was not, in short, to be without its costs. Indeed these appeared at the very outset, for there was an immediate price to pay for this cooperation. The Government agreed to delay the phasing out of the food subsidies announced in the Budget three months earlier and would limit the rent increases in local authority housing. These measures would add £150 million to public spending in 1976–77—over 10 per cent of the cuts imposed by the Budget. The Prime Minister made a lengthy statement to the House of Commons on the same day as the White Paper was published giving details of what the new policy would involve and what the Government were doing to make it palatable. He went out of his way to state that 'we reject massive panic cuts in public expenditure'.

[64] Cmnd 6151.

Public expenditure—the programmes

After the issue of inflation and wages, perhaps the most complex of the issues which had to be addressed in 1975 was that of the medium-term programme of public spending. As was the case in 1974, the annual survey in 1975 of public expenditure programmes was a protracted affair and took up a great deal of Ministerial and official time from May, when it was launched, until December, when the basis for the White Paper for 1976 was finally agreed. The starting point of this survey was not, as was usually the case, the programmes incorporated in the previous White Paper, published in January, since the Chancellor's success in getting Cabinet agreement, in the context of the Budget, to nearly £1 billion of cuts in the programmes for 1976–77 largely invalidated the spending plans so laboriously worked out in the course of 1974. But the Budget cuts left open what should be substituted for the plans for the later years, and the Treasury's immediate task in promoting the launch of the Survey was to establish what the aims should be for this period. The objective was to build on the achievement of the Budget cuts for the second year (1976–77) with unspecified consequences for the later years. The Chancellor had stated in the Budget that 'looking beyond 1976–77 there will at best only be very restricted room for overall growth'. The optimism of the White Paper of only two months earlier in which overall economic growth of 3 per cent had been taken as the central case and in which programmes were scheduled to grow by 2 per cent per annum in the years after 1976–77 had evaporated.

At the beginning of May the Treasury put forward its ideas on how the argument should be developed and what the aims should be. The object was two-fold—first to get agreement in principle to what the aggregate of public spending should be in what had been the final year of the previous PESC and White Paper and was to become the 'focus' year for the current survey (1978–79), and secondly to agree a formula which Departments would use to produce options for spending which would enable Ministers to decide how they wanted to meet a new target rate of growth for future spending. The upshot of the Treasury's thinking was incorporated in two papers the Chancellor put to Cabinet on 19 May.[65] The first covered a paper by Treasury officials which argued that the basis on which the White Paper plans had been drawn up was now invalid and that the whole medium-term outlook needed to be reviewed. Two main reasons were given. First the growth rate of the economy now seemed to be likely to be appreciably less than had been postulated a year earlier when the 1974 Medium Term Assessment had been made and had been incorporated in the White Paper as a 'central' case. Both the degree of capacity utilization and the growth rate of productive potential were likely to be lower. Secondly it now seemed that the balance of payments would have to be brought back into

[65] CAB 129/183/12 and 13.

balance more quickly than had been assumed in 1974 when the achievement of equilibrium was sought by the end of the decade. That appeared to be too leisurely a rate of progress, given the difficulties which were emerging in the financing of the deficit. The consequences of the revision of these two factors were that the retention of the spending plans incorporated in the February White Paper would entail the starvation of resources for the private sector and the increasing of taxation to even higher levels than those which, following the Budget of March 1974, now applied. Officials proposed that the spending plans for the 'focus' year, 1978–79, which had been set out in the White Paper published earlier in the year and totalled £37 billion at 1974 prices, should now be reduced by either £2.75 billion (at 1974 Survey prices) if the aim was to allow privately-financed consumption to grow at 1.5 per cent per annum over the period in question or by £2 billion if the aim was to bring the burden of taxation back to its 1974–75 level. In putting these findings to the Cabinet, the Chancellor steered his colleagues to the lower of the two objectives, although as he said 'the need for a bigger reduction cannot be ruled out'. The resulting pattern of resource use would be something like that shown in Table 3.1.

To give effect to these proposals, the Treasury proposed a formulaic scheme involving uniform cuts of 6 per cent in current expenditure and 10 per cent in capital expenditure in the focus year 1978–79—but with numerous exceptions (including notably defence which had been separately reviewed in the course of 1974 and cut significantly in the Budget exercise, industrial support and many of the demand-determined services where the government were not able to control the amount of 'take-up'). The formulaic reductions were not applied to the intermediate years and the survey took as its starting point the figures agreed in the previous year as amended by the Budget reductions (which were, of course, only for 1976–77, but had consequences for future years).

The Cabinet discussion on 22 May[66] was a long and argumentative one. It is hardly surprising that the Chancellor's colleagues found his proposals hard to stomach, coming so soon after the disagreeable fare he had laid before them at

Table 3.1 Projected pattern of resource use

Application	Average annual increase in resources (£million at 1970 factor cost prices)	Average annual increase (in percentage terms)
GDP	1,610	3.2
Balance of payments	520	
Private investment	450	8.1
Nationalized industries investment	80	5.8
Public expenditure	360	1.9
Private consumption	200	0.8

[66] CAB 129/56/25.

the Budget discussion in March. He attempted to defuse the issue by arguing that his proposals were, at this stage, only procedural and that substantive decisions were not needed until the summer Medium-Term Assessment was available and the implications of his proposals for individual programmes were apparent. His colleagues would have none of it. Some of them argued that his whole diagnosis was flawed. The economic situation, particularly for unemployment, was dire. 'If public expenditure priorities had to be replaced, this should be done in a full employment context.... There was a wholly feasible alternative policy based on import controls...combined with increased investment in the context of full employment'. The Prime Minister saved the Chancellor by summing up and stating that 'while the Cabinet were not at one on the need for cuts in public expenditure of the magnitude proposed...they accepted that only by asking officials to proceed...on the basis put forward could they ensure that they would have available sufficient options later in the year *should major cuts have to be made.*' The Cabinet, in short, were not persuaded on the basis of the arguments presented, even though, as the Chancellor's paper implied, nothing in the medium-term prospect was likely to change in the few months before the results of the Survey would have to be addressed. However officials in the spending departments had the authority now to begin the laborious business of examining the implications for policy of subjecting their programmes to the reductions that the Treasury asked should be explored.

The Chancellor was presented with the findings of the Medium-Term Assessment at the beginning of July. It did not differ in principle from the rather bleak assessment made at the outset of the Survey. Most of the optimism which had characterized the 1974 appraisals of how the economy would adjust to the huge economic changes wrought by the oil price increase had gone. However the message was that if expenditure reductions of £2 billion (at 1974 prices) could be achieved by 1978–79 the outlook for both the growth of productive potential and for privately financed consumption might not be so bad. The Chancellor put the Assessment to his colleagues on 10 July.[67] He now argued that it would be wrong to base policy 'on the assumption that we should continue to borrow from foreigners up to the end of the decade'. Even if the deficit were eliminated by 1978 (the MTA assumption) 'our indebtedness would have increased substantially by perhaps £10–£15 billion—a major burden on our balance of payments'. He proposed that 'we should accept the need for reductions in the White Paper 1978–79 programmes of at least £2 billion and preferably up to £3 billion and consider priorities against this background'.

The Cabinet discussion, on 14 July, was a re-run of that which took place on 22 May.[68] A minority of the Chancellor's colleagues thought that his whole strategy was wrong, and that the adoption of something like a National Plan, with resources allocated centrally, would be more efficient. On the other hand a majority

[67] CAB 129/184/4.   [68] CAB 128/57/5.

were apparently persuaded of the need for some adjustment of programmes. But there was unanimity that nothing should be said publicly at this stage. The TUC had only recently accepted, by appropriating the new Incomes Policy as their own, the need for what would involve a significant fall in real incomes. The Cabinet thought that they might be demoralized by an early announcement of cuts in spending, some of which might impinge on the Social Wage. The Chancellor was due to speak on 21 July in a Parliamentary debate on a motion to take note of the Government's Counter-Inflation White Paper. The Opposition had tabled a motion which regretted 'the Government's failure to reduce public spending' and it was clearly necessary for the Chancellor to respond to this charge. He could not anticipate the outcome of the PESC discussions but he could hardly say nothing. He resolved this problem by pointing out in the debate how absurd it would be to cut expenditure in the current year (1975–76) when the economy was working below capacity. But he gave a strong hint of what was to come:

Public expenditure must be firmly controlled for several years to come. The outcome of the current review, which is bound to require a new look at priorities for public spending will be announced when it is completed later this year. But it is clear that in carrying the reassessment of spending programmes forward beyond 1976–77 (*i.e. those which had been announced in the Budget*) there will at best be very little room for overall growth beyond the reduced level for that year.[69]

This was certainly an accurate statement of his and the Treasury's position, but it was one which had not yet been fully accepted by the Cabinet. Indeed when summing up the discussion of 14 July, the Prime Minister explicitly said that the Cabinet were not yet ready to take a decision on whether to cut programmes, which would certainly be required if the Chancellor's Parliamentary indications were anything to go by.

The Chancellor's paper of 10 July and the Cabinet discussion of 14 July thus did little to carry forward the process of deciding in concrete fashion the level of public expenditure in the medium term. The Cabinet's detailed involvement at this stage of the process was the result of an express wish of the Prime Minister who had outlined a new procedure for conducting the public expenditure survey in a paper to Cabinet in May which had been approved on 22 May.[70] For the most part this procedure was a codification of existing practices, but it did contain two innovations. These were that when the PESC report on the outcome of the survey was submitted to Cabinet it should be accompanied by a report by a group of senior officials drawn from several departments as well as the Bank of England (the Steering Committee on Economic Strategy—SCE) on the main issues which Ministers had to address and on the options open to them. There should also be an opportunity for the Cabinet during the expenditure round to look at the whole question of priorities in public

---

[69] *Hansard* 21 July 1975.   [70] CAB 129/183/10.

spending. Both of these were, in principle, useful developments although when the question of priorities came to be discussed by the Cabinet on 4 August[71] the discussion was at a high level of generality. As had been found to be the case when priorities had been discussed in the abstract, the conclusions did not contribute greatly to the process of actually deciding which programmes should be cut and which spared.

The PESC Survey was completed by officials early in September. It described in detail what the implications were of applying the ground rules laid down by Ministers at the outset, that is that there should be a formulaic reduction in most programmes and that departments should identify options themselves as possible candidates for cuts. It was no part of the Survey team's functions to make recommendations, but they had to highlight what the implications of particular choices were. The report made fairly disagreeable reading for Ministers. The formulaic cuts produced savings of just over £2.2 billion, but new commitments entered into by the Government since the launch of the Survey, such as the rescue of British Leyland and the measures announced as part of the new pay policy in July, reduced the formulaic savings to £1.5 billion. There were also estimating changes, some of which were in a sense perverse—the lower inflation now assumed following the new pay policy raised the real cost of the social security budget—and, more significantly, there was a very big increase in the provision required for debt interest. The policy options identified under the second part of the ground rules would produce savings of about £2 billion. Thus pretty well all the optional policy savings would be required to achieve something like the total savings which the ground rules were designed to achieve. The annual rate of increase of public expenditure in constant price terms between 1974–75 and 1979–80 would then be about 1.8 per cent. These were the bare factual findings of the Survey. They were discussed by the SCE whose conclusions the Chairman reported to Cabinet in an important memorandum on 6 November.[72] He recalled that, when the Survey had been launched, the Chancellor had proposed that it should illustrate the consequences of reductions of up to £3 billion at 1974 Survey prices in the focus year (1978–79) on the basis that the aim should be to make reductions of at least £2 billion. This aim had admittedly not been endorsed at the Cabinet on 14 July nor indeed when the question of spending priorities had been discussed on 4 August, but SCE considered that the range of £2–3 billion remained the order of magnitude of cuts which the economic outlook required (translated into 1975 Survey prices this range became £2.25–3.75 billion). The need for reductions of this order had, in the view of the Committee, been strengthened by two factors: the estimating changes caused by the improvement in the inflation outlook, which caused the resource cost of the social security upratings to be increased, and the considerable increase in the provision for debt interest,

---

[71] CAB 128/57/9.   [72] CAB 129/185/18.

caused largely by the size of the borrowing requirement for 1975–76. The arguments for a shift of resources into the balance of payments and into productive investment remained as strong as ever. The firm recommendation was that Ministers should adjust the spending programmes to secure savings of £3.75 billion (at 1975 prices) on the White Paper figures for 1978–79—as indeed the Chancellor had proposed in the first place. A list of options totalling £5 billion was displayed comprising the formulaic reductions and other possibilities which had been identified during the Survey for programmes which were not amenable to the formula as well as some suggested reductions proposed by the Treasury but not accepted by departments. It was indeed strong medicine that was offered to Ministers.

The Chancellor and the Prime Minister now had to get the Cabinet's approval to the recommendations of SCE and its identification of where the cuts should be made. This was not going to be an easy task. At previous Cabinets, on 22 May and 14 July, several Ministers had questioned the whole approach and methodology of the Treasury in relation to macro-economic policy in general and public expenditure in particular, and faced with the strong recommendation of SCE of what was something like a 10 per cent cut in the programmes agreed for 1978–79 in 1974 (after, it will be recalled, a considerable resistance on the part of some spending Ministers in the course of that year) there was bound to be a lively debate. The Prime Minister decided that tactically it was better to have a general debate about the direction of macro-economic policy before, and separate from, any consideration was given to where the additional cuts required should come from. In this way the alliance of those Ministers who were opposed to the general thrust of policy with those who had departmental responsibilities for delivering public services would be less dangerous. The Cabinet of 6 November was therefore devoted to the issue of economic policy and the expenditure issues were reserved for its meeting a week later.

For the first meeting the Chancellor put in a paper drawing on the October NIF which described the current economic situation.[73] The country was now at the very lowest point of the recession, but he saw signs of recovery, in particular in the field of international trade, which was expected to recover strongly in 1976. He wanted, however, to focus attention on the medium-term prospect rather than the outlook for the following eighteen months. Here he drew on the Medium-Term Assessment but argued that the outlook might well be worse than assumed—in particular productivity growth could be below trend. He looked at the tax implications of existing expenditures programmes, which in his view strengthened the case for the scale of expenditure reductions proposed by SCE. In an annex he set out some suggestions for further cuts to secure the desired total. In this way his paper prepared the ground for the

---

[73] CAB 129/185/14.

discussion scheduled for 13 November rather than directly justified existing policy.

The Chancellor's views on economic policy were opposed by the Energy Secretary (Benn) who put in a paper of his own arguing for an 'alternative strategy'.[74] In doing this he was continuing the approach he had begun in February when he made a similar plea to the Cabinet's Economic Strategy Committee (MES) and continued in the Cabinet discussions in May and July. The two opposing views produced a lively debate,[75] but the views of the Energy Secretary (broadly for a much greater degree of government intervention in the economy and a larger role for the TUC) did not prevail. However there was a cost to the Chancellor. Although the Cabinet accepted that there was no case for reflating the economy to accelerate the recovery from the recession, they were not prepared to rule out some reflation in the future and the Prime Minister, catching the mood of the Cabinet, said that they would want to consider this as an option early in 1976.

The Cabinet discussion also covered the issue of some selective import controls to deal with the problems of particular industries and the question of whether the UK's external borrowing policy needed to be amended. The first issue is dealt with later in the narrative under the heading 'Import Restrictions' and need not detain us here, and as regards the second, an issue raised by Lever,[76] who suggested that the emphasis should be on borrowing in foreign currency rather than in sterling, there was little discussion—most Cabinet members clearly regarded this as a peripheral matter. We return to this question in the section on external financing.

The Chancellor could reasonably hope that the issue of economic strategy would not now cloud the question of the size and distribution of the expenditure reductions in the medium term which was for discussion on 13 November.[77] In this, however, he was to be disappointed. His most forceful critic on this occasion was not Benn and the few colleagues who favoured a more interventionist approach to the economy, but Crosland, who held the portfolio of Environment. Crosland was well known for his belief in the social value of public expenditure, having given public expression to it in his book *The Future of Socialism*, written in 1956, in which he expressly said, *inter alia*, 'A Labour government should commit itself to a definite increase in the proportion of national resources devoted to social welfare'. He now came in with a paper of his own in which he argued that the Treasury's policy of seeking to eliminate the external deficit by 1978 was unrealistic and that the need to curtail the public sector's consumption of resources to provide for the external sector on the scale envisaged was not proven. He did not deny that some cuts were necessary but thought that the formulaic cuts of about £2 billion in

[74] CAB 129/185/13.   [75] CAB 128/57/16.
[76] CAB 129/185/11.   [77] CAB 128/57/18.

1978–79 would be sufficient. He was much less opposed to using tax to meet any shortfall of resources than was the Chancellor. The Chancellor came back by pointing out that his proposals to rein in spending on the scale outlined might lead to the profile of public spending on programmes being on a plateau from 1976–77 onwards, but the total of expenditure would continue to rise because of the growth of debt interest as an item outside the programmes as would the contingency reserve, which had been found to be inadequate to serve the purpose it was designed for. Crosland's objections were not the only ones made. The proponents of an 'alternative strategy' renewed their opposition. However the Chancellor did receive powerful support from most of his colleagues, who, perhaps reluctantly, accepted that he had made his case. The Prime Minister was able to sum up to the effect that 'by a small majority' the Cabinet accepted the case for cuts of £3.75 billion and that the Chief Secretary to the Treasury should pursue with the spending Ministers concerned how the additional savings (i.e. above the formulaic and agreed cuts) should be secured. It was agreed, however, that the Chancellor should seek the views of the TUC on the scale of the cuts proposed.

The Chancellor reported the outcome of the Chief Secretary's discussions in a paper to Cabinet on 28 November.[78] It was a disappointing document. Towards the Cabinet's approved total of cuts amounting to £3.75 billion in 1978–79, the bilateral discussions had led to agreed savings of only £2.6 billion, of which many were of the formulaic variety. A further £1.15 billion was required. The disputed items (and other options) amounted to £2.3 billion. The Chancellor presented a shopping list of items from several programmes and invited his colleagues to make a selection. But first it had to be acknowledged that some of the agreed savings had been lost (for technical, legislative reasons). The savings now sought were £1,205 million. After a lengthy discussion of the Chancellor's shopping list comprising a variety of programmes, but including Defence, items amounting to £1,033 were tentatively agreed. The Chancellor agreed not to press for the last £172 million and the Chief Secretary was left to sort out the issues not completely resolved.

The programmes as now agreed formed the basis of the 1976 Public Expenditure White Paper which was published early in February.[79] The programmes finally accepted by the Chief Secretary were above the levels agreed by the Cabinet and the sum incorporated in the White Paper as the reduction in the level of spending for 1978–79 was only £3 billion, not the £3.75 billion the Chancellor had targeted. Still, the total of programmes for that year was below that for the previous four years. Indeed, in constant price terms, the profile of spending on programmes after 1975–76 was virtually flat. Debt interest and a new and more realistic provision for the contingency reserve meant that total spending would grow over the whole quadrennium; but the rate of increase was small.

[78] CAB 129/186/12.   [79] Cmnd 6393.

Although the Chancellor did not get everything he sought, his achievements in the public expenditure exercise of 1975—coming on top of what he had obtained in the Budget exercise in the Spring, and given the proclivities of the Government as a whole and the scepticism some colleague felt for the basis of his strategy—were remarkable. The whole process was, however, immensely time-consuming and the Chancellor was not helped by the fact that his principal ministerial lieutenant (the Chief Secretary) was not a member of the Cabinet,[80] as had been the case with previous administrations. What it did show, as indeed 1974 had to some extent also shown, was that any attempt to obtain further cuts in public spending of any significant amount, certainly in the medium term would be fraught with frustration. It is important to bear this in mind in analysing and appraising what the UK's creditors thought should be done in 1976 —an issue we examine in the next two chapters.

Public expenditure—the system

Although the conduct of the Survey occupied most of the time and energy of the Expenditure Group in the Treasury it was, in 1975, having some serious misgivings about the whole mechanism for controlling public spending and it is to these systemic issues we have to turn, for they form an important, but largely unrecognized, element in the evolution of public expenditure in the latter half of the decade.

The first of these was to limit access by spending departments to the contingency reserve. We have seen that this accounting item had, by early 1975, become ineffective as a control mechanism whose function was simply to provide funds for items of expenditure which were unforeseen. This was partly due to the fact that in the turbulent days of the early 1970s new crisis situations were emerging by the day and Ministers were reluctant to allow them to take their course without any intervention by the Government and saw no reason to provide for them from their existing programmes. In the course of 1975 British Leyland became unviable and Ministers decided that they could not stand aside and let events take their course. Later in the year, as we shall see, another motor manufacturer, Chrysler, made it plain that they would cease to operate in the UK without some subsidy from the Government and Ministers again decided to intervene with public funds. More generally the worsening employment situation led Ministers to devise schemes, all involving public expenditure, to mitigate the situation. One such was the Temporary Employment Subsidy launched in September. This was an arrangement whereby private employers, who might otherwise be obliged to lay off parts

---

[80] This was to change, but not until 1977 after the Chancellor had weathered the experience of 1976.

of their workforce because of a temporary shortfall of orders, would be paid the costs of retaining staff for a limited period. What the Treasury wanted as a means of circumscribing the cost of unforeseen expenditure was a rule that, if a spending minister wanted to step in and spend money on a new project, he would be obliged to find offsetting savings from his other programmes. On Treasury recommendations, the Chancellor drew the attention of his Cabinet colleagues to the need for such a discipline in his Cabinet Paper for the meeting of 22 May[81] when he said the he had 'already instructed the Treasury to adopt a most stringent attitude to all such further claims'. Only when this was quite impossible should the contingency reserve be used as a source of finance. Such a rule could not of course be enforced unilaterally by the Treasury since spending decisions were effectively taken collectively and the Chancellor's edict had little effect—in any case the Treasury was itself guilty of promoting unplanned expenditure, as with the Temporary Employment Subsidy and the Burmah rescue. But the rule became a practical yardstick for Treasury Expenditure Divisions in their relations with spending Departments. It could not be rigidly applied without a fiat from Ministers, for spending Ministers usually appealed to Treasury ministers when they were thwarted by Treasury officials and Treasury ministers, as was their right, tended to be more 'political' than their officials.[82] The fruits of the Treasury's deliberations on this matter were not ripened until 1976 when a new system, described in the next chapter, was introduced at Ministerial level.

An even more important innovation devised in 1975 but also not introduced until the following year was the introduction of cash control into the public expenditure system.[83] As we have seen, the planning and control of expenditure was, following the Plowden report, conducted in resource, or constant price, terms. Departments costed their programmes over the four-year period of the review in terms of the prices obtaining at the outset of the review. The cash they actually needed to implement those programmes, at any rate in the first year of the review period, was automatically made available to them. They did not incur any Treasury displeasure provided the volume of their spending did not exceed the volume authorized in the White Paper.[84]

---

[81] C(75)63—CAB 129/183/13.

[82] Joel Barnett, the Chief Secretary to the Treasury, describes in his book *Inside the Treasury* how he had to browbeat his officials who sought to make him change his mind over a spending decision he was minded to approve.

[83] Before 1975 there had been in existence a form of cash control on many construction programmes where the nature of the contract-awarding process lent itself fairly easily to a cash basis. However, for programmes generally, the idea of a comprehensive control only surfaced in the T reasury in February 1975.

[84] T his is not strictly true. T hat part of a Department's spending which was covered by Parliamentary Votes could only be increased by the authorization of a 'Supplementary' Estimate which had to be presented to and approved by Parliament. But in practice this was largely a formality and in any case a good deal of what was classified as public expenditure fell outside the Estimates system.

The system did not, therefore, give any incentive to departments to minimize the prices at which they 'bought' their programmes; and it certainly did not give the Treasury any firm idea at the outset of each financial year what the cost, in hard cash, of the approved programmes would be. For forecasting purposes the Treasury had to make the best assessment it could of what the financial out-turn of the programmes would be. In periods of low and/or reasonably stable inflation this might not have been a serious problem in itself. But in the early 1970s when inflation reached double-digit figures and was increasing, the problems of forecasting the cash requirements of departments became acute. The relative prices of different categories of goods and services were constantly shifting, often in an unpredictable way, and putting a cash value on any particular category of public spending became well-nigh impossible. Moreover, at certain times, the level of wage inflation exceeded by a significant margin the level of price inflation and, as a considerable portion of public expenditure consists of the wages and salaries of public employees, the level of cash expenditure on programmes rose sharply. This in turn had its effect on the level of the deficit as the Chancellor himself pointed out in his 1975 Budget statement:

In the conditions of last year [i.e. 1974] the inflation caused by excessively large wage and salary increases raised public expenditure in money terms much more than public receipts and the public deficit rose sharply.[85]

In this situation the Treasury decided to attempt a system of cash provision in which the programmes of departments—or at any rate those programmes which lent themselves to such treatment—should be costed for the first year of the Survey in cash terms and that the cash cost of those programmes should be treated as a control limit, the breaking of which would attract some penalty or other disciplinary treatment. The matter was considered in some detail by Treasury officials in February 1975.[86] It was recognized that there would be both technical and policy difficulties about any scheme—Departments could be expected to argue for the full implementation of their programmes even when the cash limit was likely to be breached. But more importantly it was felt that in the absence of an Incomes Policy (which was certainly the case in February) with a stated 'norm' any attempt to put a price on a particular programme would be a matter of guesswork. It was decided nonetheless to make the attempt and an inter-Departmental Working Party was set up in April with a remit to work out in detail how such a scheme would work. The decision to make the attempt cooperatively with the spending departments proved to be a wise one, for when the report on how such a scheme might operate was delivered in July[87] it carried the support of those who would have to live with it. The success in devising a scheme in such a short space of time

---

[85] *Hansard* 15 April 1975.　　[86] T 277/3054—PCC (75)32.　　[87] IGCC (75)8.

was considerable. In the first instance the coverage of the programmes which would be subject to cash control in the first year of the Survey was limited,[88] but it was nonetheless judged to be more extensive than those operated in other countries. Ministers were invited to approve the scheme in October for introduction in the following financial year (1976–77) and on Budget Day 1976 the full scheme was set out in a White Paper[89] the contents of which are described in the next chapter. We shall see later what a big impact the system had on the out-turn of public expenditure programmes, but when it was conceived in the early part of 1975 there were few in Whitehall who expected the system to work so powerfully as a moderating influence on public spending. The reason for this success was partly that, in estimating future wage and price increases and the laying down of multiplicative factors to convert spending in Survey prices to actual cash, a very conservative approach was used. But another reason was that Departments made every effort to stay within the cash ceilings they had been given and they were encouraged to do so by a rigorous regime of regular and frequent reporting of their cash position. The introduction of a system of cash control and its extension to much of public spending was the beginning of a long period of movement towards a completely cash system of expenditure control, which was finally achieved in the early 1980s.

The whole issue of the way public expenditure control was exercised by the Treasury was the subject of a paper written for the Department by Professor Godley[90] who had been acting as an economic adviser since the government took office in 1974. Godley was very critical of the concept of 'survey prices' as the means of projecting forward estimates of spending and argued—correctly—that departments had very little incentive to control prices. Indeed he thought that the system effectively undermined Treasury control, and he advocated a reversion to a planning and control system based entirely on 'cash'. He was also critical about the extent to which choices were made between different programmes—the issue of 'priorities'. This memorandum, which Godley subsequently developed in evidence to the Parliamentary Select Committee on Expenditure, was a useful stimulus to further thinking about the system even though Godley's radical ideas of a reversion to pure cash planning for the whole survey period was deemed to be inoperable. In his evidence to the Parliamentary Committee, Godley supported his criticisms of the system by citing figures which he said showed how extensive the loss of Treasury control had become. He gave a figure of £5 billion as the extent of the extra spending which the system had allowed over a four-year period. This was a somewhat misleading figure as it comprehended not only volume changes which had occurred as a deliberate decision by Ministers (£3.3 billion), but also increases in debt interest and increases which had arisen simply as a result of the Relative Price Effect—over which the Treasury had no control—being

---

[88] The coverage is described in PESC (76)1.   [89] Cmnd 6440.   [90] GEP 9/11/01.

larger (£2.5 billion) than could have been predicted.[91] The public reporting of what Godley said did not exactly justify the implication that the Treasury had lost £5 billion of expenditure. The statement obtained a certain amount of publicity, unlike the Treasury reply which explained the reasons for the discrepancy.

The Treasury could therefore hardly be accused of complacency about the effectiveness of the PESC system. The record provides ample evidence of continuing anxiety about its weaknesses—a discussion among senior officials in early 1975 showed concern that the British system of expenditure control was more complex than that of other developed countries,[92] and, as we have seen, the abuse of the contingency reserve was another worry. The process of developing the system to meet its weaknesses as a control and planning mechanism extended over a period of many years and it was not until 1981 that something akin to the system advocated by Godley was adopted, and planning was conducted entirely in cash terms—something that had become essential to give effect to the decision of the Government of Mrs Thatcher in 1980 to base macro-economic planning on a medium-term financial plan in which expenditure plans, as well as projected tax receipts, should be publicly set out. But by that time inflation had fallen considerably, and the experience of departments in making forward estimates of the money that would be required to purchase a given quantity of output was so much greater.

Sterling and the financing of the deficit

We now have to go back and examine how the Treasury addressed the continuing problem of financing the external deficit in 1975. One of the factors influencing the shape and content of the Budget had been, as we saw earlier in this chapter, the difficulty, or at any rate the uncertainty, surrounding this problem. As the year unfolded this difficulty did not materialize quite as expected. The current account actually improved during the year and was almost in balance by the fourth quarter, mainly because, as economic activity stagnated, imports declined in volume terms and increased only slightly in current price terms whereas exports increased by just under 18 per cent. Invisible items (net) were almost unchanged. The capital account was in small surplus mainly because net private sector investment in the UK and foreign currency borrowing by the banks covered a miscellany of capital items, including a small fall in the sterling balances. The net deficit was financed by the ongoing public sector borrowing programme and from the drawing on the lines of credit negotiated in 1974, as well as, of course, by drawing down the UK's foreign currency reserves which fell during the year by just under $1.5 billion.

[91] GEP 9/11/01.   [92] Second Secretaries meeting 13 May 1975—DW 013.

In retrospect this was not a bad outcome and the worst fears, expressed both in the Treasury submission of January and by the Governor when he saw the Prime Minister privately the same month,[93] proved to be unfounded. Indeed, even in the early spring, the Treasury was making a slightly more favourable appreciation of the external financing prospect and by September the financing gap for the second half of the year which had been forecast to be £1,200 million was now expected to be only £700 million. But the underlying trend of the balance of payments and its financing remained precarious and, as the year developed, the financing problem assumed a larger dimension. There was no net inflow from the holders of the sterling balances (in 1974 these had increased by £1.5 billion) and foreign currency borrowing by the public sector was only one half of what it had been the previous year. Within the sterling balance figure was a fall of £0.5 billion on the part of the official holders (mainly the central banks and monetary authorities in Kuwait, Saudi Arabia, Nigeria, and Brunei) compensated for by an increase in private overseas holdings of sterling. In this respect 1975 was a curtain-raiser for the events of 1976.

By late July the Treasury had come to the conclusion that, despite the external borrowing that was being achieved, there would still be a financing gap for the year as a whole, and the first warnings were being given that it might be necessary to make a drawing from the IMF. The UK had a large undrawn credit balance at the Fund (the quota was SDR 2.8 billion equivalent to $3.2 billion) and the first credit tranche (25 per cent of quota) could be drawn on fairly easy terms. There was also available access to the Oil Facility at the Fund which had been established in 1974 for those countries which could establish that they were experiencing balance of payments problems caused by the oil price increase. These two provisions would provide the UK with an additional external credit of perhaps $1 billion.

But quite separately from the issue of raising new credit, the Treasury, and particularly the Overseas Finance Division and of course the Bank, were much exercised in 1975 about the stability of the exchange rate, since this was the key to ensuring that existing 'volatile' credit, that is the sterling balances, was not liquidated. There had been moments of sterling weakness in the course of 1974, in particular in the middle of December, but they had not been such as to present too much of a problem for the Bank's currency dealers though intervention had had to be on a very considerable scale; and the successful borrowing initiatives that had been taken during the year meant that the reserves at year end were still in quite a healthy state, at any rate by UK standards. But this comfortable position was not to last, and 1975 saw many periods of sterling weakness when the authorities felt compelled to step in with support buying. The question of the adequacy of the stock of currency

---

[93] PREM 16/368.

reserves to carry out this function became a major factor in the mind of both Bank and Treasury officials.

It has to be said that, in terms of a national balance sheet of current assets and current liabilities, the UK was operating on a very slender liquidity base—certainly compared with other developed countries (the US, for special reasons, perhaps excepted). The total of our 'quick' assets—that is to say the official currency reserves—fell well short of the total of the UK's 'quick' liabilities—that is to say the overseas sterling balances. At the beginning of 1975 the former amounted to about $5 billion and the latter to about £7.5 billion. Bankers are, of course, well used to having fewer liquid assets on their balance sheets than their liquid liabilities, but they do this in the knowledge that the financial system in which they operate can provide liquid assets for them at short notice to meet any run on them by depositors. In the case of the international sterling system for which the Bank of England was responsible there was no lender of last resort other than the IMF, whose facilities were strictly circumscribed and which had stern rules for the provision of finance. Nor was there then, as there is at the time of writing this history, a developed international capital market and considerable cross-border movement of funds in both bonds and equities, a market which now enables very large financing needs to be met through ordinary market developments. There were, therefore, real risks in a situation where a run on the bank could in fact lead to something not unlike insolvency. By contrast, the Federal Republic of Germany had liquid reserves many times those of the UK and had a comparatively low level of liquid liabilities.

The vulnerability of the British system to a run on sterling had led the authorities in 1968[94] to seek some safeguard through international cooperation. In the wake of the 1967 exchange crisis, the Treasury negotiated agreements with each of the official sterling balance holders whereby, for a period of five years, each of them agreed to hold minimum balances in sterling in return for a guarantee by the UK to make good any financial loss (expressed in dollars) that might occur from a hypothetical depreciation of sterling in terms of dollars. The operation was, in effect, underwritten through the Bank for International Settlements by a group of the UK's major international partners.

In the event the guarantees were never called and when the agreements finally ran out in 1973 they were not renewed in the form in which they were negotiated. But for a number of countries a continuing unilateral guarantee was given even though the recipient was not committed to any minimum holding of sterling. However this limited extension was, as we saw in the previous chapter, terminated by the British Government at the end of 1974

---

[94] There had in fact been a $1 billion facility in 1966 which was to finance 50 per cent of any fall in the UK reserves but this did not involve any commitment on the part of overseas sterling holders. The full amount was drawn, but the agreement ran for only two years and was replaced by the 1968 facility described above.

in the belief that it no longer served any useful purpose. It is fair to say that neither the Bank nor the Treasury felt comfortable with the guarantees, which in their view could be seen as a sign of weakness rather than strength. They had required complex negotiations with each of the many official holders, involving considerable administrative effort over an extended period of time. The Bank and the Treasury were not in a mood to go down this road again.

The absence of any liquidity safeguard for sterling did however become a serious issue in the course of 1975 and it became even more acute the following year. There were several episodes when sterling came under pressure, principally through official sterling holders diversifying their portfolios as a result of doubts about the parity. The Bank then had to decide how heavily to intervene in support of the rate in order to assure creditors that the value of their assets was not seriously at risk. The question of the extent of this intervention first came to the fore when sterling was under pressure in the middle of December 1974. The Governor then asked for, and received, immediate authority to spend up to $500 million (or about 10 per cent) of the reserves.[95] In January 1975 there was something of a reversal of market sentiment and the Bank were able to recover over $500 million in intervention to stop sterling appreciating.[96] This phenomenon of two-way movement was not, however, to be repeated on a significant scale as the year moved on. There was a heavy attack on sterling in the week beginning 21 April (shortly after a *Sunday Times* report that the Chancellor was prepared to let the sterling rate fall) but the weakness was disguised in part by a sudden depreciation of the dollar, so that, although sterling's effective rate fell, the cross-rate with the dollar held firm. There was a further period of weakness in early May and sentiment about sterling was not helped by the imminence of the referendum on UK membership of the EEC, due to take place on 5 June. The acceleration of inflation in the UK and the absence, until the beginning of July, of any attempt to slow it down meant that market sentiment about sterling and the UK was fragile. As we saw in the section on inflation, the Kuwaitis had actually made a demarche on the Treasury to express their fears. By the end of June the dollar rate for sterling had fallen to $2.18 from about $2.40 at the beginning of the year. Generally speaking the Treasury fell in with the Governor's judgement of what needed to be done by way of intervention. But there was some unease with the policy on two counts: first that it was the Treasury's view, which the Chancellor had endorsed, that no attempt should be made to hold sterling to any fixed parity (since some depreciation was inevitable to offset the loss of competitiveness caused by the UK's higher rate of inflation) and secondly that the size of the reserves did not permit any sustained large-scale support of the exchange rate. The head of OF wrote to the Bank on 18 June[97] and pointedly reminded it that 'the general policy aim is that the effective rate for sterling should depreciate

---

[95] T 358/132.   [96] 2F(RMSA) 98/33/03.   [97] T 277/3056—PCC (75)65.

to 30 per cent (*below the Smithsonian parity*) by the first quarter of 1976 and even a successful counter-inflation policy will not detract from this'—a clear warning to the Bank that intervention to maintain the parity was not the policy. The Bank continued to think primarily in terms of defending the sterling parity, and to this end MLR was raised in May, in July, and in October to bring it back to 11 per cent, the level it had been in January. It is fair to say, however, that the slightly different views of the Bank and the Treasury did not, in 1975, give rise to any material policy differences. This was not the case in the following year when the institutional positions differed more markedly.

The monthly published figures for the UK's reserves in 1975 do not give any indication of the size of intervention, since there were inflows into the reserves from time to time as the various borrowers (the public sector borrowers as well as the UK government) drew on their lines of credit and so fortified the reserves. Moreover the Treasury occasionally 'doctored' the true reserves figure, either by switching from spot to forward transactions or by timing the drawing on the external loans simply to bolster what might otherwise have been worrying published figures. But the intervention was at times very heavy indeed. The worst attack on sterling came, as we have seen in the context of the Government's approach to a new policy on inflation, at the end of June when the Governor informed the Chancellor of the worsening sentiment in the foreign exchange market. There was some improvement in sterling's position after the announcement of the TUC's policy on pay restraint and indeed the demand for gilts—a good test of market sentiment—was strong in July. By mid-September, however, sterling was again under pressure and the Bank felt obliged to seek authority to raise MLR in its defence.

These periodic episodes of sterling weakness, despite a considerable improvement in the balance of payments on current account, prompted much discussion within Whitehall of possible ways of strengthening the reserves and of mitigating the fears of the official sterling holders. The discussion was given a political dimension by a comment made by the Prime Minister at the Cabinet on 1 July[98] about the possibility of again giving the official holders some form of exchange guarantee against a possible further fall in the exchange rate. The thought was taken up by the Trade Secretary a week later.[99] The Treasury and Bank got to work on a paper designed to show that guarantees (of the kind which had lapsed only six months earlier) were not the answer. Both institutions, and particularly the Treasury, took the line that if the new counter-inflation policy were successful, there would be no need for guarantees and that, if it were not, guarantees would not be effective in stopping the balance holders from selling sterling. To initiate negotiations on guarantees, or to give them unilaterally, would be more likely to provoke doubts in the minds of sterling holders about the value of their assets in

[98] CAB 128/57/1.   [99] DW 036.

134

London and would give the impression that the UK Government had reservations about the success of their Incomes Policy. The Treasury also had doubts whether, even if the focus were on the three major holders (Nigeria, Kuwait, and Saudi Arabia), they would be willing to enter into any arrangement which restricted their freedom of manoeuvre. The question was discussed at a meeting with the Chancellor on 22 July and again on 5 August,[100] by which time the exchange market had quietened somewhat as confidence had been restored by the pay policy of 1 July. Indeed not only were the exchange markets quieter, but the Bank was having some success in selling gilts, whose coupon looked distinctly better as a result of improving perspectives of the outlook for inflation. The Chancellor expressed an interest in the idea of a special interest rate which would be offered to official sterling holders, but this idea did not get a favourable response from Treasury officials.

The Treasury and the Bank now saw the ingredients of an effective programme of financing the current and capital accounts as consisting of three elements:

1 effective domestic policies, including a reduction in the rate of inflation;
2 judicious intervention in the exchange markets to prevent a sharp fall which could trigger a substantial outflow of capital;
3 the raising of as much external credit as could be secured.

So far as the first was concerned, the new Incomes Policy was a welcome development, although as we shall see the Governor made discreet representations from time to time about the need to reduce public expenditure[101] over and above the efforts which were being made by the Treasury, this being a significant preoccupation of the exchange markets. The second element was dealt with on an *ad hoc* basis, the Bank using its discretion on a routine basis, and consulting the Treasury when any substantial intervention was called for. There were occasional periods after July when the markets showed some uneasiness, but these were short-lived and did not cost the reserves a great deal. It was the third item which was the main preoccupation of the two institutions in 1975.

The options considered were:

(a) further long-term borrowing in dollars by the Government or public sector borrowers;
(b) the conversion of liquid official sterling balances into some longer-term instrument, still denominated in sterling;
(c) the offer by HMG of an instrument denominated in SDRs which might be offered, off-market, to the official sterling balance holders.[102]

---

[100] Ibid.   [101] See for instance PREM 16/238 (25 July 1975).
[102] Mitchell's minute of 17 September—DW 036.

The scope for public sector market borrowing or of a special clearing bank loan in dollars similar to the one negotiated in 1974 was not judged to be great in the conditions of 1975. Earlier in the year the Treasury had examined the question whether a special loan could be negotiated for some of the nationalized industries with the Bank for International Settlements or the European Investment Bank, but these had led to the conclusion that in the prevailing market conditions and with doubts about the British economy this was not an avenue to be pursued. The Treasury and Bank doubts about the ability of the Government to raise dollar finance either in the market or on a bilateral basis were augmented by reports they received from their representatives in the United States. They were not, however, shared by Harold Lever who, throughout 1975, pursued a line of argument quite different from that of the Treasury and the Bank. Lever, who had some personal experience of the financial markets, had as early as March urged the Treasury to go for 'massive' borrowing from the United States and, although this idea did not fall on fertile ground, had returned to the external financing problem after the discussion in Cabinet on 1 July about the precariousness of sterling. He observed in a minute to the Prime Minister on 4 August[103] correctly, that it was the official holders of sterling who were the main problem and on 9 October[104] he suggested that it was worth considering 'the taking of an initiative on the sterling balances' by raising a large dollar loan on the New York market which he saw as providing the UK with the ability to meet the diversification of the holdings of the overseas official institutions. The Chancellor replied, on Treasury and Bank advice, that 'no new borrowing initiative was likely to be effective',[105] but this *douche* of cold water did not deter him from raising the whole matter at Cabinet of 6 November,[106] where again his ideas were not picked up by any of his colleagues. But, as we shall see, he returned yet again to the idea of a large dollar credit to deal with the diversification problem in May and June 1976, when he was more successful in gaining support.

As 1975 developed, it became increasingly apparent that the periodic weaknesses of sterling were due largely to the activities of the official holders—the central banks and monetary authorities, and of these those of Kuwait, Nigeria, and Saudi Arabia were the most active. By contrast, the holdings of private depositors, mainly banks and businesses, were relatively stable. These holdings were widely held and the motive for holding them was to finance business activities, not for investment. It was perhaps not surprising that the element of uncertainty about the value of sterling counted less for these depositors, whose holdings were in the nature of 'working balances' and did not generate any great movement of the aggregate deposits. In fact private holdings of sterling rose by nearly £250 million or about 8 per cent in the course of 1975; official holdings fell by nearly £500 million or 11 per cent in the same period.

[103] PREM 16/371.   [104] DW 036.   [105] Ibid 15 October.   [106] CAB 129/185/11.

The possibility of dealing with the problem of the official holders by offering them a conversion of their liquid sterling assets into a less liquid form was considered from time to time. Of the holders who might be interested, Saudi Arabia was judged to be the most likely candidate. Their balances were substantially above their liquid needs, and they might be interested in an instrument which offered them an attractive long-term yield rather than the Treasury bills or other short-term instruments in which most of their current assets were held. It was judged, however, that the approach ought to be a low-key affair, and it was decided that the idea might best be canvassed in the course of the periodic visits which senior officials from the Treasury and the Bank made in 1975 and indeed again in early 1976.

The one idea which attracted favourable attention from both the Treasury and the Bank was that of issuing an instrument denominated in SDRs. The SDR was not a tradeable currency and as a unit of account it did not exist outside the books of the IMF and the Central Banks. But it had a certain appeal to any investor who might want some stability in the currency of his investments provided its actual conversion to a tradeable currency when desired was underwritten—and this category could include the monetary authorities who held sterling. The dollar, which had traditionally been regarded as a safe currency, had suffered some reputational damage, as a result both of the removal of the gold guarantee in August 1971 and by the devaluation of February 1973 and it was thought that an instrument denominated in a unit which was linked to a basket of the major currencies as a whole, as the SDR was from 1973, would have some attraction. The idea of offering sterling holders, or at any rate some of them, a secure asset was first put to the Chancellor in a lengthy submission dated 17 September[107] which again combed over possible ideas for dealing with the official holders of sterling. It was concluded that the SDR bond was both a feasible and indeed an attractive course of action. In putting the idea forward, the Treasury remarked that the bond 'could well defuse the intermittent pressure for sterling guarantees which the Chancellor gets from his colleagues'. This comment might suggest some lack of enthusiasm for the idea, but the documentary evidence does not justify the suspicion that the initiative was simply a cynical move to avoid recourse to other measures of which the Treasury and Bank did not approve. Indeed the OF side of the Treasury argued forcefully for the SDR idea in the regular External Financing Appraisal which they put forward in mid-October[108] but by that time the focus had switched to a drawing from the Fund and the SDR idea was regarded as something which could be returned to when the negotiations with the Fund were concluded. The SDR bond was therefore quietly dropped from the agenda as consideration of an approach to the Fund as a more certain way of securing external finance took over. It was taken up again in 1976 when the

[107] DW 036.   [108] T 277/3058—PCC (75)97 Annex B.

financing problem became acute, but even then reasons were found for not actively pursuing the matter. It is not difficult to suppose that the Bank were never very keen on the SDR bond because it implicitly called into question the future stability and reliability of sterling. In contrast, a Fund drawing of a routine, as opposed to a crisis, kind had no such implications and it became, from the late summer onwards, the principal candidate for augmenting the reserves. Before we examine what was entailed, we have to look at a number of other developments which occurred in the course of 1975.

Monetary policy

We saw in the previous chapter that in 1974 monetary policy was not used to a great extent as an instrument of macro-economic policy. The growth of the monetary aggregates had been modest and interest rates were held at levels which offered creditors a negative real rate of return on their short-term monetary assets. Consideration of a change in MLR turned on what, in purely technical terms, the money market required, or to show some support for sterling on the foreign exchange markets. Much the same applied to 1975. The Corset had been removed in the Budget but this had little apparent effect on the growth of the money supply and over the year as a whole £M3, the measure regarded by the Treasury and the Bank as the one which was the most significant, grew by only 6.5 per cent. The joint Treasury/Bank Monetary Committee did not seem greatly exercised about the use of monetary policy, or lack of it, to support domestic or external policy, although there was a spirited discussion of the matter at their meeting on 23 December.[109] The Deputy Governor had told the Chancellor in August[110] that he did not think that the adoption of monetary targets would serve much purpose, and the Treasury certainly did not disagree. Both the Bank and the Treasury were conscious of the damage which high interest rates could do both to industrial investment and to the viability of some of the more fragile financial institutions, which had been affected by the property market slump in 1973 and the secondary banking crisis in 1974. Short-term interest rates (notably MLR) which were 11 per cent at the beginning of the year fell to 9.75 per cent in April under the influence of low demand for credit by the private sector but rose, as a response to developments in the foreign exchange market, in May, July, and October to reach 11 per cent. Despite these increases, they remained heavily negative in terms of their 'real' level. As we shall see later in the context of the meetings with the IMF, the latter did not have much quarrel with British monetary policy as such. Their concern was with the monetary implications of public borrowing, which they considered to be too high and which might offer

[109] MPG (75)17.   [110] DW 036.

a threat to the availability of credit for the private sector when (and if) demand on its part developed. It was however the case that the US authorities, both the Federal Reserve and the Treasury, thought that a vigorous use of monetary instruments could provide a powerful support for sterling, although they only expressed this view cogently in the summer of 1976.

The employment situation

The general state of the economy in 1975 has been referred to several times *en passant*, but macro-economic policy was by no means fashioned with very much regard to what was happening in the 'real' economy. As the year progressed, economic activity steadily stagnated under the influence of the restrictive Budget, a depressed world economy and weak private sector demand. In each of the first three quarters GDP actually fell—a phenomenon that had not been experienced hitherto in any of the post-war years. Consumer expenditure declined, in part under the influence of the operation of the pay policy (which implied a fall in real wages), in part because unemployment grew, and in part because, as the Treasury noted in its changes to its forecasting model, the personal sector showed an inclination to increase its saving—in the short-run at any rate—during a period of inflation. Gross fixed investment was flat and there was considerable de-stocking by industry. Unemployment rose from three-quarters of a million at the beginning of the year to 1.1 million at the end—a figure which had not been experienced since the beginning of the Second World War except for special periods like the 1947 and 1974 fuel crises. One of the financial effects of the fall in economic activity was that the public sector finances deteriorated, as social security benefits increased and tax receipts fell. The mid-summer NIF predicted that the forecast of the PSBR at the time of the Budget (£9 billion) would be exceeded by £1.4 billion bringing it up to £10.5 billion—a factor which was bound to limit any thought of an easement of fiscal policy on the lines of what happened in the middle of 1974.

The weakness of the economy to which the Government had made its own contribution was a source of great anxiety to Ministers for it put its relations with the TUC under severe strain. The cooperation of the unions in the implementation of the new pay policy was seen to be fundamental and yet their position, *vis-à-vis* their members as redundancies started to occur and business failures multiplied, became very strained. The Chancellor thought that the stakes were too high for the Government to be seen to be doing nothing about a matter which was so crucial to the trade unions.

On 4 August the Cabinet took stock of the worsening situation[111] and the Chancellor put forward the idea of a clutch of measures which might take the

---

[111] CAB 128/57/9.

edge off the full severity of the rate of job losses. The issue of what to do about unemployment in a situation which was unprecedented in post-war Britain received much public attention and a number of suggestions were put forward by economists and others for tempering the worst of the effects of the recession on the working population. Principal among these were ideas of a temporary employment subsidy to employers to encourage them to retain employees whom they might have to make redundant for a limited period. The hope, and indeed expectation, of the Treasury and most economic forecasters was that the economy would recover, perhaps quite strongly, in 1976 and that the rise in unemployment would stop and might be reversed. A temporary and time-limited subsidy to employers might enable them to retain staff who might otherwise be laid off. Another labour-related idea was to increase significantly the training and re-training schemes the Government ran through its agency, the Manpower Services Commission.

The Treasury attitude to these ideas was moderately favourable. The Permanent Secretary minuted the Chancellor on 8 September[112] offering a possible package of measures, ranging from a limited amount of job creation to be administered by the Manpower Services Commission, subsidies to employers to take on school leavers and grants to industrialists to embark on new factory construction. The Treasury advised strongly against anything as large as the expenditure package introduced by the Heath Government in the winter of 1971–72 and set the limit it considered acceptable as £100 million. The proposals would not do much to counter the rise in unemployment, but they would have a certain amount of political and cosmetic value. The Chancellor agreed and put the proposals to his colleagues who went along with them. The full package was announced in the House of Lords on 24 September—the Commons were not sitting. In total they went somewhat beyond the limit set by Treasury officials and amounted to £175 million. Part of this total was deliberately short-term and designed to take the edge off unemployment, but there was an element of continuing expenditure through the use of the Industry Act to subsidize industrial investment. About one-quarter of the total would be spent in the current financial year with most of the rest in the following year.

Ministers were however concerned about the general plight of the construction industry—not least because of the cuts being made to public sector programmes—and decided to supplement the measures just described with a small programme of public construction projects, limited in total to £30 million. These had to be worked out with the spending departments and it was not until 1 November that the details could be given to Parliament. The total of expenditure committed by these statements was thus about £200 million.[113] Although in relation to expenditure as a whole this was a small

[112] T 371/20.   [113] Ibid.

amount, it has to be borne in mind that Ministers were committing themselves to higher spending for particular purposes when at the same time in the public expenditure survey they were trying to reduce expenditure overall. They were also making calls on the contingency reserve for the current year, when it had already been spent.

Import restraints

One of the issues of policy which arose several times during the course of 1975 was that of adopting some administrative measures to restrict the level of imports. There were several strands to the thinking behind this idea and it is instructive to set them out, not least to appreciate the extent to which the policy of (more or less) free trade, which the UK had followed since the end of the Second World War, came under strain and to understand the importance of this issue to the core of policy as it was conceived and developed.

The commitments that successive governments had made to the principle of free trade were quite formidable. The first post-war obligation assumed by the UK was that of the GATT, the General Agreement on Tariffs and Trade, which it signed in 1948. This laid down certain principles that signatory governments accepted, one of which was not to impose new barriers to imports—existing barriers were the subject of negotiation. This, of course, included new tariffs and new quantitative restrictions. A derogation was allowed temporarily for countries in balance of payments difficulties, but a case had to be made, and other signatories were allowed to retaliate if their industries were adversely affected by such measures. The Articles of Agreement of the IMF also frowned on trade restrictions, although without formal sanction. To these international commitments were added those incorporated in the Treaty of Rome to which the UK adhered in 1973. Here again measures that interfered with the free movement of goods within the Community had to receive the sanction of the European Commission and, in turn, the European Council. Finally, as we saw in Chapter 2, the UK had signed the OECD Trade Pledge in May 1974, which expressly committed its signatories not to resort to measures restricting free trade following the onset of the Oil Crisis. All of these commitments applied to what were known as generalized restrictions, that is those applying across the board and indiscriminately. The commitments were much less binding on industry-specific restrictions and certainly on such restrictions which were applied for a limited period. At the IMF Consultations in May the head to the Fund Mission was relaxed about the possibility of limited selective import controls.[114]

---

[114] DW 013.

Against this background the application of generalized trade restrictions as an instrument of economic policy to combat unemployment or to improve the balance of payments (in the absence of a crisis in that area) was thought by most of Whitehall not to be a serious policy option. This did not, however, prevent its being examined from time to time, not least because some Ministers thought that it should be considered as an alternative to the course which the Chancellor and the Treasury were following. Nor was the Treasury wholly innocent of reflections on this matter. As early as the summer of 1974, when the possibility of some major attack on sterling and the development of a full-scale financial crisis arose, at least in the minds of some in the Treasury, serious consideration was given, admittedly on a purely contingency basis, of the introduction of import restrictions. But these were not envisaged as having any permanent basis and were simply to buy time pending the resolution of the crisis by more conventional methods. More seriously, as we saw in the passage on the 1975 Budget, the idea of some method of interference with the normal instruments of trade and payments as a means to improve the balance of payments was put to the Chancellor as a 'possibility'. But this was largely an 'aunt sally', for, when the arguments against it were set out on paper, the Chancellor came down against it and agreed with the Treasury that it would be better to have a deflationary Budget than to resort to measures, the consequences of which would have been very serious indeed. From that moment on the Chancellor needed little persuasion that generalized trade controls, as a policy option were not on the table except possibly for a limited time in a crisis situation—something the Treasury prepared for in July 1974 following a discussion in MES.[115] The idea of *selective* trade controls, against which the arguments were much less decisive, was something which he never excluded as an option, for example where a particular industry was in temporary difficulties and the restrictions would have a limited life. Indeed the Chancellor several times told his officials that he would be prepared to countenance such an approach, which he saw as having value in the relationship of the Government with the TUC. And the TUC for its part at no time pressed for generalized protection and contented itself with requests for special measures to protect particular industries in specific difficulties.

Other ministers were not so clear cut in their views. In particular the Industry Secretary (Benn), putting an alternative economic strategy to his colleagues in MES on 25 February 1975, saw import controls, admittedly tailored to particular industries, as an ingredient to a new approach. These ideas continued to surface during the several discussions of economic policy, especially as we saw in the context of the public expenditure round, and they reached their peak, for 1975 at the Cabinet of 6 November. Here both the Chancellor and the Trade Secretary both proposed very particular trade restrictions[116] to assist a small number of industries, but Benn, who was now the Energy Secretary, went further and argued

[115] DW 085 30 July and DW 033 28 October.   [116] CAB 129/185/16.

for a more generalized protective regime—although again without winning the day. The Trade Secretary emphasized that his case was at this stage for *selective* measures, but he did put his colleagues on notice that 'if there was any question of applying general import controls a decision would be needed well before May 1976 when the OECD trade pledge [not to introduce generalized restrictions] ran out'. As we shall see, he returned to the general question early in the New Year, but for the moment the issue was whether to offer some protection to particular industries. The Cabinet agreed to further work on this—in particular to examine what retaliatory action such protection might provoke—and in the course of November and early December a limited number of measures were drawn up and eventually presented to Parliament on 17 December.

The Chancellor may have been converted to the view that generalized import controls were not an option in a non-critical situation but he nevertheless thought that more work than had been done in the past on the need for crisis measures needed to be done and he asked shortly after the Budget for a full-blooded appraisal of what would be involved administratively, legislatively, and internationally by resorting to generalized import controls. A highly secret group (code name DELVE) was set up to examine a number of 'options' but all on the basis that they would not be a reversal of existing policy but rather something that might be resorted to in a crisis temporarily so as to buy time for something less disruptive to the international community. They were, therefore, all measures that would have to be implemented very quickly so as to prevent forestalling by importers and have to be within the framework of existing treaty obligations. The measures examined ranged from an import surcharge (possibly coupled with an export subsidy), through import deposits (described more fully in the next chapter) to full-blooded quantitative restrictions. The exercise was divided into two parts: the first being a study of the mechanics and the legal aspects of such schemes, and the second an appraisal of the likely economic effects. On the first, the group considered that it would be imperative that any scheme would have to be such as not to attract retaliatory action by other countries and so negate any beneficial effects. This meant that essentially it had to be within the international legal framework—something which, once again, would require full justification. The administrative and legal difficulties varied between the different schemes but none was free from serious problems. On the second matter—a purely economic assessment—the group found that, as compared with a devaluation (the yardstick taken to measure the effects) most of the measures did not have a decisive edge, although some of the schemes were marginally more effective either in improving the balance of payments or in reducing employment.

The whole exercise was completed in July.[117] It was a purely precautionary exercise and although it was submitted to the Chancellor on 4 August it did

---

[117] T 277/3056 and 3057—PCC (75)78, 79, and 80.

not lead to any ministerial discussion outside the Treasury. The Chancellor had an internal meeting with his advisers on 18 September. He said that 'he did not favour direct intervention in the balance of payments as a long-term policy' although he did not rule out resort to some form of temporary controls as a short-term expedient in certain circumstances, and he expressed interest in some selective measures of import protection.[118] DELVE was well and truly put back into the bottom drawer, but as we shall see when we look at the events of 1976, it had to be taken out and dusted off when ministers again showed interest in a different way of tackling the UK's problems.

The autumn NIF and the Treasury's response

The routine short-term forecast in the autumn of 1975 was completed in late November and it made predictably grim reading for the Treasury and for Ministers.[119] The appraisal found that events in the areas of employment and income had turned out worse than had been expected at the time of the Budget. This was partly because the world recession had been both deeper and longer than had been predicted in the Spring, and partly because businesses had substantially reduced their holding of inventories in the face of financial pressures, and partly because consumers were saving more than the model had predicted. The conventional view about personal saving had been that, in the face of rapidly rising prices, the public would accelerate their spending to avoid the higher prices they would have to pay if they deferred their purchases. In fact the reverse turned out to be the case—whether because of an aversion to spending on goods whose price had risen or whether the public felt insecure as the toll of job losses rose. At any rate the recession was exceeding expectations in its severity and the Treasury now described the outlook in the following bleak terms:

1 The balance of payments would show no improvement in 1976 and 1977—indeed the central case of the forecast showed that things would get worse.

2 Unemployment would rise throughout 1976 and go over the 1.5 million mark before falling away as GDP began to pick up.

3 The retail price index would rise to 12.5 per cent in the third quarter of 1976—well above the 10 per cent target which had been set at the outset of the pay policy in July.

4 The PSBR would be above £12 billion for three consecutive years (1974–75, 1975–76 and 1976–77). 'Quite apart from the implications this has for the volume of debt and its servicing, it cannot be financed at acceptable interest rates without a rapid and dangerous increase in the money supply.' (It was

[118] PCC (75)96.   [119] T 277/3057—PCC (75)87.

not clear whether this revealed a new attitude on the part of the Treasury to the role of the money supply or whether it simply feared that a large increase in it would trigger a confidence crisis.)

This disagreeable picture was put to the Chancellor in a submission on 24 October.[120] In addition to the unwelcome developments for the economy reported in the NIF, the outlook for financing the external deficit had been set out in a minute on 16 October.[121] The success in borrowing in 1974 and the first quarter of 1975 had not been sustained. It had been necessary to draw heavily on the reserves, which had risen to a peak of $7.8 billion in November 1974 but had fallen to $6.2 billion in June 1975 and to $5.5 billion in mid-October. The Iranian Government would probably agree to a further drawing on the loan negotiated in July 1974 and there could be further bilateral borrowing from Saudi Arabia: together with some additional public sector borrowing in eurodollars. In spite of these possibilities, there looked likely to be a financing gap of the order of £500 million over the following six months. The ideas of two-tier interest rates on certain government debt held by foreigners and of a special SDR bond were again examined only to be rejected as ineffective or unworkable.

The Treasury argued that it was now important to come to an early view on the future course of policy, 'not only because the Chancellor has to face his colleagues in Cabinet on 6 November [when as we saw earlier a discussion of the state of the economy was on the agenda] but also because any decision must be interrelated with the prior decision [which had not yet been firmly taken] on an approach to the IMF'.

The policy implications of the forecast were clear to the Treasury. The UK was not improving its price competitiveness in world markets as it needed to, and something had to be done about the exchange rate, given that the pay policy was delivering all that was, and could be, expected of it in the way of containing production costs and achieving a degree of competitiveness for UK exports. The policy of waiting for sterling to fall under ordinary market pressures was not producing the competitive improvement that was necessary, not least because of the ambivalence of the Bank (and to some extent the Treasury) about the need to resist downward pressures on the rate. Moreover it was only through net exports that the UK could do something about the unemployment situation—all other measures to stimulate employment were ruled out by the precarious fiscal situation and the impossibility of increasing imports in the teeth of the UK's deficit. This had been the view of the Managing Director of the IMF when he saw the Chancellor in April and again in August. It was also the view of respected members of the international financial community such as Dr Emminger of the Bundesbank.

---

[120] T 277/3058—PCC (75)97 Revise.   [121] Ibid, Annex B.

Before passing to the problem of manipulating the exchange rate, the Treasury briefly raised again the question of import restrictions. The DELVE exercise had established that generalized import controls were not a viable option and officials did not want to revisit this conclusion. There was, therefore, no escaping from the logic of an exchange rate change, however it might be engineered as indeed had been argued strenuously in 1974. The Treasury examined what the effect of a depreciation of 7.5 per cent[122] would have on the economic outlook. Although there would initially be a worsening of the balance of payments due to the J-curve effect, there would be a quarterly improvement in the current balance of £175–225 million per quarter in 1977 and something like a closing of the deficit in 1978 when North Sea Oil came on stream. GDP would improve by about 2 per cent in 1977 and unemployment would have fallen by 200,000 by the end of 1977. Domestic prices however would worsen by between 2 and 3.5 per cent by the third quarter of 1977. The outcome would not, therefore, be in any sense ideal for it would put the pay policy under great strain. Moreover the Treasury conceded that the recovery induced by a depreciation at a time of growing world activity and a counter-cyclical recovery of domestic demand might be so strong that supply bottlenecks could begin to appear. These, however, could be eased by an appropriate adjustment of fiscal policy. The nub of the problem, as ever, was how to get a depreciation of this amount under the prevailing international monetary system.

The Chancellor showed no greater an inclination to accept the logic of the argument than he had on earlier occasions—indeed he gave the impression that he was less certain than ever about devaluation[123] and to be fair he was not persuaded that the authorities had the instruments to achieve the end that was thought necessary. Moreover an engineered depreciation, if it could be brought about, would add to inflationary pressures and make the pay policy even more difficult to stick; it would certainly put at risk the programme of external financing on which we heavily depended. The Chancellor was sceptical that an improvement in price competitiveness of the amount that officials had in mind would bring about the improvement in the trade balance which the Treasury model predicted. In the jargon of economics, he did not accept the price elasticities for imports and exports which the Treasury economists were using. In this, as we shall see, he had an important ally in the Overseas Director of the Bank of England. The Treasury felt that the Chancellor should acquaint his ministerial colleagues with the seriousness of the economic situation, not least to forestall any pressure for premature reflation which could well develop over the winter months. Accordingly a Cabinet

[122] The 7.5% depreciation would have to be additional to the depreciation assumed in the forecast, which was of an amount which would preserve the UK's competitiveness throughout the forecast period.
[123] T 277/3058—PCC (75)100 and DW 013 28 October.

paper was prepared on the forecast,[124] although how it would deal with the sensitive matter of the exchange rate was something which exercised everybody. In the event the paper glossed over this issue by talking of depreciation as 'a feature of the situation largely determined by external events'—a Panglossian view which had hardly been borne out by events over the past two years.[125]

Within the Treasury itself, however, the serious issue was to decide on what specifically could be done to obtain the devaluation it wanted. The policy of 'gradualism'—simply waiting on events—had not achieved anything significant in the way of improved competitiveness, but that was partly because, whenever there had been a bear attack on sterling, the Bank—with Treasury approval—had intervened by buying it to shore up confidence. The Treasury now looked at what was described as a 'clean float', that is the exchange rate for sterling would simply be left to market forces and the authorities would broadly accept whatever they produced, although the *caveat* was made that decisions on what to do in any particular exchange market situation would be decided *ad hoc*. What a 'clean float' would actually entail was not seriously considered. How should the Bank react when a public sector borrower offered it the dollars it had raised on the market? Should it sell them immediately or peddle them out over a period? Or should it simply take them into the reserves? Again, how should the Bank respond to a request from a sterling area central bank for dollars? All these issues would have to be resolved if the concept of a 'clean float' were to be put into practice. They were not systematically looked at then or later.

The whole issue of the economic outlook and the options for dealing with it were discussed at a meeting the Chancellor had with his advisers on 28 October when the question of bringing his Cabinet colleagues into his confidence at the 6 November Cabinet was raised. There was clearly value in making the Cabinet aware of the seriousness of the plight the UK was in and showing why options such as a reflation of domestic demand was precluded by both the fiscal position and the external situation. The Cabinet discussion was described in the section on public expenditure and revealed considerable anxiety among Ministers at the course of events and we need not repeat the account here. The Chancellor's views, as we saw, eventually prevailed and by a small minority it was agreed to do no more than return to the issue of 'reflation' in the New Year. With the Cabinet discussion out of the way and the Chancellor still agnostic about action on the exchange rate, the Treasury came back to him in a long and seminally important submission on 21 November.[126] After a rehearsal of the salient issues facing him the minute stated that:

---

[124] T 277/3058—PCC (75)99.   [125] CAB 128/185/14.
[126] T 277/3059—PCC (75)103 Revise.

if trade restrictions are to be ruled out...the choice presented by the forecast in its starkest terms seems to us to be the familiar one of devaluation and deflation. At our present level of competitiveness we cannot balance our external books at full employment....It is of course possible that a prolonged period of heavy unemployment would provide the environment in which we would become more competitive on non-price grounds. Delivery performance might improve. Strikes might diminish. The average quality of our products might get better as the marginally inferior production was cut out. At best this would take time. At worst it might not occur. High unemployment in Northern Ireland and in the Scottish Central Belt has not led to superior industrial performance there—rather the reverse....We would all naturally prefer to take the route of a successful counter-inflation policy. But we have assumed in the forecast a degree of success [an 8 per cent norm in 1976–77] which, given the price outlook, begins to strain credulity...to achieve what we want we would have to think of a norm of one-half the assumed amount.

The paper went on to address the three questions posed by the Chancellor in earlier discussions:

1 Does depreciation, even in the longer term, improve the current balance?
2 How do we deal with the financing problem created by the J-curve (i.e. the fact that in the short-term following a devaluation we should need to borrow *more*, not less)?
3 How do we deal with the RPI effects of a lowering of the sterling rate?

The Treasury assembled some formidable empirical evidence on the first issue, citing several pieces of academic research as well as a study by the IMF and an examination of the experience of the behaviour of exports and imports following the 1967 devaluation. It also quoted the findings of CBI surveys of the experience of exporters in finding the competitiveness of their prices to be the determining factor governing the securing of orders. On the second issue, the Treasury argued that if overseas creditors saw that we had a credible path for the elimination of the current deficit we should not have too much difficulty in meeting our borrowing needs. And on the third question, perhaps the most difficult of the examination paper, the Treasury suggested that, provided something more could be found in the way of savings than had been achieved so far in 1976–77, it might be possible to offer wage-earners some *douceur* in the Budget of 1976 to offset the rigours of a strong Incomes Policy for the next wage round. The idea floated, which, as we shall see, took hold in the following Spring, was to offer some income tax concessions in the field of personal allowances which might be conditional on the acceptance of a new and demanding norm.

The problem, however, was the outlook for public sector borrowing, which, as the forecast had shown, would remain stubbornly at the level of £12 billion for three years. Quite apart from the difficulty of borrowing on this scale in a way which did not substantially increase the money supply, we could expect the IMF, with whom, as we shall see, the Treasury was now in discussion over the drawing that was being sought, to demand some firm commitment on the PSBR for the next financial year, 1976–77.

If we have to provide revalorisation [of tax allowances] as a condition for securing a second round of pay policy and this were not found by offsetting savings [in public expenditure] we should have to publish at the time of the Budget a figure substantially higher than that given to the IMF. A revalorisation which fully restored the real value of allowances to that given a year ago for the whole range of incomes would cost £1,200 million in 1976–77 and over £1,500 million in 1977–78. We see no prospect of that being afforded.

There was therefore no escaping looking at public expenditure again, and the submission examined how savings of £1.5 billion might be achieved the following year, 1976–77. The shopping list produced by the Treasury was heterogeneous in character. The qualifying requirement seems to have been a mixture of political acceptability and relevance, or lack of it, to the economic needs of the country. For instance the question of proceeding with the public ownership of the Aircraft and Shipbuilding industries and of the Ports was questioned even though they had formed part of the Labour Party's manifesto. The submission of 21 November, with its voluminous annexes and appendices was followed by a meeting on 27 November between the Chancellor and the Permanent Secretary,[127] who reported to his colleagues:

that in long talk he had with the Chancellor it had become clear that [he] had ruled out DELVE [the code word for the exercise on import controls mentioned above] and now saw the choice for policy as lying between doing nothing, which risked a deflation enforced by our creditors, and depreciating the exchange rate, which held out some hope of our retaining some control over economic management, although, as officials had made clear, it was far from certain of success. But the Chancellor was now considering how he might obtain the agreement of his colleagues to the latter course, and this was encouraging. He was grateful that he would not be rushed into a decision.

At this meeting the Chancellor asked for a more exhaustive combing of possible expenditure cuts that had low resource content. There was a brief reference to the negotiations then going on between Treasury officials and the IMF team in London about a drawing on the Fund's resources and the Chancellor's attention was drawn to the fact that the draft 'letter of intent' would be a formidable obstacle to his reflating the economy in the Spring. On Incomes Policy, an issue touched on in the memorandum of 21 November, the Chancellor said that 'he by no means ruled out a very low norm for the 1976–77 pay round', a comment which encouraged the Prices and Incomes Group to prepare a paper suggesting a 3 per cent norm (see below).

---

[127] DW 015.

The Chancellor's willingness to contemplate some action on the exchange rate—a move he had resisted on almost every occasion that it had been raised since the first submission in June 1974—led to the Treasury having a high level meeting with the Bank to establish whether a consensus on exchange rate policy could be achieved. The Bank had not been directly involved in the preparation of the submission of 21 November, but they had been sent a copy and were invited to a meeting to discuss points of difference on 1 December.

The Governor explained at the outset of this meeting[128] that 'the views of the Bank did not entirely coincide' and this became very clear as the meeting progressed. The chief dissenter from the Treasury position was the Overseas Director, who was very doubtful about the efficacy of an exchange rate depreciation in securing an improvement in the current balance, was fearful about the effect on the sterling balance holders and thought that the internal price effects would lead to a rise in pay claims. He questioned the empirical evidence produced by the Treasury about the price elasticities of exports and said that German and American experience pointed in the opposite direction to that of the findings quoted by the Treasury. The Deputy Governor shared the anxiety about the sterling balances, although the Treasury Overseas Finance head argued that confidence would be strengthened if the policies to reduce inflation were working and efforts to contain public expenditure were being made. Not all the Bank representatives seemed to share the doubts of the Deputy Governor and the Overseas Director about the wisdom of an engineered depreciation and the discussion then turned to the modalities by which, if a depreciation were to be sought, it could be achieved—an issue which had been stubbornly unresolved throughout the eighteen months that action on the exchange rate had been debated. The Bank argued that a reduction in the uncovered differential (i.e. the difference between short-term interest rates in London and New York) would be required 'and sales of sterling [by the Bank] to offset more off-market intervention'. The latter comment was a reference to the fact that the Bank frequently supplied dollars from the EEA (effectively its own resources) to sterling area central banks who wanted them and subsequently replenished the reserves when market conditions were propitious by market sales of sterling. What the Bank were now saying was that the replenishment could be more aggressive and could be carried out with less regard for the effects on the sterling rate. This comment was to resonate on 4 March the following year when the market activities of the Bank were, rightly or wrongly, thought to be driven by precisely this purpose. This issue is addressed more fully in the next chapter.

At the 1 December meeting, however, the Bank did not favour this approach. Asked to say what their prescription would be, they said that if action

---

[128] DW 015.

were required (and they were not at all sure that it was) it would be best to have an external policy 'that could be publicly stated...perhaps a step-devaluation accompanied by firm action on counter inflation and public expenditure as in 1968 and as in the French case'. The Bank doubted whether the Treasury approach of easing the rate down would achieve what was wanted. 'Three and a half years of floating offered little firm evidence to support the Treasury's recommendations'. The Treasury acknowledged this and said that simply allowing the pound to fall only in line with the fall in competitiveness would not close the deficit until 1982 and there had to be doubts whether the accumulating deficit could be financed. 'Moreover repayment of the debt incurred would wipe out the gain from the North Sea'.

The issue of the external balance was thus as unresolved as it had ever been, but it was now becoming apparent that differences were opening up both between the Bank and the Treasury and to some extent within each institution. There was not very much difference in the analysis of the problem, but judgement about the risks and the feasibility of any proposed solution (or what purported to be a solution) was not uniform; and the debate was made more confused by the absence of any hard empirical evidence to support the arguments of the different advocates. This issue is also examined in greater detail in the next chapter.

The Chancellor had not been satisfied with the assessment he had been given in October of the financing outlook for 1976 (referred to above) and had asked for something more specific. The Overseas Division accordingly produced a slightly more quantified appraisal in early December.[129] In 1975 the deficit had been reduced by a number of factors and it had been financed by a combination of foreign borrowing, both bilaterally and on the Euro-markets, and some drawing down of the reserves. In 1976 this could be repeated and, in addition, provided the current application to the IMF went through the UK, would have the benefit of the Fund drawing (about £1 billion). The Permanent Secretary in putting this to the Chancellor on 29 November[130] acknowledged that the assessment might be too qualitative for his comfort, but urged him to wait until the full assessment which would be made in February and would have the benefit of the findings of Treasury officials in the course of their planned visits to sterling holders overseas.

The year ended with an important meeting that the Chancellor called of all his Treasury ministerial colleagues and officials as well as the leading players in the Bank on 16 December.[131] The Chancellor said at the outset that he was not prepared to take a decision on a policy of accelerated depreciation 'until he

---

[129] DW 015.   [130] Ibid.   [131] Ibid.

had seen the results of the work he had commissioned[132] on the profile of the economy under various exchange rate options (which) would not be finished until the latter part of January... in addition he would want to see the NIF which would be available in February.' In the meantime he gave his preliminary reactions to the Treasury prescription. His immediate concern was that if we embarked on a policy of accelerated depreciation we might have to seek further assistance from the IMF (in addition to the Oil facility and first Credit tranche drawing then under negotiation) and this would involve deflating the economy. The options open to him seemed to be:

1 accelerated depreciation;
2 deflation;
3 a severe Incomes Policy;
4 import controls.

He would not, however, move his present policies in the direction of any of these options 'unless he was convinced that it would improve our economic prospects... he thought that there had been a change in the attitude of working people towards the country's economic problems and this meant that options in the Incomes Policy area which had previously been thought impracticable were not inconceivable.... But it would not be possible to get acceptance of such a policy unless it could be presented as a full economic strategy aimed at improving our economic performance over the next 4 or 5 years... He would start talking to the TUC about these matters in January.... The TUC (rightly or wrongly) would require a policy to bring down unemployment faster than presently forecast *as a key to the whole matter*. Without this he saw little hope of achieving an Incomes Policy norm of under 10%.... His preference among the options outlined was to go for a low norm in the next round.'

The Chancellor had thus backtracked from his earlier view that the options were only between depreciation and deflation. What he was now saying was that his main aim was to reduce wage settlements and the key to this was to attack unemployment at least as a medium-term aim. He had, by then, accepted that the economy could not be stimulated by increasing domestic demand, that is through tax cuts or expenditure increases. The logic of his position had to be that the external balance needed to be improved both to reduce our financing requirements and to increase demand. This was at heart the nub of the official Treasury's position, but at least officials recognized that this meant (in the absence of direct action on imports) some action on the exchange rate—something the Chancellor could not, yet at any rate, accept.

---

[132] The main work requested by the Chancellor was on the financing of the deficit, a Bank of England appraisal of the risks of dislodging the sterling balances and the question of using the Public Sector Deficit alongside the PSBR when publicizing the Government's borrowing needs. He also wanted a Treasury comment on a note of dissent to the Treasury's recommendation by his special adviser Lord Kaldor.

This was to become the core of the final Treasury recommendation in February which we discuss in the next chapter.

The IMF

Drawing on some of the available facilities at the IMF had, as related in the section on the external financing requirement, become an imperative as the balance of payments prospect emerged in the course of 1975 and the issue was brought to a head at an internal Treasury meeting on 1 September.[133] Treasury ministers and officials took several opportunities during the year to give tentative notice to the Fund that the UK would probably be making a request for a 'routine' drawing on its credit entitlements, that is one not involving a major review of economic policy. The facilities available to the UK were access to its credit tranches of which there were four each of SDR700[134] million and— if need could be proved—of an unspecified but large amount of the Oil Facility. The latter was an arrangement, established in June 1974 (and renewed in April 1975) whereby those member states which had experienced a sharp fall in their reserves as a result of the increased costs of imported oil could apply for help from the Fund, the latter raising the necessary funds principally from the oil exporting countries. The scheme was, in effect, a recycling of the oil surpluses to the worst affected deficit countries and was an arrangement on the lines which the Chancellor had been urging on the international community since he took office. The conditionality applied to drawings under the facility were minimal—the chief requirement being that need had to be shown. The facility was an *ad hoc* arrangement and applied only to applications made before March 1976; so if the UK wished to avail itself of this opportunity the application had to be made soon—and before the resources raised from the oil exporting countries were exhausted. Access to the credit tranches—the more normal route for obtaining Fund help—was laid down in a number of Fund decisions, but essentially the understanding was that the first credit tranche was made available with the minimum of conditions—usually the observance of the Fund's rules on trade and exchange restrictions and some acceptable statement of intent on the part of the applicant that it was pursuing appropriate (and if necessary) remedial policies. The judgement of the Treasury during 1975 was that the UK would be able to demonstrate need for access to the Oil Facility and would not have to give many undertakings or change the broad thrust of economic policy to obtain the first credit tranche. Given the imprecise nature of the size and availability of the Oil Facility, the total credit available to the UK under these fairly lenient arrangements could

---

[133] DW 062.   [134] At the time 1 SDR was equivalent to about £0.57.

not be precisely quantified in advance of negotiations, but it seemed that something like £1 billion might be borrowed.[135]

The Fund had sent a routine mission to London in May to review British policies and to examine any restrictions on trade or payments which might be held to be in breach of the Fund's Articles. But before this mission arrived, the Managing Director of the Fund, Dr Witteveen, had paid a call on the Chancellor at the beginning of April.[136] This was just before the Chancellor opened his Budget, but he decided to take Witteveen into his confidence and reveal the main measures being taken. Witteveen's reaction was broadly that although the Chancellor was moving in the right direction in seeking to contain the PSBR he was worried that the forecast for 1975–76 would still be about £1 billion more than 1974–75. But his main concern was the level of inflation (the meeting was of course before the new pay policy had been put into effect) and although he thought that the deflation implied by the Budget would help, he believed that a wages policy was necessary and he suggested that the trade unions should be confronted with the consequences of excessive wage claims. There was also a brief discussion about possible import restrictions, on which Witteveen spoke strongly, arguing that such a move would be very unfortunate and could be damaging to confidence. The Chancellor gave the first intimation of a possible approach to the Fund for a drawing on both the oil facility and the first credit tranche. Witteveen made it clear that the Fund would expect to see 'a significant start in reducing the PSBR'. He also said that he was 'not happy with the public expenditure projections in the recent White Paper and hoped that it would be possible to make reductions in 1975–76'. The Chancellor replied that his focus in the Budget was on reducing expenditure in 1976–77, although these 'could involve consequential reductions in the earlier year'. There was a brief reference to the Fund's attitude to DCE, when Witteveen said that this 'was an important indicator for the Fund, because it was one which was generally applicable to member countries. But he would not say at this stage if the Fund would place more weight on DCE or the money supply'. The question of UK competitiveness came up when he commented that the exchange rate would have to compensate for the anticipated adverse effects of the rate of inflation. He said that he would prefer to see a gradual move in the exchange rate rather than a step-change, which would disturb confidence. The authorities 'would no doubt use interest rates to produce the necessary compensating movement in the exchange rate'.

The meeting, although relatively informal and non-committal on both sides, provided each with some useful information about the likely stance of the other if there were to be negotiations. The Chancellor's meeting with the

---

[135] In a submission dated 23 October the Treasury thought that the drawing might be composed of SDR 1 billion from the oil facility and SDR 0.7 billion from the first credit tranche making SDR 1.7 billion equivalent to £975 million—IM 38/268/01.

[136] DW 062.

Managing Director was complemented by a meeting two weeks later between the Permanent Secretary and the Head of the European Department at the Fund (Alan Whittome).[137] This covered much the same ground on issues such as public expenditure and borrowing but on the exchange rate Whittome said that 'a policy of gradually floating the exchange rate downwards was the best way of securing a depreciation if it were feasible.... He had in the course of 1974 thought that a step-change... warranted serious consideration because the pound seemed stuck at too high a level... but this was no longer the case.' As to conditions which might be sought for a drawing on the Fund, Whittome said that the Fund did not have a firm position on DCE. Several other medium-sized countries might already have accepted the use of DCE in Fund negotiations, but he added that DCE would not be a performance test as such but would form part of the package of assurances that borrowing countries were required to give.

These meetings were followed in early May by the formal Article VIII consultations. These added little of substance to what had emerged from the informal discussions described above. The Fund team echoed the concern of their senior management at the level of wage inflation in the UK and at the sustainability of the path of public spending outlined in the White Paper and amended in the Budget. They sounded a strong warning against a resort to general trade restrictions but took no firm position on the question of what measures the UK should take to improve the current balance apart from making sure that resources required to do this should not be pre-empted by domestic users (notably the public sector). There was some exploratory talk about the new IMF Oil Facility, when the Fund representatives observed that contributions to it were coming in slowly: 'If both Italy and the UK sought to borrow there might be a scramble', and the Treasury was advised not to rush things.[138]

There were further intermittent and informal meetings between UK Ministers and officials and the Fund during the course of the year. The Chancellor saw Witteveen at the end of August during the Annual Meeting of the Fund[139] by which time of course the new and firm Incomes Policy was in place. Witteveen again raised the issue of the exchange rate saying allusively that 'the exchange rate must go down when inflation is higher than elsewhere'. The Chancellor said that a decision whether to seek a drawing from the Fund would be taken by October. Witteveen commented that the UK would have to show a convincing case of balance of payments need to have access to the Oil Facility and pointed out that the Italian application for a drawing had attracted criticism on the grounds that Italy did not have a serious financing difficulty.

---

[137] DW 062.   [138] Ibid.   [139] Ibid.

In late August there was an exploratory meeting in Washington between two UK officials and the Fund staff to discuss hypothetically some of the technical issues that would have to be settled before a drawing could be made. But it was emphasized throughout the contacts that any decision to seek Fund assistance could only be taken by Ministers collectively. The Chancellor clearly felt that since he might have to give some undertakings about future policy, even if he did not have to make any policy changes as a condition of a drawing, he would need the acquiescence of his colleagues and of course of the Prime Minister. In the event the Chancellor took the opportunity of the Cabinet on 6 November to inform them that, in view of the financing problem, he had decided to ask the Fund for a drawing on the Oil Facility and of the first credit tranche. No policy changes would be involved. The Cabinet did not demur. The timing of the drawing raised some interesting issues. The UK wanted to make an application for the 1975 Oil Facility in good time before it expired and in order to bolster an already fragile external financial position. On the other hand the public expenditure survey would not be completed much before the end of November, and it was likely, given what Witteveen had said, that the outcome would be of major interest to the Fund. Another reason for avoiding delay was that an agreement with the Fund would have given some assurance to other external creditors and sterling holders that UK policy was satisfactory and might well therefore act as a catalyst for further finance. In the event the timing proved to be awkward for both parties. The Fund devoted a good deal of attention to the level of future public spending and their demands were made when the outcome of the public expenditure round was still problematic. The Treasury had to negotiate in a state of some uncertainty as to whether Ministers collectively would agree to the figures for the cuts in the focus year of the Survey (1978–79) both in principle and in terms of specific action. A second complicating factor was that the Fund were insistent on the UK committing itself not to introduce trade restrictions and although there was no problem with the general principle, the discussions came to a head just as Ministers were poised to impose quantitative controls on the import of passenger cars in the wake of the decision of the Chrysler Corporation to close their UK plant and supply the UK market from other European plants. We discuss these issues in more detail later.

The main concern among UK officials in the run-up to the Fund negotiations was whether the Fund would demand stringent conditions about import restraints—not just generalized restraints, but those of a selective kind as well. The Chancellor had accepted that generalized import controls were not an option, but the position of Ministers generally and of Fund officials towards limited and selective import restraints was less clear. These would not be for balance of payments reasons but would be to help particular industries which might be in temporary difficulties. When the question of the likely attitude of the Fund to trade restrictions was raised in the routine May consultations, the

Fund staff had simply said the UK 'would have to be abiding by the terms of the 1974 Communique'.[140]

In late October when the idea of a Fund drawing had become a firm proposition the British Director at the IMF had a talk with both the Managing Director and the senior staff. It emerged that although 'at the meeting between the Chancellor and Witteveen on 31 August the former had convinced him fully of our case . . . since then there have developed doubts especially over the PSBR and public expenditure'. Witteveen followed this up with a personal letter to the Chancellor[141] stating that the avoidance of import restrictions was an important issue as were 'policies to produce a viable balance of payments in the medium-term' as well as the outlook for the PSBR. He said that he was worried about the apparent change in the emphasis of UK policies with respect to import restrictions and public expenditure. On the latter point he was repeating what he had said in April and implicitly referring to the several additions to spending programmes that had been made during the year.[142] A few days later the Fund staff told the UK Director in Washington that they would want, in addition to the issues raised by the Managing Director, to talk about monetary policy and exchange rate policy.[143]

The formal negotiations did not take place until the middle of November, but before that there was an informal meeting of Treasury officials and Fund staff in Paris on 1 and 2 November[144] and the Chancellor had a personal meeting with Dr Witteveen over dinner on 3 November.[145] There were clearly some tensions on both occasions. At the Paris meeting the Fund staff were much exercised by the revised figures of the October financial forecast which they had been given and which showed a PSBR of £12.0 billion for the current year (1975–76) and £12.5 billion for the following year. They 'were unhappy about the estimate for 1976–77 on two counts. In resource terms they thought it would be necessary to bring down the PSBR very rapidly if it was not to pre-empt resources for investment and the balance of payments in the later years . . . their other concern about the PSBR in 1976–77 was its implication for DCE, liquidity and interest rates which might be so high that they had an undesirable effect on the exchange rate.' They noted that expenditure growth for 1975–76 (following the very large increase for the previous year) would be 4.4 per cent and for the following year 2.8 per cent. They gave notice that they would want some specific assurances from the Chancellor about the PSBR after 1976–77. On the balance of payments they concluded from the financial forecast that there should be a substantial downward adjustment of the

---

[140] The Rome Communiqué of January 1974 referred to in Chapter 2.
[141] GEP 9/29/01.
[142] Since the White Paper of February there had been increases for 1976–77 of £750 million for British Leyland, £150 million for food and housing subsidies and £460 million for the package of measures designed to support the Incomes Policy announced in July.
[143] IM 38/268/01.   [144] T 371/23.   [145] GEP 9/29/01.

exchange rate. In terms which might have been lifted from papers the Treasury were themselves putting to the Chancellor at that very moment, they said 'No other course could reduce unemployment and bring about the structural improvement that was needed in the balance of payments'. They added that 'despite the difficulties a substantial real depreciation was needed'. The Fund also raised the question of import controls on which the possibility of action to protect specific industries was noted. But 'they hoped...that we were not thinking of cars'—as of course at that very moment that is precisely what we were doing.

At the Chancellor's private dinner with Witteveen on 3 November the discussion was very frank. The Chancellor asked whether the Managing Director thought that an application by the British Government would be likely to succeed. If he did, he would seek the approval of his colleagues at the Cabinet later in the week. Witteveen countered by saying that it was 'essential to secure cuts in public expenditure which would produce substantial reductions in the PSBR over the next few years.' He hoped that the Chancellor would be able to prevent any increase in the PSBR in 1976–77. The Chancellor made it plain that 'his colleagues would not be prepared to make changes of policy beyond what was implied by his own proposals'—a reference to what he was currently seeking from them in the expenditure round under progress. He revealed that he was aiming at a reduction of £3.75 billion in the focus year 1978–79 in comparison with the White Paper figures (as increased by subsequent decisions). There would actually be a fall in spending in 1977–78 as well as a fall in the following year; and there would be some feedback into programmes for 1976–77—the year which clearly worried Witteveen. The Chancellor said that he would aim for a PSBR of £12 billion in that year, 'but would not tie myself to it'. On the balance of payments Witteveen repeated what the Fund staff had said—there was a need for a real depreciation, although he conceded that for practical reasons 'any move needed to be gradual'. He added that the Fund practice in granting facilities to members was that although exchange rate policy was not explicitly the subject of conditions 'there was a form of words in Fund papers to indicate that the Managing Director had been given reassurances on exchange rate policies'. What was perhaps the most significant issue to be raised was the likelihood of the UK imposing selective import controls. The Chancellor referred to the pressure on the Government by the TUC and the CBI to protect certain vulnerable industries. The Chancellor assured Witteveen that they 'would only be considered when there was a strong case and no likelihood of significant retaliation'. Witteveen said that he must continue to advise against them. What was in the minds of both participants at this stage was that the UK might impose import controls on certain textiles under the international Multifibre Agreement. This would not have pleased the Fund, but it was not likely to be an insuperable obstacle to a Fund drawing. However, unbeknown to the Chancellor, the Prime Minister had that very day been approached by the President of the Chrysler Corporation and had had a meeting with him at Chequers where the news broke that Chrysler were going to close its entire UK operation with the loss of 27,000 jobs. This development was to raise an issue of substance during the whole of the run-up to the signature of the Letter of Application, for one option that had to be considered by the government was whether there should be any response by the Government which would have led to difficulties with the Fund.

When the formal negotiations began on 12 November, a good deal of the groundwork had already been covered in the informal discussions. Some considerable time was taken up with the form of the application, for example whether there should be two full letters of application for the Oil Facility and the First Credit Purchase, whether the latter should be a drawing or a standby and a lot of time was spent on a discussion of the timing of the announcement of the drawings and of the Board meeting. But on the substance of the negotiations it turned out that there were problems only with the nature of the British commitments on public expenditure and the question of selective import controls. For the rest the Fund accepted the general stance of policy. When the leader of the IMF team saw the Permanent Secretary on 13 November he said that he did not think that the PSBR 'would present insuperable problems' and he was fairly undemanding about commitments on the exchange rate.[146]

On public expenditure the Fund were unwilling to conclude the negotiations until Ministers had firmly committed themselves to a programme of cuts in the focus year (1978–79). They resigned themselves to what officials said was the likely level of spending in previous years and accepted the level of the PSBR that went with it. But the programme of Cabinet meetings on the Survey meant that the letter of application could not be agreed and finalized while the Fund were in London. The initial Cabinet meeting on the size of the cuts to be made took place, as we saw above, on 13 November and although it went well and the Prime Minister secured approval in principle to the level of reductions sought by the Chancellor, the detailed cuts were not agreed. As we saw earlier, there were the usual difficulties in the bilateral negotiations between the Treasury and the spending Ministers which followed and dragged on for over two weeks. By the end of the month the agreed cuts were only £2.75 billion and it had become clear that the British drawing could not be submitted to the Fund Board until the New Year. This did not matter too much provided the Chancellor could make an announcement of the agreed Letter of Intent before the Parliamentary recess. Silence on this matter would have aroused suspicion on the part of markets that the negotiations were not going well. But the level of spending for the focus year was finally fixed on

---

[146] IM 38/268/01.

11 December and the Parliamentary announcement of the application was made on 17 December.

But the other issue which troubled the Fund—selective import controls—was in some ways, and for a time, more worrying. Ministers had been undecided how to respond to the decision of Chrysler to terminate its UK operation—the choices being between doing nothing and accepting the closures, some form of bailing out at public expense and imposing import controls to ensure that the gap created by the ending of the Chrysler operation would not be met by a flood of imports from continental Europe. Neither of the latter two options would be welcomed by the Fund (or indeed by the Treasury) and when Whittome was told on 8 November in the course of the negotiations that import controls on cars was a possibility he immediately alerted Witteveen who sent a personal message to the Chancellor advising strongly against this course and referring to what had been said at the dinner of 3 November.[147] The Chancellor replied on 18 November, saying that the option of import controls was still on the table and this prompted Witteveen to repeat his objections on 22 November. The Chancellor was sufficiently disturbed by the trend of the exchanges to tell officials that 'Chrysler might call in question the whole drawing'. Indeed the Treasury prepared a letter for the Chancellor to send to Witteveen on the assumption that Ministers would opt for temporary import controls on cars. The draft referred to the dilemma that the Chrysler decision placed on Ministers and sought to justify the imposition of quantitative controls on passenger cars on the grounds that a rescue operation would have involved more public expenditure (on which Witteveen was especially sensitive). The Chancellor's difficulties in being more precise about the Government's intentions over the Chrysler development were due to collective Ministerial indecison on the course of action. The Minister responsible for the motor car industry recommended that the closure be accepted but the Prime Minister, the Chancellor, and Lever were opposed, partly on the grounds of the unemployment involved, the cost to the balance of payments and the fact that Chrysler (UK) had in prospect a large contract for the supply of cars to Iran. In the end the Government decided to step in and rescue the company by taking over the company's accumulated losses and adding bank guarantees and government loans at a cost of well over £100 million. The public rescue at least saved the government from having to introduce trade restrictions which might very well have compromised the whole approach to the Fund, for the Board of Directors, many of whom represented countries with large vehicle industries which were in difficulties, would have been bound to raise objections. The rescue was announced in the middle of December and cleared the way to an agreement with the Fund who did not demur at the comparatively minor restrictions on textiles which the UK imposed and also announced in mid-December.

---

[147] IM 38/268/01.

A large part of the negotiations with the Fund turned out to be over the detail of the description of UK policy and the intentions for the future. No binding commitments were sought, but the Chancellor was pressed to allow some mention of the intention to reduce public expenditure (as given in the White Paper) by £3.75 billion in 1978–79. He was not able to do this as the detailed decisions on how this figure should be achieved had not been reached when the Letter of Intent was finally agreed. The issue was resolved by the statement that public expenditure would be no higher in 1977–78 and 1978–79 than in 1976–77. But the staff paper which went to the Fund Board (and was not published) contained the statement that 'the authorities have decided on substantial reductions (of) . . . approximately £3.5 billion'—this being the figure which the Chancellor felt reasonably certain he would secure. The letter contained a reference to a target PSBR of £12 billion for 1976–77 as the Fund wanted, even though the Treasury forecast was that on existing policy it would be £12.5 billion. The Fund pressed for a reference to the likely growth of DCE over the following eighteen months and the annual rate of £9 billion was agreed and inserted in the letter; but it was not a commitment. The Chancellor added that 'I am ready to make further use of the monetary instruments available . . . in order to ensure that monetary policy continues to support the achievement of the Government's overall economic objectives'. Given that monetary policy had hardly made any contribution to the management of the economy in the previous eighteen months (and was unlikely to do so in the immediate future), this was by way of ritual incantation only.

One of the worries the Treasury had during the negotiations was the fact that at the Cabinet discussion of economic strategy on 6 November (before the formal Fund negotiations began) 'it had been agreed that there would be a further discussion of the possibility of *general reflation* early in the New Year' (italics added). Such a possibility did not sit easily with the statements of intent that the Chancellor was being asked to make to the Fund and, when the Fund negotiations were nearing completion, the Treasury invited him to consider the extent to which the draft Letter of Intent 'might be thought to limit his freedom of manoeuvre'. They warned him in a minute dated 3 December[148] to look with particular care at the reference to the borrowing requirement (£12 billion) and to safeguard himself against the possible criticism from his colleagues that the issue to be discussed in the New Year has been materially compromised'. At the meeting to consider this advice on 8 December the Chancellor asked officials to examine the reference to the PSBR in 1976–77 'to see if the words would be compatible with modest reflation in next year's Budget costing say £1 billion on the PSBR'. In the event the letter left a loophole for the Chancellor by stating that 'in the absence of an *unexpected* change in the timing and strength of economic recovery this implies a

---

[148] GEP 9/29/01.

PSBR in money terms in 1976–77 no more than the level for 1975–76' (italics added).

The Letters of Application for both the Oil and first credit tranche facilities were signed and dated 17 December and were published the same day. On that day too there was a Parliamentary debate on the economic situation and the Chancellor announced the import restrictions that had been decided on for certain textiles. The Fund Board met on 31 December and agreed to the UK request. There was little criticism and indeed some European members expressed satisfaction that the Oil Facility had been made available to a developed country and was thus not to be regarded as the preserve of the developing countries.

The negotiations of November and December were, in spite of the occasional *contretemps*, not in fact very demanding of the UK and the relative easiness with which the Fund agreed to the drawing was a reflection of the fact that it was only in respect of the Oil Facility and the first Credit Tranche, for neither of which did the Fund rules and practices require demanding conditions. But the negotiations did provide both participants with the benefit of a rehearsal for the much more difficult negotiations which were to take place a year later when the UK sought to make a much larger drawing and one which went well into the credit tranches of an enlarged Fund capital. The experience of 1975 led Treasury officials to have no illusions that a further drawing would involve a much more rigorous examination of British policy and the assumption of commitments which might present serious problems for Ministers. The Fund's preoccupation with the level of public expenditure, with the borrowing requirement, and the competitiveness of the exchange rate left no one in Whitehall about where the focus of attention would be.

Summary

The year therefore concluded on a somewhat uncertain note. The IMF application had not been formally approved by the Executive Board, but there was no reason to suppose that it would not go through. The financing outlook was reasonably assured in the short term. The position on inflation was encouraging. The pay rules were being respected by member unions of the TUC. But the public finances were still a source of concern to those who had to present British policy to potential creditors, and the commitment to a containment of public spending was well into the future—the spending plans for 1976–77 and the following year, given the additions that had been made during the course of the year, were hardly stringent. The UK still depended critically upon the world creditors having confidence in its economic prospects and the outlook for the raising of more external credit was uncertain. Creditors were concerned how the Government handled the sensitive question of controlling public expenditure and borrowing, whether it could sustain the success of the Incomes Policy in its first year and whether it was doing something to correct its huge balance of payments deficit. The Governor made one of his periodic complaints to the Prime Minister about the level of expenditure in mid-November when the Chancellor was still struggling to get his colleagues to agree to his proposals.[149] The expenditure issue had been settled for the time being on the conclusion of the Expenditure Survey round at the Cabinet discussion on 11 December, and it budgeted for a growth in spending of less than 3.5 per cent between the current financial year and 1978–79—an annual average of 0.8 per cent. But as we shall see in the next chapter, when the White Paper embodying the Cabinet's decisions was published in February, it was not well received by the financial commentators and indeed when the 1976 Survey came to be prepared, the Treasury sharply revised its assumptions of economic growth which had underlain the 1975 Survey. But the most intractable issue of all was the exchange rate. Sterling had begun the year at $2.35 and ended at $2.02—a sizeable depreciation, but, given the differential rate of increase of UK costs over foreign costs—estimated at well over 20 per cent compared with the OECD area as a whole—by not enough to secure the improvement in our external payments that was essential.

Although opinion within Whitehall and the Bank was not uniform, there was a consensus that some depreciation was inevitable. The unresolved question was whether the authorities should just wait for sterling to weaken of its own accord as, sooner or later, it was bound to; or whether because of the extreme uncertainty about when this would happen some positive, but unspecified, action should be taken to bring it about. It was this issue which dominated official thinking in the first two months of the new year. And the issue was still unresolved when events contrived to solve it for us.

[149] IM 34/5/01—the Chancellor observed on his own copy of the minutes of the meeting that the Governor had got the figures wrong.

4

1976 Part 1—The Markets Take Over

The Chancellor's policy questioned

The most important operational task confronting the Treasury in the early months of 1976, as in earlier years, was to offer advice on the structure and content of the Budget for the financial year 1976–77. But before that there was some political undergrowth to be cleared. Cabinet had, at its meeting on 6 November, decided to have a further discussion 'in the new year' of the issues of reflation and the balance of payments, two items on which some of the Chancellor's colleagues had decided views. The Treasury, mindful of the commitment to the IMF on the size of the borrowing requirement for 1976–77, advised the Chancellor to put in a paper opposing any suggestion of reflation and urging his colleagues to accept that the way forward was to continue broadly with the existing policy and make every effort to secure a satisfactory norm for the pay round beginning in July.[1] The Chancellor agreed, but decided that the appropriate forum for such a discussion would be MES, the small Ministerial Committee of heavyweights rather than the full Cabinet where the November conclusion had been reached. He also decided on a more emollient paper than the one the Treasury had proposed and put this to MES on 29 January.[2] While acknowledging that unemployment was continuing to rise, the paper said that early measures to reflate the economy would have little impact on the immediate outlook, and for the longer term there was an expectation that the upswing in the world economy would help to achieve his aim to reduce unemployment to 3 per cent by 1979. In the meantime while he would be prepared to agree to some micro-economic measures to help with the employment situation, including selective import controls, the Chancellor said he was firmly against general import restrictions. The discussion of the Chancellor's paper on 3 February[3] was on predictable lines. The balance of payments,

---

[1] DW 047 21 January.   [2] CAB 134/4048—MES (76)12.
[3] Ibid—MES (76) 2nd Conclusions.

and the restrictions it placed on policy options generally, was an important theme of the discussion, although the Chancellor showed a sympathy with the plight of particular industries and expressed a willingness to allocate resources temporarily to help them. A minority of Ministers took issue with the Chancellor and argued vigorously for a system of generalized import restrictions, much being made of the high risks involved in the Chancellor's rather anodyne prescription of an uncertain path of sterling depreciation. The Prime Minister decided that the Committee should return to this issue on the basis of a paper the Chancellor was asked to circulate on the balance of payments generally. This was not particularly what the Treasury wanted, but the need for it was established when on 17 February the Trade Secretary (Shore), who had been arguing for some sort of trade restrictions even at the Cabinet on 6 November, circulated a letter to the Committee making a case for a system of import controls based on a freezing of the imports of consumer goods and semi-manufactures at the 1975 level until 1980. This he argued could be obtained under Article XII of the GATT which permitted restrictions for balance of payments purposes.

The timing of this development presented something of a problem for the Chancellor and the Treasury, for they were getting involved in Budget preparations and the possibility of some fundamental change of policy in the run-up to the Budget was decidedly unwelcome. The problem was partly dealt with by delaying the paper the Chancellor had been asked to circulate, which was not in fact put to the Committee until 12 March.[4] There was one other advantage in this delay: it enabled the Chancellor to present his colleagues with the NIF which by then had been delivered to him—see later. Although this was not strictly relevant to the case against import controls, which rested on medium-term considerations, it enabled him to present his policy in reasonably optimistic terms, not least because, as we shall see, by 12 March sterling had begun to depreciate and the rather uncertain case for relying on depreciation to deal with the balance of payments problem appeared somewhat more credible. The Chancellor's main argument was of course against import controls both in principle and on international legal grounds—for reasons which had been fully explored in the DELVE exercise of the previous year—but he acknowledged that his own course of action required either a big increase in UK productivity, a strict Incomes Policy or a 'depreciation' of sterling of unspecified amount. His prescription was to seek a low norm in the next pay round and to hope for depreciation. It was not a very precise course, but, given the sensitivity of the subject and the uncertainties, it was about the most he could say. The Committee,[5] which considered the Chancellor's paper and the Shore letter on 17 March, were clearly not

---

[4] CAB 134/4048—MES (76)32.   [5] CAB 134/4048—MES (76) 6th Conclusions.

convinced by the Chancellor's case and the Prime Minister had to concede to the Chancellor's critics a proposal that officials from the departments concerned should carry out a detailed appraisal of the Trade Secretary's suggestion. We return to consider the impact of this further study later in the year (June) when the official report was delivered.

The Budget

The MES discussion had come at an awkward time for the Chancellor for he was already immersed in the preparation of his Budget. This was dominated by one overriding idea: that it should be used as an inducement to the TUC to continue with their policy of laying down a specific figure for the increases in pay which its constituent unions could claim in a second year of Incomes Policy. The norm of £6 for all workers, excepting only the higher-paid, had been widely respected, and by the beginning of 1976 it seemed quite likely that the target of achieving a year-on-year increase in the RPI no higher than 10 per cent by the third quarter of the year would be achieved, or at worst be only narrowly missed. Given that the annual increase in prices a year earlier had been more than double this figure and that with the decline in the external value of sterling raw material prices were increasing quite fast, the success of the policy was remarkable. Indeed its success was noted with admiration by many influential overseas commentators. Arthur Burns, the Chairman of the Federal Reserve Board, who was later in the year to be such a fierce critic of British macro-economic policy, paid the Chancellor a notable compliment in May about the success of the pay policy[6]—he had made the same point to the Permanent Secretary at the time of the 1975 Fund Annual Meeting.[7] Dr Witteveen was equally fulsome. But the policy did impose a significant cut in real income for ordinary people. Moreover unemployment was rising strongly in the winter of 1975–76. To expect the TUC to continue to recommend to their members a period of wage restraint which would impose a further cut in living standards was clearly going to be difficult, however much such restraint would redound to their benefit in the longer run through lower inflation, better export performance, and indeed higher employment.

The policy makers in Whitehall were of course very keen to build on the success of the first year. The Short-Term Economic Policy Committee of Permanent Secretaries (STEP) looked at the implications of a norm for 1976–77 in the range 5–10 per cent in late November 1975.[8] They decided that this was not sufficiently ambitious and that a figure of 3 per cent should be the aim. In

---

[6] IM 34/5/01 17 May 1976.   [7] DW 062 8 September 1975.
[8] STEP (75)23 and STEP (75) 10th Meeting.

the submission made to the Chancellor in late November in connection with a possible depreciation of sterling, the figure of 4 per cent had been used illustratively to show what benefits would flow from a tough policy. The Chancellor himself at first said that he 'by no means ruled out a low norm' but at a meeting with Treasury officials in mid-December he said that he had little hope of a norm under 10 per cent.[9] The TUC were deeply concerned at the trend in unemployment and this made their task of selling to their members an extension of the pay policy politically hazardous. The Chancellor decided that it was important to keep the TUC fully apprised of the constraints under which policy could be made and decided to hold a series of informal dinners with the NEDC Six at which both sides could explore the perceived options. The Prime Minister had in any case said, according to a report given to Treasury officials, at the first meeting of the Cabinet in 1976, that the TUC should be consulted over future public expenditure issues, since, with the hard stance the Government were beginning to take on departmental spending, this too had become a potential area of concern to the unions.

The Chancellor had four informal dinners with the TUC representatives[10] between late January and early March and he was able to make clear his position and the constraints under which he operated. The TUC used the occasions to air their views on the need to protect industries hard-hit by overseas competition and by the world recession. The Chancellor emphasized the need to retain overseas confidence, given the UK's continuing dependence on external credit. The defeat of inflation was an important ingredient in the policy to which he was committed. This meant that he needed continued cooperation in the continuation of pay policy and an acceptance that there was not much he could do to stimulate the economy. The Chancellor did make as much capital as he could out of a decision the Government had reached in January to introduce a limited number of micro-measures, involving the allocation of over £50 million for new industrial schemes, a similar amount on public sector housing, the extension of the Temporary Employment Subsidy Scheme and a measure of job creation. This he duly announced on 12 February[11] in accordance with what he had told MES on 3 February. At the last of the series of meetings on 2 March[12] the Chancellor took head-on the TUC argument that policy should aim to get unemployment down to 600,000 within two years and said that he could only aim at 3 per cent (750,000) by 1979. He also robustly rejected the idea of general import restrictions to protect domestic employment. He had he said studied this issue for over a year and it would simply not be possible to go down this road 'in the present international environment'. On pay restraint the Chancellor floated before the TUC the concept of what he called a 'two stage' Budget in which the

[9] DW 015 16 December 1975.   [10] DW 014—3 February and PCC (76) 3rd Meeting.
[11] *Hansard* 12 February.   [12] PCC (76) 13th Meeting.

second part, involving some personal tax concessions, was strictly conditional on a suitable pay limit to be recommended by the TUC at the meeting of the General Council in June (which would be the occasion for a decision on such a course). Finally the Chancellor stressed the need to improve the UK's competitiveness (to which pay restraint made an important contribution) saying that 'there would have to be some measure of depreciation (of £), but this would only work if the unions did not demand higher wages in compensation . . . he would welcome TUC advice on the best approach to this problem'. Very little in the exchanges at the dinners led to concrete decisions or agreements. But they had the effect of giving the TUC the feeling that their views on economic policy were being listened to and were having some influence on actual decisions. More importantly the TUC were brought face-to-face with the hard choices the Chancellor faced. Although there were some misgivings in the Treasury at the apparent power-sharing that the meetings seemed to involve, the consensual view was that the acquiescence of the TUC in the policy the Government were now following was an important asset.

Against this background the Budget was seen to have an important and unusual role and it is to its construction that we now have to turn. The starting point was, as in previous years, the February NIF,[13] although, in keeping with what the Chancellor had said about the status of the Budget Judgement in his Budget Speech the year before, the financial forecast which followed the NIF was of as much, if not greater, importance than the conventional resource forecast. The outcome of the NIF was highly dependent on two important assumptions, neither of which could be made with any confidence and could not themselves be forecast using the usual econometric techniques. These were the likely outcome of the 1976–77 pay round, where as we have seen the policy makers recognized that the TUC were in the lead, and the path of the sterling exchange rate. The behaviour of the latter over the previous two years had been erratic and unpredictable. Periods of relative stability had been followed by periods of weakness, the two being determined largely by the sentiment of overseas official holders of sterling. The assumptions made by the forecasters in respect of these two variables were the rather formal ones that the pay norm for the period from 1 July would be 8 per cent and that sterling would decline so as to keep UK competitiveness at the level of the first half of 1975. On the basis of these rather arbitrary assumptions, the findings of the forecasters were a mixture of good and bad news. Two elements of demand showed some strength: stockbuilding by business and exports. Both of these were recovering from low levels, but exports were expected to be quite strong as the level of world demand picked up in line with the expected upswing of the world economy. Consequently the deficit forecast for the current balance of payments declined to £1 billion from £1.5 billion in 1975. Personal

---

[13] STEP (76)4.

consumption was expected to decline further (partly because of the success of the pay policy which had the effect of cutting real wages) and both public consumption and public investment would contract over the forecast period in accordance with the profile for public spending set out in the Public Expenditure White Paper (see below). GDP would rise by 2.5 per cent in the year from the second half of 1975. Unemployment, however, would continue to rise, reaching 1.5 million by the end of 1976.

According to the canons of policy making in the past, this forecast might have led to consideration of some stimulatory measures. But this was hardly now an option. The financial forecast pointed to a PSBR of £11.5 billion in 1976–77 rising to £12 billion the following year. The Chancellor had told the IMF in the consultations on the drawing three months earlier that he expected the level in 1976–77 not to exceed £12 billion and this was taken by the Fund as something of a commitment. The forecast pretty well told him that this would be the case on the basis of existing policy. But it hardly permitted any increase. The Treasury put its recommendations to the Chancellor in a minute dated 3 March.[14] Senior officials thought that the economic outlook might not be quite as bad as the forecasters had suggested. Outside forecasts were less gloomy, labour market indicators were improving and business confidence was picking up. The Treasury expressed concern that the Chancellor should not 'be precipitated into an over-response to what is undoubtedly a troubling prediction'. On the other hand, officials recognized that there were dangers in being too cautious. The TUC had made it abundantly clear to the Chancellor in their four informal meetings that they attached the highest importance to policies to reduce unemployment[15] and their commitment to a continuance of the pay policy might be compromised if the Government showed an apparent disregard to the outlook for the labour market. The Treasury, however, recommended that on the basis of a pay norm of 8 per cent there should be no fiscal stimulus in the Budget. The Chancellor was reminded of the events of 1972 when a depressed economy, which was in the process of recovery, was stimulated by an expansionary budget. The world on which we still depended for credit to meet our balance of payments deficit would not be impressed by a soft Budget. The IMF to whom we now had policy obligations would be distinctly 'underwhelmed'.

There was however a qualification—one which had been passing round Whitehall for some time and indeed had been floated at the meeting of MES on 11 February[16] when Ministers had been considering a paper by the

---

[14] PCC (76) 22 and PCC (76) 13th Meeting.

[15] At a meeting the Permanent Secretary had with the General Secretary of the TUC on 8 January the latter said that the TUC had a 'target' of 600,000 for unemployment by 1978—PCC (76) 1st Meeting.

[16] CAB 134/4048—MES (76) 4th Conclusions.

Chancellor on the need to secure a low pay limit for the next pay round. The Permanent Secretary put it thus:

> I would however qualify this advice [for I think that] it would be entirely right to make some substantial income tax concessions if the TUC can be induced to go along with an appreciably lower norm than is assumed in the forecast [8 per cent].

What the Chancellor was advised was that if a norm of 3 per cent could be obtained there would be economic justification in making income tax reductions, through an increase in personal allowances, costing £500 million, or even, to clinch an agreement, £700 million. Income tax cuts of this fairly modest nature would compensate wage earners for the cut in real take-home pay which would be involved in a pay norm of 3 per cent when prices were rising at over 10 per cent. But it was important that the tax reductions should not be granted before the desired low pay norm was agreed and formally recommended to its members by the TUC.

The Chancellor accepted these recommendations, more or less as they stood, and his Budget of 6 April carried them into effect. There was little else of a macro-economic kind to be considered and the rest of the Budget discussions were about the small print of tax administration.

The opening words of the Budget statement were that this was the most critical Budget of recent times. This was perhaps something of an overstatement, for the latitude of choice that the Chancellor had was rather small. Although his commitment to the IMF on the PSBR for the financial year 1976–77 was not binding, it would have been difficult for his relations with the Fund for him to produce a Budget deficit other than marginally above the £12 billion figure given in the Letter of Intent. At best it would have made for problems over any future application for Fund credit. But just as important as relations with the Fund, was the undoubted fact that it would have been very difficult for the UK to maintain any credibility with overseas official creditors on whom it continued to depend for substantial borrowing if it had shown any fiscal laxness. By 6 April, as we shall see, sterling had begun the downward path which characterized its behaviour in 1976 and the Bank was beginning to dig into the foreign exchange reserves to an extent that seriously compounded the financing problem the UK already faced. Anything like an expansionary Budget would have greatly intensified the difficulties.

The Chancellor defined the aim of the Budget as having to 'prescribe the course for the fastest return of Britain to full employment and external balance during what is now recognised to be a period of world recovery'. The world economy had in fact begun to recover from the precipitous decline in activity in the first half of 1975. The American economy had 'bottomed out' in the second half of 1975 and by the year end most of the European economies, especially Germany, had begun to pick up. The British economy lagged behind somewhat on these external trends and the depth of the recession was only touched in the third quarter of 1975.

The Chancellor presented an optimistic view of the outlook for the financing of the UK deficit. The balance of payments had improved significantly in 1975—by about £2 billion mainly because of the fall in domestic output and an improvement in the terms of trade. He referred to the extensive borrowing by public sector entities under the Exchange Cover Scheme (by which the nationalized industries and local authorities participating in it were indemnified against any losses arising from a depreciation of sterling) and to the enlarged facilities available to IMF members under the arrangements agreed in January to temporarily increase the size of the credit tranches by 45 per cent. 'We should thus have no difficulty in meeting our external financing needs this year'. But as a rider the Chancellor warned that this would depend on our beating inflation and 'maintaining confidence in our determination to pay our way in the world'. There was more rhetoric about our success in keeping the money supply under control—£M3 had grown by only 8 per cent in 1975—and although the PSBR had risen in 1975–76 to £10.75 billion (compared with a forecast in the 1975 Budget of £9 billion) more than one half of it had been financed outside the banking system. He then launched into an eulogy of the Government's determination to give a high priority to the improvement of the national industrial performance by the introduction of an 'Industrial Strategy', the approach to which, under the auspices of the NEDC, had been described the previous November;[17] it had also led to the establishment of a new high-level post in the Treasury to deal with it. There was in addition a reference to the micro-measures the Government had introduced in the past six months or so to help selected industries and to encourage training and the retention of manpower which would otherwise be made redundant as a result of the recession.

On public expenditure the Chancellor repeated much of what had been said in the Public Expenditure White Paper published some six weeks earlier. The aim was to stabilize spending in volume terms 'at about the level reached in this financial year', that is 1976–77. The most important element in this part of the Speech, however, was its reference to the introduction of Cash Limits for a large part of public spending. A White Paper was issued on Budget Day.[18] The Chancellor stated that he 'was determined to ensure that our expenditure in the current year does not exceed the limits laid down'. We have more to say on this in the section on Public Expenditure.

Up to this point the Speech had largely been recitative—with very little that was new. But at the end the Chancellor produced his plan to encourage the TUC to persevere with the voluntary pay policy. 'I intend to guarantee that the working population as a whole does not suffer by accepting a lower pay limit rather than a higher one'. He was prepared to discuss what the limit should

---

[17] Cmnd 6315—*Parliamentary Papers* 1975/76 Vol. xvii.
[18] Cmnd 6440—*Parliamentary Papers* 1975/76 Vol. xxiii.

be, 'but it will be for the TUC to judge the size of the pay increase to which it can secure the agreement of its members'. He would not dictate what that should be. However, part of the tax reliefs he was making would have to be conditional on a low pay limit. He had based these on the assumption of a 3 per cent limit—or 'something in that area'. The tax concessions would therefore be made in full (some of the concessions were simply an adjustment of the allowances in line with inflation and were not conditional) only when he saw the outcome of the TUC proposals for the pay round beginning 1 July.

The Chancellor concluded by saying that he expected GDP to grow by about 4 per cent in the year to the middle of 1977 and that the PSBR for the coming year would be £12 billion—lower as a proportion of GDP than in the previous year. The Financial Statement and Budget Report, published on Budget Day, gave the precise figure for the PSBR as £11,962 million a figure which had been increased by £700 million by the Budget measures, including the conditional reliefs.

The Budget was therefore very much on the lines recommended by Treasury officials in February. The only significant fiscal measure was the one which was conditional on the TUC delivering something in the region of a 3 per cent pay norm—the level suggested by the Treasury. Otherwise it was a continuation of existing policy. This meant that the economic recovery would not be assisted by any stimulus and the further rise in unemployment which existing policy implied would have to be accepted.

The Budget was therefore bound to be a disappointment to many on the Chancellor's side. The TUC, which had set its sights on a reduction of unemployment to 600,000 by 1978, were bound to see, and indeed did see, the Budget as a missed opportunity. It was presented, however, against the background of a growing crisis in the foreign exchange market and it is to the problem of sterling that we next have to turn.

Sterling—Part 1

Before he was asked to consider his options for the Budget the Chancellor had, on 25 February, been presented with an updated assessment of the problems of financing the external deficit.[19] It was by no means a gloomy prediction, although of course it was surrounded by the usual qualifications. The forecast deficit on current account was put at something of the order of £1 billion in 1976, rising perhaps to £1.7 billion the following year. The structural capital account deficits for the two years were put at £0.6 billion and £1.3 billion respectively. To finance these two deficits it was hoped to raise the equivalent of over £1.2 billion in each of the two years. The official sterling holders were

[19] PCC (76)17.

expected to reduce their balances by about £200 million in 1976, but to restore them the following year. The financing gaps were therefore relatively modest—£600 million in 1976 and £1.5 billion in 1977. The joker in the pack was the extent of short-term capital inflows—mainly private sector financial investment in sterling or sterling-denominated assets. In 1975 this had been of the order of £1.8 billion, and 1976 could well see this flow continued. 'We ought,' said the Treasury, 'to be able to get through 1976 very comfortably', but confidence was an important factor and the forecast assumed a depreciation; so there was a large element of wishful-thinking about the prognosis. In the event most of the predictions given in this assessment proved to be wide of the mark.

The year of 1975 had, as we saw in the previous chapter, ended with an important submission to the Chancellor from his Treasury advisers to the effect that, if he was to have any hope of bringing unemployment down in the medium term and of reducing the UK's dependence on foreign credit to balance our external accounts, there would have to be a lower exchange rate for sterling. The submission of 21 November had argued for a depreciation of 15 per cent, without however specifying how this should be achieved. Its aim was to secure the Chancellor's agreement to this objective before examining modalities. For over a year he had shown a marked reluctance to embrace such an objective without, however, formally coming down against it. It has to be remembered that the Labour Party had been associated with two significant devaluations of sterling, notably in 1949 and 1967, and neither had added greatly to the reputation of the Chancellor of the time. The Prime Minister, Harold Wilson, had set his face against devaluation in the 1960s and was known to be unsympathetic to it as an instrument of policy. In a minute to Harold Lever dated 14 August 1975 he expressed his 'concern about the Treasury's overt desire to get the rate down'—an echo of his emphatic rejection of devaluation as a course of action in the mid-1960s.[20]

As we have seen, the Chancellor continued to show ambivalence about the exchange rate as a tool to improve competitiveness and to help to reduce unemployment, and at the meeting held with his ministerial colleagues in the Treasury, the Bank and Treasury officials on 16 December he said that 'he was not prepared to take a decision on a policy of accelerated depreciation until he had seen the results of the work he had commissioned on the profile of the economy under various exchange rate options... which would not be finished until the latter part of January... in addition he would want to see the National Income Forecast which would be available in February'. This looked to officials suspiciously like a decision simply not to take a decision, for many of the questions posed by the Chancellor were implicitly answered in the appendices to the main submission; and the relevance of the short-term

[20] BP 98/33/03.

forecast in February to what was essentially a medium-term problem was far from clear. But the aftermath of the November submission had revealed that the Bank, or at least some senior members, had doubts about the effectiveness of a depreciation of sterling as a means of improving the payments imbalance; and everyone, not excluding the advocates of depreciation, had doubts about both the availability of instruments to secure a depreciation and the effect of an engineered depreciation on official sterling holders overseas.

Notwithstanding these internal differences and indeed the doubts shared by most officials about the practical difficulties of securing a particular exchange rate change in a floating rate system, the Treasury felt that it had to return to the issue. It therefore decided to make a further substantive submission on the need for a policy change and, after prolonged discussion at various levels in the department, issued a memorandum which dealt both with the various questions put by the Chancellor in the aftermath of the November submission and with the basic question of how we could get unemployment down and restore equilibrium to the external payments imbalance. This memorandum went to the Chancellor on 24 February[21]—much the same time that the main Budget submission was being made.

The paper argued that with the development of a coherent strategy for reducing pay settlements the outlook for inflation was not unsatisfactory; that with a more resolute approach to public expenditure control and the substantial cuts for the later years of the Public Expenditure Survey period the problem of excessive spending had been tackled; and that with the development of the idea of an Industrial Strategy the endemic problem of low productivity in British manufacturing was being addressed at the micro-level. 'Where we do not have a credible programme is in the field of unemployment and the balance of payments'. The paper referred to some simulations carried out by the Treasury economists of how the economy might develop over the following four or five years on the basis of certain assumptions, notably about the level of UK competitiveness. It was taken as axiomatic that we needed to restore balance to the overseas payments by 1980 at latest. Anything less ambitious would involve our running up external debts to a level which was unsustainable. The UK's dollar-denominated public sector external debt was already over $14 billion and the external sterling balances were £7.5 billion. If further borrowing were to be incurred to cover the current account deficit in the base case (i.e. no change of policy) the total of dollar-denominated external debt would rise to $27 billion, involving interest payments of $1.8 billion in 1978, 1979, and 1980. Thus the benefits of North Sea Oil would be more or less pre-empted before it even began to flow. The unvarnished message was that this could not continue.

[21] PCC (76)18.

The paper then narrowed down the policy options to two: generalized import controls or improved competitiveness. Import controls were speedily rejected for reasons which had already been amply rehearsed. Improved competitiveness could come about in one or both of two ways: better performance on inflation than other industrial countries, or a lower exchange rate than was in prospect on the present policy of not seeking any decline (but not strongly resisting a modest decline when it occurred). The paper found on the basis of the simulations that 'we need a *very early* improvement in our competitiveness of about 10 per cent. This would mean a devaluation of about 15 per cent'. The need for action to be early was due to the well-known J-curve as a result of which the payments advantage of a devaluation might not begin to be realized until 1.5–2 years after the devaluation occurred.

The paper then addressed itself to two matters: the risks involved in the policy recommended and the modalities by which it could be realized. The risks lay in three areas: the effect of a policy of depreciation on overseas sterling holders, the effect it would have on our industrial competitors who might see it as an unfair attempt to secure a larger share of the export market at their expense, and finally the effect on wage earners and their representatives at the workplace of a further cut in their real incomes as a result of the domestic price rises which a devaluation of 15 per cent would inflict. (We must remember that concurrently with this memorandum the Treasury were recommending a pay norm of 3 per cent for 1976–77 at a time when prices were still rising at an annual rate of over 10 per cent.)

None of these risks was insignificant and the 'wrong' response of any of the three constituencies to the policy change could vitiate it more or less completely. The way out of the dilemma proposed by the Treasury was to avoid an explicit exchange rate change—such as a step-change whereby the Bank would announce to the market that it would sell sterling at a specified rate (somewhat below the existing market rate) and so put a ceiling on the market rate (probably without specifying a rate at which it would buy sterling and so avoiding the creation of a floor)—but to go for a 'slide', that is to let sterling slip by not intervening (or not intervening much) in the market when it showed signs of weakness and not to resume intervention before it had found a new and apparently stable level. The slide could, if need be, be assisted or engineered by using short-term interest rates to create an incentive to arbitrageurs to reduce the forward rate and create an expectation that sterling was declining. The paper acknowledged that such a policy was a step into the unknown. We had never tried such an approach in the past, but we could, as the paper put it, 'have a try'. To clinch the argument the paper reminded the Chancellor of the:

lack of success we have had in maintaining competitiveness over the last year by using these two instruments [i.e. interest rates and intervention] to edge the rate down. If we are to have better success we shall need a complete change of emphasis and the Bank will have to adopt quite different techniques from those employed hitherto. It may well be that a direction will have to be given to them in the field of both monetary policy and intervention policy.

The paper concluded on a sombre note:

A 10 per cent depreciation now, followed by the maintenance of price competitiveness, would only make us 3 per cent more competitive than we were a year ago. On this basis we should still have to rely on fairly substantial unemployment in order to close our external accounts. This is the unpalatable message which comes from the pages of our paper. It demonstrates in the starkest possible terms the unreality of setting a confident medium-term unemployment objective of a politically acceptable size given the availability of existing policy instruments.

The timing of this memorandum is important—24 February. It came when the TUC were making plain their anxieties about the employment situation and in the middle of the season when the Chancellor was formulating his Budget strategy, which involved a bait to secure TUC acceptance of a further period of pay restraint. It came too after a period of relative stability in the foreign exchange market. Sterling had been quiet in the period after the announcement of the IMF drawing in December, although there had been some weakness following the publication of the Public Expenditure White Paper in February, a point we touch on in the section below. It was, therefore, all too clear that, if there were to be any hope of an improvement in the long-term outlook for employment, some action to secure a fall in the exchange rate would have to be taken.

The Chancellor's initial reaction to the memorandum was ambivalent. His Private Secretary recorded[22] first some of the Chancellor's peripheral comments on the Treasury's apparent views about the level of unemployment needed to secure current account balance without a depreciation and wondered whether 'it made sense to base policy on a forward look at the balance of payments over a five year period'. But the Chancellor went on to ask for an alternative approach which consisted of shorter-term macro-economic policies and a more active micro-economic policy designed to improve industrial performance. He was not yet persuaded of the case for depreciation 'but if he were he would want to go further... probably on the basis of a step change with an immediate approach to our main overseas depositors with proposals for compensation or guarantees.' The ambiguity contained in these comments was, however, partially resolved at a meeting the Chancellor had with his advisers on 26 February.[23] He now said that he was persuaded of the need to depreciate sterling to the level of competitiveness that obtained in the first half of 1975 and maintain it at this level. But he had not yet decided to accept the

---

[22] DW 015.   [23] Ibid.

full recommendations of the Treasury of a 10 per cent depreciation by June. It would be essential to ensure that the Bank of England 'cooperated fully'.

The meeting the Chancellor had with his advisers on 26 February had not reached anything like a clear conclusion on policy, although the Chancellor's MES paper of 12 March (referred to above), when it came to be written, was reasonably specific about the need for a depreciation. The Chancellor was moving towards their position but had not yet committed himself. There had still been no real discussion about the technique to be used. There had been a preliminary review of the management of the exchange rate following the preparation of a Bank memorandum on 5 February entitled 'The Implications of Attempting to Accelerate the Depreciation of the Exchange Rate'. This was produced in response to some questions the Chancellor had posed at the meeting on 16 December and it looked at three possibilities: a step devaluation, a change in intervention policy, and the use of interest rates to discourage the holding of sterling. On the first the Bank were very apprehensive. A step change in a floating rate system was something never previously attempted and no one knew how it would work and whether it might get out of control. An angry response by the official holders might trigger a decline of unknown proportions. One possibility would be to join the system of a joint floating rate operated by the six founding members of the EEC—the 'snake'—but this was rejected (as it had been by the former Chancellor in his Budget Speech in March 1973 shortly after it had been established) as unlikely to carry conviction. Changes in intervention policy were a more promising possibility. The Bank might, for instance, freely execute sell orders by official customers whatever the state of the market instead of waiting for a propitious moment in order not to create any disturbance. All such techniques would involve, one way or another, the Bank selling sterling on a falling market or not supporting it when it weakened and this would cause considerable anxiety among official holders. Action on interest rates would consist of a narrowing of the interest differential with New York so as to make sterling a less attractive currency to hold, although care would have to be taken not to reduce interest rates to levels which were not appropriate for domestic borrowers.

The Bank concluded, in effect, by rejecting all three options and favouring existing policy which it described as 'grandmother's footsteps'—working by stealth, but doing nothing to create an impression of active management of the rate. The Chancellor discussed this with the Bank and his Treasury advisers on 13 February—he had not yet received the main Treasury submission advocating an active approach to the exchange rate—but he expressed some concern at the rather passive approach proposed by the Bank. He said that, if neither depreciation nor import controls were policy options, the degree of deflation required for the economy to secure external balance was 'not tolerable'. When it came to techniques for managing the rate down he wanted the Bank to take advantage of any weakening of other currencies, notably the franc and the lira, but he accepted that there were big risks in any overt policy of depreciation. However, in his view, the assessment of risk was a judgemental matter, not a technical one, and he asked for more work to be done on reducing the risks of dislodging the balances. He warned the Bank that some action on depreciation 'or import controls' was probably necessary—although the Bank, in reviewing the minutes of the meeting, doubted whether this was a consensual view.

There the matter lay for the time being. An appraisal of the risks of direct action had been commissioned, but no decision on action (except for the opportunism of moving with other currencies which might weaken) had been taken. The Treasury had, however, come to the pretty firm conclusion that any form of step change would carry huge risks and were inclined more and more to the use of intervention and interest rate policy to steer the exchange rate down. However, four days after the Chancellor's meeting with Treasury officials in which he had accepted that some positive action *should* be taken, that is on 1 March—a Monday—the Chancellor had lunch at the Bank of England with the Governor and the Executive Directors of the Bank. No Treasury official was present save the Chancellor's Private Secretary, who subsequently informed the Permanent Secretary[24] that 'the Chancellor had said to the Governor that he had decided in favour of depreciation, though not on either the quantum or the modalities of it'. This was exactly what the Treasury wanted and on the following day the Permanent Secretary told his colleagues that the next step would be to submit to the Chancellor advice on the modalities of a depreciation. He said that, following the Chancellor's lunch at the Bank, he had had a meeting with the Governor at which 'he had secured the Governor's reluctant agreement to prepare a thorough exploration of the various methods of depreciation'.[25] The aim would be to put the issue to the Chancellor early in the week beginning 8 March.

Events, however, decided otherwise, and the advice the Treasury were preparing turned out not to be necessary—and it was never delivered. On Thursday 4 March there was a violent upheaval in the foreign exchange market.[26] A wave of selling of sterling took place and the exchange rate fell by 3 cents—about 1.5 per cent. No one in the Treasury could explain this but the Bank later informed them what had happened. The Nigerian Central Bank had placed a sterling 'sell' order with the Bank which the Bank duly executed from the Exchange Equalisation Account in accordance with the normal drill for handling orders placed by official overseas sterling holders. The Bank, again in accordance with normal practice, then had to decide whether to recoup the Account by selling an equivalent amount of sterling in the market, something they normally did if market conditions were propitious. In this instance conditions were judged to be favourable to such a course and the sell order

[24] DW 014.   [25] PCC (76) 13th Meeting.   [26] PCC (76) 14th Meeting.

was therefore given. However, in the meantime, between the decision and the execution, market conditions weakened. The upshot was that the market, which rapidly perceived the Bank to be a seller of sterling in a falling market, leapt to the conclusion that the authorities wanted to see a further fall. The effect was inevitable. Sterling buyers disappeared and the rate fell sharply.

In many ways what happened on 4 March was in line with what the Treasury had suggested might be a way of engineering a depreciation in the memorandum of 24 February. But it seems to have happened by accident. It was certainly not based on any instructions from the Treasury, who were still without formal guidance from the Chancellor on the exchange policy to be followed. It is simply not credible that the Bank were acting deliberately on the Chancellor's remarks at the lunch on 1 March. The Bank had been showing misgivings over the feasibility, and to some extent the desirability, of a contrived devaluation since the meeting with the Treasury on 1 December, and their memorandum of 5 February was decidedly agnostic. The Governor had, moreover, been reluctant even to put specific ideas on possible measures to bring about a devaluation at the meeting with the Permanent Secretary on 2 March. The only conclusion is that the events of 4 March were indeed accidental.

But if the events of 4 March were all without intention, and the market's interpretation of them was, in formal terms at any rate, wrong, the misperception was compounded the following day, Friday 5 March. Friday is the day on which the weekly Treasury Bill Tender takes place at the Bank, when the money market makes its bid for new Treasury Bills, getting any credit it may need for bids from the Bank, usually at Minimum Lending Rate. On this occasion short-term market rates had fallen below the existing MLR and the Bank decided that for this reason MLR should be brought into line with market rates. What was intended as a purely technical adjustment was however seen by foreign exchange market operators as further evidence that the Bank wished to see a move out of sterling and a further fall in the exchange rate. Again, as on the previous day, what was a normal and relatively insignificant and technical step on the part of the Bank was seen, erroneously, as part of a new policy. Indeed in many ways the actions of the Bank on 4 and 5 March were almost exactly what the Treasury had been recommending a week earlier.

The Treasury could hardly believe its luck. It had obtained the course of action it had been advocating for over eighteen months and one about which the Chancellor had always seemed to have misgivings. In the week that followed 4 March sterling fell from $2.0149 to $1.9120, a depreciation of over 5 per cent—not quite as much as the Treasury had been arguing for, but a decided step in the right direction. In retrospect, it might have seemed that the Treasury would have been satisfied with events, but the record shows that it did not think that the bear attack would last and it continued to debate what more might have to be done to achieve the full devaluation that was required, even to the extent of preparing a draft operational plan for a step change if the weakness of sterling did not continue.

The prevailing view in the market was that the Government had embarked on a new policy and it proceeded to act on this assumption. If sterling was destined to continue to fall there was no point in investors and traders buying spot sterling and every advantage in their selling it—short if they were in a speculative frame of mind. The Bank of England responded with heavy intervention and the foreign exchange reserves fell by over $1,200 million in the course of March—on one day by over $200 million—a drop of about one-quarter of the total available. Within a few days it became necessary to say something publicly which would check this developing cast of the market's mind. An attempt to do this was by way of a press statement, but it was hardly a categoric affirmation of intent to defend the sterling parity. What is interesting is that the French government seemed somewhat concerned, no doubt because these developments might spill over into the franc.[27] The US Treasury were also anxious, and sent a senior representative to call on the Permanent Secretary to ask, pointedly, whether the fall had been engineered.[28] The UK Executive Director at the IMF also reported that the US authorities 'don't believe we didn't engineer it'.[29] The Japanese Financial Attaché also asked some pertinent questions, and Witteveen, who met the Governor in Basle over the weekend of 6–7 March, had to be persuaded that the fall in the rate was not deliberate.

Confidence in sterling was not increased by another fortuitous development a week after the beginning of the slide. On 10 March the House of Commons debated the Public Expenditure White Paper[30] which had been published on 21 February. This might well have been a routine affair as comparable debates in previous years had been. But this time a significant number of Government supporters in the House of Commons decided to show their dissatisfaction with the stance of economic policy and withheld their support for the Government's 'take note' motion, although they refrained from voting with the Opposition on a motion to reject the White Paper. The Government were put in an acutely embarrassing position, as the Leader of the Opposition made clear. The situation was, quite reasonably, treated by the Prime Minister as an issue of confidence and he tabled a motion to this effect the following day. This was, predictably, carried and the rebels in the Labour Party, having made their point, returned to the fold. In the course of his speech on the confidence motion the Prime Minister made a fairly anodyne comment on the decline in the rate which had taken place in the previous seven days:

Our inflation rate is still above that of other important countries and it was inevitable that the market should at some stage exert some downward pressure on the exchange rate which is what we have seen in the last few days.

The nervousness of the market in the weeks immediately following 4 March brought out some considerable differences between the Bank and the Treasury

[27] PCC (76) 14th Meeting.   [28] DW 036—19 March.
[29] DW 036.   [30] Cmnd 6393.

about the extent to which the Bank should show a presence in the market by vigorously supporting sterling. The Treasury were unhappy about the Bank's desire to spend substantial sums of the reserves, and there were several instances of the Bank's requests for authority to intervene being refused or scaled down. By early April the market had reached a state of some fragile stability. The exchange rate was down to $1.85, but thereafter was reasonably stable. The Bank had spent some $2.5 billion of the reserves intervening in the open market as a means of steadying the rate and showing that the Government was not pursuing a policy of active and sustained depreciation—but, in response to Treasury pressure, not overdoing its support. When the Chancellor opened his Budget on 6 April he did not feel the need to say anything special about sterling beyond stating, by way of assuring the market, that the events of early March were not deliberate, that 'depreciation . . . is no answer to our problem'. This might have been a little disingenuous, but the Chancellor was only making the point that our competitiveness should be thought of in terms of quality and reliability of delivery of goods both for export and home delivery and that the new Industrial Strategy was aimed at improving performance in these areas. In spite of these reassurances, by late April market confidence in sterling had declined again and had become an issue which the Treasury now recognized had to be addressed as a serious matter. The question of restoring confidence to a badly shaken market was to become the burning issue for the remainder of 1976 and we deal with this at length later in the chapter. But now we need to look at how two very important domestic matters—both relevant to the question of overseas confidence—were being handled in the early months of 1976: pay policy and the public expenditure survey.

Pay policy

The Chancellor had thrown down the gauntlet to the TUC in his Budget speech with the proposition that, if the latter would agree to recommend to their constituent unions a pay norm of 3 per cent, he would implement income tax reliefs amounting to some £700 million. As we saw there had been some informal hinting at such a proposition in the conversations between the Chancellor and the NEDC Six in early March, and the Chancellor clearly felt that his proposal had some likelihood of success. The degree of success it had was, in the event, quite impressive. In the negotiations which took place in late April and early May the TUC, who perhaps inevitably saw the Chancellor's proposal as an opening gambit in a negotiation, began with a counter-proposal of a pay limit of 6 per cent with a floor of £3 per week and a ceiling of £5 per week together with a number of 'frills'. They wanted a commitment by the government to hold the rise in prices over the following year to 5 per cent, something the Chancellor dismissed out of hand. The TUC's bid would have increased the national wage bill by 5.6 per cent, which the Chancellor said immediately was too high. There was hard bargaining in which the Chancellor, following the decline in sterling that had occurred, made much of the confidence factor. Three long meetings with the NEDC 6 in the run-up to the weekend of 30 April–1 May were followed by informal talks with the General Secretary and a further meeting with the NEDC 6 which concluded, rather dramatically, in an agreement with the TUC representatives in the early hours of 5 May with an endorsement by the General Council later in the morning.[31] The terms of the agreement were somewhat less satisfactory to the Government than the aims set out in the Budget Speech, but the outcome was still a considerable achievement. The TUC agreed to recommend a norm of a 5 per cent increase in pay rates with a minimum of £2.50 per week (intended to protect the low paid) and a ceiling of £4 per week which would apply to all levels above £80 per week. It was estimated that this formula would result in an increase in the wage bill of 4.5 per cent in the year beginning August 1976. In presenting this deal to Parliament later the same day[32] the Chancellor claimed that the '4.5 per cent level... is likely to be below that in practically all the Western developed countries this year. Even the Germans, with their excellent record, are seeing a rate of increase of about 5.5 per cent'.

Provided the agreement was endorsed by a special conference the TUC were convening on 16 June, the Chancellor said that he would recommend to Parliament the enactment in full of the conditional tax reliefs specified in the Budget. Apart from the income tax concessions, the price the Chancellor had to pay for this agreement was the introduction, on the same day, of a number of micro-measures aimed at relieving some of the worst effects of unemployment and at rescinding one of the public expenditure cuts which had been incorporated in the Public Expenditure White Paper, that is an increase of 5p in the charge for school meals which had been scheduled for September. The Chancellor was thus continuing with his policy of spending relatively modest sums of public money to assist those worst hit by unemployment or to placate some social constituency which he had begun in September the previous year. We saw in the previous chapter that he had had, in effect two mini-Budgets in 1975 (September and December) and he had introduced another in February 1976.[33] It is not perhaps necessary to go again into the *minutiae* of these measures—they involved assistance in training and re-training, a temporary employment subsidy to enable employers who had short-term problems with production to retain workers who would otherwise be laid off, and, as in the February announcement, the making of payments under the

---

[31] A full account is given of these meetings in the minutes of the second and third meetings of the new EY Committee—CAB 134/4015.
[32] *Hansard* 5 May. [33] *Hansard* 12 February.

Industry Act of 1972 to selective industries to modernize and rationalize the production base.

These were all measures which were high on the TUC's agenda and they all had some value in helping to secure the agreement of organized labour to the policy of pay restraint. This is not to say that they had no value except as placatory gestures to the TUC. Many qualified economists had argued for some action on the part of the Government to improve industrial training and, in the interest of efficiency, to take the worst off the edges of unemployment. But the measures did not come without a public cost. The Chancellor conceded this but said that the important thing was to ensure 'that there is no risk of expenditure slipping into future years when public spending must be contained so as to permit the movement of resources into exports and investment'. But the four statements did add appreciably to public spending in the current year (1975–76) and to an extent into the following year.[34] He knew from his discussions with the Managing Director of the IMF the previous November how concerned the Fund were with the fiscal prospect in those two years and these concerns were shared by the markets. The achievement of a successful outcome to the pay negotiations did not therefore come without some cost to the Chancellor's (and the Treasury's) reputation for soundness in the ongoing task of keeping spending down and it is to the issue of public expenditure control that we now have to turn.

Public expenditure

Although there were, of course, many issues concerning the UK economy which attracted criticism both at the time and since, it was the level—and trend—of public spending planned by the Government for the second half of the 1970s which became the dominant issue affecting the confidence of many of the players in the events of 1976. The IMF had made it plain that public expenditure was their principal concern about British economic policy in the course of the negotiations on the 1975 drawing, and their worries were taken up by financial and economic commentators and, as a result, by the markets. We have to scrutinize in some detail what lay behind those worries and what was done to allay them—and indeed what was done to correct what many saw to be a serious imbalance in the distribution of resources within the UK. But before we look at the public spending decisions taken by Ministers at various times in the course of 1976, it is worth examining the systemic issues which arose in the course of this year, for they had more than a marginal influence on the actual outcome of those decisions. They may not have had much impact at

---

[34] The total increase in spending involved in the four statements was in the region of £400 million, spread between 1975–76 and 1976–77.

the time on the perceptions of outside observers of what actually was happening in the fiscal area, but with hindsight it is clear that the greater rigour introduced into the planning and spending process had a significant effect on the out-turn.

Perhaps the most important measure of the tightening of control was the introduction of cash limits on public spending generally. We saw in the previous chapter that the decision to embark on this course was taken in early 1975, but the planning and preparatory work had to be extensive. The Treasury was in no position by itself to determine how decisions to implement a given level of volume spending approved by Ministers for a department for a particular period should be translated into a cash provision for that period, for the prices of the goods and services being bought by departments moved in uncertain and differential ways, and reliable and realistic decisions about the money required to purchase those goods and services needed the collaboration of the spending departments themselves. This did not mean giving departments a free hand in determining what the multiplicand of the agreed volumes should be for each programme, but it did mean that the process had to be a collaborative one and as we saw earlier it was handled interdepartmentally. The Treasury was naturally concerned to protect itself if the estimates of the price movements underlying the cash provision were too generous. It was also determined that the system should not be abused by the failure of departments to keep within the cash limits provided. To this end a system of regular monitoring of departments' spending was incorporated as a strict requirement.

The procedure was described in some detail in a White Paper issued on 6 April.[35] Cash limits applied solely for the year immediately ahead—1976–77—the idea of budgeting in cash terms beyond the first year of the Survey as advocated by Godley was not adopted. Moreover there were certain areas of public expenditure which were not easily amenable to strict cash control—notably those where policy and rates of payment had been laid down in statute as an entitlement, for example for social security benefits. Local authority current spending was also excluded as the government's involvement in this was already controlled by the rate support grant (and supplementary grants), which were negotiated each year. The nationalized industries were to be cash controlled through limits on their financing—not their investment which was then the element subject to volume control, although this too was to be changed later in the year. In all, cash limits were applied in the initial year to over 65 per cent of central government expenditure (including the rate support grant to local authorities). It was made clear that cash limits would be strictly enforced—only minor exceptions being admitted and then only after first applying every possible means of absorbing the extra expenditure. But the public reaction to this innovation was sceptical. The *Financial Times* Principal

[35] Cmnd 6440.

Economic Commentator had said on the occasion of the publication of the 1976 White Paper in February that 'the value of the much advertised cash ceilings ... has been heavily overstated' and this was—and remained for some time—the prevailing view of the markets.

A second area of reform lay in the treatment of the contingency reserve—the provision made in the Survey system for items of expenditure which could not be foreseen at the planning stage but which emerged during the course of the year. This provision was normally about 1 per cent of total programmed spending for the year ahead and by the mid-1970s came to about £700 million, rising somewhat for future years to take account of the unpredictability of the likely needs for those years. We have seen that in both 1974–75 and 1975–76 the contingency reserve tended to be exhausted quite early in the financial year as Ministers and spending departments found irresistible reasons for additional expenditure. Although the Chancellor decried this tendency[36] he was not immune to it. His mini-Budgets of September and December, 1975 as well as February and May 1976 involved expenditure, not all of which by any means could be accommodated within the spending plans of the relevant department. This process of 'creep' was of serious and increasing concern to the Treasury and early in 1976 it put forward some specific ideas for avoiding, or at least greatly reducing, it. But of course it knew that no amount of rule-making was of much avail if spending Ministers were insistent on breaching the rules and the Chancellor or Chief Secretary went along with the breaches. The matter was discussed among senior officials at a meeting on 13 January.[37] It was agreed that the aim should be to ensure that claims on the contingency reserve should be considered *together* by the Cabinet as a whole rather than as a set of individual issues; and that the Treasury should present to the collectivity of Ministers every four months a list of claims which, in the period covered, it had neither approved nor rejected and on which it wanted Ministerial decisions, together with a list of possible savings to offset those claims which had to be conceded. The contingency reserve was to be seen as a last resort, not, as hitherto, an easy 'first port of call'. It was also argued that the issue of public expenditure should be discussed by the Cabinet well before the end of the Survey process to avoid the situation which occurred at the very end of the previous year's exercise, when an element of crisis was injected into the process by Ministers' being unable to translate a collective view of what the level of spending as a whole should be into specific consequences for their own programmes. The Cabinet as a whole discussed these matters when they considered the publication of the 1976 Public Expenditure White Paper on 5 February.[38] It was the Prime Minister himself who took the initiative in

---

[36] See particularly his comments at the Cabinet on 20 May 1975 referred to in the previous chapter.
[37] DW 014.   [38] CAB 128/58/4.

proposing an important procedural change, very much on the lines the official Treasury had in mind when they discussed the issue at the end of 1975.[39] Who put these ideas to him, or indeed whether they were his own, is not clear, but the fact that they closely resembled the Treasury's own thinking is unlikely to have been coincidental. What the Prime Minister proposed was that, if a spending Minister succeeded in persuading his colleagues in a Cabinet Committee on the rightness of some particular expenditure which could not be accommodated within his programme, but failed to obtain the consent of the relevant Treasury minister, the issue should be referred to the whole Cabinet, who would consider, systematically and at regular intervals, the accumulation of 'unaccepted' spending claims and decide which could be made a claim on the contingency reserve. This system was implemented forthwith, and the Chief Secretary subsequently submitted reports to the Cabinet at roughly quarterly intervals on the size of the outstanding claims. The records of the Cabinet discussions of the Chief Secretary's reports in 1976 show very clearly how serious Ministers, collectively, had now become about the need for a much more rigorous system of expenditure control.

Two other systemic changes were made in the course of 1976 although they were not to come into effect until the 1977 Public Expenditure White Paper was published. These were the calculation of 'debt interest', that is the cost of servicing the totality of public sector debt, and the treatment of the nationalized industries as spending entities. Debt interest had hitherto been shown as the gross amount paid, or expected to be paid, by the public sector by way of debt servicing, even though the greater part of this did not have to be financed from taxes or further borrowing. The beneficiaries of the spending financed by borrowing met a large part of the cost of borrowing through the prices, rents, or charges they paid for the goods and services provided for them by the public sector—and some was met by interest receipts. Some interest payments of course had to be paid on borrowings applied to finance current deficits or to finance investment in roads, schools, hospitals, etc. for which no charges were levied. In the new presentation the former category would be excluded from the presentation of public expenditure, and only the latter would be included. The effect of this presentational change on the perceived total of public spending was considerable. For 1976–77 debt interest on the old basis would have been shown as about £6.5 billion, whereas on the new basis it fell to £1.8 billion and the comparable figures for the previous year would have been £5 billion and £1 billion respectively.[40] This was purely a presentational change, but it had the effect of reducing significantly the publicly quoted figures of public expenditure as, for instance, the proportion it bore to GDP.

[39] DW 014—13 January 1976.
[40] Note to the Treasury Select Committee in PESC (76)42 and GEP 8/9/03.

It did not affect the planning totals, which were the sum of departmental programmes and had always excluded debt interest.

For the nationalized industries the planning total had been the total investment programme no matter how it was financed. This was what the Plowden Report[41] had recommended in 1961 and its recommendations had been implemented. But a good deal of the capital spending of the nationalized industries was financed by their borrowing abroad under the Exchange Guarantee scheme (which was outside the definition of public borrowing) or by their trading surpluses (when they had them). To take account of this, the element of nationalized industry spending in the programmes would in future consist only of the cash advances the government made to them by way of loans, public dividend capital (effectively equity) or grants. Cash limits, however, would continue to apply not only to these items but to foreign borrowing as well. The case for this change rested on the need for the industries to have a reasonable degree of freedom in the way they financed themselves commercially. It was not the intention to reduce in any way the Treasury's grip on that element of public spending which had to be financed by taxes or central government borrowing and indeed the cash limit system applied to all their net borrowing, not just their borrowing from the central government. Moreover the Treasury continued to scrutinize the whole investment programmes of the industries as it had in the past and these programmes would remain under collective Ministerial control in the annual expenditure survey. As we shall see, when the IMF were apprised of this accounting change in the course of the negotiations later in the year they were slightly suspicious that the motive behind it might be to allow the total of public expenditure to be reduced without any change in the 'real world'. In the event they were persuaded that this was not the case and they accepted it as a sensible change.

The 1976 Survey was launched very shortly after the publication of the annual Public Expenditure White Paper which gave public expression to the statements made to the IMF in the course of the negotiations of November and December.[42] It was not well received by the commentators, who seized on the fact that the plans were based on growth projections which assumed that unemployment would be reduced to 3 per cent by 1979. But at that stage the attack on sterling had not yet begun and the White Paper did not provoke any new manifestation of doubt on the part of sterling holders about the viability of British economic policy. The Chancellor's presentation to the Cabinet of the economic background[43] to the launch of the Survey was a sober affair, based as it was on a discouraging note[44] by the Head of the Expenditure Group dated 27

---

[41] Cmnd 1432.

[42] The figure published for 1978–79 was about £500 million above the target set for 1978–79 because Ministers were at that stage unwilling to credit social security savings which had been agreed but not announced.

[43] CAB 129/187/25.   [44] GEA 14/01.

February, advising him that the economic assumptions on which the previous survey were based were no longer valid and that it was no longer realistic to take as the central planning case the reduction of unemployment to 3 per cent by 1979. The Chancellor's paper acknowledged that many of the assumptions about the growth of economic potential and of the world economy now looked optimistic but—again on Treasury advice—did not call for any radical review of the public expenditure plans of the White Paper. What he suggested was that the Cabinet should simply accept that, until a new and more realistic MTA could be presented, they should do no more than instruct officials to hold to the difficult decisions they had taken in November of the previous year and incorporated in the White Paper. The figures to be used for the new final year (1979–80) should be the same as for the previous year, that is that the cuts made in the latter year in November should not be restored. For the intermediate years the figures would be those set out in the White Paper, adjusted to 1976 prices. As had become usual, new spending bids and options for cuts should be explored during the Survey so that when Ministers came to make decisions they would be aware of all the implications of the choices open to them.

The Cabinet discussed this approach on 11 March and agreed the guidelines set out by the Chancellor and the Survey was launched on this basis. But it was becoming clear to the Treasury that the 1976 MTA, on which final decisions on public spending would to some extent be based when it became available in June, would have to incorporate some unpalatable assumptions about the potential of the economy—even more unpalatable in fact than the message given to him in March had been. The Chancellor was told, as indeed he had already been advised, by his officials on 9 April[45] that in preparing the new Survey the Treasury economists could no longer treat as a central case the 3 per cent unemployment target for 1979 underlying the White Paper—nor indeed could they support the growth potential of 3 per cent which also underlay it. They discussed a number of options for the base of the new MTA one of which, the preferred one, would see unemployment remaining a problem for the rest of the decade. The clear implication was that when it came to the taking of decisions about the path of the total of public expenditure for the new quadrennium at the end of the Survey there would be some unpalatable choices to be made.

At this stage the main focus remained on the final year of the Survey, now 1979–80. But it was becoming increasingly clear that the crucial question that Ministers would have to address was going to be the level of spending in the intermediate years, in particular 1977–78, for this, rather than the later years, was the time horizon of many of the players on the domestic and international scene. They were looking at the fiscal position in the period immediately ahead—in particular the PSBR—and they were not impressed by Augustinian

---

[45] PCC (76)25.

promises to stabilize or even reduce expenditure in three or four years' time. The previous survey had settled the figure for 1977–78 at just under £44.5 billion at 1974–75 out-turn prices and the Chancellor had not explicitly considered the need for this, adjusted to 1976 Survey prices, to be reduced in the paper he put to Cabinet in March—although of course, as we saw, his presentation of the economic outlook was a sober one. The Survey was completed in mid-June. It was essentially a non-political exercise; its main purpose being to indicate to Ministers what new commitments (additional to those incorporated in the White Paper) were being sought by departments and what the options were for making cuts, either to accommodate the new proposals or to reduce spending in total. The guidelines given to the Survey Committee were to display options adding up to cuts of 2.5 per cent in 1977–78 and 5 per cent in later years. At 1976 Survey prices the White Paper programmes stood at £53.6 billion in 1977–78 and £53.0 billion the following year. But since the publication of the White Paper the demand-determined programme requirements had grown by £0.25 billion (mainly due to higher unemployment) and new proposals by spending departments came to a further £1 billion. To offset these and hold to the White Paper levels, cuts in programmes amounting to about £1 billion in 1977–78 and just over £2 billion the following year would be required. The illustrative reductions were spread widely over departments and we need not examine them at this stage. They certainly involved some retreat from what had become accepted standards, like the uprating of social security benefits in line with earnings, and the availability of such items as school meals and prescriptions at heavily subsidized prices. It suffices to say that at this stage of the expenditure round the Treasury divisions responsible for departmental spending felt that simply holding levels at the White Paper levels would, given the propensity of Ministers to incur new commitments, be a significant achievement. It also goes some way to explain why, when (as we shall see) the question of cuts in 1977–78 below the White Paper levels came to be considered, the Expenditure side of the Treasury took a cautious—indeed pessimistic—view about what Ministers could be persuaded to accept.

We return to the narrative of the part that the control and reduction of public expenditure played in 1976 later when Ministers considered the conclusions of the Survey in the light of what had by then become an unusually difficult economic environment: the issue of public expenditure became caught up in the more general problem of economic management and the defence of sterling—an issue we now have to consider in some detail.

Sterling—Part 2

While the planning for the Survey was going on, the attack on sterling began to take on a life and momentum of its own. Whereas breaks in confidence in 1974 and 1975 had been fairly short-lived (or, as in June 1975 been repaired by a firm policy move, i.e. the introduction of a strong Incomes Policy) the bear attack of 4 March did not peter out. In part this was because no policy move was made to restore confidence, and the press guidance was not very robust in character. The only action taken to steady the market's nerves was to intervene in the foreign exchange market to moderate the fall. It has to be remembered that up to the end of April the rate had not fallen below the level the Treasury wished to see to achieve the desired competitiveness. In early April—a month after the attack began—reports came in that the depreciation had not led to any diversification of assets by overseas official sterling holders.[46] The hope was that selling was confined to professional speculators who would sooner or later judge that their open positions should be closed. Indeed the Treasury put an up-dated external borrowing assessment to the Chancellor on 29 April[47] which made only marginal adjustments to the one given in February. OF commented that the assessment 'offers comfort only until the end of 1976—and qualified comfort at that'. It added prophetically 'we could have to restore external confidence by a change of policies—or borrow from multilateral sources [clearly the IMF]'. Something of this nervousness crept into OF's thinking as April drew to a close. It reported that the pound was now 'fragile'; the Second Secretary in charge of OF expressed the view that 'the Treasury should now consider whether cuts in public expenditure should be made and when'.[48] He said that the Head of the European Department of the Fund said that the Fund had in mind a cut in the PSBR for 1976/77[49] of £3 billion'.[50] The idea of proposing an arbitrary cut in spending ahead of the delivery of the new forecast and of the PESC report was not taken up by other officials, who felt that the Chancellor would not be persuaded of the need to go back to his colleagues so soon after putting in his proposals for the PESC survey without some stronger argument than 'confidence', important as that issue was. But before the question of what stance the Treasury should adopt towards public expenditure in advance of the completion of the Survey could be addressed,

[46] We see later that these reports were not correct.
[47] BP 32/100/02.
[48] DW 014 29 April.
[49] This is almost certainly a misreporting and the reference should be to 1977–78. The Fund would have known very well that cuts of the order of £3 billion in the current year of any programme were not possible without violent disruption. Moreover in all subsequent exchanges with the Fund the focus of their attention was 1977–78 and even more strongly 1978–79.
[50] DW 014 12 May.

the department had to submit to the annual Article VIII consultation by the Fund which was carried out during a visit between 17 and 25 May.

The IMF routine consultation

The Fund staff had submitted a list of questions about the stance of policy and the outlook for the economy and they had a series of meetings with Treasury and Bank officials. The detailed examination was a largely technical and fact-finding matter, but at the conclusion the Fund gave their verdict. The leader of the Treasury team gave the Chancellor his assessment of the Fund's position.[51] According to him the Fund now recognized the opportunity for export-led growth and they were generous in their views about the contribution that pay policy and improved industrial performance were making to the UK's external trade. They thought that with this development there was a likelihood of excessive demand from the public sector. They thought that the Treasury had underestimated the speed of economic recovery from the recession and they were worried about the growth of DCE and of the money supply, which they saw growing at an annual rate of 13 per cent (compared with only 8 per cent the previous year). On the PSBR their hope—and belief—in December when the oil facility and first credit drawing was negotiated was that the Chancellor's acceptance of a limit of £12 billion for 1976–77 would oblige him to take action to cut borrowing—but this did not in fact seem to be the intention. They noted the size of external finance the UK still needed—the Treasury had put the requirement in 1976–77 at over £3 billion and doubted whether this could be obtained. They added that, sooner or later, a substantial further reduction of net public sector demand would be needed and they concluded with a warning. Even to draw on the remainder of the first credit tranche[52] would need some action, which need not be immediate, but might well involve an undertaking to adopt measures to deflate the PSBR by £2–3 billion in 1977–78. Their closing statement was explicit: 'We would expect the scale of discretionary fiscal action appropriate to the evolving situation to be quite large'. On 25 May the team leader had a meeting with the Chancellor and made much the same points. The Chancellor's comments were illuminating. For him it was important to keep public expenditure within the published limits—there was no hint that he thought that these were already too high; on the question of a change in policy he said that, although

---

[51] GEP 9/29/01B.

[52] Following a special meeting of the Interim Committee of the Fund in Jamaica in January all the tranches of the Fund were temporarily raised by 45 per cent, so the UK found itself in the position of having some SDR 3,360 million undrawn (New quota SDR 4,060 million less SDR 700 million drawn from 1st credit tranche in 1975) of which the undrawn 1st credit tranch was SDR 313 million.

some countries might welcome external pressure to change policies, this was not the case with the UK. 'If any change were needed he would prefer to make them independently... in that case there would be no need to draw on the additional IMF tranches'.[53] This was a quite defiant message and suggested that he thought that existing policy, possibly adjusted, would enable the UK to avoid an application for substantial IMF support.[54] At the concluding meeting of the consultation the Fund continued to press for cuts in the PSBR, and were not impressed by the arguments put forward by the Treasury that the level of public expenditure was an important ingredient in the acceptance by the TUC of a further measure of pay restraint. After the Fund team had returned to Washington, on 2 June, the UK Executive Director at the IMF reported a talk he had had with the Managing Director, who had clearly been briefed by the Fund team. Witteveen picked up the theme of a reduction in public expenditure as well as 'monetary measures to mop up liquidity'. The Fund staff report to the Board at the beginning of July[55] contained many of the worries expressed during the consultation, but it also dealt at length with the role of the exchange rate, which it regarded as important to the recovery. The staff sought to allay any suspicions the UK competitors might have had by accepting that the substantial decline in sterling since March had been strongly resisted by the UK authorities and 'that in no sense do the results reflect aggressive market behaviour. Indeed they noted that there had been hardly any improvement in the UK's competitiveness since the second half of 1973'. This was a helpful comment in the sense that it reinforced the assurances the UK had been giving to its competitors (notably France) that it was not seeking to gain an unfair trade advantage by conniving at the depreciation of sterling. But on the question of domestic policy the staff report was critical. 'The situation requires a substantial reduction in the fiscal deficit... there could be different views about timing (but) the staff favours an early and major commitment to action'. There could have been little doubt in the minds of UK policy makers that if recourse had to be made to the IMF for help later in the year the terms would involve a big fiscal policy change.

Sterling—Part 3

The sterling situation continued to deteriorate in May. In the course of the month of March the rate had fallen by 5.4 per cent, and in the first sixteen working days of April it fell by a further 5.0 per cent. In response to this on 26

[53] DW 062.
[54] The Chancellor hinted that the UK might seek to get the balance of the enlarged first credit tranche but the IMF team leader made it clear that this would require a new application and would not be treated as a minor addition.
[55] SM/76/153.

April MLR, which had remained at 9 per cent since the reduction at the beginning of March, was raised by 1.5 per cent. This action temporarily relieved market pressure but the respite was short lived. Nor did the Chancellor's statement on 5 May that the TUC had agreed to a further year of pay restraint have any noticeable effect. By the middle of May the rate was back to where it had been and later in the month pressure again began to build up. 21 May was a particularly bad day. The Governor came to see the Permanent Secretary[56] and expressed his anxieties about the adequacy of policy to satisfy the market and, if nothing else was to be done, there should be an immediate increase of 1 per cent in MLR—to be achieved not by an administered change but by persuading the discount market to lower the price of their bids at the Treasury Bill tender the following day (a Friday). The Treasury, no doubt concerned that the competitive gains achieved by the depreciation so far should not be lost, were not persuaded that an increase of 1 per cent was justified—they preferred 0.5 per cent. The 1.5 per cent increase at the end of April had not had much effect and the level of activity in the economy, with the improving outlook for inflation, did not justify a rate of 11.5 per cent. The matter was referred to the Chancellor who sided with the Governor[57] and agreed to his request for a full 1 per cent increase. In fact the rate hardly responded to this move and within a week it had fallen a further 1 per cent. It thus became clear to both the Treasury and the Bank that confidence in sterling was not likely to be much affected by movements in short-term interest rates. The fears—and expectations—of sterling holders that sterling was on a downward path were not likely to be mitigated by small movements in interest rates. (The Chancellor had at one point specifically asked if interest rates might by used to compensate official holders of sterling for the losses they were incurring through sterling's decline, and was firmly advised that the increases that would have to be made by way of compensation would be enormous.) If by this time markets were interested in domestic monetary policy it was in the rate of growth of the money supply, and it was in part in acceptance of this fact that, after the rise in MLR on 21 May, short-term interest rates were left untouched for four months, during which period sterling was under more or less continuous pressure. The adoption of monetary targets, rather than the level of interest rates, came in 1976 to be the issue which was thought to be relevant to stability and we examine how this was addressed in the context of the policy actions that were eventually taken in July.

What did materially dominate the thinking of the Treasury and the Bank as well as senior ministers from May onwards was the rate of spend of the UK's foreign exchange reserves to support sterling in the markets. At the outset of the crisis in early March the reserves totalled just under $5 billion, and were augmented shortly after by a drawing (about $1 billion) on the 1975 standby

---

[56] HF 9/02.   [57] Ibid.

with the IMF under the oil facility and the first credit tranche. The current account of the balance of payments was still heavily in deficit but the capital account was not far out of balance and some borrowing by the banks and by public sector entities more or less brought the accounts into balance in the first quarter. But later on the accounts could only be balanced by heavy intervention in the markets. In the first few days of the crisis, from 4 to 11 March, intervention by the Bank amounted to $910 million—nearly one-fifth of the total held: and although this scale of spending was not kept up, there was a steady haemorrhaging of the reserves, even as they were augmented by the proceeds of the borrowing by public sector bodies, as the overseas sterling holders divested themselves of their sterling short-term assets and the Bank met the market supply of sterling by buying it up. Who these sellers of sterling were was not known for some time. The Bank's intelligence of the movement of the balances was limited, as a large proportion of them, including some of those held by central banks and monetary institutions, were deposits in commercial banks who only reported their levels to the Bank of England at mid-month dates and at quarterly intervals. From what the Bank knew, it seemed that the main sellers were not the official holders, although subsequent information showed that this was not the case.[58] Indeed the Chancellor was briefed to tell his colleagues at the Cabinet meeting on 20 May[59] that the balances of the oil-rich countries were not being reduced, and he said much the same thing in reply to a Parliamentary Question on 7 June. By the end of June the Bank became aware that this was not the case. In a minute dated 16 June[60] the Overseas Director confessed to 'being unhappy about the speed and adequacy of our knowledge of the sterling holdings. When we took the External Financing Report last week all we had were the mid-April figures'. He added 'I should not in fact like the mid-May figures to go to the Treasury before next Monday [21 June] because they will contain some shocks to them in relation to a number of holders—particularly probably Nigeria and Kuwait'. It was, therefore, not until late June that the Treasury became aware that the problem of the balances was in fact the official holdings not the private ones. This could have materially affected the Treasury's response to the crisis as it developed, and, as we shall see, officials concentrated their attention on the behaviour of the official, not the private, holders when they came to advise the Chancellor on policy changes in late June. (Per contra, the American officials who later in the year expressed views about British policy concentrated on monetary measures designed to change the behaviour of the *private* holders—another issue examined later on in the narrative.)

---

[58] Sterling balances held by official institutions fell by £1 billion, or one-quarter, in the second quarter of 1976.

[59] CAB 128/59/6.

[60] Band of England file 4A 100/7.

Be that as it may, the issue of how much of the UK's currency reserves should be spent in defending the rate was not addressed in a systematic way, largely because, at any rate in the early days, officials believed that the attack would, as on previous occasions of weakness, burn itself out. Equally importantly, given the uncertainties, it was impossible to devise a system which would guide the Bank and the Treasury on the degree of intervention in the market at any one time and in any one set of circumstances. But the experience of April and May when the scale of currency intervention (including sales of dollars to central banks) reached nearly $2 billion[61] while the rate fell more or less steadily by over 8 per cent revealed that there were underlying differences of opinion and approach, notably between the Bank and the Treasury. The amount to be spent on intervention was decided *ad hoc* on a daily, sometimes an hourly, basis usually in accordance with the size and scale of the selling of sterling that was taking place. But it was becoming evident that the Bank were more concerned to defend the rate and to be seen to be doing so, while the Treasury was worried about the draining of the foreign exchange reserves. It would be wrong to say that there was at this stage a sharp policy difference, although later on, in particular when the issue of intervention was raised with Ministers, the positions of the two parties became visibly rather more polarized. One person who was greatly exercised about the rate of depletion of the reserves was the new Prime Minister. James Callaghan had succeeded Harold Wilson in early April following the latter's resignation in March—almost coincidentally with the onset of the crisis. He had been the Chancellor of the Exchequer in the 1960s and had had personal experience of at least one sterling crisis involving a heavy loss of reserves, an approach to the IMF and eventually a devaluation. Almost from the outset of his assumption of Prime Ministerial office he showed an anxiety about the fall in the UK reserves which was taking place and he communicated this anxiety to the Chancellor and the Governor on several occasions—notably through a minute from his private secretary on 21 May to the Chancellor and again when the latter reported the progress on the Central Bank credit on 4 June—see below—and indeed further in discussions at Chequers on 26 June.[62] The debate about the scale of intervention assumed important dimensions early in June, but first we have to look at a development which, for the moment, took precedence in the preoccupations of the main players in the drama.

The Chancellor and the Prime Minister may have been alarmed by the rate of spend of the reserves but there was at least one Senior Minister who was not—Harold Lever, and at this point he made a significant intervention. Since the formation of the Government in early 1974 he had been loosely attached

---

[61] The published reserves loss was only $500 million, as some $1.5 billion of foreign currency loans was taken into the reserves to disguise the gross fall.

[62] DW 014 29 June.

to the Treasury, and had received all the important papers that had been put to the Chancellor. He had frequently engaged with Treasury officials on matters (usually of a purely financial character) on which he had had some experience and, as we have seen, he played an important part in the genesis of the mini-Budget of July 1974 when he had been a keen advocate of using public finance to reduce prices in order to moderate wage increases. On 24 May he wrote to the Chancellor[63] and argued that the exchange market situation had become so serious that the Treasury had to intervene strongly to restore equilibrium. He recognized that the reserves were exiguous and argued that we needed additional foreign exchange credit. He put the figure required at $3 billion and urged that we 'go for credit from our major partners'. The Chancellor was clearly somewhat taken by this suggestion, and at a meeting with the Governor and Treasury officials on 27 May he said that 'he wanted to reach a view on the possibility of a big loan from the United States'.[64] Market sentiment by then had reached a new low ebb and a telegram from the UK Director at the IMF reported that 'the market was completely demoralised'. The Chancellor called a meeting with Lever, Treasury officials and the Bank (including of course the Governor) on 3 June to discuss the loan idea. Lever set out his views as follows[65]:

The pound should be defended at or near its present rate.[66] A further fall would jeopardise the Government's central economic policies and it would be disastrous to lose the support of the unions for pay restraint which would demonstrably have failed to stabilise the pound...the defence of sterling required money—at least $3 billion...the obvious source was the US Federal Reserve.[67]

The Chancellor agreed with Lever's worries about the unions. 'The loss of union support would have wide effects and would probably lead to a general election from which Labour might emerge as the largest party but weaker than now in Parliament....His conclusion was that it was desirable to defend the rate by means which would not break the relationship with the unions. This criterion ruled out an immediate cut in public expenditure in present circumstances...though this would not apply in a major foreign exchange crisis....*He did not rule out a significant public expenditure cut for 1977–78*'.

[63] DW 036.
[64] BP 98/33/02.
[65] Ibid.
[66] The rate was then $1.79.
[67] The New York Federal Reserve Bank had at that time a network of swap arrangements with the central banks of other G10 countries, totalling some $20 billion. The swap with the UK amounted to $3 billion. It could be drawn upon, but not necessarily on demand. The consent of the Americans was needed for any drawing on the New York bank and indeed they had agreed to an Italian request—but only for one quarter of the available size of the bilateral swap.

The Permanent Secretary said that the general view of the Treasury was close to the Chancellor's, provided a cut in public expenditure for 1977–78 was envisaged.[68] The Second Secretary (Public Expenditure) said that in his view public expenditure cuts as large as £3 billion (the figure which had been mentioned by the Head of the European Department of the IMF) would not be compatible with the Government's present relations with the unions.

Lever's preference for more international credit to support sterling was not shared by all at the meeting. The Treasury were apprehensive about mobilizing a large short-term credit facility and then spending it without significant effect. The borrowing programme the Bank and Treasury had embarked upon in 1974 was strictly for long-term credit intended to take care of the financing needs until North Sea Oil revenues began to flow and the current balance of trade improved. A short-term credit could not help unless it led to an improvement in the confidence of the market. The Treasury's preference was to wait a little longer and then change domestic policies if the pound continued to fall. The Governor expressed a preference for an immediate drawing from the Fund (which would of course have provided the credit on a medium-term basis but, on the scale required, would have involved substantial changes of policy). The Chancellor said that his view was that in the present situation a policy of doing nothing was too risky. He accordingly authorized the Bank to explore the possibilities of a Central Bank operation on the lines suggested by Lever.

The meeting was therefore important in a number of respects. It showed that opinion in the Treasury at official and ministerial level was already in favour of cuts in expenditure for 1977–78 even though neither the short-term forecast nor the MTA which would provide the rationale for cuts was yet available. Cuts of some sort were necessary to restore confidence. On the other hand the figure attributed to the Fund of £3 billion, if implemented, would have serious effects on the TUC's further support for the Government. (The Second Secretary who expressed this view was subsequently to argue that this figure would simply not be accepted by the Chancellor's Cabinet colleagues—see below.) But the meeting was equally significant in that it revealed subtle differences of opinion about the right course of action in a deteriorating situation. Lever wanted to explore the possibility of short-term credit without any policy change. The Bank wished to see a policy change and some longer-term credit (from the IMF). The Treasury were worried about the idea of short-term credit which might well be spent without effect and would have to be repaid from depleted reserves. They thought that a policy change was the right remedy—when and if the situation deteriorated further.

---

[68] This seems to have been the first time that the Treasury told the Chancellor that it now thought that action would be required on spending in 1977–78.

The Chancellor discussed the issue with the Prime Minister the following day. He said that of the three views he was disposed to accept Lever's course—on a contingent basis. The Prime Minister's first reaction was to agree with the Treasury, but he eventually came round to the view that an exploration of the swap facility was acceptable, such exploration being done urgently on the telephone. He added that he was in favour of a long-term funding of the sterling balances for instance by substituting SDR bonds for them. There was some discussion of the need for a cut in expenditure in 1977–78 on which the Chancellor said that this would have to wait for the completion of the PESC exercise later in the month.

Following the meeting of 3 June the Governor[69] began his exploration with the Chairman of the Federal Reserve Board of the possibility of activating the $3 billion swap with the New York Federal Reserve Bank. The reaction of Arthur Burns, then Chairman of the Board of Governors of the US Federal Reserve System, was to doubt whether this was what was required. He thought that the right course was to cut the fiscal deficit. But if the swap idea was to be pursued, there should be an agreement that the UK would go to the IMF for a drawing if need be to repay the swap on time (i.e. after three months). Moreover he was against the idea of a full drawing on the swap line. The Italians had been able to draw only one-quarter of their swap facility. Later that evening Simon, the US Secretary of the Treasury, telephoned the Chancellor to say that Burns wanted to help and he himself was in favour, but only on the basis that there was 'a Fund take-out'. He said that the Governor should take matters further with Burns the following day. The Chancellor mentioned, for the first time, the possibility that he might 'ask the Europeans for $1 billion'.

The American unwillingness to agree to a full drawing of the swap was probably the reason which led to the next, somewhat unexpected, development. Early in the afternoon of Friday 4 June the Governor received a telephone call from the Chairman of the BIS, the 'head prefect' within the central banking community. The current occupant of this position was Zjilstra, who was also the President of the Netherlands National Bank. Ziljstra must have been approached by Burns with the information that the UK was in need of short-term credit and was proposing to activate the 'Fed' swap. Whether Burns added that the Chancellor had indicated to Simon that he might want to turn to the Europeans for a contribution, or whether he suggested of his own accord that the BIS might also provide some help in order to soften the impact of Simon's opposition to a full activation of the swap, or indeed whether the idea of a full BIS credit was Ziljstra's own idea is not clear. At all events Ziljstra told the Governor that he would try to organize a Group of Ten (G10)[70] support operation for sterling. In this he

---

[69] BP 98/33/02 and DW 036.

[70] The group of ten leading industrialized countries which also formed the source of additional finance for the IMF under what was known as The General Arrangements to Borrow (GAB), see Glossary.

achieved a remarkable success in a matter of hours and by Monday morning he had obtained the unanimous agreement of his colleagues to such a collective credit. However, whereas all the other participants were prepared to supply credit from their central bank's assets, the Americans decided that rather than activate the swap they would supply their funds from the US Treasury's own resources. The reason for this tactic was not clear at the time—Burns spoke of difficulties he was having with Congress over help for other countries (Italy was a case in point) but it seems as much as anything to have been a decision taken in the US Treasury to ensure that the question of renewal and repayment should be in its hands and not in those of the Federal Reserve. The US Secretary to the Treasury and his Under-Secretary were to become important players in the resolution of the financial crisis later in the year and by giving a role to their own institution in the Central Bank credit they were staking out their claims to a voice in what the terms of the credit should be and whether it could be 'rolled over'.

The total credit obtained by this exercise was $5.3 billion, made up as shown in Table 4.1.[71]

The terms of the credit were crucially important—to the creditors and to the debtor alike. The maturity was three months, although there was provision for renewal for three months, but not more. For its part the UK agreed to an important condition laid down by the creditors, that is that if it were necessary to obtain credit to repay the credit it would seek a drawing from the IMF.

The operation accordingly changed significantly the character of the drama which until then had been played out largely on the national stage. From 7 June, when the credit was finally agreed and announced, the scene widened considerably. The creditors, particularly the US Treasury, felt, not unreasonably, that their participation gave them an authority to monitor the British

Table 4.1 Composition of $5.3 billion credit obtained in June 1976

Source	Amount
United States	$2 billion
Belgium	$200 million
Canada	$300 million
France	$300 million
Germany	$800 million
Japan	$600 million
Netherlands	$200 million
Sweden	$150 million
Switzerland	$600 million
BIS	$150 million
Total	$5.3 billion

[71] BP 98/33/02.

Government's economic policy and to comment on it in a way which, except perhaps in international fora like the OECD and the IMF Board was, to say the least, unusual. But the Fund too were implicitly brought into the scene, for it immediately became apparent that recourse to its resources by the UK—on a substantial scale—was now well within the bounds of possibility.

The taking of the credit, with all its implications, was done with very little consultation of Ministers outside the Treasury—apart of course from the Prime Minister who consented to the exploration of the idea. A meeting of the Economic Strategy Committee was informed, *ex post facto*, on the morning of 7 June[72] shortly before the credit was announced to the House of Commons. What is perhaps surprising is that there was very little debate within the Treasury about the consequences of the credit. The view expressed by Lever at the meeting, that the UK should take a large international credit and spend it to defend the sterling rate, was accepted without any serious appraisal of the alternatives, or of the implications. It is perhaps true that the conclusion drawn by most Treasury officials involved was that the credit probably made recourse to the Fund later in the year very probable but this was an idea which had already begun to take shape within the Treasury. It is also true that there was, at the time, some slight hope that the combination of the breathing space bought by the credit, the degree of confidence it might inspire in the minds of the official sterling holders and the announcement of a fiscal package sometime in mid-summer would at least stop the haemorrhaging of the re-serves and perhaps promote an inflow of currency into the UK. But the failure of the announcement of the credit to shore up confidence and the subsequent unwillingness of the Treasury to draw on the credit[73] because of its short maturity meant that it had little real effect on the situation. We discuss later the importance of the Central Bank credit and the counter-factual issue of whether there was, as the Treasury seemed to argue at the time, a credible alternative to it. Here it suffices only to rehearse the facts and the consequences.

The effect of the announcement of the credit on the markets was initially favourable, but short-lived. The Treasury had prepared itself for some upward movement in the exchange rate and even contemplated that it might go above $1.80, but it acknowledged that the pressure might go the other way and proposed that if necessary intervention should be made to prevent it falling below the rate on 4 June. Sterling did in fact rally from $1.7170 on the morning of 7 June to $1.7699 the day after. But the recovery was not achieved without cost. In the first week following the announcement the scale of intervention was heavy. It became immediately apparent that confidence had not been restored by the credit, which could easily be used up to little

---

[72] CAB 134/4025.

[73] In all, during the currency of the swaps, only just over $1.5 billion of the $5.3 billion was drawn, and that mainly to bolster the monthly published figures for the reserves.

effect. If an inflow of money did not occur the Government would be faced with the inevitability of having to go to the Fund to repay the debt and take the medicine which the Fund would insist on. The Chancellor and the Treasury were clearly worried where we were now going, and a meeting was called with the Bank on 10 June[74] to assess the prospects. Discussion focused on the question of how much more to intervene in the markets to support the exchange rate and what to do if intervention failed to stabilize the situation. The Treasury, represented only by the OF Division, thought that the Bank should continue to support sterling. No conclusions were reached, but the Bank said that MLR would be raised the following day and this might have a steadying effect.[75] On 11 June Lever wrote to the Chancellor[76] suggesting that he should make a statement to the effect that 'we should be cutting public expenditure next year to permit a shift of resources into the balance of payments'.[77]

The Treasury was now becoming increasingly convinced that the only effective measure to stem the reserve loss and the decline in sterling would be to take policy decisions which would satisfy market expectations. The case for a policy change was expressed at some length in a personal note which the Permanent Secretary sent to the Chancellor on 14 June.[78] He had spent the end of the previous week in Paris at a meeting of the OECD Economic Policy Committee, attended by the senior officials from the Ministries of Finance and Central Banks, and had had the chance to discuss the British situation privately with his colleagues from the Group of Seven. His note was, therefore, based on some solid evidence of opinion in the main creditor countries. 'Every indication is', he said, 'that a budgetary package will need to include reductions in the Government's planned target for public expenditure from at least 1977–78 onwards if it is to carry conviction with our creditors... we need a major change in fiscal policy as the necessary condition for IMF support. The precise timetable is exceedingly difficult to predict at this stage. On fairly optimistic assumptions we might have till July; at worst it could be this week. On any basis it seems essential that Cabinet should be in a position to take major decisions for 1977–78 and publish a special White Paper before the summer recess.... I have asked the Department to bring to a high state of readiness contingency plans for a budgetary package... including substantial cuts in public expenditure in 1977–78'.

The argument put to the Chancellor was in essence that the Central Bank credit had failed to reassure the markets and that only fairly urgent action to

---

[74] DW 036.

[75] MLR was not in fact raised, but the reasons for the change in intention does not emerge from the Treasury or the Bank files.

[76] Ibid.

[77] It is interesting that Lever was advocating this, since by the time expenditure cuts for 1978–79 came to the Cabinet at the time of the Fund drawing in December, he was fiercely opposing them.

[78] Ibid.

reduce the Budget deficit would satisfy them. It was no longer a case of looking at what the domestic UK situation called for, and therefore of making a careful appraisal of the state of the economy. That would be done on the occasion of the MTA and the NIF, both of which were not as yet finalized. But it was unlikely that this analysis would weigh very heavily with Treasury officials.

The Chancellor had a meeting with his advisers later the same day and discussed both the timetable and the tactics to be employed in the foreign exchange market pending any substantive policy decision. Cabinet was due to discuss the MTA and its implications for the public expenditure survey on 6 July. This would be the occasion for the decisions which the Treasury wanted and would enable a 'crisis' White Paper to be published later in the month. One difficulty, however, was that the NIF would not be completed before 6 July and it would not be possible to give the Cabinet a PSBR forecast for 1977–78, still less for the following year—something that might well be essential to getting Cabinet endorsement to the cuts that the Treasury would be seeking. Meantime the tactics to be used in the foreign exchange markets would have to be decided. The exchange rate was unlikely to be helped by the publication on 14 June of poor trade figures for May[79] and there would be a temptation to spend more of the reserves. The Treasury, and indeed the Governor himself, suggested that one way of husbanding the reserves would be for the Chancellor to give the Bank a fixed sum of foreign exchange to use until the policy measures could be announced and leave it to the Bank to decide on day-to-day tactics.[80] The target for the rate should be \$1.715–1.80 (the current rate was \$1.77). The Chancellor went even further; there should be no intervention unless the rate fell to \$1.70. Meantime the US Treasury was beginning to flex its muscles over UK policy and let it be known that monetary policy, in the form of a call for special deposits, should now form a part of the strategy. The Bank and Treasury were inclined to dismiss this idea on the grounds that the monetary position had been tightened by some successful selling of long-dated gilt-edged stock and no further action was called for.

Public expenditure—Part 2

From the middle of June senior officials in the Treasury concentrated their attention on the establishment of the case that Ministers might be prepared to accept for public expenditure cuts in 1977–78—cuts that would bring the

---

[79] They showed a deficit on visible trade of £342 million—well above the average monthly deficit for 1976.
[80] Ibid.

total of spending below the White Paper level for that year and bring some reassurance to a demoralized market. The Chancellor had made it plain that, certainly in the light of the options displayed in the PESC report to which we refer later, he would need more than an appeal to confidence to persuade his ministerial colleagues to see their spending programmes cut yet again. As previous discussions had shown, they saw an economy operating below capacity with unemployment well over 1 million and would see little rational justification in reducing economic activity by cutting spending. In any case the political difficulties in reducing some important social service programmes needed no emphasis. By the middle of the month the first indications of the MTA became available and the PCC examined it at its meeting on 14 June. As expected, the outlook it showed for the immediate future was not an economy which was supply-constrained and the case, on supply and resource grounds, for restrictive action was not an overwhelming one. On the other hand some members of the committee thought that the rise in output in the following year could be quite strong and precautionary reductions in public spending for that year were a reasonable response—an argument that the IMF team had made in forceful terms in May. Others argued that, rather than rely on purely resource arguments, the Treasury should base its case on financial grounds, in particular the size of the borrowing requirement (still estimated at some £12 billion for the following financial year—1977–78—and possibly leading to a growth in the money supply which might add to inflationary pressures).

The PCC resumed its discussion of the MTA and the implications it had for policy on 21 June and again two days later.[81] By this time the Treasury case was taking firm shape and the Chairman spelt out the arguments that would have to be used with Ministers:

1 The main official sterling holders,[82] who had now been identified as the source of the problem, thought that the PSBR was too high and they had a strong preference for reducing it by cutting expenditure rather than by increasing taxes.

2 The outlook was that the economy would be growing quite strongly in 1977 and it was important that the volume of UK exports should not be held up by supply constraints or by buoyant home demand augmented by strong public sector demand.

3 If the opportunity to cut public expenditure were not taken now, that is at a critical phase of the PESC cycle, and an adjustment to fiscal policy in 1977–78 had to be made later on, it would be necessary for the whole burden of that adjustment to fall on taxation, with clear implications for net personal incomes and hence for the future of Incomes Policy.

[81] PCC (76) 24th and 25th Meetings.
[82] Most of the overseas central banks would have known, from their representative directors on the Fund Executive Board, that this was also the view of the Fund staff.

The question which had to be answered, however, was how big should the cuts in spending in 1977–78 be. It was this question which began to expose differences within the Treasury hierarchy. The Overseas side wanted to go for cuts of £2 billion, on the grounds that only a figure of this order would impress the markets; moreover the IMF had been talking of cuts of £3 billion earlier in the year. The Industrial Strategy side also wanted to aim at this figure, but on the grounds that this would enable interest rates to be reduced and would in any case free resources for the manufacturing sector during the upswing. But, as is so often the case, it was an Horatian situation—those behind cried 'Forward!' and those before cried 'Back'. The side of the Treasury (the Expenditure sector) which would have to deliver the cuts had serious reservations on practical grounds. The head of the sector said 'that it was very doubtful whether the Cabinet could agree on cuts amounting to more than £1 billion, which would do real damage to the fabric of the public services'. He had already told the Committee at its meeting on 27 May[83] that the main aim of the PESC round had been the *holding* of spending to the White Paper figure for year 1 (i.e. 1977–78) and as we have seen, at the Chancellor's meeting with Lever on 3 June he had said that cuts of £3 billion were out of the question. The Chairman of the PCC judged that the majority of the Committee were inclined to limit the objective to £1 billion. It was conceded, however, that cuts of this order would translate only to about £600 million reduction in the PSBR—mainly because tax receipts would fall to some extent with the decline in government spending. There was clearly anxiety that a reduction of so small an amount might fail to convince the markets that the UK had its problem under control.

On 3 June[84] the Chancellor had been given a preview of what the MTA, whose revised basis had been described to him in the submission of 9 April referred to above, would be likely to imply. 'A certain picture is beginning to emerge,' it said, 'that despite the improvement in our competitive position in the past three months, we have problems with the balance of payments right up to 1979 and could well fail to reduce unemployment to 3 per cent unless we can expand the supply of manufacturing output much faster than in the past.... The blunt fact is that our financing prospect over the next few years may be such as to raise a question whether we can afford to maintain, let alone, increase our present spending plans'. The paper went on to discuss how the prospect should be presented to Cabinet for the planned debate on the results of the PESC appraisal. The idea was that the Chancellor should not spare his colleagues and should give 'an unconstrained realistic assumption forecast' but to 1979 only—not as was usual to cover the final year of the PESC report. 'We had in any case envisaged that in the Treasury paper to accompany the PESC report the emphasis would be on decisions about 1977–78 and to a lesser

---

[83] PCC (76) 21st Meeting.   [84] PCC (76)37.

extent 1978–79 on the practical grounds that the credibility and success of the existing White Paper plans and in consequence our creditworthiness in the world depend on getting through this year and next within at most the White Paper limits.... We should be reverting to the previously accepted concept of firm decisions for one year (1977–78) and near firm decisions for 1978–79'. The Treasury were getting well away from Plowden and asking for a quite different Cabinet debate about the problem of public spending.

The formal submission on the MTA and its implications for spending decisions was put by the Treasury to the Chancellor on 24 June[85] and it covered a draft paper for him to present to his colleagues, first the Economic Strategy Committee on 2 July and subsequently, on 6 July, the full Cabinet. The two-stage process would enable the Chancellor, it was hoped, to win a substantial proportion of his colleagues over at the first meeting and then, with their support, to take on the main spending colleagues in the full Cabinet. The covering note by the Permanent Secretary summarized the MTA as shown in Table 4.2.

There was, of course, a certain amount of artificiality in the assumptions underlying the assessment and a huge leap of imagination required so far as exogeneous factors (like the future of the Pay Policy) were concerned. The bias was clearly still towards favourable assumptions in spite of the attempt to make the assessment more realistic. But, even so, the outlook was bleak and unlikely to inspire confidence on the part of the UK's overseas creditors. The nub of the submission was, however, on what this admittedly doubtful assessment implied for policy. Looking at the balance of payments forecast, with its remorseless growth in external debt, the paper said 'Further depreciation over and above the modest depreciation assumed in the MTA does not seem to be a desirable option for the time being... our principal aim must be to establish the conditions in which it will be possible to finance the deficits. This means satisfying our creditors about the conduct of our domestic policies.... Any thought that we should "soldier on" and borrow are academic with a forecast PSBR of £12 billion in both calendar 1977 and 1977–78'. Big reductions were

Table 4.2 Summary of MTA submission of 24 June 1976

Main Case	1976	1977	1978	1979
GDP growth (%)	2.5	4.3	4.0	3.9
Unemployment (%)	5.5	5.9	5.3	5.1
Price increases	14.9	10.0	7.6	5.1
Balance of Payments (£b)	–1.9	–3.2	–2.7	–0.8
PSBR (£b)	10.2	12.2	10.9	9.6

[85] DW 015.

called for and it would be 'wrong to put it all on tax . . . decisions on spending in 1977–78 need to be taken now.' The paper ended with the view, which as we saw was not universal, that the Chancellor should seek cuts of £1 billion that year. The Permanent Secretary put to the Chancellor a separate and private note in which he gave his advice on how the Chancellor should play the difficult cards he had been dealt with his Cabinet colleagues. There were two legs to the argument: the confidence factor and the need to provide resources for the likely upswing in world demand in 1977. The confidence argument was paramount, but there were grounds also on the availability of resources for creating spare capacity for exports. The note warned the Chancellor that if the Cabinet rejected his advice 'the adjustment will have to be greater and more disruptive when forced upon us'. It also revealed that the Governor favoured cuts of £2 billion as did some Treasury officials. The figure of £1 billion was very much what those who supported it thought to be the most that would get Cabinet agreement.

There was an interesting aside to this issue when the Prime Minister, the Chancellor, and the Foreign Secretary (since April, Anthony Crosland) had a briefing meeting at Chequers on 26 June just before their departure to the Economic Summit hosted by President Ford at Puerto Rico.[86] Although not formally an issue for the Summit, the question of the stance of British economic policy was bound to come up and was briefly discussed by the three Ministers. The Foreign Secretary showed considerable doubt about the need on economic grounds for any cuts in public expenditure and the Prime Minister himself expressed anxieties about his ability to get the Cabinet to agree even to cuts of £1 billion. It was at this meeting also that the Prime Minister repeated his doubts about the wisdom of spending so much in the currency markets defending sterling and he instructed the Bank (the Governor was present at the meeting) not to spend any more. The Governor protested about the wisdom of a blanket ban, and asked that the interdiction should be put on hold pending a formal submission by him on the subject when he returned from the Summit.

The advice given by the Treasury to the Chancellor to seek £1 billion of public expenditure cuts in 1977–78 was, as we have seen, based partly on confidence arguments, partly on the need to reduce the PSBR to something approaching what the IMF would think to be acceptable and partly on the economic need to ensure that domestic demand in 1977 did not hold up the expansion of exports which would become possible with the upsurge in world economic activity. The Chancellor wanted to make as much as possible about the 'real' as opposed to the 'confidence' reasons.[87] But it was not until the NIF was completed early in July that the Treasury was in a position to substantiate

[86] Chancellor's Private Secretary note of 28 June on DW 062.
[87] PCC (76) 24th Meeting.

these arguments. It forecast a strong cyclical recovery of the economy with annual growth of 5 per cent in the eighteen months from the first half of 1976 to the second half of 1977. Compared with the post-Budget forecast three months earlier, economic growth was expected to be stronger, unemployment lower, and the balance of payments, thanks largely to the depreciation of sterling which had occurred since March, much improved. The economic case for some reining in of demand was therefore not an unreasonable one. The forecast for the PSBR for 1977–78 at £10.5 billion was somewhat better than had been suggested by the MTA. The proposed expenditure cuts would therefore go a good way towards reducing the borrowing requirement to single (billion) figures.

The timing of the advice to the Chancellor that he should seek the agreement of his colleagues to spending cuts amounting to £1 billion was fortuitously convenient, for it fitted in well with the timing of the Cabinet's consideration of the report of the Public Expenditure Survey Committee which had, as already stated, set out illustrative options for cuts amounting to £969–1,047 million for 1977–78. It was reasonably clear to the spending ministers, therefore, what the impact of the Chancellor's proposals would be for them. This was not to be a case of the Cabinet agreeing in principle to a specific size of total cut and then finding it difficult to accept the consequences for each programme.

The sequence of Ministerial meetings to consider the issue of expenditure cuts began with a meeting of EY (the Ministerial Committee on Economic Strategy) on 2 July.[88] The Chancellor chose not to put in a paper at this stage but used the occasion to brief his colleagues on the economic situation and what it was likely to entail in the way of a response. But his colleague, the Energy Secretary (Benn), was not similarly restrained and put in a paper of his own[89] which anticipated that the Chancellor would be asking for expenditure cuts and argued against them, as an immediate option if not later on. He recognized that there was a confidence issue but claimed, without much supporting evidence, that the IMF could be persuaded to agree to endorse the UK's general policy on the basis of an orderly examination of the expenditure and tax priorities without immediate action, which could easily damage the government's relations with the trade unions. But somewhat illogically it went on to argue for direct action on imports, which would certainly not have carried the IMF's endorsement. The Chancellor was robust in the presentation of his case, which he made on economic, financial, and confidence grounds. He explicitly called for cuts of £1 billion in 1977–78 although he recognized that commentators were asking for double that amount. The Committee displayed a range of positions, with some members arguing for even greater discipline than the Chancellor seemed to be calling for, but with others doubtful. But it was acknowledged that only the Cabinet could take decisions

---

[88] CAB 134/4025.   [89] CAB 129/190/18.

on public expenditure. The Prime Minister wisely asked that, when the Cabinet considered the question, the position of expenditure levels in *1978–79* should be considered as well as those in the previous year.

The EY Committee meeting was followed on 6 July by a full meeting of Cabinet[90] which took both a background paper by the Chancellor on the economic situation and a paper by the Chief Secretary[91] giving the results of the PESC round together with the spending reduction options described above. The Energy Secretary again put in a personal paper[92] repeating what he had said in his paper to EY. The Chancellor now called for expenditure cuts that would cut the PSBR in 1977–78 by £1 billion, acknowledging that this would mean cuts of about £1.25 billion. The Chief Secretary listed what he thought were feasible cuts, totalling £1 billion, although he admitted that, if the contingency reserve were to be increased to a realistic level, this would require additional cuts. There was, thus, something of a difference between the two Treasury ministers, but perhaps not such as to create a problem. In presenting his paper the Chancellor reduced his bid for spending cuts from £1.25 billion to £1 billion, but this had little impact on his opponents. The initial discussion was inconclusive although the Prime Minister concluded that a majority of the Cabinet were persuaded by the Chancellor. He did not however press for a formal conclusion, but reserved that for a later meeting, which was held on 15 July,[93] and like its predecessor was given new papers by both the Chancellor and the Energy Secretary.[94] But for this meeting the Environment Secretary (Shore) joined in the written debate with a paper, also criticizing the Chancellor's proposals not least on the grounds (which subsequent events confirmed) that the measures would be unlikely to convince the markets and that it would be necessary to go to the IMF later on and end up with even larger cuts. The discussion was now more conclusive than its predecessor and the Prime Minister was able to sum up to the effect that a majority of the Cabinet were prepared to go along with the Treasury. The question now was how to make up the package—and this proved to be a time-consuming business. Between 19 and 21 July no less than five Cabinet meetings took place as Ministers went through the list of proposed cuts and either assented to them or rejected them—or simply postponed a decision. The experience amply justified the scepticism of the Expenditure side of the Treasury, which had predicted that even to secure £1 billion of cuts would put immense strains on the cohesion of the Cabinet.

Before the final marathon meetings of 19–21 July and even as it appeared probable that in the end the Chancellor would get his £1 billion cuts, the Treasury began to have cold feet about the adequacy of the package to convince the market. (It was also apparent that the resulting PSBR for the critical

[90] CAB 128/59/13.   [91] CAB 129/190/17.   [92] CAB 129/190/28.
[93] CAB 128/59/15.   [94] CAB 129/190/25.

year (1977–78) would be some way off the target the Treasury believed might be acceptable to the Fund.) The reaction of Cabinet colleagues to what the Treasury regarded as the minimal expenditure package made it clear that there was no hope whatever of increasing the proposed cuts. On 13 July the senior members of the Treasury looked at the scope for accompanying any announcement of expenditure cuts with an immediately announced tax increase. (The Chancellor had told his colleagues that he might have to raise taxation in the following Budget in the Spring of 1977, but he had not asked for a decision there and then, on the grounds that that would depend on how events developed in the economy.) The Finance Bill was not yet on the Statute Book, and could be amended to incorporate tax increases. The head of the Industrial Sector of the Treasury, who was also responsible for taxation, said that his preference would be to go for the announcement of an increase in the employers' contribution to the National Insurance Fund to take place in the following spring.[95] This was supported by others, and accordingly a submission to the Chancellor was commissioned which argued the case and made specific suggestions. The relevant division prepared a paper[96] which looked at the timing and the legislative requirements and concluded that a 1 per cent increase was possible. This was submitted to the Permanent Secretary who put the whole issue to the Chancellor in a minute dated 16 July. He conceded that to raise taxation by way of a payroll tax, even of a small amount, which this was, had substantial disadvantages.[97] It would be strongly resented by business even if the tax was passed on in prices, for the interval between the imposition of the surcharge and its recovery by business from its customers would mean a cash loss to industry. The impost would worsen the outlook for prices, which was already worrying given the fall in the exchange rate. Finally the market would regard the surcharge as a poor substitute for cuts in expenditure.

In spite of these disadvantages the Permanent Secretary argued that the Government had to make the package look credible. The present forecast a £9 billion target for the PSBR in 1977–78—the highest figure that might be acceptable to the IMF—would only be hit after the expenditure cuts if taxes were raised for that year. He did not think that a general forward commitment to raise taxes in the 1977 Budget, if it were necessary to achieve the target, would carry any conviction. A firm decision now was essential. He therefore favoured an increase in employers' national insurance contributions—but he went even further than his colleagues and proposed that the increase should be 2 per cent. This would yield an increase in revenue *ex ante* of

---

[95] DW 014—13 July.

[96] GEP 8/9/03.

[97] Senior officials in the Treasury had looked at the pros and cons of a payroll tax as a useful possible new source of revenue at the end of June and had concluded that its disadvantages severely outweighed its advantages. But that was on the basis of a permanent new tax yielding a significant amount of revenue.

£1 billion—that is before the revenue and expenditure consequences of the measure were taken into account.[98] What was important was that if the Chancellor accepted this advice he should not tell his Cabinet colleagues, at least until they had delivered the expenditure cuts he was still seeking. 'Spending ministers ought not to see a soft option for themselves'. The Chancellor accepted this advice, pending the outcome of the expenditure discussions and at their conclusion, when the decisions were taken, he formally committed himself to the surcharge and its inclusion in the package.

The Cabinet returned to take final decisions on the package on the morning of 21 July[99] apparently to settle the few outstanding expenditure issues—the total of agreed cuts was still £100 million short of the target agreed. However, the Prime Minister finally threw his weight behind the Chancellor but said that the limit of the cuts would have to be £954 million and that the composition of the package would be put for approval later the same day. It was at this point that the Chancellor pulled the National Insurance Surcharge idea out of the hat by circulating a memorandum at short notice, proposing the 2 per cent increase in employers' contributions. The Cabinet reconvened at 5.30 p.m. and the discussion was clearly very heated. Even the normally restrained Cabinet Office reporting of Cabinet discussions leaves the reader in no doubt that the Chancellor's colleagues were furious at this development. The Energy Secretary circulated a note round the table denouncing the move as deflationary and liable to do grave damage to the Government's relations with the trade unions. His objections were echoed round the table and it must have been very difficult for the Prime Minister to sum up at the end to the effect that, although the measure would put a great strain on the Government's general policy, the Cabinet were willing to accept the Chancellor's recommendations. Those who voiced their criticism felt, exactly as the Treasury had predicted, that they had been asked to take extremely difficult political decisions on public expenditure in ignorance of one particular option, which could have been regarded as an alternative, not an addition, to the measures they had reluctantly agreed to.

Monetary targets

There was another new ingredient to the package that was now being assembled: the inclusion of a qualified target for the growth in the money supply. References in Chancellorial speeches to the rate of growth of £M3 (the preferred choice of the definition of money) were not new. They had occurred

---

[98] The net effect on the PSBR of the expenditure cuts of £1 billion and the NI surcharge yielding a further £1 billion was estimated at only a little over £1 billion.

[99] CAB 128/59/20.

in his Budget speeches but always without any normative connotation. The Treasury and the Bank were profoundly sceptical whether there was any reliable link between the rate of growth of the money stock and the subsequent rate of inflation and there were few in either institution who thought that by controlling the rate of expansion of money (if this could, in fact, be done in any reliable way) the authorities would secure a benefit in the shape of a reduction in the rise of prices. At a meeting the Chancellor had with the Deputy Governor of the Bank as early as 5 August 1975[100] on external financing the latter said that 'it was not really worth while to have monetary targets'—a view very much in line with what the Bank had been saying publicly for several years. This hardly displayed a commitment to expressing monetary policy in terms of monetary expansion. The technical Bank/Treasury Group on Monetary Policy (MPG) was similarly agnostic about numerical targets. It focused much more on such issues as the behaviour of bank liquidity as an indicator of a potential for an upsurge in asset prices. However, it did briefly look at the existing practice of publicly presenting the Government's expectations about the money supply when a paper was presented to it on 23 December 1975[101] stating that 'the existing monetary objective, expressed as keeping the growth of the money supply below the rate of inflation is ill-founded and is insufficient to ensure that monetary factors do not jeopardise counter-inflations policy'. This bland statement left open the question of whether something more definite would in fact be supportive of counter-inflation policy, but it did at least put the issue on the table, even though it seems not to have been seriously considered by the Group as having any policy implications.

In the course of 1976, however, the question was posed as to whether something a bit more 'monetarist' in the way of public statements might not be of value if confidence had to be shored up. A meeting of senior Treasury officials debated whether to put the idea forward as early as 23 March,[102] possibly prompted by the MPG paper referred to above, but it seems that this was not pursued. The question that the adoption of a numerical target posed was what action would be taken in the event that the target was not hit. It was not obvious that a rise in short-term interest rates would restore the path of monetary expansion to the desired path; indeed the only tested measure which might affect the money supply figures was the 'Corset', a direct control of the growth of the banking system's eligible liabilities which had been in operation between December 1973 and February 1975. Treasury officials were left in the rather ambivalent position of wanting to reassure the market on this point but avoiding having to make a mechanistic response to any particular path for monetary expansion. The Chancellor's statement to the House of Commons on 7 June announcing the central bank credit provided

[100] DW 036.   [101] MPG(75)17.   [102] DW 014.

an opportunity to re-affirm his commitment to caution concerning the rate of growth of the money supply but it did not go any further than the previous references.

As the July package came to be assembled, however, the firming up of the statement of intention regarding monetary expansion was an inevitable candidate. At the Second Secretaries meeting on 13 July the Permanent Secretary reported that the Chancellor wanted to incorporate a monetary target in his forthcoming statement.[103] The question was what form should the commitment to such a target take. The preferred route was to strengthen what had been said previously without committing the Government to doing anything specific if the announced target or path were not achieved. To the believing monetarist this left a lot to be desired. On the other hand a great many market operators, while not fully subscribing to the monetarist creed, did believe that a high rate of monetary expansion led to some unwanted consequences, of which the stimulation of inflation was probably the most likely. The Bank had certainly come round to the view that a fairly strong statement about monetary intentions would be a useful addition to the July package and proposed a target range of 8–12 per cent for the financial year 1976–77—this being the highest which would give any help with confidence. The Treasury were concerned at the risks this posed for some fiscal action later in the year if, for instance, gilt sales flagged. The financial forecast which accompanied the NIF[104] suggested that £M3 was likely to rise by 14.7 per cent in the current financial year—so a target of 8–12 per cent would imply some policy change before the expenditure cuts and NI surcharge being considered came into effect. For the following year the rate of increase would decline to about 9 per cent and this would mean that without further action there would be difficulty in setting a lesser target for 1977–78 than the 8–12 per cent being contemplated for the current year.

The Permanent Secretary, who had been chairing meetings with the Bank on this issue, put his views to the Chancellor on 16 July,[105] which he said represented the majority, not the unanimous, view. He argued against 'targetry' in general, citing the failures there had been in the areas of prices, unemployment, etc. and said that, if the situation were not now critical, he and most of his colleagues would argue against one for the money supply—for the reasons that fortuitous events, such as a failure to sell government debt even for a short period, could lead to an overshoot of the target. But the issue now was whether 'notwithstanding the pain a target could inflict on us later on, the confidence-raising value in the package could make all the difference between success and failure. Since we cannot afford failure we must have a target'. He was, however, against a range of 8–12 per cent for the current year and recommended a single figure—12 per cent. There was some discussion as to whether the monetary

---

[103] DW 014.   [104] PCC (76)45.   [105] HF 35/04.

target might not be DCE rather than £M3 and the latter was chosen on the rather cynical grounds that the Fund were likely to go for a DCE target and it would be less obvious that the government had had to tighten monetary policy in response to outside pressure if it were, in effect, to switch from one target variable to another! The Chancellor had a meeting with the Bank and senior Treasury officials on Tuesday 20 July[106]—two days before the statement. The Bank argued for a fairly firm commitment. The Treasury did not demur but baulked at the idea of a target for the *following* financial year and continued to advocate a 12 per cent limit. The Chancellor agreed a qualified target of 12 per cent but for only one year. The actual words used by the Chancellor in his Parliamentary statement were 'For the financial year as a whole money supply growth should amount to about 12 per cent. Such an outcome would be fully consistent with our objectives for reducing inflation. I repeat the assurances I have given that I do not intend to allow the growth of the money supply to fuel inflation either this year or next.' Whether this statement of intent constituted a monetary target is a matter of opinion. The Treasury seemed inclined to think that it was no more binding a commitment than had been previous declarations about the monetary variables.

The Bank, however, clearly took it more as a firm commitment and began to prepare for action if the path looked like leading to an overshoot. This was to take the form of a resuscitation of the Corset, about which we have more to say later. For the rest, the statement summarized the extent of the expenditure cuts which had been decided upon for the following year and announced that the PSBR would be reduced to £9 billion in 1977–78—some 6.2 per cent of GDP compared with 9.3 per cent for the current year and 9.8 per cent the previous year.[107]

Sterling—Part 4 the examination of import controls

The public expenditure measures and the intentions for the money supply were duly announced on 22 July. They may have been all that the Chancellor could get out of his colleagues and it may indeed have been all that was necessary to deal strictly with the macro-economic situation, but it did not satisfy either the expectations or the requirements of those players in the drama who now had it in their collective power to dictate the shape of British economic policy. The press, both in the UK and abroad, were at best unenthusiastic about the statement. The Washington correspondent of *The Times*

---

[106] Ibid.

[107] The financial forecast made by the Treasury in the light of the measures of 22 July was that the PSBR in 1977–78 would be reduced from £10.6 billion to £9 billion and that DCE for that year would be reduced from £9.9 billion to £8.1 billion. The rate of growth of £M3 would decline from 13.2 per cent to 9.2 per cent.

reported that the IMF saw the expenditure cuts 'as only a start' and when the Managing Director of the Fund was apprised of the contents of the statement by the UK Director he said, politely, that the statement was 'obviously a step in the right direction . . . but the staff will have to study it'. The US Treasury Undersecretary was similarly lukewarm when told of the measures. Surveying the whole foreign government reactions, the Treasury found that 'reactions have been goodish . . . but with an undertone of doubt in some quarters as to whether more may not be needed later . . . there was no discussion at Monday's meeting of the EEC Finance Council . . . foreign press reaction has been mixed'.

The Prime Minister had invested a substantial amount of personal capital in promoting the statement, with messages to his counterparts in the United States, France, and Germany. To President Ford he was anxious to describe both the extent of the measures and at the same time to reassure him that the Defence cuts which formed part of the package would not damage the capacity of the UK to play its full part in the NATO alliance. The recipients of these messages were suitably polite in their replies and President Ford told the Prime Minister that he thought that he had persuaded Simon (the Treasury Secretary) to support the statement. It is difficult to interpret the replies as very much more than diplomatic courtesies, and there could be little in them to give confidence to London that it was carrying international approval.

The Chancellor had, by eventually securing the agreement, or at least the acquiescence, of his colleagues to the retrenchment measures of July, won a significant victory, for, as the record shows, a small but vocal element of the Cabinet had considerable reservations about the strategy he was pursuing. There were really two elements to these reservations. The more moderate view was that it was wrong to be deflating the economy when it was still depressed, even though according to the Treasury an upswing was in sight. The more critical view was that the whole strategy was wrong and that a more interventionist policy was called for, a part of which would involve some restriction on imports, whether by way of import duties (or import deposits) or quantitative restrictions. The Chancellor had attempted to rebut these calls at the meetings of the Economic Strategy Committee meetings earlier in the year, but the Trade Secretary (at that time Shore) had modified his original suggestion of a regime of generalized trade restrictions so as to consist only of a standstill on the imports of consumer goods and semi-manufactures at the levels obtaining in 1975. Although less restrictive than the original idea it would—because of the depressed levels of manufactured imports in that year—have contributed to an improvement in the trade balance over the medium term and, as the Trade Secretary said, have permitted some modest domestic reflation of the economy. Ministers had, as we saw, agreed that this idea should be looked at by officials in an interdepartmental context— a step which ensured that the Treasury would not be in sole control of the examination.

The interdepartmental group looked at the issue, postulating that the regime would last for five years.[108] The regime they considered was one which applied to a number of consumer industries such as textiles and footwear, consumer electronics, instrumental engineering, and so on. They considered the legal implications, the effect on consumers and the likely international reactions. Their conclusion was decidedly negative. 'Generalised, but short-term, measures of restraint might be countenanced (as in the case of Italy)... but there is no likelihood whatever that in any circumstances the EEC Commission or Council would acquiesce in the UK taking generalised measures of import control on a medium- to long-term basis'. Retaliation would be certain. 'We could not expect to get international agreement to any scheme of import restraint except on a short term basis and only then if we were in a very much worse employment and balance of payments situation than at present.' This interdepartmental conclusion might be thought to have disposed of the issue, but it did not. The report was considered at a meeting of EY on 15 June[109]— ahead of the discussions on public expenditure in July. The Chancellor spoke strongly in favour of the rejection of generalized import controls in whatever form they might take, and a majority of his colleagues agreed with him, although the Prime Minister in siding with the majority said that the option of adopting them should remain on the table; and indeed during the course of the discussions on the July package the dissidents in the Cabinet again put forward the idea of some administrative control over the level of imports.

As it became apparent in the days following 22 July that the statement had not produced a lasting change in market sentiment and had not won anything like enthusiastic endorsement by foreign governments or the Fund, the weakness of sterling, occasioned largely by the resumed diversification of their sterling assets by the official holders, resurfaced. This outcome prompted the Treasury to dust over the contingency plans for action in the event of a further sharp decline in confidence. Because of the almost universal opposition of the international community, as well as the legal constraints, the idea of generalized import controls was not favoured, except perhaps in the most extreme emergency. What was not forbidden by the international community nor was likely to provoke reaction was a system of import deposits and it was just such a system which the Treasury presented to the Chancellor[110] as a fall-back position if the market situation should show no response and in fact deteriorate sharply. It is worth describing what such a system involved, for the use of import deposits became, later in the year, not only the Treasury's defence of 'last resort' but also the preferred course of some of those of the Chancellor's colleagues—including the Prime Minister—who were reluctant to take any further restrictive economic measures. The essence of a scheme of import deposits was that importers (possibly excluding importers of food and raw

[108] STEP (76)11.   [109] CAB 134/4025.   [110] DW 039.

materials) should be required to lodge a financial deposit with the Customs and Excise of a proportion of the value of the imports. The deposit would be repaid to the importer after a specified period (which could vary from a few months to a whole year) and the size of the deposit could be anything from 25 per cent of the value of the goods imported to 100 per cent. The scheme could in fact be of a severity which could match the requirements of the situation. The main effect of such a scheme was thought to lie in the expectation that importers would seek—and obtain—the credit they needed to pay the deposit from their overseas supplier. The scheme would therefore induce a large inflow of finance into the UK which would strengthen the reserves or offset the selling pressure in the foreign exchange markets. The scheme was not thought likely to have very much effect on the volume of imports, although of course by adding to the cost of imports it would curtail some of them. At this stage the parameters of a possible scheme, that is the size of the deposits and their maturity were not specified. The main purpose in apprising the Chancellor of the scheme was to assure him that *in extremis* some emergency action was to hand.

The Chancellor had a meeting with his officials from the Treasury and the Bank very soon after the statement on 26 July.[111] Discussion was mainly about market tactics should confidence not be restored. The exchange markets had been reasonably quiet in the remainder of the week of the announcement, but the mood as we noted above was disappointing, if not hostile. The Chancellor agreed that the sterling rate should be defended 'for a day or two' but avoided any commitment thereafter. The Bank continued to favour an approach to the IMF and held out the prospect that for a drawing of the enlarged first credit tranche no policy change might be required. This sat somewhat oddly with the attitude of the Fund mission in May when the Chancellor had been sternly warned that such an application would have to be supported by suitable fiscal changes and with the lukewarm reaction of the Managing Director to the July measures.

Sterling—Part 5 the emergence of the safety net

The month of August was a fairly uneventful one, at any rate in comparison with the turbulent and dramatic days of June and July, although even so to hold the rate the Bank had to spend some $0.5 billion of the reserves. Parliament rose, and Ministers went on holiday. The foreign exchange markets were uneasy but quiet and the mood in the Treasury was to wait and see how events would unfold when normal business resumed in September. This interregnum provides a suitable cue for us to look in more detail at how the Treasury—in

[111] DW 039.

this case OF assisted by the Bank—saw the external financing problem, for the appraisal led both to the conclusion that an approach to the IMF would be necessary and to the emergence of a plan to deal with the official balances somewhat on the lines of what had been done at the time of the 1967 financial crisis—these being now firmly identified as the source of the problem. The rather tortuous path to the solution of this problem began in 1975, when, as we saw in Chapter 3, the Treasury looked comprehensively at ways of securing external finance. The new approach focused on the official balances and put forward a number of possibilities for dealing with them:

- to 'sterilize' the volatile official balances by some form of guarantee;
- to offer some holders a higher rate of interest on the securities they held in sterling;
- to borrow a substantial sum in dollars in the New York market, the proceeds being used to match any run-down in the balances;
- to offer some holders a special long-term bond, in sterling, into which they would convert some of their liquid sterling assets;
- to issue a special instrument for them denominated in SDRs;
- to seek a drawing from the IMF again to provide funds for dealing with reserve losses.

When some of these possibilities were considered in 1975 most had been ruled out for one reason or another. The idea of offering the official sterling balance holders some form of incentive to stay in sterling, for example by guaranteeing the capital value of their sterling assets, was briefly looked at in February 1976 but the conclusion was that such an offer would be more likely to sow doubts in the mind of holders about the value of sterling. This was the very time that the Treasury was recommending some form of depreciation and the Chancellor himself expressed doubts about the feasibility of a guarantee being given just as sterling was being, in all but name, devalued, possibly by a step change. Of the remaining candidates, the last had actually been implemented at the end of 1975, and the idea of an SDR bond, which had been shelved pending the outcome of the IMF negotiations, was still in the mind of both the Bank and the Treasury. Of immediate interest was the limited idea of offering selected official holders a long-term asset in sterling to replace some at least of their liquid holdings. Most monetary authorities holding sterling regarded them as part of their reserves, to be used in emergency or to stabilize their own exchange rate. As such, they wanted liquidity and the suggestion that they lock up these assets in some long-term security was not likely to be well received. But one or two of the holders had reserves of such a vast size and had such little need for liquidity that the offer of a higher rate of interest and less liquidity might have been of some interest. The obvious candidates were Saudi Arabia, Kuwait, and Brunei. It was decided to raise the idea in the course of a visit which a small Treasury/Bank team made to Riyadh in the middle of January 1976. The suggestion put forward was that the Saudi Arabia Monetary Authority, the custodian of the country's foreign currency assets, might invest in a bond issued by one of the nationalized industries. A figure of $300 million was mentioned and this modest contribution was secured, but it was all that could be raised from this source by direct action.

The scope for borrowing from the market for funds to deal with the balances was considered several times later on. The Treasury had, at the outset, budgeted to raise some $900 million in 1976 and, although the reaction of the Saudis to the ideas put forward during the January visit were not discouraging, nothing concrete (apart from the relatively small public sector loan) had emerged. The first survey of the scene was prepared by OF in early May,[112] by which time sterling had been under some pressure. However, in the wake of the TUC agreement on pay, announced on 5 May, the Treasury judged that sentiment had improved and the scope for some non-market borrowing, in particular from some of the American banks in a syndicated form, became a serious possibility. The sums that might be raised were not negligible—figures of several hundred million dollars were mentioned by a leading US commercial bank in particular—but the difficulty the Bank saw was that the maturity of any such credit would be shorter than was appropriate. The banks were thinking in terms of a three-year credit, whereas the Treasury and Bank wanted five years as a minimum. A full External Financing Assessment was made several times during the course of 1976 as the currency situation deteriorated. At the outset, although a good deal of anxiety was expressed, the Treasury thought that the deficit could just be met from existing sources and existing methods, although the situation was fragile. By the middle of the year, as the reserves loss developed—a gross loss of $5 billion in the four months to the end of June was reported[113]—the outlook had darkened considerably. A submission to the Chancellor on 9 July[114] looked again at all the sources available. There might be some further bilateral borrowing by the same bodies from the Saudi monetary authority and there was still some unused facility from the Iranian loan of two years earlier. However, the scale of intervention likely to be required to stabilize the rate and meet the expected draw-down of some of the official sterling balances was expected to be of the order of £750 million in the remainder of the year. The note concluded 'The principal message on the assessment taken is that recourse to the second tranche of the IMF will be unavoidable before the end of the year'. Indeed the head of OF followed the assessment up in a minute on 12 July in which he went so far as to suggest that it might be desirable to make the application as soon as possible.[115] One of the large American investment banks did raise in August[116]

---

[112] DW 198.   [113] BP 98/16/02.
[114] Ibid.   [115] OF 32/100/02.   [116] DW 198.

the question of whether the Government would be interested in obtaining a credit rating from the US credit-rating agencies, but the Bank advised strongly against this on the grounds that the UK would not at that time be classed as AAA and a lower rating would have damaging effects on creditors generally. In any case the New York market for overseas borrowers was not large—a typical issue was only $200–250 million—and the effort and risks involved did not justify such a course. Borrowing from the banks was again looked at in the early autumn, but by this time the leading US players had decided that until the UK had completed the negotiations it had committed itself to with the IMF they would not participate. But their willingness to consider the matter after an agreement suggested that a standby with the Fund would unlock some important possibilities.[117]

As the currency crisis developed in the second quarter of the year, the only surviving candidate for action to strengthen the reserves and neutralize the official balances was the SDR bond, but on this the Treasury argued in a note put to the Chancellor on 14 June[118] that, in the prevailing circumstances of weak market confidence in the UK, the time was not suitable for a market operation. However the Treasury and the Bank had now come to the conclusion that another, and different, initiative involving some or all of the main industrial countries might be a way forward. The thought was that no one in the Group of Ten countries would want to see a collapse in sterling which could have repercussions throughout the international monetary system nor would they want to see UK exports at a big price advantage and therefore they might be willing to consider a collective approach to help to stabilize the rate. The template in mind was the Basle facility which had first been put in place in 1966 in which the UK was given access to a credit of $1 billion set up via the BIS by the main creditors—the credit being available for one year to be drawn upon if and when the official sterling holders ran down their balances—one half of the fall being the amount available. A second BIS facility was negotiated in 1968 for $2 billion but this time with guarantees about minimum balances to be sought from the sterling holders.[119] Only limited use was made of this second facility—$600 million being drawn in October 1968, which was fully repaid a year later. The guarantees proved to involve a long process of negotiations with each of the many official holders and, as we saw, were allowed to lapse soon after the facility itself came to an end in 1973.

The possibility of some other measure to stabilize the sterling balances was looked at by the Treasury early in the year—before, in fact, the currency crisis developed and we examine the Treasury's approach in a moment. But first it

---

[117] Shortly after the announcement of the Fund agreement at the end of the year, it became possible to raise a syndicated loan of $1.5 billion.

[118] DW 036.

[119] The 1968 Basle facility is described in Cmnd 3787 and is the subject of a Treasury Historical Memorandum—No 19—T 267/33.

has to be said that one very perceptive critic of the Treasury's passivity to the problem in the early years of the Wilson government was Lever. The Chancellor of the Duchy of Lancaster (Lever) frequently referred, in notes to the Prime Minister and the Chancellor to the fact that 'too many of our liabilities are in sterling'[120] and he recommended a massive programme of borrowing in foreign currencies to enable them to be paid off. Neither the Bank nor the Treasury thought that this was a viable option. Throughout the period covered by this study, the two institutions were scouring all the possibilities for overseas borrowing in foreign currency (or in SDRs) and judged that finance of the sort and scale advocated by Lever simply did not exist.

The first serious Treasury review of ways of dealing with the balances was made in a submission dated 19 February[121] in which OF examined a number of theoretical options, all of which had been on the table at various times over the previous two years. It added one which had been toyed with before—that of giving the official sterling balance holders some compensation in the event of a step depreciation. But the problems of taking overseas holders into the UK's confidence on the issue of a devaluation were seen to be insuperable. The issue was not seen to be critical and the paper led to no further discussion.

The initiative for a further attempt to deal with the sterling balance problem came, perhaps surprisingly, from the IMF. There had been some consideration of this issue in the context of the comprehensive review of the Fund's role in the supervision of the world's international payments system conducted between 1970 and 1972 by a special group known as the Committee of Twenty. The outcome of that study was, so far as the future of the sterling balances was concerned, inconclusive. However, in the course of a routine conversation in Washingrton in May 1976, the head of the Fund's European Department told the head of OF[122] that the IMF itself had been looking again at the problem of the 'overhang' of the balances. The conversation did not lead to anything and later in the year when the matter was again broached with the Fund the latter were distinctly cool. Later on in May, possibly inspired by what the Fund had said, the Chancellor asked his officials for a note on the reserve role of sterling and on the possibility for funding the sterling balances. The Treasury response to this request was thorough but not very encouraging.[123] It conceded that funding had for long been an important UK goal and that the idea now had greater significance than ever and 'if a medium-term credit facility could be negotiated it would be worth having.... But it was a matter of extreme delicacy and the worst outcome would be for [any initiative to this end] to become known and to fail'. The issue was however taken forward in a more concrete way when the head of OF put forward to the Chancellor two papers on 4 June,[124] one by

[120] See for example Harold Lever, 12 March 1975 in DW 036.
[121] DW 036.   [122] BP 98/16/02.   [123] Ibid.   [124] DW 036.

the Treasury and one by the Bank, examining the form of a possible scheme and considering the likelihood of its being acceptable to those who would be required to underwrite it. The Bank paper entitled 'Coping with the Sterling Balances' looked at the available options only to dismiss those hitherto considered, in particular the idea of guarantees. In practice it said 'a safety net was the only device open to us'. The two big questions were the amount which should be sought and the uncertainty over whether the Americans and the Germans, the key players, would be willing to cooperate. On the first the Bank thought that $10 billion would be required—although $5 billion might just be enough. The Bank answered the second question prophetically. The US and Germany would say 'Let the UK satisfy the Fund's conditions and draw from the Fund: then, with the UK economy set on as good a course as possible, if the sterling balance problem still remained, it could be looked at'. We have seen that even as early as the beginning of June, when the central bank credit was under consideration, the Bank had a preference for immediate recourse to the Fund, so it was perhaps not surprising that they should have structured their advice around this course of action. Nevertheless their assessment of the conditions under which a new Basle facility to underpin the sterling balances could be arranged proved to be well-founded. Although the Treasury did not at this stage urge an immediate approach to the Fund as a precondition of a new 'safety net', it did not think that there would be any advantage in opening up the idea with the Americans. The possibility of taking an initiative on the sterling balances was discussed with the Chancellor on 10 June,[125] but both the Treasury and the Bank argued that the time was not ripe. The Chancellor put the interesting question whether, if the recently negotiated central bank credit achieved something like stability, that would be the occasion to seek either the funding of the balances or a safety-net. The Treasury again opposed this, for it would signal to those from whom help would be required that the UK was trying to avoid making the adjustments that, in their view, were needed. The outcome of this meeting was reported to the Prime Minister in a minute dated 16 June[126] headed 'Sterling Holdings' which again counselled no immediate action. 'I am sure,' said the Chancellor, 'that most, if not all, of our creditors under the current standby hoped to see policy action in one or a combination of the public expenditure or monetary fields, either during the life of the facility or as a condition of recourse to the IMF. . . . I think it would not be wise and could be counter-productive to raise it with President Ford at Puerto Rico[127] . . . I will be seeing Simon (the US Treasury Secretary) and if a suitable opportunity arises I would not think there would be any difficulty about my having a quiet word'. When the Chancellor left for

---

[125] MPG(75)17.   [126] Ibid.

[127] This was a reference to the forthcoming Economic Summit which President Ford was to host.

Puerto Rico he had a Treasury brief which advised him to tell Simon that the issue 'was not being aired in any sense of urgency'. The head of OF said that he rated the chance of a response from Simon as being 'very low to nil'. In the event neither the Prime Minister nor the Chancellor took the matter up with their counterparts at the Economic Summit though according to American sources there was a discussion of the general economic predicament of the UK.[128] When, in the middle of July, the Chancellor of the Duchy urged a more immediate initiative to achieve a Safety Net, the Chancellor replied that, although he did not rule out raising the matter with his German and American counterparts, he did not want to do so at that time and he said that he had asked for a paper in September. The Prime Minister, in his reply, made it clear that, although he might accept the constraints posed by the domestic circumstances of his German and American counterparts, he did not look with favour on the rather leisurely approach he sensed that the Treasury and Bank were taking.

However, after Puerto Rico the issue of the sterling balances inevitably faded into the background, for the main emphasis of action was on the July public expenditure measures, which it was hoped would have a calming effect on the markets and might indeed lead to a period of stability, making the setting up of a new facility both easier and in one sense unnecessary. When the US Treasury Undersecretary (Edwin Yeo) met the Chancellor in London in early August[129] he made much the same point. He had, he said, done a lot of work on the sterling balance question but 'he did not see a convenient way of handling this. . . . If the UK turned the corner the balances would be an advantage' and he urged the British 'not to put it on the table at this stage'. The record of the discussions in Whitehall of the idea of a 'solution' to the sterling balance problem gives a very strong impression that the Treasury and the Bank were at one with Yeo in regarding it as out of the question while the fundamental problem of confidence was unresolved. It would not of itself restore confidence and those whose help would be essential would not be prepared to make their contribution until that fundamental problem had been addressed. The Prime Minister clearly did not share this view, but except for a brief reference to the idea at the Cabinet Meeting on 3 August[130] when Ministers collectively reviewed the economic situation in the aftermath of the July statement, the 'safety net' as a major new initiative did not come on stage again until September when the Treasury delivered its appraisal of the possibilities and options which the Chancellor had requested in July. We deal with the development of this initiative and how it fitted into the negotiations with the Fund in the next chapter.

---

[128] Fay and Young.   [129] Ibid.   [130] CAB 128/59/22.

An approach to the IMF

By early September it had become all too clear that none of the measures adopted in the summer—the central bank credit, the public expenditure package or the adoption of a qualified form of monetary target—had dealt with the underlying problem, that is market confidence: and although there was to be no difficulty in obtaining a single renewal of the central bank credit on 7 September, it was plain that an extension beyond 7 December was not going to be possible. The only option now inevitably seemed to be a new approach to the IMF and it was with an appraisal of this course that the Treasury began what was to be an eventful autumn.

On 3 September it produced for internal purposes an extensive study of all the options for dealing with the financing issue. It now identified the financing gap as £900 million in the second half of 1976 rising to £1,500 in the second half of 1977. The size of the reserves, now just over $5 billion, were simply insufficient to cover these sorts of deficit and provide a backing for the external liabilities. The effect on the market of allowing the reserves to fall would cause consternation among official sterling holders. Moreover, the reserves had been bolstered by a drawing of $1,030 million of the central bank credit, which would have to be repaid on 7 December. Intervention in the currency markets had been extensive in July and August—over $800 million had been spent in those two months alone—and anything like that rate of spend without some augmentation of the reserves would pose a difficult presentational problem. The Treasury paper looked yet again at the borrowing possibilities. There was still about $200 million of the 1974 Iranian loan to be drawn and a $300 million loan by the Saudi Arabian Monetary Authority to one of the nationalized industries would be taken into the reserves. The credit facilities in the EEC had all been exhausted by the Italians, who had had similar foreign exchange difficulties to those of the UK in the course of 1976, and a new Support Fund which was in process of being set up by the OECD was not yet operational. A bilateral loan from the G10 countries would, it was thought, simply not be negotiable in advance of a new approach to the Fund. Every opening, in short, save that of a Fund drawing, led to blind alley. The only question in the mind of the Treasury was that of timing and on this there was, perhaps surprisingly, some flexibility. While on straight financing grounds the case for an early approach seemed overwhelming, there were some voices which counselled delay. The US Undersecretary of the Treasury (Yeo) had suggested to the Chancellor that a deferment to the Spring might be worth considering: and from Washington the UK Executive Director said that the Fund might find the UK borrowing requirement of £9 billion in 1977–78 (the figure given in the July statement) more acceptable in the Spring than in the previous autumn. How serious these siren voices were it is not easy to assess. But the Treasury was not disposed to listen to them. For one thing the financing requirement did not permit any more delay than was absolutely necessary. The Central Bank credit had to be repaid in December. What is more, a delay to the early part of 1977 ran the risk of coinciding with negotiations with the TUC about the third year of the Incomes Policy, which were not expected to be easy as it would involve a further cut in real incomes. The conclusion was that the earlier the approach to the Fund the better, and a provisional timetable, geared in with the central bank credit expiry date, involving negotiations in November was set out.

It is interesting to note that, at that time, the Treasury thought that the negotiations could be concluded in two weeks—the normal length of a Fund consultation. But the paper drily noted that this timetable 'did not leave much time for Ministerial discussion'—an observation which subsequent events amply confirmed. On the question of conditionality, the paper simply noted that commitments would have to be given on limits to the growth of DCE and of the borrowing requirement in 1977–78 and 19/8–79—although at this stage, when the UK forecast for the PSBR in the year ahead was £9 billion, these did not seem to present insuperable difficulties. The paper looked at how the Fund would finance a large drawing by the UK and noted that the GAB would have to be activated and that some members of the arrangement might prove difficult. Finally it asked the unanswerable question of what would happen if the negotiations became deadlocked. There was little likelihood of the Group of Ten stepping in with a rescue package. On this uncertain note the paper was finalized and put to the Chancellor on 10 September[131] with the expression of the firm view that an application to the Fund was unavoidable. We resume the narrative of how the Cabinet were put in the picture and apprised of the consequences of a Fund drawing later on. But first we have to look at how the exchange markets behaved in September, for it was what happened there in that month which released the cascade of events and created the atmosphere of crisis which made 1976 such a traumatic year for those involved.

We saw earlier that the markets had been reasonably quiet—though nervous—in August, but early the following month pressure on the rate began to build up. Although the markets had developed a pathology of their own, they were not helped by one disturbing development in the industrial relations field. Early in August the National Union of Seamen sought the approval of the TUC for the negotiating of a special pay increase in excess of the second round norm agreed in May. The TUC refused, whereupon the union called a ballot of its members which, early in September, voted in favour of industrial action.[132]

---

[131] BP 122/24/01.
[132] The threatened strike was in fact called off on 22 September, but only after heavy intervention by the Prime Minister and senior trade union figures.

The exchange rate reacted adversely to this development and was held at just above $1.77, only at significant cost to the reserves. Wednesday 8 September was a particularly bad day and the Treasury decided that continued intervention on the scale the Bank were employing was simply not tenable. After seeking the Chancellor's and the Prime Minister's approval, a decision was taken to cease intervention altogether. The course favoured by OF was to accompany the withdrawal from the market with a sharp tightening of domestic credit conditions so as to drive domestic borrowers into foreign currencies and indeed to make it expensive for operators with bear positions to remain open. The Home Finance Division argued, however, that there were no domestic reasons for tightening credit, and said that the domestic side of the Bank agreed. One course briefly considered was the immediate imposition of import deposits. The Treasury had no enthusiasm for such a scheme except as a fall-back, emergency response.

The Bank were most unhappy with the decision to withdraw altogether from the market and strenuously protested, as they had done in June when the Prime Minister had instructed them to withdraw. At the very least, however, some tightening of monetary policy was called for and on 10 September MLR was raised from 11.5 per cent to 13 per cent. A week later, on 16 September, the Bank decided to tighten credit conditions further by making a call for Special Deposits: £350 million immediately and a further £700 million three weeks later. In spite of these monetary measures, sterling's weakness persisted and it was not long before the Treasury had to accept that complete withdrawal from the market could lead to a free fall in the exchange rate. At the end of the following week the policy of limited and cautious intervention was resumed. But by this time the rate had fallen below $1.72 and by the end of the month it went below $1.67. It was not just the absence of any sign of a policy tightening which disturbed the market. One important element which did not help was the Labour Party annual conference that was held in the week beginning 27 September.

It is no part of this narrative to go into the details of the events which took place at Blackpool, but it was abundantly clear from the motions put down that there was widespread unhappiness in the Party with the economic policies being followed by the Government. We saw how in Parliament in March a sizeable rebellion of back-benchers took place on the motion to approve the Public Expenditure White Paper. Sensing that the Party Conference might be a difficult one, the Chancellor made a presentation to the TUC/Labour Party Liaison Committee at its meeting on 20 September arguing the case for the continuation of existing policy, borrowing abroad so as to maintain living standards and rejecting generalized import controls as long as economic growth could be maintained. The Chancellor felt that the TUC accepted this—but of course the Party Conference was less predictable, although the National Executive tabled a resolution broadly endorsing the Government's economic strategy. In the event the Conference proved to be a rather turbulent one and the Prime Minister made a strong speech on 29 September in which he effectively rebuked his fellow Party members for supposing that the Government enjoyed much latitude to modify its policies, particularly its policies for controlling public expenditure. The Prime Minister was subsequently to get considerable plaudits for this 'realism' from his fellow Heads of Government when they were approached for help with the UK application to the IMF. President Ford sent a personal message congratulating him on his courage in making such a strong statement. The Chancellor himself made a speech the following day defending his policies, but he was received with less than the customary deference—*The Times* reported 'booing and hissing from the floor'.

Despite the rather rough treatment he received at the Party Conference, the National Executive resolution was carried by a large majority, and the Chancellor was given a quite sympathetic hearing at two informal meetings he had subsequently with the NEDC 6 of the TUC on 11 and 28 October. Once again he laid out the arguments for the course he was following and asked for the policy to be judged as having a three-year horizon. The TUC could hardly contradict the Chancellor, but they made plain their unhappiness with the consequences of what was happening to the economy and to their members. The Government's measures in 1976 (a reference to the July statement) had reduced confidence in the outlook for inflation. One point made with particular feeling was that the trade union movement had made a strenuous effort with its members to save the pound in 1975 and had repeated the exercise in 1976; but it now saw sterling falling despite having done what the Government asked. The leader of the important Amalgamated Engineering Union, Scanlon, gave 'a warning that if his members were asked to bear further cuts in living standards [whether directly or through the social wage[133]] the union leaders would not be able to help to win support for giving the Government further help'. The two meetings served as a stark reminder to the Chancellor of the political difficulties he would face if he were to seek further cuts in expenditure.

The strategy reviewed

The Treasury had by then, in its paper of 10 September,[134] made it clear to the Chancellor that there was no escape from an application to the IMF, and the only question was when the Cabinet should be brought to accept this and

---

[133] The social wage was the term then used by the unions and to some extent by government ministers to denote the benefits citizens received from the state, for example housing and food subsidies, education and social security benefits—all financed by public expenditure.
[134] PCC (76)59.

when the decision should be announced. To help the Chancellor secure the approval of his colleagues, the Treasury prepared a strategy paper, from which a Cabinet memorandum could be derived. This rehearsed what by now were familiar themes. A substantial current account deficit continuing for at least a further two years was likely, but there was a good prospect of a turn-round occurring before the end of the decade. Between 1977 and 1982 the current account could improve by as much as £12 billion; roughly one half of this would be due to the flow of North Sea Oil but an equal improvement was expected from better trade performance due to improved competitiveness. There was, therefore, a huge medium-term financing problem, but if this could be resolved the longer-term outlook was not unfavourable. The key to the solution to the external financing problem was a Fund drawing, which would not only provide substantial finance but also give encouragement to other creditors.

Two issues were identified as important. The first was the successful negotiation with the TUC of a third year of pay restraint. The second was satisfying the Fund on the key areas of importance to them, that is the growth of DCE and the money supply and, underlying these indicators, the level of the PSBR and, one of its drivers, the level of public spending in the two years ahead. What the Fund's requirements would entail was not yet known with any precision and for this reason the extent of the cuts that might have to be made could not be estimated. Although major public spending cuts now would certainly help with confidence, it was difficult to see how the Chancellor, after the bruising experience of the Cabinets of July, could get the acquiescence of his colleagues in the absence of unassailable evidence that they could not be avoided. The strategy paper looked, as had so many of its predecessors, at the question of whether there was in fact an alternative strategy, one not so much of seeking a greater degree of self-sufficiency but of amending somewhat the present approach. The main element of such a policy would be to cease intervening in the exchange market and so preserve the level of the official reserves. The exchange rate would of course fall, but, as the Treasury economists were inclined to argue, sooner or later an equilibrium level would be found at which the demand for sterling balanced its supply. The Bank and the overseas side of the Treasury were less sure that the process of adjustment would be so smooth and feared that a 'free float', as it was known, would not be a smooth process. The paper inclined to the latter view.

On the question of import controls, it was acknowledged that a scheme of import deposits would have the effect of both tightening domestic, and promoting overseas, credit and of reducing imports, although on the latter the effects were not thought to be significant. The effect of such a scheme on corporate liquidity would be serious and there would be a problem of 're-entry' when the scheme ended. (It was thought that international approval would be conditional on the scheme having a short and finite life.) The conclusion, yet again, was that the best course was to stick to the present policy and negotiate a satisfactory deal with the Fund. The Chancellor was offered a draft paper to put to his colleagues on EY in which these points were made, with the additional information that he had authorized the state of readiness of an import deposit scheme, previously at six weeks notice, to be reduced to one week. The whole set of papers was covered by a note from the Permanent Secretary which again advised extreme caution in the way the Government handled its financial affairs. Other objectives (than the achievement of stability and viability) might have to be sacrificed and every public expenditure issue would have to be fought to the bitter end.

The Chancellor put these thoughts to his colleagues on the EY Committee on 22 September. He took them through the arguments that led to the conclusion that an approach to the IMF was now inevitable and should be made in the course of October so as to complete the negotiations before the Central Bank credit had to be repaid on 7 December; he held out the prospect that it might be possible to reach an agreement with the Fund on the basis of existing fiscal and monetary policies. He also reported progress on some contingency planning which officials had been carrying out since the EY Meeting on 2 August whereby some form of import restraints would be introduced. But he ruled these out except in extreme emergency. He did, however, describe a scheme of import deposits which could be introduced at fairly short notice in something perhaps short of a complete emergency.

The Chancellor's paper was discussed at EY on 23 September when, as had become routine, doubts were expressed by a minority of his colleagues about the viability of existing policy and the need for a more draconian, interventionist approach. The Prime Minister had little difficulty, however, in summing up that, although the Committee should continue to be involved in the oversight of policy, the Chancellor had authority to make an application to the Fund for a standby covering the whole of the UK's entitlement. But he had to acknowledge that the case for an 'alternative strategy' remained on the table and the Cabinet Office (in effect the CPRS) were asked to produce a paper giving the 'objective' case for and against import controls.[135] The application to the IMF was made and announced on 29 September having been brought forward, as a means of reassurance to the markets, following the cancellation of the Chancellor's attendance at the IMF Annual Meeting in Manila, the proceedings of which we examine below.

---

[135] The CPRS did in fact put in two papers to EY Committee in mid-October giving the case for and the case against import controls. These were subsequently discussed at a meeting of the Committee on 20 October when the usual arguments for and against the existing strategy were produced, but again the Prime Minister was able to conclude that there should, in existing circumstances, be no change of direction, although the issue would be reviewed from time to time.

The IMF annual meeting

The World Bank and International Monetary Fund annual meetings for 1976 were scheduled to take place in Manila in the week beginning 4 October, and a number of unofficial meetings were arranged among the participants for the previous weekend. The Chancellor was to lead the UK delegation in accordance with a practice stretching back to the foundation of the two institutions. He had been planning to leave London on 28 September so as to attend the Commonwealth Finance Ministers' Meeting in Hong Kong later that week but it so happened that on this day there was another devastating attack on sterling. The prospect that the following few days might require action in London to deal with a critical situation led him to decide to cancel his attendance at the annual meeting. The Governor, who had been intending to accompany him, made a similar choice. The Chancellor's decision was entirely understandable in the circumstances; it was unlikely that any action would be required in Manila that demanded his attendance. His speech to the Meeting was to be a rather formal affair, although it could have been made the occasion to explain to the international community the reasons for the application for a stand-by and to assert the government's commitment to an orthodox approach to macro-economic policy. However, the meetings he would have with his counterparts from other countries and with the Fund Managing Director would not involve negotiations or indeed statements that the various parties had not been rehearsing at length in the previous months. But the manner of the Chancellor's decision did attract criticism for it had the appearance of panic, being taken as he was literally on his way to Heathrow Airport to take the flight to Hong Kong. And the fact that, at the annual meeting, the UK, then in prospect of being a heavy debtor to the Fund, would be represented by officials with no Minister present was not likely to have a favourable effect on world opinion.

In the event the officials from the Bank and the Treasury who represented the UK at Manila were able to have a number of useful meetings with the Fund and, among other members, US and German officials, and it is instructive to examine how these constituencies were then regarding the UK and whether they were, or were not, in sympathy with its general conduct of economic policy. We have recorded the views of the Managing Director of the Fund on several occasions: in 1975 at the time of the first UK drawing and in the wake of the July measures to name only two. He was disturbed by the high borrowing requirement of the public sector and the effect he expected this to have on the growth of DCE and hence on the pressure on resources. The position of other important members of the Fund, whose approval would be necessary for any large drawing by the UK, not only because of their general influence on the Fund Board but also because they would have to put up specific credit through the GAB to finance a UK drawing, was less clear cut, at any rate up to the time of the annual meeting. The Central Bank credit had, however, given them an additional lever on the UK, and it was clear that the US Treasury, which had quite deliberately given itself a role in that credit even though all the other participants were the relevant central banks, was going to exert its influence to the maximum extent possible.

Contacts between UK and US officials during the course of 1975 and early 1976 had not been marked by any very strong criticism of British economic policy. The two leading members, Dr Arthur Burns, Chairman of the Board of Governors of the Federal Reserve System, and William Simon, Secretary of the Treasury, were both committed Republicans who had an avowed preference for liberal free market policies with minimum interference in economic activity by the State. Burns had been an economics professor, and at one time Chairman of the President's Council of Economic Advisers: Simon was a Wall Street bond trader. Simon's deputy, Edwin Yeo, was a newcomer to the scene, having left commercial banking in Pittsburgh for Washington in the summer of 1975. In spite of the lack of doctrinal empathy between American Republicans and British Labour Party Ministers on policy, their personal relations were amicable, and for a time the Americans did not voice any disapproval of the trend of British policy making. When the Permanent Secretary met Burns in Washington early in September 1975, that is after the introduction of the pay policy, Burns expressed admiration for what the Government had achieved. 'UK policy is marvellous if it works' are his reported words. He visited London in May 1976 and saw both the Chancellor and the Permanent Secretary, telling each of them that he admired the government's success in the fight against inflation. But he added that the pay policy needed 'to be accompanied by the right fiscal and monetary policy',[136] implying that on both fronts the policy was lax.

Both Yeo and Simon were in London on several occasions in the course of 1976 and although the flavour of the meetings was of mild questioning of British policy, notably on the level of public sector borrowing, there was not a great deal of pressure for a policy change.[137] However, as we noted above when the UK Director at the IMF saw Yeo on the day of the July statement, he was told in no uncertain terms that the measures did not go far enough. Yeo was, however, only expressing a view that was widely held in the USA. When Yeo had a meeting with the Chancellor and Treasury officials in London on 3 August[138] there was little policy criticism. Yeo expressed worries about the effect of unemployment on the unions and went so far as to say that 'it was vital that the Government should not be forced to take action which would

---

[136] IM 34/5/01.

[137] Some histories (e.g. Burk/Cairncross) claim that the Americans made sharp criticisms of British policy at the Puerto Rico summit, but there is no documentary evidence on the British side that this was so.

[138] Ibid.

damage its relations with the unions'. The one point he made which he was to repeat more forcibly later in the year was that the UK ought *not yet* to raise at the international level the question of the sterling balances (i.e. the safety net). No doubt the Americans sensed by then that the UK would have to apply to the Fund for a large drawing, if only to repay the Central Bank credit, and decided that the best way to apply pressure was through the Fund. But they did not want this course to be complicated by what they regarded as a secondary matter, that is a support operation. At all events it was not until the annual meeting at Manila that the Americans came out strongly with a face-to-face criticism of British policy.

In Manila British officials from the Bank and the Treasury had a number of important meetings—with Fund staff and the Managing Director and with delegates from several senior member governments and central banks. Of the meetings with government officials, the most important were with the Americans. On 3 October the Overseas Director of the Bank had a talk with Burns when the latter came out with a very strong criticism of British economic policy. After expressing sadness at the UK's plight, he launched into what was little short of a diatribe against the policies of the Labour Government. The UK should abandon 'this nationalisation nonsense and give the people some incentives'; Britain should 'reduce its awful deficit'; 'It had to satisfy the world's banks... Denis Healey does not understand this'. No doubt this was only the off-hand talk of a semi-private conversation, but the message was essentially the same when the Permanent Secretary accompanied by his Treasury colleagues and the Overseas Director of the Bank saw Simon and Burns on 3 October and again the following day.[139] The Americans were blunt in their criticisms of UK policy—much more so than they had been to British Ministers and more indeed than they were at future meetings. Perhaps they saw no need to be polite to officials. The report sent back to London was stark. 'We (i.e. the UK) had,' the Americans said, 'now run out of time. Our failure to take sufficient action on the PSBR and monetary policy earlier meant that our options were now much more limited and the action needed now was more drastic... the margin of credibility had narrowed.... Simon said that tough monetary action might be of some immediate value but would be ineffective... unless backed by a change in fiscal stance.' So much for the view that a drawing from the Fund could be made on the basis of existing policies. When the British side spoke of the efforts which had already been made in the July measures and of the enormous political difficulties the Chancellor would have in making further big cuts in expenditure, these considerations were unceremoniously brushed aside. The Americans were told that if the demands made of the UK were too great there could be a huge political crisis. None of this cut any ice. The meeting left the British

---

[139] PREM 16/798.

with the clear understanding that the negotiations with the Fund were going to be tough—probably very tough indeed.

The meetings with Fund officials and the Managing Director were more emollient—and more productive—concentrating as they did on the technical aspects of a drawing. The Permanent Secretary had a general talk with the Managing Director[140] who spoke of the need for the UK to free financial resources for the private sector when the upswing in economic activity (which could be expected) developed and therefore to cut the PSBR. He said that he regretted that the Government had not taken more action in July. On the question of what the Fund would be seeking, he said that he thought it unfortunate that the talk in London was of the drawing being on the basis of existing policies—a clear warning that there would have to be policy changes, as indeed Treasury officials well knew. Witteveen was told of contingency planning that had been carried out for the emergency introduction of import deposits. He hoped that the UK would not go down this road, but if they did, it should be with the aim of tightening credit, not of restricting imports. When the UK delegation saw Fund officials separately[141] the same day, one question which came up was whether there would be any difficulty in the UK drawing 145 per cent of quota—the new temporary upper limit following the Jamaica meeting in January.[142] The Fund pulled a rather long face at this and said that a very strong case of need would have to be demonstrated—Witteveen had been less emphatic about this at the separate meeting. If the UK balance of payments were going to improve with the flow of North Sea Oil, this prospective improvement would have to be taken into account. Another question raised was whether the UK would be able to draw a substantial proportion of the funds as soon as the agreement was reached—an issue termed 'front loading' in subsequent discussions. The Fund again were cautious and recalled that when the British had secured a drawing in 1967 there had been a strong reaction from other members of the IMF at the concession made to allow the whole drawing at the outset of the term of the agreement. There might even be difficulty this time in making an initial drawing of $1.5 billion—the sum by then drawn on the Central Bank credit of June which would have to be repaid on 7 December. The meeting discussed how the question of the sterling exchange rate would be handled—an issue taken up at a separate meeting with senior Fund officials. It became evident that, although this would not form part of the published Letter of Intent, the Fund would want to have assurances that there would be no erosion of the improvement in competitiveness that had taken place during 1976. At a subsequent meeting with the Bank on 7 October the Fund were even more explicit.[143] The question was not whether sterling should be further devalued but how. The British side

---

[140] PREM 16/798.   [141] IM 1/33/02.
[142] This would be SDR 3.36 billion.   [143] DW 036.

rehearsed all the arguments that had been made in Whitehall during the previous twelve months about the lack of any instrument for engineering a depreciation and, although the Fund staff expressed an understanding of this, they did not seem to be convinced. The question of the exchange rate became an important issue during the subsequent negotiations and we reserve an examination of the intellectual basis of the Fund's position till later. Suffice it to say here that at Manila the Fund made it quite clear that the views they had expressed in consultations of the need for a sterling devaluation over the previous two years were as strongly held as ever. How the commitment they wanted from the UK on this matter was to be expressed was open to debate— but pressure for the commitment itself was not likely to be dropped.

Other matters raised in discussion with Fund staff were whether the UK had it in mind to introduce import deposits, as the Italians had done, to deal with the reserves question. The Fund were told only that there was no present intention, but the possibility could not be ruled out. On other issues of economic policy, the Fund said that the PSBR would certainly feature prominently in the discussions. They acknowledged that the deficit in the current year (1976–77) could probably not be reduced but they would certainly want to look at the following year 'and perhaps 1978–79 as well'. This was the first intimation that the Fund might want to look at a *two-year* programme for a drawing as large as the UK had in mind. The Fund were not prepared at this stage to say what their target would be, but 'on present policies and forecasts they would be inclined to think that a target of £9 billion [the figure given after the July measures for 1977–78] was too high'.

The experience of British officials in Manila was a sobering, albeit a very useful, one. It gave the clearest indication yet of what the Fund would want in the way of policy commitments and signalled that the negotiations would be difficult and might well result in demands for public expenditure cuts which Ministers would find politically unacceptable. It was also clear that the Fund would be strongly pressed by the US Treasury not to bow to political pressure and to concede terms which neither they nor the Fund thought appropriate.

The head of the British team reported his experiences to the Chancellor and the Prime Minister immediately on his return on 6 October, particularly what had been said by the Fund and the Americans about the need to tighten monetary policy. By that time Yeo had had a telephone conversation with the Chancellor (29 September) and had followed it by coming to London for a meeting with him on 3 October[144] on his way to Manila. It was then that he expressed the strong view that a 'bear squeeze' on the creditors would benefit the exchange rate. The markets had been in some disarray since the abandonment by the Chancellor of his proposed attendance at the IMF meeting ten days earlier. The pound that day fell by nearly 2 cents to its lowest level

[144] BP 98/16/02.

so far—$1.65. Following several meetings between the Governor and the Chancellor, it was immediately decided that a drastic increase in interest rates was essential if only as a holding measure, and MLR was raised a full 2 percentage points to 15 per cent the following day.[145] By any standard this was a crisis measure. MLR had not been at this level ever before—and was to exceed it in the future only twice—in late 1979 and on the occasion of Sterling's ejection from the ERM in 1992. But the move was effective. The interest rate increase was supplemented by a call for Special Deposits from the banks. This was in two stages, the first with more or less immediate effect and the second a month later. Sterling stabilized almost immediately and remained quiet until the next blow fell, on 24 October, with a press story, the details of which are given later in the narrative.

Public expenditure—Part 3

Meanwhile the Public Expenditure side of the Treasury was finding that departments continued to put in bids which made claims on the contingency reserve for the current year and for 1977–78 and they prepared the third of the quarterly papers which the Chief Secretary put to the Cabinet on the 'state of play'.[146] The reserve had been fixed at £1,050 million, but already agreed claims amounting to £412 million. A variety of additional claims had been staked, including a further employment package of £89 million. The Head of the Expenditure Group minuted the Chancellor, highlighting three areas where spending was becoming worrying: the employment and industry area, housing (both subsidies and house building), and local authority current spending. Ironically the employment proposals stemmed from the more sluggish growth of the economy. At a meeting with his advisers on 6 October[147] the Chancellor gave expression to his frustration at the course of events. 'The big problem the Chancellor had with his colleagues', runs the record, 'was that while he had told them in July that cuts were needed because the economy was growing faster than planned, he now faced the prospect of telling them that cuts were needed because the economy was growing slower than planned'. This was perhaps an oversimplification of the Treasury's position but the comment was an indication of the problem the Chancellor would face if he had to deny future bids for expenditure related to the level of unemployment. But the Treasury was already thinking that actual cuts, even of the reduced programmes which emerged from the July exercise, would be

---

[145] MLR had been raised by 1.5 per cent to 13 per cent on 10 September following the heavy fall in the rate following the disengagement of the Bank from the foreign exchange market the day before.
[146] CAB 129/192/10.
[147] DW 056.

necessary. Although their explicit position was that holding to those pro-grammes and not exceeding the provision for the contingency reserve would be an achievement, they began (at divisional level) to assemble a shopping list of further measures should the need arise; but the case would have to be over-whelming. The hypothetical list contained very big reductions in housing expenditure and in social security spending. As an illustration of the radical nature of the content of such a programme, the suspension of all social security uprating was included. The total of the list came to £1,950 for each of the two years 1977–78 and 1978–79. At a meeting of the most senior Treasury officials on 12 October[148] the judgement made by those who had been to Manila and talked to the Fund and to the US administration was that a Fund package would certainly have to contain substantial fiscal action. The expenditure Division's precautionary move was therefore entirely justified and did, in fact, prove to be a necessary preliminary to the negotiations with the Fund which took place the following month. It was clear, however, that a further expenditure policy change made *after* the conclusion of the PESC round and based on options not included in the PESC report would be highly disruptive to the whole planning process of fixing Parliamentary Estimates, cash limits, and the Public Expenditure White Paper. These bureaucratic considerations no doubt would pale beside the political difficulties of implementing any of the cuts, but to the people who had to ensure an orderly process in the annual round they posed quite a problem. The Head of Expenditure put it feelingly in a minute to the Permanent Secretary:

Having long doubted the sustainability of a high public sector deficit over a whole series of years, naturally I accept that, if the need for a major adjustment is now decided upon, public expenditure will have to play its part. But this will not overnight overcome the problem of feasibility and practicability. We can offer no suggestions from this side which do not involve severe administrative and political difficulty.[149]

The dilemma the Treasury faced was whether to advise ministers to go to the Cabinet immediately with proposals for decisions affecting the recently agreed programmes for 1977–78 or simply aim to hold to the agreed levels and the containment of new commitments within the contingency reserve, and then take further action when it became necessary. There was also the question of how far the cuts of July, which applied solely to 1977–78 should be carried through to later years. The Chancellor raised the issue with the Prime Minister on 14 October[150] in which he argued that at this stage the Cabinet should be asked simply to stick to the White Paper levels of spending as adjusted for 1977–78 (and only that year) by the July measures and be asked to consider only those cuts which might be necessary to accommodate new proposals. This was agreed and the Chancellor put a paper over the Chief Secretary's

---

[148] DW 014.   [149] DW 056.   [150] Ibid.

name to the Cabinet to his effect on 20 October.[151] The Cabinet considered this on 26 October[152] but, although the Prime Minister supported the Treasury, when it came to looking at the individual programmes where additional bids were being made, it proved difficult to get Cabinet agreement even to this limited objective—particularly in the area of housing, where the rise in interest rates generated a need to raise rents to offset the financing charges and this was deemed to be politically difficult. The Treasury were left, therefore, with Cabinet agreement in principle but insufficient authority to implement that principle. The Chancellor, however, took the opportunity of the Cabinet of 26 October to alert his colleagues to the likelihood that one of the consequences of going to the IMF was that further cuts in expenditure might be needed. He therefore asked the Cabinet to agree to officials carrying out some contingency planning designed to explore the implications of further cuts. This was agreed without much discussion—the doubters were clearly keeping their powder dry for the real debate when and if the Chancellor came back with firm demands. On 5 November the Treasury was becoming worried that the PESC round was nearing completion and departments had no knowledge[153] of the possibility of further cuts involving the financial year which was to begin only five months later. The top officials in the Treasury decided, however, that tactically it would be better to wait and see what the IMF team had in mind when the negotiations began rather than carry out any planning with spending departments in anticipation of the Fund's ideas, even though this would add to the problem of implementation when cuts had to be made. The path of public expenditure over the following two years would become the major issue in the negotiations with the Fund which began in early November and we deal with this in the context of those negotiations in the following chapter.

Preparations for the Fund negotiations

While all this was going on and the Treasury was preparing the ground for the negotiations with the Fund, the markets continued to be uncertain about the future of sterling. During the course of October the exchange rate stabilized at about $1.65 following the increase to 15 per cent in MLR on 7 October. On 24 October it was dealt a heavy blow by a report which appeared in the *Sunday Times* to the effect that the IMF were understood to have as their requirement of help for the UK the depreciation of sterling to $1.50. The author of the article appeared to have had good contacts with the Fund staff, and the

---

[151] CAB 129/192/91.   [152] CAB 128/60/6.

[153] Knowledge of the Chancellor's proposal was not disseminated outside Ministers' offices because of its sensitivity, so the Treasury had to proceed on its own.

markets acted on the following day as though the report was reliable. Despite heavy intervention, sterling immediately fell 5 cents to $1.59 and continued to weaken all week, touching $1.57 on 28 October. Both the Treasury and the Fund put out statements strenuously denying that there was any substance in the report and the market did rally somewhat the following week, helped by considerable intervention. What lay behind the *Sunday Times* report is not clear. Its author was a highly respected economic journalist with good contacts with the market and the various official bodies at national and international level. It would have been completely out of character for him to have manufactured the material on which his article was based, although it is not impossible that he made inferences from material that was available to him which led him to the conclusion that the Fund had the intention he attributed to it. The Fund Board had in early July approved a Staff paper[154] which argued that in a floating rate environment member countries should use domestic policies, notably interest rates, to move their exchange rates so as to reflect the purchasing power parity. And we have seen that at meetings with Fund staff in Manila British officials had been told that some form of commitment on the exchange rate would be necessary as part of a package— something which did indeed turn out to be the case, although the figure of $1.50 did *not* form part of the Fund's ideas when they came to present them in London in November. It is difficult to escape the conclusion that the story was written in good faith and had many elements which were true but that the core assertion was not valid. But true or not, it was decidedly unhelpful to both the Fund and to the British Government. Whether the professional ethic of a journalist to publish material which he believes to be true should override some consideration of 'the national interest' is not a matter for this narrative and we leave it to others to reach a judgement.

The *Sunday Times* article did not have a lasting effect on market sentiment. By the end of October, with the imminent arrival of the IMF team, the market had stabilized. To some extent this may have been due to the monetary measures taken in the course of early October, but it was also helped by the market's undoubted conviction that the outcome of the Fund's visit would be both an economic programme that was viable and a supply of foreign exchange which strengthened the ability of the authorities to deal with any market weakness. One of the consequences of this change of sentiment was that the Bank had considerable success in selling gilt-edged. This development itself had the effect of tightening credit conditions, already made restrictive by the call for special deposits. No doubt the savings institutions had been very liquid during the late summer, having been reluctant to invest long term during the development of the crisis, and they now saw an opportunity to make firm investment decisions. At all events, the large-scale movement of

[154] SM/76/153.

funds into public sector debt led to a liquidity squeeze in the banking system, which was now feeling the effect of the call in October for additional special deposits. The authorities decided that the implementation of the second call, timed for 15 November, should be postponed for a month. At the same time a modest reduction of MLR (of 0.5 per cent) was announced on 18 November, but this move was accompanied by the reimposition of the Corset, which had been removed at the beginning of 1975. The purpose of this latter move was simply to establish a path for the growth of the non-interesting eligible liabilities of the banks which was consistent with the Government's monetary target (12 per cent for £M3) and to counter any possibility that the easing of interest rates would lead to a monetary explosion. The Bank had been working on the idea of reintroducing the Corset as soon as the Chancellor announced his qualified target of 12 per cent growth of £M3 in July, and it was only natural that they should advise its reintroduction as soon as some untoward expansion was detected. It was also useful in dealing with some anxieties which the Americans and Germans expressed when they heard of the postponement of the second call for special deposits. The Americans, Yeo in particular, firmly believed that the UK had not used the monetary weapon aggressively enough to deal with the weakness of sterling earlier. On 18 November a tightening of exchange control took place through the banning of bank financing of third country trade in sterling, but this was less to make credit more restrictive than to save foreign currency.

We now have to go back to the situation at the end of October when the entire scenery in front of which the preparation for the Fund negotiations was taking place was violently rearranged by what was yet another unexpected and adverse development. The autumn NIF, which examined the likely course of the economy over the following eighteen months, was delivered to senior members of the Treasury on 27 October.[155] The principal finding of the forecasters was that, compared with the previous forecast in the wake of the July measures, the economy was now and prospectively much more depressed. Whereas in mid-summer the forecasters had talked of rapid growth and a balance of payments improvement, economic growth in 1976 and 1977 was now expected to be only about 2.5 per cent in each year and the expected upswing in the later part of the period did not materialize, mainly because export volumes did not expand as had been hoped in the wake of the depreciation. Consequently the improvement in the trade balance also failed to come through on the scale which had been expected and the deficits now anticipated in both 1976 and 1977 were of the order of £1.5–2 billion. Unemployment was forecast to continue to rise throughout 1977 reaching a peak of 1.75 million and only then, in 1978, to decline somewhat. This gloomy prediction was crowned by an even more sombre financial forecast. The PSBR

[155] STEP (76)17.

for the year 1977–78, which had been forecast at £9 billion in the wake of the July measures was now put at £11 billion—the deterioration being ascribed to the slacker state of the economy and hence to lower tax receipts and to higher expenditure (principally on social security benefits). Given the importance attached by the Fund to the PSBR, this development was bound to cast a dark shadow over the forthcoming negotiations. It has to be said that the reliability of the financial forecast was open to a good deal of doubt. The team responsible for it made it clear that they had had the greatest difficulty in producing an internally consistent set of numbers owing to the huge uncertainties surrounding the external outlook. It was however the best that could be done. The Chancellor immediately saw the significance of the forecast to the prospect ahead and sought an audience with the Prime Minister at which he revealed the dire outlook.[156] The Prime Minister was not pleased, but his concern seems to have been with the employment prospects revealed rather than with the problems it was going to lead to with the Fund. 'The prospect revealed was one which the Government could only regard as intolerable. . . . The Government would have to break out of it by a major initiative designed to promote industrial growth and in this connection he attached importance to interest rates' (which had only two weeks earlier been raised to 15 per cent). The two ministers reflected on the likely impact of the publication of the forecast, as was now required by statute.[157] The Prime Minister thought that it was quite unacceptable to publish it in the form in which it stood, although the Chancellor thought that this difficulty could be overcome by choosing the context.

A meeting of EY Committee had been arranged for 3 November and it had to be decided how to present the forecast to them. The Chancellor resolved to be completely frank and in his paper to the Committee[158] he gave them the full forecast: but he emphasized that there were many uncertainties, as indeed there were. When it came to the question of how the Fund negotiations should be handled, he asked for authority to be given to Treasury officials 'to take the Fund frankly and realistically through the economic prospects and the respective variants and *through the implications of possible policy adjustments*' (italics added). In his concluding paragraph he said that further fiscal action looked now to be necessary for 1977–78 but he did not specify whether this would be through taxation or public expenditure. At the EY meeting[159] the Chancellor, having taken his colleagues through his paper, told them that he was looking at ways of improving both the balance of payments and the PSBR outlook in the light of the forecast and he mentioned specifically the possible sale of the

---

[156] DW 036.
[157] An amendment had been made to the Industry Bill 1975 at the initiative of Jeremy Bray MP which required the Treasury regularly to publish its forecasting model and to provide comprehensive forecasts of many economic variables.
[158] CAB 134/4026.   [159] CAB 134/4025.

BP shares which the Bank of England had acquired in early 1975 as part of the rescue of the Burmah Oil Company,[160] a limitation on the sterling financing of third-country trade and some limitation on the public support for fixed-rate export credit. The discussion was predictably wide-ranging, with markedly differing views of the right way forward being expressed. Considerable emphasis was given to the importance of finding some solution to 'the sterling balance problem' without, however, very much being proposed that was specific. The Prime Minister felt able to sum up in a way which did not go against the grain of the Chancellor's case, but he did put a strict limit on the extent to which the Treasury could conduct the negotiations with the Fund. 'The opening discussions with the IMF must take place on a very tight and restricted brief and . . . the Chancellor of the Exchequer should return to the Committee for a further discussion as soon as the first views of the IMF were known.' The Chancellor was firmly put in commission.

The IMF arrived in London early in the week beginning 1 November and concluded their work on 10 December. The six weeks of their stay was packed with drama and tension, and the events that took place in that comparatively short space of time merit a chapter in their own right. But as we explain below, they were complicated by being linked with the separated question of the future of the sterling balances and it is to these two linked issues in the closing months of 1976 that we now have to turn.

---

[160] The issue of the BP shares became important during the Fund negotiations and we describe exactly what was involved in the next chapter.

5

1976 Part 2—Resolving the Crisis

From the beginning of November 1976 the focus of attention in the Treasury and the Bank, and perhaps above all in the Cabinet, was on the resolution of the crisis. There were two strands to this preoccupation: the putting in place of some mechanism to deal with the official sterling balances, which as a short-hand we label the safety net, and the completion of negotiations with the International Monetary Fund (IMF) for a drawing or a stand-by of a substantial amount. The two issues were handled at the same time with considerable cross-referencing. But they were essentially different matters and, although some players on the stage sought to link them, others, with equal determin-ation, sought to separate and distinguish them. But in purely historic terms they were contemporaneous and no account of the climacteric events of 1976 can avoid dealing with them as related issues. We deal with the Safety Net first, although in doing so, and in separating the two matters in the narrative, we have to allude occasionally to events which have not yet been fully described.

The Safety Net

Before the summer break the Chancellor had asked his officials to produce a considered appraisal of the options for dealing with the sterling balances in September. On 9 September the PCC discussed a paper prepared by OF outlin-ing the case for an initiative and how it could be presented.[1] The important premise was—as had been repeatedly said by officials—that the facility was in no sense an alternative to the Fund drawing which had now been accepted as inevitable by the Treasury. Moreover it was not to be regarded as an alternative to a general long-term borrowing programme, which also would remain a necessity even with a Fund agreement. Rather it was a measure for bringing some stability to the sterling balances and reducing the risk of a repeat of what had happened so often in the past, that is their sudden run-down in

---

[1] PCC (76)53 and PCC (76) 31st Meeting.

conditions which were least propitious for the UK. It was, therefore, a useful supplement to, but not a substitute for, other measures. The Treasury argued that both a Fund drawing and a 'safety net' would involve the G10 countries putting up or committing very large sums, for the size of a full UK drawing would mean that the IMF would not be able to handle it with its own resources but would have to seek reinforcement from the GAB, whose members, of which the three most involved would be the USA, Germany, and Japan, would be the very countries who would have to underwrite the safety net. The task of enlisting their double involvement was likely to be formidable, and the Treasury considered how the case for international support for sterling might be presented. It was decided that it should rest on the two propositions that, with the UK an important part of the fabric of international trade and payments (and sterling still an international currency), it was in everyone's interest that 'the UK should not go under', and secondly that stabilizing the sterling balances would be a major contribution to the achievement of exchange rate stability generally, an objective which, following the five years of instability after the dollar went 'off gold' in 1971, was still firmly on the international agenda. As to the size of a new facility, the Treasury thought that $5 billion would suffice, although in the earlier paper the Bank had argued that $10 billion might be required to achieve the task of fully underwriting sterling. At this stage the paper did not discuss the modalities for bringing about the facility; this was something which would have to be taken forward when it was apparent that an agreement with the Fund was in sight.

The paper was put to the Chancellor[2] who, in the light of the conclusions of the Cabinet meeting of 3 August, forwarded it to the Prime Minister on 22 September.[3] The Chancellor said that he agreed with the paper's conclusions and added that he felt 'inclined not to circulate to EY [the Ministerial Committee on Economic Strategy]'. The public announcement of the UK application for a drawing, made on 29 September, was the next occasion for progress to be made on the safety net. The Prime Minister decided to make a personal telephone call to President Ford the following day, explaining the context of the decision to go to the IMF. The Prime Minister disclosed the outcome of this conversation when, on 30 September, he replied to the Chancellor's minute of 22 September. 'As you know', he said,[4] 'I touched on the problem of the sterling balances when I spoke to President Ford following the announcement of our application, and registered the point in my follow-up letter. We must keep up the momentum gained and not be inhibited by the timing of the elections in the United States and Germany'.[5] The Government, he thought, should go for a larger facility than the $5 billion mentioned by the Treasury.

---

[2] BP 32/24/01.   [3] BP 98/16/02.   [4] Ibid.

[5] The American Presidential and Congressional Elections were to be held on 2 November, and in Germany the Bundestag elections were timed for 3 October.

'The main point we shall need to get across to the USA and Germany in particular is the very real threat to our position as an ally in a number of fields such as trade, political alliances as well as defence', he said. The issue should be discussed in EY—a clear reminder to the Chancellor that the important issues which were now on the table were not to be regarded as his preserve. (The Chancellor, however, did not take up this suggestion immediately, but waited until early November, when he sought the Committee's authority to embark on the Fund negotiations before apprising it of his plans for a safety net.) He must have had a further conversation, not recorded, with the Prime Minister for he told the Governor on 30 September that Ford had been non-committal on the subject of the safety net although he had been extremely forthcoming about help from the IMF.[6]

Two conclusions can be drawn from this conversation. First the Prime Minister was going to play the political card of the UK's continued involvement in the Western alliance and the economic framework on which it was based to secure some help on the safety net from our allies, and secondly President Ford had evidently been briefed by the US Treasury not to be encouraging about the safety net, at any rate in advance of the Fund drawing. On 3 October Yeo—at the Chancellor's request—was again in London,[7] having come primarily to discuss his ideas for strengthening sterling. When the safety net was raised in the discussion Yeo was distinctly unforthcoming. 'There is no prospect of additional help for the UK. ... Any action on the sterling balances would be counter-productive', to which the Chancellor replied that the UK would nonetheless continue to pursue the idea. The subject was discussed between Yeo and the head of OF on 7 October[8] when the former arrived in Manila and the message was repeated. 'The White House might like the idea at first—but would drop it when they saw the realities of the US domestic policies'. What Yeo seems to have been alluding to was the likelihood that, if Congressional approval had to be obtained, the President might have difficulties. He noted that the mood in the Republican Party was becoming more, not less, hostile to interventionist economic policies and to providing financial help abroad.

Manila saw another, less unpromising, development. A senior official at the Bank for International Settlements (BIS) revealed to an old colleague from the Bank of England that his institution had been considering some possibilities for stabilizing the balances:[9] and the Managing Director of that institution raised with a member of the Treasury the matter of guarantees.[10] These developments suggested that, outside the United States, the leading players were themselves beginning to entertain the idea of some action on the balances. But, as we shall see, although the idea of by-passing the USA if they were

---

[6] Ibid.   [7] Ibid.   [8] Ibid.   [9] DW 036.   [10] Ibid.

intransigent had some attractions, it soon became apparent that the Americans' involvement was absolutely essential.

The divergencies between the Prime Minister's ideas for making progress and those of the Chancellor and Treasury were beginning to become more sharply defined and they were not narrowed by another development. On 3 October the German Social Democrats, with their political allies, won a narrow victory in the Federal elections to the Bundestag, and their victory gave the Chancellor, Helmut Schmidt, a further three years in office. Schmidt and Callaghan had been colleagues for a number of years and the Prime Minister had, in his capacity as Foreign Secretary, had several occasions to meet the German Chancellor after they both took office in 1974. Schmidt, since his experience as a British prisoner of war in 1945, had been something of an anglophile, and as a Social Democrat had a natural affinity with the moderate wing of the British Labour Party. At all events the two men were comfortable with each other and there was probably also something like friendship between them. The Prime Minister saw Schmidt's victory as an opportunity to cement the relationship between them and he put a congratulatory telephone call to him on 4 October as soon as the electoral results came in. The conversation did not end with the congratulations however, and the Prime Minister quickly got on to the issue of the application for a Fund stand-by and what the Germans could do to help. 'I think the immediate help we can have, Helmut, if I may say so, is if the IMF can give us the loan *on the basis of existing policies* which we intend to stick to. . . . Your people should indicate . . . that Germany feels that the existing policies are of sufficient character to enable the loan to be granted' (italics added).[11] Schmidt was suitably polite but non-committal. Two days later the Prime Minister put another telephone call through and this time he was more specific. He told Schmidt that he would like to have a talk with him the coming weekend. 'We have got a problem and I would really like to talk it over with you in a political sense without officials and the rest of it . . . talk about the economic and financial position'. He would not, as he put it, 'bring Healey along'.[12] The whole meeting would be kept quiet and Schmidt, who at first seemed reluctant to fall in with the idea, pleading reasonably enough that he was exhausted by the election campaign and wanted to rest, agreed, but on the basis that the visit was simply to have an exchange of thoughts over dinner. The two heads of government had a long and discursive talk late on the evening of 10 October. No officials were present, but the Prime Minister gave an account of the discussion to his Private Secretary who immediately made a record. Part of the discussion was about the geopolitical situation and need not concern us. However, in the area of economics and finance it was not the Fund application which was discussed, but the question of the sterling balances, something Schmidt raised unasked. The Prime Minister seized on the

[11] PREM 16/895.   [12] Ibid.

reference and immediately suggested that the answer was to create a safety net in the order of $10 billion to be financed by those countries with ample reserves. Schmidt responded by talking about the size of Germany's foreign exchange assets and suggested contributions in about equal proportions from the USA and Germany. Schmidt said that he would talk to President Ford about this. After the talk the Prime Minister directed that the contents should not be divulged outside No 10 Downing Street. The Prime Minister did, however, reveal what had been said when he held a meeting of senior ministers and officials on 1 November, see below.

One must be careful not to ascribe too much significance to one particular episode, and the Chequers meeting may not have had the importance the Prime Minister subsequently suggested. But two observations may be made. The first is that, whatever Schmidt may have said, he simply did not constitutionally have access to the German foreign currency reserves, which were the assets of the independent Bundesbank. The State Secretary at the German Ministry of Finance (Karl-Otto Pöhl[13]) subsequently told the Treasury[14] that if the German Chancellor wanted himself to give overseas aid or contribute to a safety net he would have to do so from Government funds or borrow to do so. He also said that when Schmidt had returned from Chequers he was 'in a pessimistic frame of mind'. It is hard to escape the conclusion that the Prime Minister read more into whatever Schmidt said than was intended. But what is important is that the Prime Minister took encouragement from the meeting and felt the need to follow it up.

The follow-up took an usual form. On 18 October, in accordance with what he had said at the dinner on 10 October, the Prime Minister sent the Cabinet Secretary to Bonn for a private talk with Pöhl, a close confidant of Schmidt's and a key player on the international financial scene. What it was hoped would be achieved from this move, which was revealed to the Treasury Permanent Secretary on a private basis only the day before it took place, is not clear. No doubt the Prime Minister wanted to learn at first hand, and not via the Treasury machine, what the attitude of the Germans at the technical level was. Whatever the motives, the outcome was very much as the Treasury would have predicted.[15] Schmidt might be willing to help but the terms of any deal would have to satisfy the markets.[16] Some form of safety net was a possibility but the Germans would be opposed to a purely bilateral deal or even one based

---

[13] Pöhl, although a civil servant, was in fact a political appointee having been a member of the SPD. His background was as an economic journalist and in this capacity he had formed a close relationship with Schmidt, closer probably than that between Schmidt and his Finance Minister, Hans Apel. He subsequently was appointed President of the Bundesbank.

[14] BP 98/16/02.

[15] Indeed Pöhl telephoned the head of OF, with whom he had close relations, to ask him what the meeting was all about and to add that 'talk of a bail out was premature', BP 98/16 02.

[16] PREM 16/895.

solely on the EEC. There could be no possibility of an extension of the central bank credit—Yeo, said the Germans, would be strongly opposed. Instead Pöhl suggested that the UK should explore the scope for using the OECD Support Fund or for developing a network of sterling guarantees. These were not very helpful suggestions: the OECD Fund was not in being, the US Congress having declined to ratify it, and the idea that a system of sterling guarantees would stabilize the market seemed to the British to be fanciful. Pöhl made one further comment. Why didn't the British speed up the timetable for the Fund negotiations? He had become aware that there had been some delay in setting up the Fund mission which was to carry out the necessary consultations but did not seem to understand that this was for technical reasons. The Cabinet Secretary made two important points in reply. The first was that a failure to find a solution to the problem of the sterling balances might lead to political difficulties a plain hint at the implications for the British contribution to Western Defence—and the second that the British Government would have to know, before it signed up to the IMF, that a safety net would be in place. This latter proviso was to constitute a serious stumbling block later on when the Americans revealed their objections even to the *preparation* of a safety net in advance of a Fund agreement. The visit to Bonn was not without some value however. Four days after it took place Pöhl telephoned to say[17] that Schmidt had it in mind to call the US Secretary of State, Kissinger, presumably to test how opposed the US were to any preparatory work on the safety net. But he had heard from Yeo that he would like to talk privately to Pöhl—no doubt to ensure that there would be no breaking of ranks among the main creditors.

The battlelines were now clearly drawn up. The British wanted clear assurances about the delivery of the safety net before they committed themselves to the Fund. The Americans, that is to say the US Treasury and the Federal Reserve, were unwilling to take the heat off the UK to settle with the Fund and to this end would not contemplate anything which looked like a soft option. The Germans wanted to help the British, but knew in their hearts that there was no escape from a tough agreement with the Fund. They might, however, be willing to look at the safety net on a provisional and tentative basis. What the British dearly wanted was that the Germans should persuade the Americans at least to declare that a safety net was a possibility and to participate in the necessary planning. The Prime Minister held a council of war with senior ministers and officials including the Foreign Secretary on 1 November[18] just as the Fund team were arriving in London. The Cabinet Secretary reported on his talk in Bonn and commented on Pöhl's dismay at the leisurely pace of the Fund Mission (which of course had not yet left Washington). The Chancellor agreed that the important point was now to complete the Fund negotiations as soon as possible. The Prime Minister referred to his meeting with Schmidt three weeks earlier and said that he

---

[17] DW 036.   [18] Ibid.

remained convinced that the Germans wanted to help with the safety net. He wanted to keep further developments in the political arena—another dig at the Treasury and an expression of his view that the political card would at the end of the day take some tricks. The Treasury were not by any means as opposed to this as the Prime Minister supposed. In his brief to the Chancellor for the meeting, the Permanent Secretary said[19] quite categorically that 'sooner or later, if the idea of a multilateral safety net to be negotiated during the course of this month [November] is to be pursued, contact will have to be made with the Americans at the highest level. Perhaps a prime ministerial approach to Kissinger is desirable.' But the Treasury did not think that this would let the UK off the hook. 'My own view is that a *masse de manoeuvre*[20] would be very difficult to negotiate on the basis of minimal changes in policy and the publication of a large PSBR for next year'.

The Prime Minister's concern to keep personal control of the developments and not to leave the running to the Treasury burst into the open in a rather unusual way. On 25 October he gave an interview to the BBC Current Affairs programme, 'Panorama',[21] in the course of which he was asked what could be done about the sterling balances. Most politicians, asked at a delicate point in international diplomacy such as this, would have ducked the question. The Prime Minister was not an unastute politician, but he chose to deal with the matter openly.

I would love to get rid of the reserve currency. I am not sure that everybody in the Treasury would or maybe in the Bank. . . . From the Bank's point of view I see no particular advantage of being a reserve currency at all. . . . I would very much like to see us get into a situation where these liabilities of ours which we have as a reserve currency were taken over in some form or other. Whether that can be achieved of course isn't only for me . . . I do say this. I think that Germany and the United States, and perhaps Japan, have got some responsibility here. They have got vast reserves. . . . If the IMF were to try to force us into policies which would be harmful to the economy, that we would go into a downward spiral, then we would have to say to some of those other countries 'Look, the IMF and you yourselves must accept the political consequences of what you are doing'.

To the journalist's subsequent question whether the object of the search for a solution to the sterling balance issue was to avoid being forced by the IMF or by events to pursue policies against 'our better judgement', the Prime Minister replied:

Right! And you see I think this is where the IMF will have to be very careful because they have got a great responsibility here. . . . They will have to say is it right to force Britain into courses which unless the sterling balances are met in some other way could be very harmful to the whole politics and whole structure, not only of Britain but of the West.

---

[19] Ibid.
[20] The term *masse de manoeuvre* was that of Lever. It seems to have consisted of the raising of very large dollar loans which would then be used to underwrite the official sterling balances.
[21] The full text appears in BP 98/16/02.

This statement, containing the first public intimation of the desire of the Government to seek a 'solution' to the sterling balance issue and the first public warning of the dire consequences of a failure to reach an agreement with the Fund, aroused a good deal of interest, indeed concern, among overseas countries. The New Zealanders came to the Treasury to ask what this meant to them as sterling balance holders and the Japanese, who had not, unlike the Germans and the Americans, hitherto been informed of what the UK had in mind, also put some pointed questions to the Treasury. But on a rather more parochial level, the Prime Minister's public doubts about the commitment of the Treasury and the Bank to the search for a solution to the problem did cause some upset among officials who felt that their professional commitment to serve the Government of the day, whatever their private inclinations might be, was being questioned. As our narrative has brought out, the doubts of officials about the wisdom of pursuing a solution to the sterling balance problem ahead of the Fund negotiations were based on an objective assessment of the likelihood of this being achievable, not on any doubts about the aim as the Prime Minister had implied.

On 2 November the Prime Minister spoke on the telephone to Schmidt[22] and the following day the German Chancellor took up the points in a personal letter. Schmidt said that he had spoken to President Ford, who had indicated that the United States would like to help over the safety net and take part in any solution, but only 'if the IMF negotiations went well'. The Prime Minister replied that he was determined to persevere with his present course and said that he thought that the two of them 'should keep political control'. Schmidt made some cautious noises about the need for the UK to do something about the fiscal position, but otherwise he showed a disinclination to get too involved himself. On the same day the head of OF had a meeting in Brussels with Pöhl,[23] who was much less forthcoming than his political chief about the usefulness of a safety net. The UK must, he said, adjust to the markets, which would want to see evidence that the balance of payments was improving. It would be wrong—and damaging to the Fund's credibility—for the Fund to soften its position on the UK for political reasons. What would be its position on Italy, Mexico, and France if it let the UK off lightly? It was clear that German officials would be unlikely to encourage their ministers to bow to the pressures of the British Prime Minister to secure softer terms from the Fund than the latter thought appropriate. A few days later the Chancellor of the Exchequer himself met Pöhl in Brussels[24] and emphasized the need for the Germans to appreciate the political aspects of the British problem. The Chancellor said that there was a growing readiness (presumably among Ministers) 'to go for a siege economy'. His own credibility with his colleagues had been weakened by successive cuts in public expenditure which failed to do the trick. (Moreover)

---

[22] BP 98/16/02.   [23] Ibid.   [24] Ibid.

the IMF borrowing might not be enough and the Prime Minister had therefore forced the pace on the safety net. He (the Chancellor) would welcome anything the Germans could do to influence the United States or enable progress to be made without them. The discussion between them then addressed the question of the Bundesbank, the German institution which would be involved in any safety net and which enjoyed a large measure of independence from the Federal Government. The Chancellor was clearly concerned that German cooperation should not be put at risk by a failure to bring the Central Bank into the picture in good time.[25] Throughout the conversation Pöhl showed some scepticism about the importance of the sterling balances to the problem the British faced. He had told the head of OF that the British would be wise *not* to resist an inflow of sterling and a rebuilding of the sterling balances once agreement with the Fund was reached; and he now told the Chancellor that 'rather than reduce the sterling balances why don't you try to attract capital (*and inferentially let the balances build up again*).' He had indeed made much the same point to the Cabinet Secretary at the secret meeting in Bonn on 18 October.

While all this was going on the Treasury were looking again at the idea of an SDR bond as a possible ingredient in any solution to the sterling balance problem. In a minute dated 21 October OF judged that it might now be possible to approach three or four of the main sterling balance holders[26]— those in fact with liquid resources which were surplus to their current requirements—to test the temperature of the water. The Chancellor was not enamoured of this however and, following a meeting with the Bank and Treasury on 29 October, he sent a minute to the Prime Minister recommending that the SDR bond should be kept in reserve pending the outcome of the safety net negotiations. This was virtually the last that was heard of the idea, for the financing problem came to be comfortably resolved by the combination of a Fund drawing and an underpinning safety net.

The scene now shifted to one dominated by central bankers. The latter had hardly surprisingly been talking among themselves about the issues which some solution to the sterling balance problem might involve. The Bank prepared an appraisal of each of the technical variants which were on the table—a safety net on the lines of the 1968 facility (but without guarantees) and a BIS bond.[27] The latter was an idea conceived by BIS staff, whereby the UK would offer official sterling balance holders the option of converting some or all of their sterling reserves into a bond of perhaps ten years maturity with an interest rate which was market related and would be an obligation of the British government but

---

[25] In fact the Bundesbank were by then well aware of what was going on, as the discussion between the Bank of England overseas director and his opposite number on 27 October showed.

[26] DW 036.

[27] S. Payton, 7 October BP 98/16/02.

would be underwritten by the BIS (and implicitly all its member central banks). The Bank and the Treasury both preferred the former not least because it would not involve the sterling balance holders themselves. The Overseas Director of the Bank talked to his opposite number at the Bundesbank on 27 October[28] when the latter made encouraging noises about achieving simultaneity with the Fund drawing and the safety net. Moreover the Germans were willing to start preparatory work straightaway and not to wait for the Fund negotiations to be completed.

Preparations now began for the forthcoming meeting of the BIS Governors, over the weekend of 6–8 November. A meeting was arranged between the Chancellor and the Governor on 4 November[29] to deal with both the Basle meeting and the regular monthly meeting of EEC Finance Ministers, which was to be held on 8 November. The Chancellor, conscious of the American reluctance to engage in even preliminary discussions on the sterling balances, said that, if a safety net of only $5 billion was likely, this might be handled by the Europeans themselves, although he must have known from what Pöhl had told the Cabinet Secretary in Bonn two weeks earlier that this was something the Germans were not prepared to entertain. The Prime Minister also decided to get involved in this matter and called a meeting[30] with the Chancellor and the Governor the following day to discuss tactics. The Governor argued that it might be best to leave the running to the BIS itself which had, as we said earlier, been looking at two ideas, a safety net and a bond underwritten by the BIS which might be offered to those sterling balance holders who wished to reduce their holdings of sterling. The Prime Minister was not keen on this. He repeated that it was important to get international agreement on a scheme, whether the safety net or the BIS bond, in parallel with the IMF negotiations (which by then, as we shall see, had begun, albeit in a rather hesitant way). He pressed the Governor to go for a speedy development of the technical aspects of a scheme and he would personally ask Schmidt to get Klasen (the President of the Bundesbank) to cooperate.

The Governor reported the outcome of the Basle meeting to the Chancellor at a meeting on 9 November.[31] The Governor said that he had made clear to his colleagues that the UK did not regard the safety net, if it could be agreed, as a substitute for a successful outcome to the Fund negotiations—to which the Chancellor replied that although the two issues were separate 'there was something in the argument that the provision of a safety net would allow us to get away with somewhat softer terms for the IMF loan which would not need to be tough enough to satisfy the market'. By this comment the Chancellor was echoing what the Prime Minister had said in the 'Panorama' interview, but it was not a proposition which either the Treasury or the Bank thought had much validity. The Fund were unlikely to see the safety net as

---

[28] BP 98/16/02.   [29] DW 036.   [30] Ibid.   [31] Ibid.

having much relevance to what they clearly thought were fundamental flaws in British economic policy; and the Americans were most unlikely to go along with any inclination which the Fund, however improbably, might have to bow to political pressure. The Chancellor also broached the idea that the contacts and influence that Harold Lever had with some members of the US Administration might be used by asking him to pay a personal visit to Washington.

The Basle meeting of 6–8 November did highlight the difference of approach of the Americans from the others. The Federal Reserve Board—the nearest thing to an American central bank—refused to be represented itself, and only deputed the President of the New York Federal Reserve Bank to attend the meeting and he clearly had instructions not to get involved in anything like negotiations. By contrast the President of the Bundesbank played a helpful part, no doubt encouraged by the German Chancellor. This was, however, of little relevance to the technicians in the BIS who were now given the job of fleshing out the concept of a safety net into a formal, but still hypothetical, presentation of the issues which would have to be decided by the Governors at their next meeting (in mid-December). The assumption was that by this time the participants would know, one way or another, whether the UK had reached an agreement with the Fund.

This was not exactly what the Prime Minister wanted. The timing of the next Basle meeting and the possibility that, through the absence of cooperation from the Americans, the safety net would not be in place when a decision had to be taken whether to accept the Fund's terms for a stand-by, placed him in an awkward position. He felt very strongly that the safety net would be a powerful selling point to those of his colleagues who might have reservations about the terms sought by the Fund. The meeting of EY on 3 November had given him a foretaste of the opposition he would encounter to an agreement with the Fund which involved a significant change in policy.

The Prime Minister decided that the key to any progress with the safety net lay in Washington, and to a lesser extent in Bonn. It was not absolutely clear what he hoped to achieve by some new initiative at this stage. Ford and Schmidt had both told him at various times that the key to everything was a Fund agreement, after which the sterling balances could be dealt with. Neither of them had shown much inclination to exert pressure on the Fund to become softer in its approach to the UK. The most that they had seemed willing to contemplate was a speeding up of the safety net preparations so as to secure their completion simultaneously with the Fund agreement. Whatever it was that the Prime Minister hoped to achieve, he authorized a visit, which the Chancellor had hinted at at his meeting of 9 November, of the Chancellor of the Duchy of Lancaster (Lever) to Washington in the week beginning 15 November.[32] Lever's chief target was the American Secretary of State

[32] Ibid.

(Kissinger) whom he knew on a personal basis. But he also had meetings with the President and with Simon and Burns. Lever's formal bid was that there should be early action on the safety net without it being specified that this would not be seen in any way as a substitute for a Fund drawing. Kissinger seemed to have little grasp of what Lever wanted—he even confused the idea of a safety net with the OECD support facility—and it was the meetings with the experts on the financial side that were revealing. Neither the President nor Simon rose to the suggestion of accelerated progress on the safety net, and Burns said flat-footedly that he was not even prepared to discuss the safety net until the Fund agreement was reached.[33] The initiative of the Lever visit was therefore unproductive. It certainly achieved nothing concrete, and it may well have confirmed the Americans in their impression that the British were seeking softer terms from the Fund and were hoping that the Americans would use their muscle with the Fund to help with that. In that sense it may well have been counter-productive.

In the meantime the Prime Minister had been working on Schmidt, sending him a personal letter by special courier on 10 November. What precisely this said was not known outside the Prime Minister's office, and the Treasury were certainly not given a copy—even the Ambassador in Bonn was not put in the picture. It now emerges,[34] however, that it was largely a political appeal to Schmidt to help to achieve the objective of putting the safety net in place at the same time as the Fund drawing and both by the end of the month. It is not easy to understand why this document should have been thought to be so sensitive. Schmidt's reply, on 16 November,[35] was circulated in Whitehall and stated that he had been in touch with the Americans and had concluded that they simply were not prepared to enter into even technical discussions of a support facility in time for the next meeting of the BIS on 12–13 December. Without the Americans, said Schmidt, no progress could be made. As far as the Germans were concerned, this was the end of the matter.

It was, therefore, clear beyond any doubt that the chances of a successful outcome to the safety net discussions before any agreement with the Fund could be announced were non-existent. The Prime Minister sent a personal message to the President on 27 November but this was largely about the difficulties the Cabinet were then having with the Fund's terms and it drew the polite but discouraging response that the 'United States would not interfere with the IMF negotiations but would move sympathetically (on the safety net) when substantial agreement has been reached with the Fund'. Meanwhile the UK Director in Washington was confirming independently that Burns was not willing even to discuss the safety net until the Fund negotiations were finished.[36]

---

[33] DW 036.   [34] PREM 16/800.   [35] DW 036.   [36] Ibid.

The concern of the Treasury and the Bank was now to get as much agreement as was possible at the Basle meeting on 13 December so as to allow the Government to make a definitive statement about the sterling balances at the same time that the Fund agreement would be announced. The need to repay the $5.3 billion central bank credit on 7 December made it almost imperative that agreement with the Fund should be reached then or very soon after, and the important question was how much could be said about a safety net having been agreed, if only in principle.

The first task was to make a critical appraisal of what the BIS staff had produced in the way of a position paper. It was very much on the lines expected and offered the choice of either a safety net on the model of the 1968 facility or of a special bond to be issued by the BIS, denominated in dollars, to official sterling balance holders who wished to convert their sterling assets. The one problem the paper presented to the British was that of a UK guarantee being given to official sterling holders. We have seen that this idea was anathema to both the Bank and the Treasury. The purpose was, of course, to minimize the exposure of the creditors who stood behind the whole facility. A guarantee, if credible, made it less likely that the balances would be run down and the safety net invoked. To the British the guarantee looked like a vote of no confidence in sterling, which was not how they wanted a facility timed to coincide with a successful Fund drawing to look. Moreover, harking back to the 1968 precedent, a guarantee, which was an uncovenanted benefit to the holder, ought to be associated with a commitment to hold a minimum sum in sterling. To resurrect the idea of guarantees and minimum balances reawakened the memory of difficult and prolonged negotiations with each of the selected holders. Negotiations could only be avoided by offering the guarantees unconditionally and this did not appeal to the British at all. As the Bank memorandum[37] of 30 November on the paper put it 'guarantees must require a *quid pro quo* for holders to maintain a minimum amount of sterling'. But in the last analysis on 9 December, the Treasury recognized that guarantees could not be made into a breaking point.[38] The need to have an agreement obliged it to swallow some of its principles.

As the Basle meeting approached, another problem cropped up, linking the Fund negotiations with the safety net preparations. Although in early December agreement on the main body of the points at issue with the Fund had been settled, there was still a problem over the amount the UK could draw at the outset of the term of the agreement. As we shall see, the Fund, for good reasons, saw difficulty in what would have been a breach of normal practice in allowing a member who had agreed a programme covering a period of one or two years to draw a significant part of the total credit at the outset. In the British case they were firm that, of the total credit agreed, the initial drawing

---

[37] BP 98/16/02.   [38] Ibid.

should be only $1 billion—their opening position had been only $0.5 billion. This was firmly contested by the Treasury and the matter was not finally resolved until the eleventh hour and even then with only a minimal increase. But it also caused concern among the likely creditors of the BIS facility. They felt that they were being asked to underwrite a commitment to $5 billion immediately the safety net was in place, whereas the Fund were phasing in their commitment—which in any case was subject to performance criteria and was for a smaller sum. Thus both the UK and the creditors were unhappy with the Fund's intransigence and the Germans applied some pressure on the Fund to modify its position. At one point according to Pöhl[39] the Bundesbank felt that if the Fund held out for an initial drawing of only $1 billion it would undermine the position of the participants in the safety net arrangement. Fortunately this issue was resolved by the Fund moving somewhat in the closing stages of the negotiations in London.

A much more serious problem was the participation of the Americans. As we have seen, from the very outset of the initiative, Burns in particular, but also Simon and Yeo, were strongly opposed to doing anything, even of a purely preparatory kind, on the safety net until agreement had been reached with the Fund. In the course of November it became steadily clear to the British that the President and his senior political advisers were not prepared to overrule the US Treasury Department: and constitutionally they had no means of overruling the Chairman of the Board of Governors of the Federal Reserve System. The most that they could have done would have been to ask Congress to authorize the Treasury Department to commit itself and accept on the Federal Budget the liability inherent in a safety net. But a new Congress had only just been elected and would not convene until the New Year. Moreover, by that time, a new President would be in the Oval Office,[40] and Ford could clearly not commit him. As we have seen, the Germans did what they could to persuade the Americans to participate in the preparations if only on a contingent basis; but their efforts were not successful. The most that could be expected now was that the Americans would sit in on the discussion of the BIS paper at the Basle meeting and that if by then agreement with the Fund had been reached the scheme could be agreed. But in a conversation he had with the head of OF on 9 December[41] Yeo said emphatically that he, Simon and Burns were 'at one, and believed that any "intermediate" (i.e. non-short-term) scheme, greater than about six or seven months, would involve either Congressional approval or the use of the Exchange Stabilisation Fund', neither of which were attractive courses. This was a more extreme statement than anything that had gone before. The Americans were making objections of principle and not of timing.

---

[39] BP 98/16/02.
[40] The Presidential election had resulted in the victory of the Democratic candidate, Carter.
[41] Ibid.

They were saying more explicitly than hitherto that there was really no need for a safety net now that agreement with the Fund had virtually been reached. The Chancellor broke this news to the Prime Minister on 10 December,[42] by which time he had secured the reluctant agreement of the whole Cabinet to the Fund's terms, but on the understanding that a safety net would be part of the whole package. The head of OF was despatched to Washington at the end of the week beginning 6 December and had several meetings with the leading players: Burns, Simon, and Yeo. By now Burns had agreed to send a senior Governor of the Board to the Basle meeting of 13 December, but only on the basis that he would not participate in the examination of the scheme. Burns and Simon were particularly hostile to the messages the Prime Minister had sent to the President at the end of November. The National Security Adviser (Scowcroft) was more sympathetic and said that he was pressing Yeo to relent.[43] But Yeo was now saying that the US was opposed to doing anything through the BIS and that the most they would contemplate would be some bilateral agreement with the UK covering the official balances only. He did, in the event, produce the textual outline of such a plan, but when Burns heard of this he was critical—it would require a great deal of work. By this time the Governor of the Bank of England was in Basle for the BIS meeting. He telephoned the Chancellor to say that 'it was impossible to imagine the other countries involved operating separately from the United States'. The US representative took no part in the substantive discussions but merely observed that there was no need for a scheme at all; but if there was to be one, it should provide for the phasing out of the sterling balances. This was a theme which struck a chord with other countries. The Europeans recalled that the UK had promised to do this at the time that it acceded to the European Community; so they were only asking the UK to deliver on its promises. The meeting also thought that a scheme of $5 billion was unnecessarily large and contrasted with the $3.9 billion the Fund were providing. It was now painfully clear that the BIS would not produce a workable scheme at this meeting. It could pick up the threads at a subsequent meeting and it did in fact commission the BIS deputies, who were due to have a meeting in Paris on 20 December, to continue the study of the question.

The events described above left the Chancellor with little to say about the safety net when he made his announcement of the Fund agreement to the House of Commons on 15 December. His actual words were:

Considerable work has already been done on the problem of the sterling balances in the BIS where central bank governors have had constructive discussion over the last weekend. At the same time, the matter is under discussion with the Treasury and the Federal Reserve in Washington. These talks have revealed a general desire on the part of those

---

[42] Ibid.   [43] Ibid.

concerned to achieve a satisfactory arrangement for the sterling balances, and I believe it will be possible to reach an agreement before long.[44]

The Chancellor took the opportunity to also inform the House of his intention to take a $0.5 billion swap with the US Treasury and the Federal Reserve—see below. He also mentioned the availability of the Bundesbank stand-by facility of $350 million without expressing any intention at that stage to draw on it.

There is no doubt but that the failure to secure the safety net simultaneously with the Fund drawing was a disappointment to the British and something of a humiliation for the Prime Minister, who had expended a considerable amount of personal capital in an effort to obtain an international agreement in good time. It was left to the Chancellor to beg him not to send a recriminatory letter to President Ford.[45] By then the Americans had agreed to activate the Federal Reserve Swap to the tune of $500 million to dispose of the front-end loading issue with the Fund. Bitter words would not have been appropriate, particularly as at the January meeting of the BIS Governors of 9–10 January the safety net was agreed in principle with the Americans withdrawing their opposition to it and participating in a facility of $3 billion. The arrangements were formally adopted after the completion of some technical work at the Governors' meeting of 6–7 February. The Chancellor was therefore able to justify the optimism of his December statement on 11 January when he announced to the House of Commons the successful reaching of an agreement in principle and the availability of foreign exchange bonds for those official sterling balance holders who wanted them. He made a further statement on 10 February when the agreement finally came into effect.

The foreign bond alternative was, in the event, an arrangement implemented by the UK on its own, but with the blessing of the members of the BIS, who stipulated that no more than 75 per cent of the bonds should be in dollars—the rest being in Deutchmarks, Swiss francs, and Yen. But it had to be sold to the overseas monetary institutions and to this end the Bank of England had to conduct bilateral discussions with all the potential participants—over 130 in all. This took two months, at the end of which the Bank had persuaded a number of overseas official holders to diversify their sterling holdings. All told £395.3 million of official sterling was converted into non-sterling liabilities. For the Bank the exercise was not wholly free from regret and irony. As the briefing note put out to his staff by the Overseas Director put it, the Bank, having spent most of the previous decade persuading sterling holders of the benefits of sterling, now had to tell them that they might be better off in other currencies. It was to all intents and purposes the end of the sterling area.

---

[44] *Hansard*, 15 December.   [45] BP 98/16/02.

The negotiations with the Fund

We now have to go back in time and pick up the narrative of the negotiations with the Fund. These embraced several issues, which although enjoying a loose connection, were really separate items. They were of differing importance to each of the parties and they presented differing problems: some considerable, some relatively minor. Without an appreciation of each of those problems, a strictly chronological narrative of the course of the negotiations would run the risk of missing some of the subtleties of those differences, and we begin this section with an appraisal of what, in the event, the main issues of contention proved to be.

It was, as we shall see, the Fund which set the agenda, and for reasons which will emerge from the narrative, and the items they chose to dwell upon were the following:

1 the 'adequacy' of existing UK macro-economic policy, in particular the government's budgetary stance in relation to the monetary outlook;
2 the size of the budgetary adjustment which the Fund thought necessary;
3 the Government's policy on the exchange rate;
4 the amount of credit which the UK would be able to draw immediately the negotiations were completed and the application was approved by the IMF Executive Board;
5 the nature and extent of the financial performance targets which would be prescribed in the agreement with the Fund;
6 the term of the agreement, in particular whether it should embody a programme of commitments for one year or for a longer period.

On all these issues the British government, at any rate at the outset of the negotiations, took a different view from the Fund—in some cases a significantly different view—and, although at the conclusion the two views on all these subjects were reconciled by shifts in position by both parties, the bridging of the gap took a great deal of time and even at the end, although an agreement which both parties accepted as reasonable was reached, some significant intellectual differences remained. It was the second, and to some extent the fourth, of the six issues which posed big political difficulties for British ministers both inside the Treasury and in the Cabinet generally. The remaining issues were of a more technical nature and the negotiations on them did not involve departments or Ministers outside the Treasury.

The Fund had made its views on all six issues reasonably clear, although not specifically in quantitative terms, well before the consultations began in London at the beginning of November. On the first two matters the Fund, at Managing Director as well as staff level, had expressed doubts early in the year about the 'adequacy' of fiscal and monetary policy, both currently and prospectively, and these doubts persisted after the July measures. At the meetings in Manila at the beginning of October the Fund had indicated that they would be seeking some reduction in the prospective borrowing requirement in the fiscal year ahead (1977–78) and this was before the substantial upward revision in that figure which the NIF produced at the end of October. They had also expressed strong views for a considerable period of time about the need for the sterling exchange rate to depreciate—and they even wanted a rate below the low level reached in early October. They had made discouraging noises about the likelihood that the UK would be able to draw the full amount of any stand-by agreed immediately. They had talked of a two-year programme with phased drawings over its period and they had given a firm indication that the performance criteria would embrace DCE and the path of the PSBR. The Treasury could hardly say that it had not been warned.

Structure of the negotiations

A straightforward and strictly chronological account of the progress of the negotiations through to their conclusion would make for a certain confused reading, for the six issues of contention mentioned above were raised, discussed, dropped, and picked up again at various stages and only at the end were they all brought together and resolved. This perhaps is the nature of any complex negotiation between two parties in which several discrete issues are involved. A certain amount of 'give and take' becomes inevitable and there are trade-offs between one objective and another—trade-offs which do not have much logical connection but which give each party something of what it is seeking. In spite of this untidiness the negotiations did fall into four reasonably distinct phases and it may be helpful to the reader to treat each phase as a separate entity, irrespective of the precise sequence of events which made up that entity. The four phases may be described, albeit simplistically as shown in Table 5.1.

There were of course political issues within Phases I and II, and there were technical issues in all four phases and the rather neat labels attached to them must be treated with some reserve. It is important, however, to distinguish

Table 5.1 The four phases of the negotiations with the IMF, November–December 1976

Phase	Dates	Nature
I	1 November to 14 November	Procedural
II	15 November to 28 November	Technical
III	29 November to 6 December	Political
IV	7 December to 15 December	Detailed specifications

between the technical and the political in all four, for, although they interacted, they were dealt with by different players on the UK side, with officials being concerned with the technical aspects of the analysis and the detailed specifications and Ministers with the political. We may describe the two aspects broadly as follows:

- *Technical.* The principal technical issue was that of 'how the economy works'. The Fund had a conception of the likely economic response to a given policy change which was fundamentally different from that of the Treasury; this difference was perhaps the main reason why officials found it difficult to make a clear and unambiguous recommendation to Ministers to meet the Fund's policy prescription at the outset of a large fiscal adjustment in both of the two fiscal years ahead of 1976–77.

- *Political.* Ministers outside the Treasury were not involved in the technical discussions but they did have a real problem with the fiscal policy prescription of the Fund and indeed with that of the Treasury when the negotiations had progressed to the point that an agreement to the satisfaction of both parties on technical grounds seemed possible. Ministers considered that both the original Fund proposal and the modified Treasury proposal for a settlement would damage the Social Contract and the future of the Pay policy as well as create big problems with their own supporters through the cutting of social benefits and the raising of the level of unemployment. Many also thought that no fiscal retrenchment at all was called for.

In the narrative which follows we deal with the technical issues in Phase II and the political in Phase III. However, before we look at any of the four phases it is useful to summarize how the Treasury prepared for the negotiation. It was, as we have said, perfectly clear to officials, particularly in the light of the October NIF, that the Fund was bound to require policy changes which would greatly reduce both the rate of monetary expansion and the PSBR in the two fiscal years ahead. They would also probably wish to reach an understanding that there would be an 'active' exchange rate policy, in that the UK would have to agree not to allow competitiveness to be eroded as it had been between early 1974 and early 1976. Against the background of this expectation, the Treasury had some internal deliberation as to whether it would be better to await the Fund's proposals or to take the initiative by making some of their own. In the event the latter course was ruled out by Ministers who, at the meeting of EY on 3 November, had laid down that there should be no discussion with the Fund of policy changes without specific authority. The Treasury was therefore constrained to a purely reactive role, commenting on the Fund's ideas, but not making any suggestions of its own. The Treasury had recommended to the Chancellor, in a briefing note[46] on 1 November for this meeting, to ask his

---

[46] DW 036.

colleagues for a mandate to explore policy changes with the IMF, but the Chancellor decided not to take on his colleagues on this issue.

As to what the Treasury's expectations of the Fund's specific requirements were, there was little in the way of considered analysis. Among the Second Secretaries the figure of a reduction in the PSBR for 1977–78 of £1 billion was mooted,[47] although several thought that a much higher figure would be necessary—the head of OF had expressed the view when he saw the forecast that savings of £2 billion would be necessary. But these estimates were not based on what, left to its own devices, the Treasury would have recommended on grounds other than confidence. The October NIF did not lead to any collective policy recommendation before the Fund's arrival. It is true that during the Fund's visit the Chief Economic Adviser did put forward a hypothetical package of measures[48] which could be justified on the grounds that some acceleration of the improvement in the balance of payments was a pressing requirement, not least to re-create the lost external confidence, and other packages were discussed by the PCC which would have improved the external outlook and reduced the PSBR by between £1 billion and £3 billion. These included substantial public expenditure cuts and in some cases tax increases and a surcharge on imports. But none of these were put to Ministers or of course to the Fund. And it was not until 24 November that the Treasury was authorized to examine with the Fund some ideas of their own for dealing with the situation. But this is to anticipate the unfolding of events.

Phase I—procedural issues

The Fund team arrived in London in the first week of November. The leader of the team was Alan Whittome, the head of the Fund's European Department. He was a former Bank of England official and had been in the Fund over ten years. He was greatly experienced in consultations with those European members who had been in financial difficulties over the previous decade—notably France and Italy. His principal lieutenant was David Finch, an Australian national, also with a great deal of experience, but his base in the Fund was the Exchange and Trade Restrictions Department, whose remit was to examine and pass judgement on breaches by members of the formal rules governing the free movement of goods and finance across international borders. But it was also heavily involved in Fund consultations with members, and Finch, like Whittome, had a wealth of experience behind him.

The first formal meeting between the two Fund leaders and the UK team took place under the Chancellor's chairmanship on the morrow of the EY

---

[47] DW 014 28 October.   [48] HF 33/04, PCC (76)70 and 72.

meeting—4 November.[49] The meeting was a low-key affair and was concerned largely with procedural matters. The only specific issue raised was that of the exchange rate. The Chancellor said that he wanted a stable rate without specifying precisely what this meant. The Fund, for whom this was an important issue, countered that the criterion should be the maintenance of price competitiveness of UK exports—not quite the same thing. But Whittome took the opportunity to say that the target figure of $1.50 mentioned by the *Sunday Times* in its article on 24 October had not even been discussed inside the Fund. Among the procedural issues raised was that of a meeting between the Fund and the TUC and CBI. Whittome was quite willing to go along with this, but would want to say, if asked, that this was the Chancellor's idea. Finally the Chancellor, carrying out EY's mandate, put down the first of a series of markers on the extent of any restrictive thoughts the Fund might have. 'Deflation', said the Chancellor, 'would affect everything, notably the relationship with the TUC'. The TUC had only recently, at its annual conference, passed a resolution in favour of continuing the attack on inflation. Later that day there was a meeting between the Fund and Treasury officials, where the former stated what they would want to focus on, again the exchange rate but also public expenditure and the duration of the programme. On the exchange rate the Fund were unhappy with the way sterling had behaved over the previous year. There had been plateaux of stability followed by periods of serious weakness when the rate had precipitated. Over the next twelve months sterling would have to continue to depreciate to compensate for the excess of the UK's rate of inflation over that of its competitors. The IMF wanted 'an openly stated policy of gradual adjustment of the inflation differential'. The current rate, $1.70, was not in their view 'an undervaluation'. There were going to be difficulties here. An open statement of policy to depreciate was the last thing that the Bank of England and the Treasury thought possible (although at this stage they did not voice this thought). The Fund also expressed a desire to clarify the technical question of what 'the base figures [for public expenditure in 1977–78 and 1978–79] were'. They wanted to go into this in some detail with the expenditure division. The Fund indicated that they would probably want to focus attention during the consultations 'very heavily' on the PSBR. Moreover they were firmly thinking of a two-year programme, as they had said in Manila.

Next day, 5 November, the Permanent Secretary had the first[50] of some six or seven informal meetings with the Fund team leader—some of these on a one-to-one basis. The first meeting was, like that with the Chancellor the day before, partly of a procedural kind, but Whittome took the opportunity to identify what he thought were going to be the difficult issues. The first was the exchange rate and the Fund made exactly the same point that they had with the Chancellor. The second was the PSBR. The Fund had not yet seen the NIF

---

[49] BP 122/24/01.   [50] DW 062.

with its worsened view of this variable for 1977–78. Whittome said that his 'back of an envelope' calculation suggested that if the target were for money supply to grow at about 8 per cent in that year, the PSBR would have to be of the order of £6–7 billion. (The forecast, it will be recalled was £11 billion, although subsequent revisions of a technical nature reduced this to £10.5 billion.) At its face value this intimation by Whittome of his objectives implied a huge fiscal adjustment. The Treasury, under instructions not to discuss policy changes, made no comment on the figures, but the Permanent Secretary expressed reservations at aiming at a PSBR target constructed from a desired path for the money supply. As he put it 'there are intellectual objections to projecting an estimate from a money supply target in view of the heroic assumptions required. [Moreover] the PSBR could only be changed by very large shifts in expenditure and tax *ex ante*'. Whittome again referred to the two-year programme idea.

The next development was an informal lunch on 10 November between the Head of OF and the UK Executive Director at the Fund on the one hand and Whittome and Finch on the other.[51] Again the exchange rate and the PSBR for 1977–78 came up but the difference between the two sides seemed somewhat less, except on the issue of a publicly stated commitment. Finch seemed keen on a policy of a 'smooth slide' although Whittome, as befitted his background, was more pragmatic. On the PSBR again there had to be a ceiling for 1977–78 and the fiscal adjustment required would be heavily in the public expenditure area. The lunch did, however, provide one new thought. The Fund said that, if it was absolutely essential (presumably to hasten the correction of the balance of payments), the UK might introduce 'for a few months' a surcharge on imports. This was quite a surprise. The Treasury had for some months regarded import *deposits* as the least objectionable measure to support an adjustment pro-gramme, or even as an alternative *in extremis*, but had supposed that anything in the way of a tariff would not be countenanced either by the Fund or by the international community. Later that day there was an informal dinner between senior Treasury officials and the whole of the Fund team. No record exists as to what was said, but from the briefing it seems that the Treasury, who were of course still labouring under the handicap of not being allowed to discuss policy changes, intended to confine substantive discussion to that of the exchange rate and the technical aspects to it. It seems reasonable to conclude—and this is the author's recollection—that the conversation at the dinner had very little of substance to it and was confined to background issues.

Another development occurred on 10 November, but the Treasury were not for some time aware of it. The Prime Minister privately invited Whittome to call on him in Downing Street and saw him alone except for a Private Secretary who was instructed not to take notes. A record was subsequently produced, but

---

[51] BP 122/24/01.

not circulated to the Treasury. This record[52] shows that the Prime Minister wanted to impress on the Fund his own personal involvement in the negotiations and to stress the considerable difficulties he would face if the Fund's prescription involved an increase in unemployment. There was some discussion of the problems presented by the NIF and Whittome gave the fiscal adjustment he thought would be necessary as £3–4 billion, although the record does not reveal which year he was referring to. The Prime Minister said that he was not seeking soft options on the outcome of the negotiations. Perhaps he had an afterthought, for it seems that he got in touch with the Chancellor to say that he might have given the Fund the impression that a big fiscal adjustment was a possibility, which was certainly not the case.

The Chancellor had a meeting with the Fund staff the following day and he took the opportunity to put the record straight. This meeting[53] was in all respects a good deal less low-key than the first meeting. Picking up what the Fund had told officials on 5 November and Whittome had said to the Prime Minister, the Chancellor had to say that reductions of £3–5 billion in the PSBR were 'not on'; what was more, officials had no authority to discuss any policy changes. The Fund countered by saying that they had been horrified at the NIF, which they had now seen, and that it would be impossible for them or their constituency to accept the prospect it revealed. They also had reservations about the prospective growth in £M3 put at 14 per cent in 1977–78. On a more emollient note, the Chancellor assured the Fund that import deposits were not in his mind except in an emergency. There was a brief mention of the initiative on the sterling balances, on which of course there had been no discussion with the Fund for some time, and the Chancellor asked whether the Fund could play a part. The Fund were not responsive.

On the same day, 11 November, Whittome also saw the head of the Expenditure Group, but it was a fruitless meeting.[54] Whittome wanted to explore what were the options for reducing public spending in the medium term, but the Treasury officials involved pleaded that they were not authorized to do this.

At the end of that week, on 12 November, Whittome returned to Washington, no doubt to report to the Managing Director on the slow progress of the consultations and inform him that the Chancellor had given no authority to officials to discuss policy changes. He had expressed his disappointment to the Head of OF at the way that 'everyone seems to have clammed up'.[55] A normal consultation for a drawing took about two weeks, but in this case the first two weeks had produced nothing in the way of substance. The British were making it clear to the Fund—and this had emerged at the dinner on 10 November—that the running was with them. What the Fund wanted was for the British to

[52] PREM 16/800.   [53] BP 122/24/01.   [54] GEP 9/29/02A.   [55] DW 062.

come up with some ideas that the Fund could then comment on and criticize, but this was ruled out.

Over the weekend of 13–14 November the Chancellor had one of his regular dinners with the NEDC members of the TUC.[56] He was joined by the Employment Secretary and the Prices Secretary. The Chancellor took the union members into his confidence and warned them that the PSBR was likely to be a problem with the Fund. Even the £9 billion given after the July statement might be too high, but the Cabinet had insisted that there should be no negotiations with the Fund at this stage. The TUC members expressed their worries. If the PSBR correction were made through indirect taxes, they would regard this as 'a foul in terms of the Social Contract' since they would raise the price level. The leader of the Transport Union said that 'excessive action would break the Social Contract' and that 'it was important to maintain social welfare'. All this was predictable stuff and was scarcely new to the Ministers who just listened.

Phase II—technical issues

Whittome arrived back in London on Monday 15 November and a meeting was arranged with the Prime Minister and the Chancellor the following day. Before Whittome appeared the two ministers had a private talk about the timetable for further Cabinet meetings and for the outlook for the negotiations.[57] The Chancellor had received a brief from the Permanent Secretary which expressed the view that the Fund would not accept a PSBR for 1977–78 of more than £9 billion[58] and he passed this opinion on to the Prime Minister. The Chancellor went on to say that he thought that the cuts in expenditure would have to be found 'one half from social security and one half from "shrimping"'—that is small contributions from a large number of programmes. When Whittome joined the two ministers he laid out the intellectual basis for the Fund's position. Although he did not quarrel with the basic message of the Treasury forecast, he and his colleagues 'gave more weight than the Treasury to financial variables'. Accordingly he thought that the Government's existing strategy could be derailed by the sort of growth in the money supply which was predicted (15.5 per cent growth of £M3 in 1976–77 and 14 per cent the following year[59]). To bring this down, the PSBR must be reduced and this should be done mainly through public expenditure savings. He suggested that Stage 3 of the TUC's pay policy should be brought forward and 'tied in to the programme [to be agreed with the Fund]. The exchange rate would have to come down. If need be an import surcharge could be introduced to hasten the improvement in the balance of payments' although

[56] BP 122/24/01.   [57] Ibid.   [58] Ibid.   [59] MPG (76)8.

when pressed Whittome agreed that this would have to be agreed with the EEC. The Prime Minister asked whether, if the Government went along with the Fund's prescriptions and they proved in the event to be 'overkill', they could be 'undone'. Whittome was non-committal.

The same day, 16 November, the Permanent Secretary had another informal meeting with Whittome[60] who briefly outlined the contents of a memorandum he had prepared describing in general terms what the Fund wanted. Public expenditure should be held 'in real terms' at its present level until 1978–79. There should be 'a continuing substantial reduction in the nominal amount of the PSBR in both 1977–78 and 1978–79' and £M3 should be held to a growth rate of 10 per cent. The Fund acknowledged that the sort of policy changes involved would present difficulties, 'but it was not possible to do nothing'. 'A two-year programme offered the prospect of a better outlook in twelve months time'. Whittome said he now wanted to engage in detailed discussions with the Expenditure Division to find out what could be cut 'without causing acute short-term problems'; and he wanted to discuss with the Home Finance Division the implications of an abrupt curtailment of the money supply growth below 12 per cent. The Fund clearly wanted to be able to rebut the charge that they were unmindful of the consequences of their prescription. The meeting briefly discussed the timetable and on this Whittome made it clear that this was now in the hands of the Government. There was a post-script to this meeting the following day[61] when the Permanent Secretary sought clarification of some points made by Whittome and, in particular, how far the Fund would want the expenditure policy changes to be announced in Parliament before the credit could be agreed. Whittome was firm that there would have to be a firm public policy statement before the proposal could be put before the IMF Board. A further new point emerged. Whittome was mindful that the Government might want to meet any commitment on the growth of the money supply by reintroducing the Corset, as indeed it did two days later (18 November).[62] Any action in this area would upset the Fund's calculations for the Corset had the effect of reducing the money supply without necessarily reducing overall credit growth. The point was a technical one but it showed that the Fund were not going to leave any loopholes for the Government to exploit.

An important development now took place, the full import of which we discuss under Phase III, the political argument. Following his private meeting with the Prime Minister on 16 November, when it will be remembered the Chancellor passed on to him the advice of the Treasury that the Fund would

---

[60] DW 062 and PCC (76) 40th Meeting.   [61] DW 062.

[62] The fact that Whittome raised this issue at this point suggests that he had been privately informed of the Bank's intention to reintroduce the Corset, but there is no documentary evidence for this.

certainly not accept a PSBR for the following year of more than £9 billion, the Chancellor, on advice, decided to seek the authority of EY for the opening of exploratory discussions involving the consideration of policy changes. He accordingly gave an oral account of the development of the Fund discussions to a meeting of EY on 17 November and, by suitably describing the target PSBR as *his own* view of the limit of what the Government would be able to finance by market borrowing, persuaded the Committee to agree to exploratory discussions with the Fund in which, *in extremis*, a borrowing requirement of *at most* £9 billion could be explored with the Fund.

Before the Treasury could take advantage of this new authority, Whittome played a card which enabled some analytical discussions between the two sides to take place. On 16 November he sent to the Chancellor the memorandum[63] to which he had referred at an earlier meeting and in which he set out the reasons why the Fund believed that 'a change of policy is now imperative'. In doing this he was departing from the usual procedure of leaving it to the applicant country to make its own prescription, which the Fund would then examine. The Fund now broadly accepted the findings of the NIF for the period it covered, but thought that the economic outlook was even worse than predicted because of the failure to hold even to the announced financial policies. 'The monetary forecast is not consistent with a stable exchange rate . . . the present rate of DCE will lead to exchange rate instability' and the consequent rise in the price level would cause interest rates to rise. The problems with the exchange rate would put at risk the continuance of the pay policy. Any attempt to maintain the rate in present conditions would mean that the 'inevitable eventual failure would be interpreted as a battle lost. . . . Success in the field of pay policy and the exchange rate is critically dependent on firmness of financial policy. . . . In our opinion an immediate review of public expenditure programmes leading to policy decisions will be required to give assurance that a substantial release of resources will be obtained in the near future. . . . It is also essential to establish a continued and substantial reduction in the nominal amount of the PSBR in 1977–78 and 1978–79'. This policy would have to be supported by early and firm action in the area of credit policy—'to control recent excessive increases in bank advances to the private sector'. A two-year programme was required but it 'must include present action on an adequate scale'.

The Fund memorandum was unspecific about the size of the adjustment that the Fund wished to see—their views on this were forthcoming only in a second memorandum they sent to the Permanent Secretary the following week—but at least they now set out the reasons why they were convinced that both a two-year programme was needed and some action had to be taken immediately. These reasons were essentially financial, and the argument was

---

[63] GEP 9/29/02.

broadly that the expansion taking place in the field of public and private borrowing was leading to a monetary explosion which would aggravate inflation, wreck the exchange rate and thereby damage the prospects of being able to continue the pay policy. These were not the sort of arguments that had been put to the Chancellor by the Treasury for a policy adjustment, although by now the Treasury were giving more weight to financial factors. The real clash between the two different frameworks of analysis was to come later when the Fund set out in numerical terms the scale of action they had in mind.

The Prime Minister, who had of course been closely involved not least because he had seen the Fund staff himself and been briefed by the Chancellor, had used the meeting of EY on 17 November to link the negotiations in the mind of his colleagues to two other developments: the search for a solution to the sterling balances and the possibility of 'some action on imports'. It is not clear where the second of these ideas came from, unless it was the suggestion that Whittome himself had made at his meeting with the Prime Minister. There is some evidence that the Cabinet Office had been thinking along these lines, but the Treasury was unaware of it. Some Ministers immediately seized on this, no doubt thinking of something significant, and it may indeed have been a factor in the Committee's willingness to go along with what the Chancellor and the Prime Minister were seeking, that is authority to explore some fiscal adjustment with the Fund. The Prime Minister said that he would have to ask the Committee to give him and the Chancellor a free hand to explore the safety net issue as well as action on imports (whatever that might have meant) but in the meantime he suggested that, as regards the Fund negotiations, 'the Treasury could, if necessary, discuss the implications of a number of alternative figures [for the PSBR in 1977–78]—£10 billion, £9.5 billion and, if absolutely necessary, £9 billion'. The aim should be to get agreement at the highest level of the PSBR that both the Fund and the markets would accept. But on no account should officials commit Ministers. The Committee assented.

This authority given to the Treasury by EY on 17 November now paved the way for the first full formal meeting with the Fund and this took place on the afternoon of 18 November.[64] It was attended by a large number of officials from the Treasury and the Bank as well as the entire Fund team. The form of the meeting was such that it could not lead to any useful discussion of detail and both sides set out their positions rather in the fashion of two opposing armies on a medieval field of battle. The Treasury did, however, in accordance with the authority of EY, make its first cautious move in the direction of the Fund. The Permanent Secretary described the Government's basic strategy of achieving a reduction in inflation through the engagement of the TUC in the design and implementation of the pay policy and of improving industrial

[64] OF 122/24/01.

performance through the industrial strategy. Macro-economic policy involved a strict control over public spending and the achievement of external balance over the medium term. Any action which undermined the understanding with the TUC would jeopardize the whole strategy. Commenting on the memorandum the Fund had sent to the Chancellor, he said that the IMF seemed to overstate the risks of a deterioration of the economic outlook stemming from a failure to meet the Government's financial targets. It was, of course, possible that the publication of a high PSBR would cause a hiatus in the sale of gilt-edged stock and this could lead to an expansion in the money supply, but this was rather problematical. The weakness of the Fund's approach was that it assumed a unique relationship between DCE and the money supply growth on the one hand and the PSBR. A given rate of growth of the monetary variables was possible with a range of figures for the public sector deficit. Turning to the Fund's proposals, he said that there were enormous constraints on any fiscal adjustment, but the Government had authorized him to explore the scope for reaching an agreement on the basis of a lower PSBR in ways which did not jeopardize the economic strategy, and he suggested that this could involve a reduction in the current estimate for 1977–78 by rather more than £1 billion, leading to an out-turn PSBR of £9.5–10 billion—a suggestion which was well within the authority the Treasury had. This produced a negative reaction from the Fund, who thought that if that was the Government's position 'the gap was unbridgeable'. The meeting ended with no further movement on either side, even though officials had authority to go lower than £9.5 billion—an authority which for tactical reasons they decided not to use at this stage.

The full meeting was followed the next day, 19 November, by a small meeting between Whittome and the Permanent Secretary which was a little more fruitful but still led to difficulties.[65] Whittome explained that he simply could not sell the sort of action the Government had in mind 'even to himself, let alone to the creditors'. He said that the Fund were thinking in terms of a different approach to policy rather than of specific quantities. They wanted to see space created for manufacturing output to expand and he repeated that he was seeking a sizeable reduction in the nominal PSBR for 1978–79, that is the year following the one on which negotiations had so far focused; but, significantly, this would be on the understanding that the figures could be reviewed in the light of performance. Turning to the immediate future, Whittome suggested a number of options, including that of a pause in the negotiations for a few weeks for reflection. This was clearly out of the question for the Treasury, and the Permanent Secretary took a rather softer line. 'It was important,' he said, 'not to exaggerate unnecessarily the differences between us'. He went on to develop the possibility of an understanding on the exchange rate and he understood the Fund's desire not to get involved in a bargaining

[65] BP 112/24/01.

process. But he needed to be specific about the quantities. Whittome then described how the Fund had arrived at their ideas. They started with a desired DCE expansion of £5 billion in 1978–79. If that were agreed, the PSBR for the previous year could be £6.5 billion. The latter figure was a balance of what was needed to satisfy the markets and what was needed to get on track for the following year. Of the two the former was the more important, and his judgement on this was that *ex ante* public expenditure cuts in 1977–78 of £3 billion were required or 'if the PSBR figures are the basis, well below £9 billion'. He ended with a figure of £8–8.5 billion. Finch added that the figure would depend to some extent on how it was made up, but the Fund would want 'policy changes that are ongoing and they would want a still lower PSBR in 1978–79'. This was hard stuff, and the Permanent Secretary expressed his anxieties about the impact on the economy. There would be an adverse effect on the price level (because some cuts would have to reduce price subsidies) and cuts could not avoid damaging the construction industry, which was already in recession, and the defence supply industries. He counselled against the idea of disengagement and suggested that the Fund should now examine with the Expenditure Division how the Fund's ideas would affect particular programmes. Whittome responded positively to this and a series of technical meetings took place with the relevant officials during the following week. But first it was necessary to clear with the Prime Minister that it was all right to begin to look at expenditure options.

The Chancellor and the Permanent Secretary went over to No 10 early in the afternoon of Friday 19 November and described the Fund's position, including their threat to adjourn the discussions. When told that the Fund were wanting expenditure cuts of £3 billion the Prime Minister said that this simply 'wasn't on'.[66] The meeting looked at the sort of policy changes that would be necessary—a zero uprating for unemployment benefits, a £2 per week increase in local authority rents and cuts in the UK's contribution to NATO. The Permanent Secretary said that Whittome seemed to be more interested in 1978–79 and that it might be possible to negotiate something much less than the figures mentioned for 1977–78. This led the Chancellor to suggest that they look at cuts for that year of about £1.5 billion. At all events it was vital not to stop the negotiations and it would now be important to bring the Fund up against the consequences for UK policy if the sort of cuts they were seeking were to be imposed. The Prime Minister agreed that the Fund could be taken through the policy decisions that would have to be made and that this should be done at the technical level by the Expenditure Division of the Treasury. But the Chancellor should himself now see the Fund and explain the difficulties their suggestions would entail. A meeting was arranged with Whittome for 7.00 p.m. that evening. This proved to be significantly fruitful. The Chancellor set the scene by

---

[66] PREM 16/802.

saying that he was now persuaded that some fiscal action was desirable on economic management grounds, but 'the Fund's target of £6.5 billion for the PSBR in 1978–79 would be acceptable only if it could be shown that the prospect for the economy with such a target would be better than that embodied in the NIF'.[67] Any target must be consistent with achieving a growth rate of 4 per cent in 1978–79. If that could be shown, then it might be possible to persuade the Cabinet to agree to the fiscal implications. But the Chancellor had no authority to discuss a PSBR of less than £9 billion in 1977–78. Towards that figure he might be able to seek expenditure cuts of £1.5 billion consisting of £1 billion of actual savings and £0.5 billion from the sale of the Burmah shares in BP (on which we have more to say later). Whittome replied that the Fund would certainly be able to demonstrate how their estimates of growth of 4 per cent were arrived at and were consistent with their financial targets. There was then some inconclusive discussion about exchange rate policy, with the Chancellor expressing his scepticism about whether the Fund's recipe for lowering the rate for sterling would be acceptable to the UK's trading partners. There was also a reference to some action to restrain imports, but the Fund were very discouraging on this point and it did not resurface in the negotiations.

We turn now to the technical discussions—now authorized by the Prime Minister—of the public expenditure adjustments which were implied by the Fund's targets, but before the technical meetings got under way, the Fund were treated to a general homily about the difficulties of cutting expenditure by the Head of the Expenditure Division.[68] He began by describing the Government's strategy for containing public spending in the medium term. The profile of spending was broadly flat, although there was a 'kink' in 1977–78 as a result of the July measures which had not yet been carried through to later years. The UK public spending pattern was in 'the same ball park' as other industrialized countries, and it would be wrong to think of a multi-billion pound package. There was some discussion about the uprating of social security benefits, but as these had just been announced for the year beginning April 1977, a cut here could have little immediate effect. Other options examined were a moratorium on capital projects to save £1 billion, although at considerable damage to the construction industry, a reduction in the subsidies of nationalized industry prices and foodstuffs (although these were in the process of being reduced anyway), a reduction in local authority current spending (which was not under central government control, although it could be influenced by a reduction in the Rate Support Grant from its existing level of 65.5 per cent), a cut in housing subsidies (which would require legislation), in local authority mortgage lending and new housing construction, a cut in export credit refinance, a cut in overseas aid, some reduction in education expenditure, and some increases in the charges for publicly provided services, for example

[67] PREM 16/802.   [68] GEP 9/29/02.

prescription charges. This shopping list was intended to show the Fund how extensive the programme adjustments would have to be if they continued to argue for a big fiscal adjustment. As was stated in the previous chapter, the Cabinet had had an inconclusive meeting on 26 October when the Chief Secretary had sought to obtain the agreement of ministers to making *offsetting* savings (amounting to about £1 billion) to accommodate, within the White Paper totals, the additional bids for expenditure in 1978–79 which had been made in the PESC round. This would only have brought aggregate spending back into line with the White Paper figures. The Treasury were, therefore, fully seized of the difficulties which the Fund's proposals would involve for the Cabinet and they left them in no doubt about the size of the political problem that would have to be resolved if a big fiscal adjustment were required. All these savings would[69] accrue only from 1978, but the Fund now wanted to explore the scope for earlier reductions, affecting the current year. At the next meeting however, later the same day,[70] Whittome decided that the best course would be to focus on the second year of the programme, 1978–79, and examine what would be involved in a reduction of £3–4 billion—the figure he had given the Permanent Secretary *for the previous year* at the earlier meeting on the same day. The head of the expenditure division reacted adversely to this suggestion which he said would be 'wrecking and would not be attainable . . . it might be possible to carry through into 1978–79 the cuts made in July for 1977–78 and consequential policy changes which might produce further savings in 1977–78. . . . Even this would mean that no major programme could be spared, but it would still not amount to £3–4 billion'. The meeting went over the shopping list of options again and ended inconclusively, although Whittome made two conciliatory remarks. The first was that his goal of £3–4 billion of cuts was 'not the last word' and that the Fund would not 'pack their bags and go if there was not agreement on that figure'. The second was that he had been starting from a figure by which the PSBR should be reduced and the fiscal mix was 'open'. But for the moment they wanted to explore exactly what was involved in cuts of the size they wanted and they asked for a precise list of what the Treasury would propose for (i) a total package of £3 billion and (ii) a total of £4 billion.

The next development was the arrival of the Fund memorandum which the Chancellor had asked to see at the meeting he had had with Whittome on 19 November. This was presented to the Treasury at official level on 22 November[71] and it contained the technical rationale for the size of the adjustments the Fund were aiming at. We have seen that they had outlined their position in general terms in the memorandum of 16 November which they had sent to the Chancellor: and this had been briefly commented on by the Treasury at the plenary meeting on 18 November. But the new memorandum presented to

[69] Ibid.　　[70] Ibid.　　[71] BP 122/24/01.

officials was a much more articulated description of their analytical position and gave rise to some important, although in the end unproductive, examination by the technical experts. The memorandum was accompanied by a second letter in which Whittome gave some examples of major countries adopting policies similar to those suggested by the Fund and realizing strong economic growth as a result. We look at the two documents as a whole.

The memorandum began by acknowledging that 'any model of the UK economy built up by conventional methods is undoubtedly going to suggest that the outcome, given the policy changes being considered, will be very much worse than anything we believe to be at all likely'. It accepted that the Government's medium-term strategy was appropriate and should be supported, 'but we believe that the present financial and exchange rate policies are not compatible with that strategy... [and] the risk of failure is considerable indeed'. It went on to make some sharp observations about exchange rate policy and the need for domestic policy to support it. 'The exchange rate was overvalued for many years' and a 'continuously competitive rate is essential'. The memorandum gave some examples, derived from previous Fund experience covering the United States, Canada, and France, where a competitive exchange rate had led to a strong recovery in the balance of payments. It did not, however, make any reference to a publicly stated policy on the sterling rate and was therefore in many ways a confirmation of the views the Treasury had been canvassing for two years. It was in the field of domestic policy that the Fund was more controversial. A competitive rate had to be supported by domestic policies which would release resources for the balance of payments, and this should be phased in over the following two years. The heart of the memorandum was, however, on two issues:

1 Why the Fund believed that the Treasury forecast on the assumption of a continuation of existing financial policies was wrong in predicting a pessimistic outcome.

2 How the Fund had built up its own model and reached the conclusion that the PSBR needed to be cut substantially in the two years 1977–78 and 1978–79.

On the first of these issues the Fund thought that a competitive exchange rate would increase the profitability of exports on a scale which was 'unprecedented in the post-war world'. Given a change in policies 'we see every prospect of a dramatic improvement in both the current and capital account of the balance of payments. ... Improved profitability of exports and a turn round in the public sector deficit would engender a sharp improvement in confidence and expectations which would lead to a turning point which will invalidate the conclusion that would be put out by any normal model of the economy.' The Fund gave four areas of economic activity where they thought that the Treasury model was wrong:

1 It predicted too small a response of exports to the opportunities presented by a better exchange rate and the release of domestic resources.

2 It was too pessimistic in believing (as it undoubtedly did) that the *trend* rate of import penetration would continue.

3 The Fund expected a considerably faster rebound in manufacturing output than was in the forecast, aided by an adequate supply of credit made available by reduced credit demands of the public sector.

4 It thought that business confidence would be strengthened by the improvement in the external and public sector accounts and by the lower interest rates which would be possible as a result of the cut in domestic credit expansion.

Finally 'we also wonder whether the Treasury forecast takes adequate account of the spillover effect into other private non-manufacturing sectors which results from an exchange rate that suddenly becomes more competitive'.

Having savaged the Treasury model, the Fund then described how they had built up their own financial proposals. They started with the target expansion of DCE in 1978–79 which they put at £5 billion, a figure that was consistent 'with an evolution of the economy... which would include a growth of GDP of 4 per cent, a rise in manufacturing investment of some 20–25 per cent and an increase in total private investment in real terms of 8 per cent, induced by the growth of net exports... and a current account surplus in excess of £1 billion... a rise in the retail price index of 9 per cent and a PSBR of £6.5 billion'. 'Put more simply there is reason to believe that a DCE target is likely to be adequate to accommodate the demand for credit by the private sector for investment because with a PSBR of £6.5 billion the credit requirements of the public sector would be reduced to a level in which it can be financed from expected personal savings without forcing up interest rates. If however there is a larger increase in the credit needs of the private sector it would be possible to borrow from abroad, given that the implementation of the policies being discussed will create an environment in which this will become possible'.

The Fund illustrated how their financial model had been constructed in the form of Table 5.2.

Table 5.2 IMF financial model (£ billion except where otherwise stated)

Variable	1976–77	1977–78	1978–79
1 PSBR	11.3	7.5	6.5
2 Sales of public sector debt to non-bank sector	–4.9	–5.3	–6.3
3 Bank lending to private sector in £ and to overseas sector	3.7	4.5	4.8
4 DCE (1+2+3)	10.1	6.7	5.0
5 External financing of public sector and banking sector	–3.75	–1.6	1.3
6 Increase in banking non-deposit liabilities	–1.2	–0.9	–1.2
7 Increase in £M3	5.15	4.2	5.1
	(13.7%)	(9.8%)	(10.9%)

The precise logical processes by which the Fund arrived at the figures in this table were not apparent from the memorandum, and the Treasury economists had several meetings with the Fund to elucidate some of the points which were not clear. It emerged that the 4 per cent growth postulated in the memorandum was 'illustrative' and a 'hope' rather than a forecast. Whereas the Treasury were forecasting GDP growth in 1977 at 2.5 per cent, followed by 3 per cent in 1978 (on the basis of existing policies), the Fund assumed that (on the basis that their financial policies were implemented) growth would be 1.5 per cent and 4 per cent respectively. They were taking it, therefore, that the programme would be deflationary at first but would be followed by strong growth driven by faster net exports and rising manufacturing investment which more than offset the fall in public consumption and investment caused by the expenditure cuts. Having postulated this pattern of projected growth, the Fund proceeded to fix, somewhat arbitrarily, the expansion of DCE which would be sufficient in the second year of the programme (1978–79) to meet the growth objective. This approach to Fund-designed stabilization programmes was a general one in that it was applied, in one form or another, to all applicant countries. It has been described, most recently, in an IMF Occasional Paper and in a paper the former Chief Economist at the Fund wrote after leaving the Fund.[72] It was known as 'financial programming' and took as its starting point the consolidated balance sheet of the national banking system, from which it extracted the expansion of DCE as a policy variable and took that as the starting point for the policy prescription. In the case of the UK, the Fund decreed that £5 billion was the appropriate figure for the second and focus year of the programme, and from this, by making assumptions about the sales of public sector debt which could be expected to take place outside the banking system and about the level of bank lending to the private sector, they arrived at the 'allowable' amount of public sector bank credit that could be accommodated and hence the size of the PSBR. A target of £5 billion for DCE expansion in the focus year was, on this arithmetic, shown to be consistent with a PSBR of £6.5 billion. All this figuring was, however, contingent on the achievement of a growth rate of 4 per cent in that year, which, as stated above, was an assumption whose validity depended on improved confidence and lower interest rates. The Treasury economists were not impressed with this approach, for which there was little empirical support—in the UK at any rate—and which seemed to be largely an act of faith. They continued to argue that the *ex ante* reduction in the PSBR (and hence in public spending) in 1978–79 proposed by the Fund—with substantial 'lead-in' cuts the previous year—output growth would decline from the 3 per cent in the NIF to perhaps 2 per cent. To

[72] IMF Occasional Paper 55 (1987) and 'The Changing Nature of IMF Conditionality' by Jacques Polak.

them it was an enormous act of faith to suppose that the qualitative factors invoked by the Fund would raise output growth to 4 per cent p.a. The Treasury economists were therefore highly sceptical about the internal consistencies of the Fund's case. However, turning back to the policy implications of the Fund's analysis, the economists calculated that since the Treasury were estimating the uncorrected PSBR in 1978–79 at £12.5 billion the Fund were proposing a reduction in public spending in that year of £4.5–5 billion, of which about £1–1.5 billion would occur anyway as a result of lower interest charges on the public debt as a result of lower borrowing in the previous year. To achieve this *ex ante* cuts of £3.5–4[73] billion would be needed by 1978–79, which would involve a 'lead-in' of cuts of £2 billion the previous year. What struck the Treasury was what a large margin of error there was in the calculations and how tenuous were the linkages in the Fund's calculations between the DCE targets—the starting point—and the suggested package of spending cuts. If there was one conclusion to be drawn from the technical discussions, it was that there could be no meeting of minds on the logic. The negotiations would therefore inevitably have to become, from then on, little more than a 'horse trade'.

The Fund had given their views and it was now the turn of the Treasury to offer a counter-proposal. At the meeting on 18 November the Treasury had gone no further than to suggest a cut in the PSBR for 1977–78 of £1 billion without specifying how it might be achieved or what the consequences, according to the Treasury model, might be. It was felt by officials that, in order to counter the proposals put forward by the Fund in their technical memorandum, the Treasury should describe what, in their view, would be the consequences for employment, the trade balance, and the monetary aggregates of some hypothetical adjustments to the fiscal balance in 1977–78. It was of course the case that the Fund would not accept the outcome the Treasury predicted for these packages but at least they would provide a basis for technical negotiation. It was necessary to obtain Ministerial approval for such a course and the Chancellor sought this first by an approach to the Prime Minister in a letter[74] to No 10 dated 23 November, in which he suggested that the Treasury should be authorized to explore 'without commitment' a less demanding objective than the PSBR targets of £8.5 billion and £6.5 billion for 1977–78 and 1978–79 respectively set by the Fund in their memorandum, and they might look at a figure of £9 billion for the first year and 'a corresponding one a year later. . . and if this was not negotiable stop short at £8.5 billion'. This request, so far as the first year was concerned,

---

[73] This was broadly the range which Whittome had put to the Treasury on 19 November before the memorandum arrived.
[74] BP 122/24/01.

was in line with the summing up made by the Prime Minister at the EY meeting on 17 November but it went farther by seeking to extend the discussions to the second year.

One ingredient of the package, designed to make the expenditure impact less, would be to sell some of the Government's BP shareholding—this had been referred to at the Chancellor's meeting with the Fund on 19 November. This item became an important and useful element in the package eventually agreed and it is worth saying a word or two about it. The original shareholding of 51 per cent of the total stock of what was then the Anglo-Persian Oil Company had been acquired by the Government not long after its foundation in 1909—a measure designed to protect the oil supplies of the Royal Navy, then building ships to be fired by oil as well as coal. In 1967 the Government's shareholding was allowed to slip to 48 per cent, but it still had a controlling interest. A second large shareholder of the Company was the Burmah Oil Company, but as we saw earlier Burmah had fallen on hard times in early 1975 and had to resort to a forced sale of its unfettered holding (about 20 per cent) to the Bank of England—the only conceivable bulk buyer at the time. The Bank acquired the shares with the resources of the Issue Department whose assets backed the fiduciary note issue. The assets were legally the property of the Bank, but any profits and income generated by them accrued to the Treasury—as of course did any losses. Thus, although the Bank was the legal owner, it was the Government who were the beneficial owner—so the Government became in effect the beneficial owner of BP as to 68 per cent of the total stock. However, the Burmah shareholders launched a legal claim against the Bank for what was argued to be a forced sale and this in effect placed the 20 per cent shareholding in baulk. The idea conceived by the Treasury was to sell 17 per cent of the shares held in the name of the government (likely to yield some £485 million at current market prices) and rely on the Bank winning the legal case, after which the Burmah shares could be transferred to the Government in exchange for government stock, restoring its holding to 51 per cent of the total stock. The cost of the Bank's acquisition of the shares had increased the PSBR for the year in which they were acquired (1974–75) even though it was not formally counted as public expenditure, and the proceeds of any sale of the stock would correspondingly decrease the PSBR. Such a sale could, therefore, count as a useful contribution to the reduction of the PSBR without in fact reducing the government's spending programmes.

As we shall see when the political aspects of the negotiation are examined, the Treasury proposal to explore three packages, each containing the BP element, was agreed by the Prime Minister and in principle by the Cabinet later that day, 23 November and the Treasury were authorized to put forward three hypothetical packages, as follows:

1 *Package 1.*
- Public expenditure cuts of £0.5 billion in 1977–78 carried through to the following year
- The PSBR is reduced to £9.5 billion in the first year, but rises in the second
- DCE rises by £10 billion in 1977–78 and by even more in the following year

2 *Package 2.*
- Public expenditure cuts of £1 billion in 1977–78 and £1.5 billion in the following year
- The PSBR is £9 billion in the first year and again is higher the following year
- DCE rises by £8 billion in the first year and somewhat higher in the following year

3 *Package 3.*
- Public expenditure cuts of £1.5 billion in the first year and £2 billion in the second
- The PSBR is £8.5 billion in the first year and 'somewhat lower' in the second
- DCE rises by £7.5 billion and about the same in the following year.

In all three cases the BP sale was treated as a contribution to the expenditure cuts, although formally it only reduced the PSBR without affecting spending programmes.

Before the packages were discussed with officials, the Prime Minister had told the Cabinet that he proposed to meet the Fund himself and he did this on the evening of 23 November. It was a critically important occasion for it led to a partial breaking of the log-jam. The Prime Minister[75] said that the Cabinet had now authorized the Treasury to discuss policy changes involving reductions in the fiscal deficit in the two following years. He went on to assure the Fund that he was seized of the idea that if the outcome of their visit was a small adjustment the markets might find it unsatisfactory and respond accordingly. On the other hand too big a move would put the Social Contract, and with it the future of a voluntary Incomes Policy, in jeopardy. He had no doubt that the union leaders would protest strongly at a deflationary package involving a worsening of their members' living standards but at the end of the day they might be brought, reluctantly, into line. His big worry was that by the time the union conferences took place in the spring of 1977 there would be a rank-and-file revolt against further cooperation with the Government. The challenge was, therefore, to strike the right balance between too little and too much. At present the Cabinet were not persuaded intellectually of the arguments which the Chancellor was putting forward. In his view the most that could be expected for 1977–78 was a reduction of £1 billion in the PSBR, bringing it

---

[75] DW 062 and OF 122/24/01.

down to £9.5 billion—but even on that the Cabinet would have to discuss the detailed impact on spending programmes. The Chancellor intervened to say that, in the light of the Fund's target of £6.5 billion for 1977–78[76] he wanted to explore with the Fund team a PSBR of either £9.5 billion or even £9 billion and would be willing to explore the implications for the following year. Whittome was very diplomatic in his reply. It was no part of the Fund's remit to bring down the Government of the day and indeed it was in recognition of the political problems that the Fund were putting its emphasis on 1978–79 and regarding the previous year as a 'lead in'. However, to the IMF—and indeed to the bankers—a PSBR of £9.5 billion for 1977–78 was not convincing. With a two-year programme based on the Government's industrial strategy and on a strong export policy, they had concluded that the programme required a PSBR below £9 billion next year, in which case 'there would be very little more to do in 1978–79'. They had thought it politically helpful to have attached to this programme the possibility of an import surcharge on a temporary basis, although the acceptability of this to others was uncertain.

The way was now clear for the Treasury to have some concrete discussions with the Fund about the area of possible agreement. The three Treasury packages were put hypothetically and 'without prejudice' to the Fund and examined with them during the course of 24 November.[77] The meetings were long and the going was hard. As could have been predicted, the Fund were interested only in Package 3 since this was the only one which came anywhere near their own proposals, at any rate for the first year. They were worried about the adequacy of even the large package in 1978–79 since it envisaged no further action beyond the consolidation of the measures of the previous year and a PSBR of £8.4 billion, compared with the figure they had put forward in their memorandum of £6.5 billion. The Treasury had an internal meeting late in the afternoon of 24 November and the Permanent Secretary had a stock-taking meeting with the Fund team that evening.[78] Whittome said that the Fund were not sure about the internal consistency of the Treasury's figures (a criticism the Treasury made of the Fund's) and they were worried about the monetary expansion implied even in the large fiscal adjustment case. The real difficulty, however, lay with the second year and the PSBR figure for it. The Permanent Secretary commented that 'it was an odd world in which one had to take firm decisions on a PSBR target two years hence, given the inherent uncertainty in forecasting this variable. A better approach would be to think in terms of taking action which . . . would put us into the sort of area on the financial variables that we would think right . . . but with precise commitments to the first year only'. Whittome was at first not convinced but the Permanent Secretary made a specific suggestion. 'The two year programme might be more fruitfully discussed in terms of fiscal action [i.e. how much

[76] This is clearly a mistake. The Fund figure of £6.5 billion applied to 1978–79.
[77] DW 062.   [78] Ibid.

adjustment would be taken rather than what the financial consequences would be] over two years.... If agreement were to be reached on public expenditure, the Government would be in a far better position to give firm commitments for two years expressed in these terms.' This proved to be a breakthrough in the negotiations. Whittome immediately took it up and even went so far as to say that the PSBR figure for 1978–79 could be given in general terms and 'could be related to a proviso about the level of activity'. It meant that henceforth the negotiations could be solely about the fiscal adjustment that each side thought necessary or adequate and the public expenditure cuts that would be required and that the discussion of the monetary consequences could be treated as a consequential, although not a subordinate, issue to be resolved when the text of the agreement came to be examined. It is not perhaps too much of an exaggeration to say that from that moment on the negotiations acquired a sharpness and a definiteness that had not been present hitherto, and that the differences between the parties could be described in terms which permitted a resolution that broadly met the objectives of both.

The Treasury now prepared a memorandum for the Chancellor to send to the Prime Minister reporting how the discussions had gone. The memo, dated 25 November,[79] first described the three packages and explained that in all of them it was assumed that the sale of the BP shares in January 1975 would form part of the package—that is that within the total of public expenditure cuts the proceeds of the sale, estimated at £0.5 billion, would count as an expenditure cut. Another point which needed explanation was why, according to the Treasury simulations, expenditure cuts in the third case produced PSBR and DCE paths which were much higher than the Fund assumed would flow from such action. The reason the Chancellor proffered was that the Fund gave much greater weight to the recovery of confidence and the effect it would have on investment. Accordingly employment would be higher than the Treasury forecast and the PSBR lower (as a result of higher tax receipts and lower social security payments). The Chancellor went on to take up the point made by the Permanent Secretary that it would be unwise for the Government to commit itself to firm targets over a two-year path. 'We must,' he said, 'resist any attempt to tie us irrevocably to precise quantified targets'. He suggested that he should now seek Cabinet authority to explore the possibility of reaching agreement with the fund on the following basis:

(i) an agreed fiscal package;
(ii) reasonably firm commitments to quantified objectives for the PSBR and DCE for 1977–78;
(iii) no commitment to objectives for those two variables for 1978–79;
(iv) a fiscal adjustment which was as far as possible composed of expenditure items;
(v) however, any balance arising from (iv) to come from tax increases.

[79] Ibid.

The Chancellor went on to say that the exploratory discussions of the previous few days had revealed that it would at best be very difficult to reach agreement with the Fund on any basis other than Package 3, consisting of a fiscal adjustment of £1.5 billion in 1977–78 and £2–2.5 billion the following year. Even that basis envisaged a PSBR for 1978–79 of £8.4 billion—well above the target the Fund had given of £6.5 billion.

The Prime Minister agreed that the Cabinet should be asked to endorse this approach and there was then some discussion about how much detail should be gone into about the areas of expenditure which would be affected by an agreement with the Fund on the lines described by the Chancellor. Both ministers felt that at this stage 'it would court disaster to circulate now' a paper prepared by the Treasury on possible packages. This draft listed cuts to programmes up to £3 billion in 1978–79 and offered two illustrative packages drawn from this list—the first consisting of total cuts of £1 billion in 1977–78 rising to £1.4 billion in 1978–79 and the second of £1.5 billion rising to £2 billion. (Both of these totals *excluded* the sale of the BP shares, so that the actual fiscal adjustment involved would be £0.5 billion higher in 1977–78.) The head of the Expenditure Division commented that the possibilities envisaged incorporated bigger cuts than any of the illustrative programmes drawn up by the Chief Secretary to the Treasury in the context of the PESC round in October. The strategy decided by the Prime Minister was, therefore, to take the Cabinet through the process of choice by having two meetings—the first on Wednesday 1 December and the second the following day. The first would be to persuade the Cabinet of the political necessity of reaching an agreement with the Fund and the second to decide which programmes would have to bear the brunt of the savings required. In this, as we shall see in the following section, the timetable expectations of the Prime Minister were not to be realized.

Meanwhile Treasury officials and the Fund were still some way from reaching an agreement which met the essential requirements of each. On the evening of 24 November it had looked as though Package 3 came reasonably close to the Fund's ideas so far as the fiscal adjustment was concerned for Year 1, but there was little negotiation about Year 2. An important development took place on Saturday 27 November when Whittome telephoned the Permanent Secretary[80] to give his considered reactions to the whole of Package 3. He said that he wanted to make it clear that *so far as he was concerned* the figures envisaged for 1977–78 in that package were satisfactory. A difference remained however for the following year. He suggested that 'there might be some trade-off' between the two years—that is that smaller cuts might be possible for the first year in exchange for larger cuts in the second. Whittome was here showing what he had argued throughout: that the programme was essentially a

---

[80] DW 062.

medium-term one and that it was more important to get the longer-term question settled properly even at the expense of an immediate policy change, which he saw mainly in confidence terms. The Permanent Secretary said that a switch of the sort suggested would not be easy to achieve. He felt that the first year was what 'other people would be looking at even if the Fund were more concerned with the second'. He added that statements in 1976 about action to be taken in 1978–79 might not be convincing. He suggested that one way forward would be to express the additional fiscal adjustment the Fund wanted in the second year as a contingent matter related to some performance test, which could then take the form of a tax increase. The matter was allowed to rest there. Whittome had now decided to return to Washington to put the Managing Director in the picture and to indicate to him what the areas of disagreement were. It would then be for him to explain to British ministers what the breaking points were. Before he left at the end of the weekend he sent the Permanent Secretary a personal letter dated 28 November[81] in which he reverted to the issues discussed on the telephone the day before. He felt that if the Cabinet were to approve the first year contents of Package 3 (essentially cuts of £1.5 billion including £0.5 billion for the BP shares) that would be satisfactory. But for reasons of monetary stability as well as those of resource allocation and confidence, he thought that a further significant reduction in the PSBR must be secured for the second year. It was vital, given the time lags and the ease of stimulating demand (if the proposed adjustment led to over-kill), that there should be a programme of further cuts in 1978–79 *unless the economy were markedly weaker than expected*. He also very firmly believed that the confidence factor required a two-year programme and planned cuts over that time span. No doubt this was the message he delivered to the Managing Director when they met in Washington on 29 and 30 November. At this stage there was a surprising intervention by no less than the US President, who had been apprised by the Prime Minister in his telephone conversation of 23 November of the difficulties he was having in Cabinet. President Ford strongly advised Witteveen to intervene personally and travel to London for a meeting with the Prime Minister himself. Witteveen, with some misgivings, acquiesced[82] and he presented himself in London on Wednesday 1 December for what was to turn out to be perhaps the most momentous series of meetings during the whole episode. But before we examine the record, we have to see

---

[81] Ibid.

[82] Witteveen's misgivings were justified. Under Fund rules the Managing Director did not make an overseas trip without informing the Executive Board. In this case such a step would have compromised the secrecy of the visit and Witteveen kept the mission a secret. Later, when knowledge that he had made the visit came out, there were recriminations from the Board. The Fund's historian (ref De Vries) states that the Managing Director's relations with the Board were never the same after this incident.

how the Cabinet discussions went, for they had a decisive effect on the outcome of the discussions between Witteveen and the Chancellor.

Phase III—the political argument

Our account of the discussions with the Fund have concentrated on the technical aspects and have referred to the political dimension only to show the authority under which officials operated. If that treatment gives the impression that the general Ministerial involvement in the progress of the negotiations was peripheral, this would be a serious distortion of the whole picture. From the very outset the Prime Minister had insisted that the Cabinet, or the relevant Cabinet Committee (EY), should be in command of events, and at every turn the Chancellor and the Treasury sought collective Ministerial authority to take the negotiations forward. Ministers collectively had had very little say in the negotiation of the Central Bank credit in June and had been irritated by the way that the national insurance surcharge had been levied in July without any notice to them that this was an option for reducing the PSBR. The Chancellor was therefore scrupulous in keeping his colleagues informed— and they took full advantage of the opportunities this gave them to criticize the way things were going and to make counter-suggestions. It has to be said that Ministers collectively did not receive much briefing independently of what the Chancellor gave them. Apart from the Prime Minister, who had his own Policy Unit, and one or two like Benn who had Special Advisers with an economic background, the Cabinet had to be guided by what the Chancellor, and to some extent the Prime Minister, told them. They needed little guidance on the political aspects of what was on the table but when it came to hard economic appraisal of both the policy options put forward, and indeed of alternatives which the Chancellor did not canvas, they had little to guide them. Some were aware of what independent analysts were saying, for example the so-called New Cambridge economists and outside 'think tanks' like the National Institute; but for the most part the ordinary Cabinet Minister had to accept what the Chancellor was saying, or question it on mainly political grounds.

The first general involvement of Ministers collectively was, as we saw, at the EY meeting on 17 November[83] when the Chancellor reported the progress to date and asked for a mandate to open serious and concrete discussions with the IMF and in particular to suggest that a PSBR of £9 billion for 1977–78 was about the right figure that could be financed. (The Treasury had given him a speaking note which represented their views of what might possibly be achieved in the negotiations with the Fund as they then stood. The assessment

[83] CAB 134/4025—EY (76) 19th Conclusions.

they made was that it might just be possible to reach agreement on a PSBR of £9 billion, with cuts of £1.5 billion, comprising £1 billion of 'real' savings and £0.5 billion from the BP shares—a package the Chancellor was to suggest to the Fund two days later.) The mood of ministers at this meeting was fairly relaxed, perhaps because the Prime Minister and the Chancellor put the Fund negotiations into a wider context and revealed not only the possibility of a safety net for the sterling balances but 'some action on imports'. The Chancellor had perhaps contributed to the mood by circulating a paper[84] outlining some, fairly painless, measures for improving both the balance of payments and the fiscal balance—these included the sale of the BP shares referred to above, possibly to a foreign customer, a banning of UK banks' financing of third country trade within the sterling area, and a further reduction in the proportion of local authority spending financed by the Rate Support Grant. The Chancellor also notified his colleagues that the Bank would be reimposing the Corset the following day. None of these measures was commented on by EY, which, as we saw, focused on the size of the fiscal adjustment to be targeted. The Prime Minister summed up by saying that Ministers agreed with the figure of £9 billion for the PSBR but stipulated that this was to be the minimum. The position was reported to the full Cabinet the following day.

The next collective ministerial discussion of the negotiations took place a week later at the Cabinet of 23 November on the basis of a memorandum by the Chancellor[85] which reported on the discussions he had had with the Fund on 19 November. The memorandum provoked a much sharper reaction than the one his earlier paper to EY had. The Chancellor now reported that the Fund wanted to see a fiscal adjustment for 1978–79 of £3–4 billion. He said that they foresaw a rate of growth of 4 per cent and for 1977–78 wanted a PSBR below the figure produced at the time of the July cuts (£9 billion). 'They are looking,' said the Chancellor, 'for a PSBR of about £8.5 billion to be achieved principally by means of public expenditure savings. . . . In my judgement the broad scale of the action they now suggest is about right if we accept their view of the pattern of growth in the next two years (1.5 per cent in 1977–78 and 4 per cent in 1978–79)[86] . . . in any case we need to take action on this scale to restore confidence and re-establish control of our currency.' The Chancellor's comment is significant. He was now saying not just that the Fund wanted a significant fiscal adjustment, but that he agreed in principle with the Fund's case for them using as his argument that the growth of the monetary variables on the basis of existing policy was likely to fuel inflation. It was this concession to financial orthodoxy which took some of his more moderate colleagues by surprise and it may have been a tactical error—the Treasury always wanted to

---

[84] CAB 134/4027 EY(76)64.   [85] CAB 129/193/111.
[86] This was a big proviso, for the Treasury economists were advising that the growth rates postulated by the Fund were largely an act of faith.

rest the case for action primarily on 'confidence' grounds, something which might not be provable but was the consensual view of everyone involved. The Chancellor went on to inform the Cabinet that he had prepared a shopping list of cuts amounting in total to £3 billion. Some would be relatively painless, like the reduction in the subsidy for the fixed rate export and shipbuilding credit schemes, but others, such as a big increase in local authority rents, and changes 'in the planned levels of benefits and public sector pensions' would have political implications. (There was at the time considerable public criticism of the fact that public service pensioners were protected from the rigours of inflation while their private sector counterparts had no such benefit.)

The Chancellor's proposals produced a quite violent reaction.[87] The chief critic turned out to be the Foreign Secretary (Crosland) who, as he had in the past, took a strictly Keynesian line, contrasting it with the financial orthodoxy the Chancellor had expressed, and argued that the whole package proposed by the Fund, and now substantially endorsed by the Chancellor, was deflationary and would pose big risks to the Social Contract and to the Parliamentary Labour Party. He had previously written to the Prime Minister supporting the Lever idea of borrowing heavily abroad.[88] His own proposals were that the Fund should be told that a PSBR of £9.5 billion for 1977–78 was the lowest the government could accept and that it should be achieved by £1 billion of cuts made up of £0.5 billion from the sale of BP shares, £0.25 billion from 'cosmetic' cuts (i.e. those having little effect on demand), and £0.25 billion from demand-rich cuts. The Foreign Secretary received substantial support from his colleagues. There were also the usual siren voices of those who favoured an 'alternative strategy'. The record shows that the Chancellor did receive some support, but it must have been modest, for when the Prime Minister came to sum up he was no longer able to stretch a point and say, as he so often had before, that the balance of argument was in the Chancellor's favour. Instead he said that he would send messages to President Ford and Chancellor Schmidt urging them to put pressure on the IMF to be more accommodating to the UK. He did, however, promise to come back to the Cabinet in two day's time with a recommendation jointly endorsed by himself and the Chancellor.

The Prime Minister promptly sent messages to his two principal counterparts, Ford and Schmidt.[89] They amounted to little more than a description of the reluctance the Cabinet had shown to any sort of agreement with the Fund involving a fiscal adjustment of the size proposed. The Prime Minister said that the Fund were asking for PSBRs of £8.5 billion in 1977–78 and £6.5 billion the following year. The Chancellor had thought that he could get agreement with the Fund at £9 billion for the first year, but the Cabinet had not accepted this.

---

[87] CAB 128/60/11.   [88] DW 036.   [89] Ibid.

The Prime Minister went on to describe the risks posed of a rupture of the agreement with the TUC if the Government adopted severe measures.

The Treasury had much earlier in the process considered the merits of an appeal to the Germans and Americans for some help with the negotiations, but had discarded the idea as unlikely to be fruitful. This indeed turned out to be the case. President Ford replied to the Prime Minister on the following day to say that 'interfering with the Fund would be inappropriate' and he fell back on the point, not raised by the Prime Minister in his message, of help on the sterling balances 'when substantial agreement has been reached with the Fund'.[90] Clearly the Lever visit of the previous week had had little effect and the US Treasury and Federal Reserve continued to be in command of the American position. Schmidt was a little more responsive. The British Ambassador in Bonn saw him on 24 November,[91] but he was apparently little impressed with the economic arguments for not meeting the Fund's proposals. However he noted that the Americans, and Burns in particular, seemed to be reluctant to help and that was about as far as he was prepared to go. He did, however, decide to send the State Secretary (Pöhl) to London to discuss the situation with the Chancellor and a meeting between him and the Chancellor took place on the evening of 24 November. The Chancellor outlined where matters stood with the Fund[92] but Pöhl was non-committal, and indeed he was implicitly critical of the way that the British were dramatizing their differences with the Fund. 'He regretted' says the record[93] 'that the discussions with the Fund were being dramatized to look like the "Battle of England"'.[94] It was evident thereafter that neither of the two major creditor countries would be willing to put any pressure on the Fund, and the UK would have to argue its case alone. This was indeed the message which came through at a meeting the Chancellor had with Simon and Yeo during a brief visit they paid to London over the weekend of 27 and 28 November.[95] The Chancellor informed them where matters then stood but the only matter on which he obtained any help was on the question of how much the UK would be able to draw once an agreement had been reached. On this the Fund had already indicated that the initial drawing would be limited to $1 billion and this did not appeal to the British. The drawing on the central bank credit had reached over $1.5 billion and there was some anxiety that the repayment of this, not being fully offset by the Fund drawing, would lead to a fall in the published official reserves in the first week of January. Simon was sympathetic to the Chancellor's concern on this point and the British took some comfort from the sense that he might be prepared to use his influence to persuade the Managing Director to relent.

---

[90] Ibid.   [91] Ibid.   [92] BP 122/24/01.   [93] Ibid.
[94] Pöhl spoke quite good English, but here the idiom escaped him—he obviously meant 'The Battle of Britain'.
[95] Ibid.

Apart from that indication, the meeting with Simon was without effect. The Americans continued to oppose any move on the sterling balances until the Fund agreement was in place.

The Prime Minister came back to the Cabinet, as he said he would, on 25 November,[96] but not with a joint proposal from himself and the Chancellor. Instead he recounted his exchanges with Ford and Schmidt and described the meetings he had had with the Fund staff on the same day. He informed the Cabinet of the three packages the Treasury had put to Whittome and said that there would be an opportunity to discuss the options in full the following week, after his return from a meeting of the European Council on 29 and 30 November. The Cabinet made it plain that they were in no mood to accept a Treasury fiat. What they asked for (and duly got) were alternative proposals *on paper* from other sources within Whitehall than the Treasury. In the meantime they ventilated the usual nostrums about the situation not calling for deflation and the need for policies which would not jeopardize the Social Contract. According to the political memoirs of some Ministers,[97] this was a period of feverish informal consultation among those of them who were alarmed at the way the Chancellor was proceeding. They seem, however, to have been occasions for them to express their concern and frustration at the way things were going rather than to the formulation of specific proposals to which they would, more or less collectively, commit themselves: and in practical terms these informal discussions led nowhere.

The fact that so many Ministers were unhappy meant that by the weekend of 27–28 November the Chancellor's position had become very isolated. He had not persuaded his Cabinet colleagues to accept the adjustment of £1.5 billion in the fiscal balance for 1977–78, which he thought might secure agreement with the Fund, and he could look to no help from his fellow Finance Ministers to get the Fund to soften their terms. By this time the Treasury had established that, although there would still be problems with the second year (on which the Cabinet had had very little discussion), an adjustment of £1.5 billion in the first year would in fact go a long way to meeting the Fund's conditions for the following year. The Chancellor had, as we saw in the previous section, reported this to the Prime Minister in his minute of 25 November which summarized the state of the discussions about the three Treasury packages, of which, it will be recalled, the largest involved a fiscal adjustment of £1.5 billion in the first year (including the sale of the BP shares valued at £0.5 billion) and a further adjustment of £2 billion in the second year. This package, however, did not come anywhere near meeting the Fund's objectives for the PSBR and the DCE targets for the second year. By this time the Fund had, as the Permanent Secretary had suggested to them, ceased to conduct the negotiation in terms of the monetary variables and were focusing more or less solely on the size of

---

[96] CAB 128/60/12.   [97] Benn, Crosland, and Dell.

the fiscal adjustment. The Chancellor put it to the Prime Minister that he should now put to Cabinet a paper based on the three packages arguing that the third looked to be the one which could be negotiated.

The Cabinet Secretary informed the Treasury that the Prime Minister would want to have two Cabinets the following week to take matters forward—the first on 1 December and the second on the following day. The first would be devoted to the major political issues involved in how big an adjustment should be made and the second to questions of detail, including of course the impact of any agreement with the Fund on particular expenditure programmes. Over the weekend of 27–28 November Treasury officials prepared three Cabinet papers for the Chancellor to circulate. The first was a statement of how far the negotiations had got and how the Fund had reacted to the three packages discussed. The second, and perhaps the most important *apologia* for the policy the Chancellor was advocating during the whole IMF episode, set out his intellectual position and justified his acceptance of the case for a significant shift in policy. The third set out the areas of public expenditure, which in the Chancellor's view would be candidates for reductions if his policy proposals were accepted.

The first paper, as circulated,[98] set out the implications of the three packages put forward to the Fund by the Treasury and made it clear that only the third approached what the Fund wanted and even this fell well short of the target for the borrowing requirement for 1978–79. The second paper[99] went more fundamentally into the *objective* reasons for some adjustment, although not necessarily to the full extent the Fund wanted: the question of confidence, the need to secure a great deal of external finance before the deficit was closed, and indeed the need to make progress on closing the deficit itself. It was, even by the Chancellor's standards, a very cogently argued piece of advocacy. The Chancellor portrayed himself as by no means unsympathetic to the medicine the Fund were proposing although he jibbed at the size of the dose, at any rate for the second year. He said that he would now want to go for a PSBR of £8.5 billion in 1977–78 and a similar figure for the following year—achieved largely through expenditure savings. At the previous meeting of the Cabinet he had said that this could be achieved by cuts of £1.5 billion in the first year rising to £2 billion the following year. Further work by the Treasury in which account was taken of the lower interest rates which such a package would achieve (with consequent savings of public sector debt interest) suggested that the cuts need only be £1 billion in the first year (supplemented by the £0.5 billion from the BP sale) and £2 billion in the second—and in the second year he would not rule out some modest tax increases. The paper went on to examine whether one solution would be to confine the fiscal adjustment to 1978–79 and leave the previous year alone, introducing a programme of import deposits to deal

[98] CAB 129/193/12.   [99] CAB 129/193/13.

with the situation in the previous year. But this was of dubious value as import deposits would only affect the PSBR for the current year (1976–77) and would do little for the following and critically important year. The Chancellor went on to deal with three alternatives to what he was proposing:

1 a scheme of import controls and a *dirigiste* approach to the economy;
2 little change and recourse to considerable external borrowing;
3 a scheme of import deposits and a wage freeze.

After dismissing these as chimeras the Chancellor invited his colleagues to support him in his basic proposals.

The Chancellor's examination of hypothetical alternatives to what he proposed was, of course, occasioned by the ventilation of such ideas at the Cabinet of 23 (and to a lesser extent that of 25) November. But he now had a more pressing need to take on the opposition, for three Cabinet Ministers outside the Treasury had put in papers proposing something like the policies which the Chancellor was at such pains to repudiate. They were the Energy Secretary (Benn),[100] the Foreign Secretary (Crosland)[101] and the Environment Secretary (Shore).[102] None of these spoke to a departmental brief, and each took somewhat different positions from the others, although all were opposed to the Chancellor. Benn staked out the position he had put forward on several occasions over the previous two years—this was in essence the first of the three suggestions addressed by the Chancellor. Crosland had also consistently taken a Keynesian line in the past, arguing that the economy did not need any more deflation. He now repeated the argument he had used at the Cabinet meeting of 23 November that only a modest programme of cuts should be put forward and that the UK could, in effect, use its considerable bargaining position as a major player on the world financial scene to blackmail the Fund and the major creditors into accepting only a token adjustment. Shore argued his own particular line of a programme of planned expansion coupled with import controls, which he argued could be introduced on a temporary basis even under existing treaty obligations.

All these papers were taken at the Cabinet of 1 December[103] which was inevitably a long-drawn out affair. The three dissenting ministers spoke to their papers, although Crosland was at pains to distance himself from his two colleagues, in that he remained broadly in favour of existing policy and only wanted to make an adjustment smaller than that proposed by the Chancellor—and to use the threat of a siege economy only to 'frighten' the Fund. The other two ministers argued their cases strongly. But the Chancellor now obtained a fair amount of support for his position and his opponents fell back in disarray. The Prime Minister was in the end able to sum up to the effect that

---

[100] CAB 129/193/7. [101] CAB 129/193/8.
[102] CAB 129/193/14. [103] CAB 128/60/13.

the Chancellor's general approach now had the support of the Cabinet, but that the latter would want to look at 'the fine print' of what precisely an agreement with the Fund would entail, both in aggregate and for individual spending programmes, before they assented to an agreement.

The Chancellor was nearly out of the wood, but he had yet to take on his spending colleagues—and this was the theme of the Cabinet on the following day.[104] He now supplemented the third of the three papers referred to above which had been prepared over the weekend of 27–28 November on public expenditure with a fourth[105] of a more specific nature. The third paper was a covering note to a Treasury paper listing a range of options for expenditure cuts from which a selection could be made to give whatever total of cuts Ministers eventually decided upon. It clearly went well beyond the list from which the Cabinet had on 26 October, after enormous difficulty, agreed the cuts designed to bring the aggregate of programmes back to the path set out in the White Paper in February. The fourth and more specific paper invited the Cabinet to address itself to the problem created by the legislative obligation to uprate social security benefits and public service pensions in a particularly rigid fashion. The Chancellor had for some time, as had Treasury officials, reservations about this matter. Social security benefits constituted 22 per cent of the total of public spending, and yet the Government had, in effect, no control over it as the amount of annual uprating was laid down in statute. Public service pensions were also governed by statutory provisions. The general effect of these rules was that public service pensions and long-term social security benefits had to be uprated annually at the rate of the rise in earnings (or prices if they rose faster) and short-term benefits in line with prices. The effect of these provisions had been to add £1.5 billion to the Budget in 1976. But it was not only the cost, and the lack of control over it, that bothered the Chancellor. He saw the protection of those on benefits as providing a disincentive to work when earnings were rising slowly and prices faster—the situation in 1976.

The Cabinet of 2 December presented almost as formidable a challenge to the Chancellor's skills as had that of the previous day, for he now had to take on his colleagues on their own ground and cajole them into accepting the medicine which was implied by their (albeit reluctant) acceptance of his general prescription. In short, they had to deliver the necessary expenditure cuts. The three colleagues who had proposed a different policy approach from that of the Chancellor might have shot their bolt, but there were several colleagues who had not. The Chancellor opened the meeting by again setting out his proposals (cuts of £1 billion plus £0.5 billion from the BP shares in 1977–78 followed by £1.5 billion in 1978–79 plus £0.5 billion that year either via more cuts or some tax increase, the whole yielding a PSBR of £8.7 billion in

---

[104] CAB 128/60/14.   [105] CAB 129/193/11.

1977–78) but added to them a view that it would be proper to reduce income tax rates at the lower and the upper end of the income range. This was too much for the Lord President of the Council (Michael Foot) who launched into a strong attack on the whole package, finding the further call for spending cuts after the July measures unacceptable and objecting to the proposal to cut the higher rates of tax. He thought that the entire package was inconsistent with the Labour Party's priorities. The Prime Minister, however, was in no mood to reopen the discussion of the day before, and threw his weight behind the Chancellor in an unqualified way. He raised the question of import deposits as a supplement to the package and reminded the Cabinet that he had mentioned this possibility to the Americans and the Germans, but having done so he was doubtful about them. On the question of changing the basis of social security and public service pensions, he said that the Chief Whip had advised him that there would be a revolt among the Government's back-benchers: it would require careful thought. The Prime Minister's support for the Chancellor had the effect of finally swinging a good many Cabinet colleagues, and the meeting ended with broad approval for the Chancellor putting his ideas to the Fund, although the Cabinet would not take a final decision until it saw all the expenditure proposals in detail. This would be at the beginning of the following week.

We now have to go back in time somewhat and pick up the threads of the discussions the Treasury were having with the Fund, all of which were taking place against the background of considerable Cabinet unhappiness with the direction in which the Chancellor and the Treasury were going. Whittome had returned to Washington on 28 November at the end of the week, which saw the Chancellor subjected to a great deal of opposition. His purpose was to brief the Managing Director on the state of play in the negotiations and to advise him how to deal with a suggestion, mentioned above, that the US President personally made to him to intervene in the negotiations by going to London to talk to the Chancellor and the Prime Minister.[106] Witteveen arrived on 1 December with Whittome, having travelled overnight from Washington, and had an immediate meeting with the Prime Minister and the Chancellor— before the Cabinet, referred to above, that had been arranged to decide what negotiating authority the Chancellor could have. The Prime Minister warned the Managing Director of the huge risks of the Government opting for some form of protectionist policy if the financial terms sought by the Fund were too severe and the British economy were forced into a deflationary mode. Witteveen countered that the Fund's prescription was not deflationary and that a curtailment of the public sector's absorption of resources would release resources for the private business sector. He thought that public expenditure cuts of £1.5–2 billion in 1978–79 were required. Both the Chancellor and the Prime

---

[106] De Vries.

Minister said that this was simply not possible. The meeting ended inconclusively and the Ministers went into the Cabinet meeting. Immediately after this the Chancellor had a working lunch with Witteveen and there was a further meeting (apparently between courses) with the Prime Minister before the Chancellor's lunch resumed and the Managing Director then departed for Heathrow. The substance of the discussion at these meetings was essentially political, with both the Prime Minister and the Chancellor stressing how impossible the Fund's terms were. (The Cabinet had, as we saw, very reluctantly gone along with cuts of £1 billion for 1977–78, and Witteveen's demands of £1.5–2 billion were not negotiable—the Prime Minister said he would not even consider putting them to the Cabinet but would go down the protectionist road.)

On the question of a fiscal adjustment, the Chancellor told Witteveen that he was proposing £1 billion of cuts in public expenditure in 1977–78 (supplemented by the sale of the BP shares) and £1.5 billion in 1978–79 with the possibility of indirect tax increases in that year of a further £0.5 billion. Witteveen commented that this implied a PSBR of the order of £9.5 billion for 1977–78,[107] and was not satisfactory. There was then some skirmishing about the outcome for 1978–79, Whittome suggesting that the idea of assured cuts in expenditure of the size the Chancellor had mentioned and an 'aspiration' for a satisfactory level of the PSBR in that year 'looked promising'. The Chancellor responded by saying that he might be willing to go for a PSBR in 1978–79 of £8 billion, but Whittome commented that the Fund were looking for a target of £6.5 billion—otherwise the growth of M3 would be a problem. Witteveen, who as we shall see, was somewhat irritated by Whittome's suggestion, said that the Chancellor was in effect offering Package 2 of the three variants illustrated by the Treasury, and this was not acceptable. Witteveen said that he wanted something as large as Package 3. The Chancellor replied that a larger package than the one he had put forward was not possible. The debate now focused on the first year. The Chancellor repeated that £1 billion of 'real' cuts was the limit of what was possible politically; Witteveen continued to hold out for an extra £0.5 billion. With this difference still unresolved, and no agreement on Whittome's suggestion for the second year, the meeting broke up and Witteveen returned to Washington. It remained to be seen what progress could be made in negotiations with Whittome given the intransigence of the two principal negotiators.

The meetings may have been dominated by the size of the adjustment the Fund were seeking in the first year, but there was a brief discussion (at the Chancellor's lunch) of the issue of front loading. The Chancellor said that if all the Fund were prepared to make available immediately an agreement was

---

[107] This seems to be a faulty calculation. The combination of £1 billion cuts plus the sale of the BP shares would have brought the PSBR down to £9 billion.

reached was $0.5 billion[108]—the figure that the Fund had suggested at the outset—the Cabinet would simply not be willing to consider a fiscal adjustment. Because of the refinancing of the central bank credit the UK would need at least $1.6 billion. When he had raised the smallness of the initial drawing with Simon at the weekend, the latter 'had been shocked'. Witteveen was not impressed and refused to be drawn. He had had a different impression of the American position from Yeo (to whom presumably he had spoken before leaving Washington). A drawing of as much as $2 billion at the outset was too much by the Fund's normal standards. There the matter was left for the time being.

A small meeting was arranged between Whittome and the Permanent Secretary and their immediate colleagues at noon the following day[109] to take stock of where matters stood. Whittome recalled that, at various stages of the discussion with the Prime Minister and the Chancellor, Witteveen had said that public expenditure reductions of £1.5 billion were necessary in the first year and the Prime Minister had replied that £1 billion was the maximum that could be secured. This difference had existed throughout the day and Whittome said that he had 'received short shrift from Witteveen when he suggested that perhaps £1 billion of cuts in 1977–79 were not so bad'. Witteveen was apparently very worried about getting through the next six months and his fear was that the package would be inadequate and consequently that there would be a run on the pound perhaps within two or three months. Nevertheless Whittome was prepared to try to persuade the Managing Director to accept £1 billion in 1977–78 (plus the BP shares) provided the adjustment was larger than £2 billion in the following year. A £2 billion adjustment in 1978–79 did not look adequate in that it implied a PSBR of the same level as in the previous year and the money supply growth would be 14 per cent.[110] Whittome emphasized that he was talking without any authority from the Managing Director or indeed any encouragement from him but he would do his best to persuade him to move on the first year. The Permanent Secretary asked whether, if the British Government could not move further than its present position on the fiscal adjustment for each of the next two years, a possible compromise might be to accept its figures but require them to be buttressed by a firm commitment to declared targets for DCE and the PSBR—something of a backtracking of the position he had taken earlier. Whittome did not think that

---

[108] The Fund wanted eight equal instalments of $0.5 billion spaced out over the two-year length of the programme, with of course conditionality on the achievement of performance targets attached to each instalment.

[109] DW 062.

[110] These figures were derived from the Treasury's simulations and were not those the Fund was using on the basis of their memorandum of 21 November. But of course the Fund was supposing that the forecast the Treasury would publish at the conclusion of the negotiations would be their own and not the Fund's; so Whittome's argument was a reasonable one.

this would do. What he wanted was *announced cuts in public expenditure* which would give credibility to the whole programme.

Whittome was summoned to a meeting with the Chancellor in the afternoon of 2 December[111] and was told what the outcome of the Cabinet that morning had been. The Chancellor said that, by a significant majority, the Cabinet had now authorized him to tell the Fund that the Government were willing to take significant action to reduce the PSBR in 1977–78 from £10.4 billion to £8.7 billion by means of expenditure cuts of £1 billion and the sale of £0.5 billion shares in BP. That should lead to a fiscal adjustment in the following year of £1.5 billion and he had proposed a further £0.5 billion reduction 'whose nature could be settled later'. The Cabinet had not yet reached a final decision on the second year. There would be a further Cabinet meeting on the following Monday (6 December) to give formal clearance to the £2 billion adjustment for 1978–79. The question of Import Deposits had been discussed, but a number of Ministers were unenthusiastic. Whittome said that he would report this to the Managing Director. As far as he was concerned he was satisfied with what was proposed for the first year, but he thought that the scale of action in the second year should be more than £2 billion. The position of the Cabinet did not represent the acceptable minimum for the Fund. He made the further point that, when it came to the Letter of Intent, it would not be the figures it contained but the actual measures (by which he meant the nature of the expenditure cuts) that mattered. The discussion touched on the unresolved question of 'front loading'. On this Whittome was adamant that an initial drawing of $1.5 billion was out of the question but he came up with a compromise. Although it would be in excess of the normal initial drawing, the Fund might be prepared to go to $1 billion—an improvement on the initial proposal of $0.5 billion. He also made the helpful suggestion that the Americans and the Germans might be persuaded to activate central bank swaps to provide the additional funds temporarily until the UK was able to make its second drawing (probably four months later). Whittome took the opportunity to remind the Chancellor that the question of the UK's management of the exchange rate remained unresolved—it had hardly been discussed except at a high level of generality—and this had to be settled. Clearly the Government still had quite a few hurdles to surmount.

On the following day, Thursday 3 December, by which time the Chancellor was fortified by a firm Cabinet mandate to negotiate, there was a series of meetings which went far to resolve the main disputed issues, subject of course to the overriding need for the agreement to be endorsed by the Cabinet. At noon Whittome called on the Chancellor[112] to tell him of Witteveen's reaction to the Cabinet's position as reported on the previous day. This was bleak news for the Chancellor. The package acceptable to the Cabinet for the first

[111] Ibid. [112] Ibid.

year and the Chancellor's proposals for the second 'were not adequate'. He wanted expenditure cuts of £1.5 billion in 1977–78 and 'a substantial addition for the following year'. By this he meant cuts of the order of £3 billion. It was this which caused the Chancellor to explode with understandable fury. If that was the Managing Director's position 'he could take a running jump'. Whittome, who had played a very constructive and conciliatory role throughout, saw that an impasse had been reached. He said that he would go back to the Managing Director and try to persuade him to accept the £1 billion expenditure cut for the first year. 'But he had no chance whatever of success except on the basis that the measures for 1978–79 would be about £1 billion larger than the Chancellor had suggested', that is cuts of £2.5 billion. In this Whittome was repeating what he had always believed—that the second year was more important than the first. The Chancellor's reply was that the Cabinet had not yet reached a decision on the second year, but he said the Prime Minister was very worried about £2 billion of expenditure cuts in that year and did not think that he could go beyond that figure. He recognized that failure to agree a programme with the Fund could lead to the fall of the government, but equally to accept Witteveen's proposal would lead to the same outcome. The Chancellor said that he was prepared to fight his colleagues for his own proposals, but he was not prepared to do so for the Managing Director's. It was at this point that the Fund came up with a proposal which was to break the deadlock. Whittome suggested that perhaps the additional fiscal adjustment the Fund wanted in the second year could be expressed in a contingent way— an idea that the Permanent Secretary had thrown out earlier—and Finch added that, since the Fund wanted a large adjustment in the second year because they foresaw a vigorous upswing in the UK economy in the course of 1978–79, the contingency could be expressed in a form which acknowledged this. This idea was seized on by the Chancellor and he asked the Fund and the Permanent Secretary speedily to find a form of words which would express this thought and which might be incorporated in the Letter of Intent. Over lunch officials worked out a draft and this was considered by the Chancellor with Whittome early in the afternoon. The form of words proposed was:

In preparing my Budget for 1978 I shall take full account of the prospective growth of output and ensure that nothing stands in the way of the resource shift described above. In particular if the forecast rate of growth from the beginning of 1978 to the end of 1979 is in excess of 3.5 per cent I shall make a further fiscal adjustment in 1978–79 of £500–£1,000 million at 1976 prices.

This looked a safe bet for the Treasury, whose forecast even before the cuts agreed with the Fund were taken into account was of growth in 1978–79 of only 3 per cent. The Chancellor felt so encouraged by this development that he wondered whether the contingent idea could be applied in the first year. Whittome dismissed this suggestion without even arguing against it.

The Chancellor said, however, that he would like to be able to do something in the 1977 Budget if the economy did not develop according to plan and the PSBR looked likely to be lower than the agreed figure. Whittome gave a diplomatic, but non-committal reply to this.

There matters were left between the two parties. Technical discussions were proceeding between the Fund and the Treasury about the wording of the Letter of Intent and on the profile over the two years of the programme of the main financial variables (notably DCE and the PSBR) and these we look at later in the narrative. There was also the undiscussed matter of the exchange rate and the stumbling block of 'front loading'. But for the moment we have to concentrate on the problem the Chancellor and the Prime Minister now had to convince their colleagues that they had an acceptable deal which should be clinched. Whittome announced that he was returning to Washington but would be back early the following week to hear of the Cabinet's final decision and to resume consideration of matters outstanding.

The crucial Cabinets to reach a final decision on the main points of principle were fixed for Monday and Tuesday (6 and 7 December). There was now little or no room for delay, for the central bank credit had to be repaid on 7 December and, if a paper was to be presented to the IMF Board before the end of the year, the text of the Letter of Intent had to be agreed within a matter of days.

The Prime Minister asked the Treasury to provide a brief setting out again the arguments for the agreement with the Fund and, perhaps even more importantly, a brief on what fall-back was open to the government if an agreement was not reached. He also asked the Foreign Office and the Cabinet Office to set out what political and defence measures the government could take to reduce expenditure if a drastic programme had to be implemented. The choice of these two areas for possible retrenchment were clearly designed to show the UK's allies what the consequences were for the Fund's 'intransigence' if in fact the Cabinet failed finally to endorse the proposed agreement and the allies failed to intervene in the negotiations. We need not go into the detail of these briefs[113] although they do perhaps provide evidence of how catastrophic, at any rate in the eyes of the Treasury and the Foreign Office, the situation would be if the negotiations broke down.

The Cabinet resumed discussion of the issue on 6 December and continued the following day with two further meetings,[114] the final one being taken at 8.00 p.m. on 7 December—the day the central bank credit had to be repaid. The meetings had before them a shopping list of possible spending cuts, prepared by the Treasury, and the job of Cabinet was to go through this, agreeing or not agreeing to each in turn. The Prime Minister prefaced his introduction by saying that this time there would be no question of the

---

[113] PREM 16/807.   [114] CAB 128/60/15, 16, and 17.

Chancellor springing a surprise on his colleagues by introducing a new measure at the last minute. We need hardly go into the details of the discussion of the shopping list, but two or three items may be noted. The first was that the Chancellor returned to his proposal to break the automatic link between social security benefits and public service pensions and prices or earnings. The relevant ministers had been thinking about this and came up with a formidable array of objections, partly Parliamentary but also more widely political. It was decided to drop this item from the package and pursue the issue outside the context of the Fund agreement. No more was heard about it either during the negotiations or subsequently. The second issue was that of introducing a further limited package of industrial and employment measures to deal with some of the particular problems of certain industries and elements of the labour force. These would cost about £200 million, and it was felt that it would be extremely difficult to find further spending cuts to offset this. So the idea was put forward that this should be financed by some tax increases. There was some apprehension about this, but in the event ministers overcame their scruples and accepted this suggestion. The third issue was that of import deposits. The Prime Minister had raised this as a possible component of the package several times at previous Cabinets and had warned the Americans and Germans that this might turn out to be the case. He took the question up again at the Cabinet of 6 December, but the Chancellor was lukewarm and spoke of the delay this might cause in view of the need to give prior notification to the European governments.

The Cabinet broke up late on 7 December, and their job was really over. They had provided the Chancellor with the authority he had sought to clinch an agreement with the Fund and, although they had not accepted his proposals on social security, he had got the programme. He had avoided any direct action on imports. He had at the same time greatly softened the original terms the Fund wanted. He had demonstrated to his opponents that, however much they might dislike the terms, there really was no credible alternative. It was a huge personal achievement. It has to be said that it was also a huge personal achievement for Whittome, whose skill and diplomacy throughout had made such a contribution to the deal. His contribution and the professionalism he displayed throughout the episode were implicitly acknowledged some years later when a knighthood was conferred on him.

There were, however, still some troublesome loose ends, but they hardly involved the Cabinet, and the Chancellor felt able to settle them by himself (subject only to clearance with the Prime Minister). He saw Whittome on the morning of 8 December[115] to tell him of the outcome of the Cabinet meetings of the previous two days, including the decision to include some additional spending on industrial matters, financed by a tax increase. There was a brief

---

[115] DW 062.

discussion of the front-loading issue. Whittome said that Witteveen was resisting attempts by the USA to increase the initial drawing from $1 billion.

The Prime Minister sent messages to President Ford and Chancellor Schmidt on 9 December[116] reporting the Cabinet's decision, which would now lead to an agreement with the Fund. He raised with both of them the issue of front-loading. This produced a telegram from the German Finance Minister (Apel) to the Chancellor to the effect that he personally would welcome it if the Fund would pay the first three instalments (amounting to about $2 billion) at the outset. He said that he would use his influence with Witteveen to secure this. This may have been the cause of the last minute improvement in the Fund's offer for the initial drawing which we describe later on.

Phase IV—residual issues

The acceptance by the Cabinet of the Chancellor's proposals for the fiscal adjustments in the two years 1977–78 and 1978–79 virtually sealed an agreement with the Fund, but three important technical issues had to be resolved: the nature of the government's future policy on the exchange rate, the form of the commitments to be embodied in the Letter of Intent and in supporting documents about the performance targets (in particular the path of DCE and of the PSBR), and finally the precise nature of the commitment on public expenditure reductions in terms of those programmes that would be reduced.

The exchange rate

The issue of the exchange rate had been raised as early as the first meeting the Fund had had with the Chancellor on 4 November and it had been referred to on and off at meetings over the following four weeks, but without any concrete formulation of a policy statement. The Fund had made it abundantly clear that they wanted a commitment to 'manage' the rate to ensure that the UK did not lose the improvement in competitiveness that had been secured in the course of 1976 as a result of sterling's sharp decline. This was integral to their whole plan for the UK economy, for they argued that it was because there would be a strong demand for UK exports as a result of this policy that room had to be found from the resources consumed by the public sector. The Bank and OF, who conducted most of the discussions with the Fund in the early stages, were reluctant to commit themselves to anything specific about 'intervention policy'. They essentially wanted stability, particularly after the turbulence of the previous months. Indeed they were reluctant to commit themselves not to allow sterling to rise—at any rate temporarily—if confidence

---

[116] Ibid.

were eventually restored. The Fund were impatient with this and at one point suggested that there ought to be some form of monitoring of the exchange rate in future Article VIII consultations, but this too was resisted by the Treasury. By the beginning of December, as the discussions on the rate took centre-stage with the agreement on the fiscal adjustment reached, the Fund expressed their exasperation in a letter to the Permanent Secretary:

We want to be firmly assured that the strategy in this area is that it should be constantly ensured that net exports should be competitive—or, as the Chancellor has twice previously told us, 'the rate should always be slightly undervalued'. We would want this assurance to be given for as long a period forward as possible.

As regards tactics, we want to know the range within which policy now seeks to operate, and we most decidedly want an upper limit—I think that $1.65 is as high as is acceptable.

We accept that the theoretical idea of a steady downward path may present difficulties though the operators have not always spoken with one voice on this subject. Nevertheless, we want to be assured that the seductive appeal of exchange-rate stability will not be allowed to keep the rate on a plateau for any length of time.[117]

In the detailed negotiations, the Fund at first proposed a form of words which stated:

Intervention will be designed to minimise disruptive short-term fluctuations in the rate along an appropriate path that safeguards, on a continuing basis, the maintenance of the competitive position of UK manufacturers both in foreign and domestic markets.[118]

Although in substance this was what the Treasury had been arguing for over the previous two years, they saw difficulties in an explicit and public reference to it. There were some internal exchanges on this point in the first week of December and the Treasury sought a much blander statement of intent, with no reference to 'competitiveness'.[119] The Chancellor agreed with this approach when it was put to him on 6 December and a meeting took place the same day with Fund officials. The Fund still wanted something stronger in the way of commitment than the Treasury was prepared to make and suggested as a compromise that it might be made in the form of an unpublished *aide mémoire*.[120] The Treasury did not like this, on the grounds that the Chancellor could not be put in the position, if asked in Parliament, of having to deny that there was any undertaking concerning the exchange when there in fact was one. The idea was then put forward by the UK Director at the Fund that the difficulty could be got round by having a meeting to discuss the exchange rate and to embody in the minutes of the meeting a general statement of intent by the Chancellor as to how he saw developments in this area. This, in fact, was what happened and the Chancellor took a formal meeting with the Fund on 10 December,[121] the minutes of which had actually been written before the meeting took place. They read as follows:

[117] OF 122/24/01.   [118] DW 062.   [119] Ibid.   [120] Ibid.   [121] Ibid.

The Chancellor agreed that a necessary condition for securing a shift into net exports will be an exchange rate which ensures the continued maintenance of price competitiveness...exchange rate policy will be conducted so far as possible with a view to maintaining the present degree of competitiveness as measured by the appropriate relative price and cost indices.

The Chancellor said that he thought that an exchange rate in the region of $1.60 to $1.65 was probably sufficiently competitive to give exporters confidence and indeed might permit a period of stability...He was however concerned to avoid a situation in which the rate appeared to have become fixed at an unsustainable level....*He felt that it would be inappropriate for the rate to appreciate from present levels.*...His intention would be to take the opportunity offered by a tendency for the rate to strengthen to cream off dollars to strengthen the reserves.

Mr Whittome said that this was satisfactory. (italics added)

The Fund had got something of what they wanted, but the commitment embodied in these minutes was much weaker than the one they had sought at the outset. The minutes were not disclosed to the IMF Executive Board when the standby was submitted for approval and neither they nor their content were revealed publicly in the UK. We shall see in the following chapter how far the implicit policy was executed in the year that followed and how easily the UK was in effect to backtrack on the general understanding reached at the meeting.

The performance criteria

After the hard political decisions had been taken on 7 December—the size of the fiscal adjustments and the consequential expenditure cuts for the two years in question—the detailed consequences of these decisions had to be translated into firm, monitorable commitments, the fulfilling of which would govern the UK's entitlement to draw on the successive instalments of the credit. These technical matters comprised the following issues:

1 the profile over time of the drawing rights over the life of the credit;
2 the profile, again over time, of the monetary and financial consequences of the agreement;
3 the conditionality which should apply to the right to draw upon the credit;
4 the precise expenditure programmes which would be reduced and the degree of commitment to them.

These matters took up a great deal of officials' time and effort in the interval between the conclusion of the basic agreement on 7 December and the Chancellor's statement to the House of Commons on 15 December. Some of these issues had been addressed in a hypothetical manner in the period before 7 December, and indeed some had been resolved, but there was still much to be done in a very short space of time.

Before the first item could be resolved, it was necessary for the economic forecasters to make a revised forecast of what the agreement with the Fund was likely to entail both for the economy as a whole and for the main financial variables which would be incorporated in the Letter of Intent. A summary of this forecast[122] is worth examination, and later on we shall want to examine how far, in the event, this forecast was borne out by events (Table 5.3).

Table 5.3 Summary of the forecast consequences of the agreement with the Fund

Item	Period/time	Quantity
PSBR	1976–77	£11.2 million
	1977–78	£8.7 million
	1978–79	£8.6 million
GDP growth (% on a year earlier)	1976 (H2)	2.5%
	1977 (H2)	1.8%
	1978 (H2)	2.8%
Unemployment	1976 (Q4)	1.3 million
	1977 (Q4)	1.7 million
	1978 (Q4)	1.9 million
Balance of payments (current account)	1976–77	–£2.3 billion
	1977–78	–£1.0 billion
	1978–79	+£2.9 billion
Retail price index (increase on a year earlier)	1976 (Q4)	14.9%
	1977 (Q4)	15.1%
	1978 (Q4)	8.5%
DCE	1976–77	£9.3 billion
	1977–78	£7.7 billion
	1978–79	£6.0 billion
£M3	1976–77	11.4%
	1977–78	12.0%
	1978–79	14.2%

The Fund did not necessarily accept the consequences of the agreement for real economic growth, for unemployment or for the balance of payments, for they had made plain their view that the freeing of resources created by the expenditure cuts and the reduction in monetary growth would lead to an increase in investment and exports—a view that was not reflected in the Treasury forecast. The Fund was, however, prepared to use the financial and monetary forecast as the basis for calculating the performance criteria and it is to this issue that we now turn.

The profile over time of the drawing rights on the stand-by followed standard Fund practice. This was that the credit should be drawn upon gradually over the life of the agreement, this gradualism being the discipline that obliged the drawer to comply with its commitments. In the case of the UK, this did not present any difficulty save in the matter of the initial drawing, which, as we

[122] BP 122/24/01.

Table 5.4 Profile of drawings from the IMF December 1976 to November 1978

Initial drawing (million SDR)	May 1977	August 1977	November 1977	February 1978	May 1978	August 1978	November 1978
1,000	320	320	310	360	350	350	350

have seen, was a matter of some concern to ministers as soon as they became aware that the whole credit would not be available from the outset of the agreement. The Fund initially proposed that the first drawing should be only $0.5 billion with the remainder spread over two years at quarterly intervals. Following strenuous representations by the Chancellor to the Fund and to the Americans and Germans, the Managing Director relented on the initial drawing and agreed that it should be $1 billion with consequential adjustments for the size of subsequent drawings. At the very last minute, on 15 December, the Managing Director relented further and agreed that the initial drawing should be raised to SDR 1 billion—the equivalent of $1.15 million. This of course still presented the UK with the problem of finding additional finance to enable it to repay the Central Bank credit without showing a worrying depletion in the reserves, but at least it was a gesture. The agreed profile was then as shown in Table 5.4.

The next task for the negotiators was to specify the performance criteria which should be used to determine whether the UK was eligible to draw the instalments as they became available.

From the outset the Treasury had known that the test would be the observance of the intentions on the growth of DCE. This had, after all, been the test applied at the time of the 1968 drawing and had been regularly used by the Fund in stand-bys with member countries for some time. In the early stages of the negotiations some important technical issues regarding the definition of DCE and the manner of accommodating unevenness in its path over a prescribed period had been discussed, mainly with the Bank, and largely resolved. The definition of DCE need not perhaps detain us as the effect on the commitment was small, but the unevenness was a matter which took some time to be resolved. Historic observation of the growth pattern of DCE over any time period, for example a year, showed that it could be quite uneven. Seasonal factors could be allowed for but there were other extraneous influences which could cause unpredictable unevenness. The Fund acknowledged this and the discussions about how to accommodate it were purely technical and hardly presented a serious stumbling block. In the end it was agreed that, while the annual commitment to the growth to DCE for the two years, 1977–78, would be regarded as firm, the quarterly path could be given some flexibility by allowing a disproportionate level of growth for the first quarter of each year. The Fund insisted, however, that the commitment to containment of DCE should apply with immediate effect, not from the beginning of the year

1977–78. But they also agreed that the quarterly path should at the outset be defined only for the period until July 1977, with the proviso that the commitment for later periods should be the subject of discussion at the time of the next Article VIII Consultation in May 1977.

One aspect of the definition of DCE which was of considerable concern to the Fund was the effect of the Corset on the figures and it is necessary to look at this matter fairly closely. It will be recalled from Chapter 1 that the Corset, or to give it its proper title The Supplementary Special Deposits Scheme, required the banks to take active steps to discourage inflows to them of interest-bearing deposits since, if for a particular bank, these exceeded a defined level at a defined time the bank had to pay a penalty to the Bank of England. The scheme had operated from December 1973 until February 1975 when it was judged that it had served its purpose. Interest-bearing deposits which the banks would otherwise have acquired found their way into other non-bank interest bearing instruments such as Treasury Bills and Local Authority short-term debt so that bank credit (and money supply too, the other side of the banks' collective balance sheets) was constricted. In response to the reduced inflow of interest-bearing deposits, the banks tended to reduce their holdings of short-term market paper. To the extent that this was the effect, the result was to reduce the two monetary variables—DCE on the assets side of the collective balance sheets of the banks and £M3 on the liabilities side—without much effect on underlying economic conditions. Even the monetarists acknowledged this, although there was some dispute as to whether this was the sole effect. But for the Fund the availability of the Corset presented a possible escape hatch for the UK from the full rigour of the DCE discipline. The matter was brought to a head on 18 November, when, in order to ensure that the Chancellor's target for monetary growth in the current year (1976–77)—12 per cent—was hit, the Bank of England reintroduced the Corset. There was a good deal of discussion between the Fund on the one hand and the Treasury and the Bank on the other, which was finally resolved by the parties agreeing to moderate the agreed and conditional path for DCE in the first six months which was fixed at £4,500 million, slightly less than one half the estimate for the whole year—£9,300 million.[123]

If the discussion of the performance figures for DCE were relatively smooth, those for the PSBR were less so. It came as something of a surprise to the Treasury when, as the commitments and performance criteria were being discussed, the Fund said that they would want a similar discipline for the PSBR as that for DCE.[124] The Treasury felt that, as the DCE was regarded by the Fund as the controlling factor in the behaviour of the economy and quite properly should be regarded as the performance criterion for future drawings, it was unnecessary to have a second criterion which would have a similar control function. Furthermore the quarterly path of the PSBR, which the

---

[123] BP 122/24/01.   [124] Ibid.

Table 5.5 Projected PSBR October 1976 to March 1978[125]

	Limit (£ million)
Six months to end March 1977	5900
Three months to end June 1977	3100
Six months to end September 1977	5200
Nine months to end December 1977	7700
Twelve months to end March 1978	9200

Fund wanted to specify, was very difficult to predict for a variety of reasons. The Fund, having extracted a firm commitment from the Government for the PSBR for two financial years, were not prepared to abandon the incorporations of this variable into the performance criteria and the Treasury had to give way.

The agreed path of the PSBR for the period up to the end of the first financial year (31 March 1978) is shown in Table 5.5.

It will be seen from these figures—particularly the first and the last—that the Fund, while insisting that the PSBR should be a firm commitment, was allowing quite generously for margins of error, in particular by making the first quarterly figure for 1977–78 well over one-quarter of the full year figure and the first half well over one half of the full year figure. Although the negotiation of these figures was carried out by technical experts on the Treasury side, the Prime Minister had made it clear that he wanted to see whatever commitments were made to the Fund and the proposed performance criteria were duly cleared with No 10.[126]

The next issue was to decide on the degree of confidentiality of the commitments made on these two performance criteria. The Treasury and the Bank were concerned at the possible effect on confidence if the figures became public, particularly if the limits were exceeded and the UK became technically ineligible to make a further drawing on the stand-by. It was agreed that the commitments could be incorporated in a Memorandum of Understanding which would not be published, but would be made available to the Fund's Executive Board. Even this degree of restriction was thought by the Treasury to be inadequate, but they acquiesced. With hindsight the Treasury's preoccupation on this point seems somewhat excessive.

The public expenditure issues

The second issue upon which the Fund wanted to satisfy themselves was that of the expenditure programmes that were to be reduced to meet the commitment to reduce the fiscal deficit in the two years of the programme. They felt that the credibility and durability of the programme turned on the nature of the cuts and whether they might be eroded by subsequent political pressure or

[125] Memorandum of Understanding OF 122/24/01.   [126] BP 122/24/01.

public acceptability. As we saw earlier they had had a number of meetings with the Expenditure Division in the days following the first examination of the list of candidate programmes for cuts on 19 November, but, now that the Fund had settled for reductions a good deal less than those that were mooted at those meetings, it became possible to look at what the Treasury regarded as a feasible programme of adjustments. There was, however, one technical matter in the expenditure area which worried the Fund, that is the change in the treatment of nationalized industry spending. We have seen that a few months earlier Ministers had agreed that instead of counting all their investment as expenditure, only that part of it which was financed by loans or grants from the central government should be included. The Fund smelt a rat at this,[127] and they perceived, correctly, that the change would enable the Treasury to obtain a cut in the presentational figures of future expenditure by driving the industries into market borrowing. The Fund wanted to use the old definition but the Treasury were able to satisfy them about the desirability of making the change, which was simply to accommodate the commercial objectives of the industries themselves. The Fund did not press their objections since, although the change led to a presentational reduction in the published figures for future expenditure programmes, it had no effect on the total borrowing of the public sector, which was the variable the Fund was primarily concerned to reduce.

The Treasury's detailed proposals for cutting expenditure by £1 million in the first year with a follow-through of £1.5 billion in the second year were the subject of considerable discussion within the Treasury and, as we saw, they were scrutinized with the utmost care when they were put to the Cabinet on 6 and 7 December. They were spread over a multiplicity of programmes. There were two general reductions which were not specific to programmes. The first was a cut in the size of the civil service and the second was a reduction in the percentage (from 65.5 per cent to 61 per cent) of local authority current expenditure which the central government agreed to finance (the Rate Support Grant). For the rest the cuts were widely spread. Heavy reductions were made in capital expenditure from housing to investment in water supply. The construction industry, already in recession, was to feel the full severity of the industrial impact and went into severe decline (from which, as we shall see in the next chapter it had to be rescued by a government expenditure package in the course of 1977). Food subsidies were phased out and minor savings were made in the school meals programme. Overseas aid, which had been spared the cuts in July, made its contribution too. There were however two glaring omissions. As we reported, during the run up to the agreement the Chancellor, and to some extent the Prime Minister, thought that the social security programme should make a significant contribution. The Chancellor had seen the removal of the statutory entitlement of social security beneficiaries as a reasonable move at a

---

[127] GEP 9/29/02—26 November.

time of stringency. The savings which could have been achieved by this step (and the associated change for public service pensioners) could have been considerable—over £100 million in 1977–78 and over £300 million in the following year—but they were removed. The Cabinet decided at the meeting on 6 December that these moves were too politically sensitive and both were omitted from the final package, although in his statement on the outcome of the Fund negotiations on 15 December the Chancellor, in commenting on the exclusion of benefits from the cuts, said 'we are concerned about the narrowing gap between them (the beneficiaries) and the income of those in work.' The matter was, however, left on the political agenda and it was agreed by the Cabinet that there should be consultations with the TUC on the issue of the automatic uprating of the two categories of benefits.

The crisis resolved

The Chancellor made his statement to Parliament on 15 December and the following day the Fund staff submitted to the Executive Board[128] a full appraisal of the UK economy and of the measures contained in the Fund agreement. There was little in the staff report that had not been amply discussed in the negotiations and incorporated in the Letter of Intent and the Memorandum of Understanding,[129] which contained the performance criteria. The treatment of the exchange rate was suitably coy. It had for some time been the policy of the Managing Director not to discuss exchange rate issues in quantified terms with the Board on grounds of market sensitivity and there could, therefore, be no mention of the band of $1.60 to $1.65, staying within which the Chancellor had agreed was appropriate for the immediate future. The staff report repeated the general statement of intention regarding stability and the maintenance of the competitive position of the UK but that was as far as it went. There was a brief attempt by the Managing Director to strengthen the commitment of the Chancellor to make the undetermined £0.5 billion of fiscal measures in 1978–79 and the contingent £0.5–1 billion measures fall as much as possible on expenditure and not tax, but the Chancellor would go no further than to say that 'he would prefer to do as much as possible on public expenditure'.[130] This satisfied Witteveen.

The Executive Board discussed the UK application on 3 January. It was a low-key affair and the general tenor of the discussion was generous approval of the content of the UK programme, although there were one or two dissenting voices, from Directors who thought that the measures did not go far enough.

Before the Board discussion, arrangements had to be made for the activation of the General Arrangements to Borrow (the GAB). This was the facility provided

---

[128] IMF—EBS/76/519.   [129] OF 122/24/01.   [130] DW 062.

by the Group of Ten countries to augment the Fund's resources when especially large demands on them were being made by members. It had been established in the early 1960s and had been activated first to provide funds for the UK drawing in 1965. The Managing Director did not feel able to provide more than $0.5 billion of the stand-by from the Fund's own holdings of the currencies the UK was likely to require and there was therefore a need for the G10 to commit themselves to some $3 billion of extra funding should the UK draw on all the credit tranches for which it had applied. A meeting of the G10 was held in Paris on 21 December but its proceedings were largely a formality. On the previous day a meeting of Working Party Number 3 of the OECD (most of whose members were from the G10 and included the Central Banks) had given a warm welcome to the UK programme and to the application and it was virtually unthinkable that the mobilization of the GAB would be withheld.

The first drawing by the UK took place early in January in time to fortify the foreign exchange reserves which of course had been depleted by $1.5 billion on 7 December to repay the central bank credit. The effect on the foreign exchange markets of the conclusion of the British application and the announcement of the measures to reduce the public sector deficit and the growth of the monetary variables was extraordinarily favourable. The Bank of England was able to take in over $2 billion by selling sterling and the exchange rate rose to over $1.70. Consequently the figure published for the reserves for the end of December—$4 billion—was not a problem. The Bank felt able to reduce interest rates and MLR fell from 14.25 per cent at the beginning of the month to 12.25 per cent at the end. On the capital markets the Government, thanks to the efforts of the Bank of England, had no difficulty in raising a syndicated credit of $1.5 billion from a group of British, American, and German commercial banks. On 24 January the Chancellor felt able to announce that, in view of these developments, he did not now need to draw on the swap of $500 million with the US Treasury—which of course remained available as did the $350 facility with the Bundesbank.

Witteveen paid a visit to London at the end of January and had meetings with the Prime Minister, the Chancellor, and the Governor. The tenor of the meetings was mutually-congratulatory, as indeed it had every right to be. The only jarring note was that of the exchange rate, which then stood at over $1.70. The Prime Minister defended this state of affairs by pleading that 'we can hardly drive the rate down'.[131] Witteveen did not press matters, accepting, perhaps too readily for his staff, that 'it will fall'. In this his judgement was wrong. Sterling remained above $1.70 for the remainder of 1977 and indeed went above $1.80 in October and above $1.90 in December. But discussion of the aftermath of the Fund drawing is one of the subjects of the next chapter.

[131] DW 062.

6
Some Conclusions

The announcement of the agreement with the IMF led to a sharp improvement in market sentiment both towards sterling and towards the economic policies of the British Government. The pound appreciated several cents against the dollar, and there was a massive inflow of foreign currency to the reserves as the Bank of England 'creamed off' dollars to prevent the exchange rate from rising, or at least from rising significantly. Government stock, gilt-edged, was much in demand, from overseas as well as domestic investors, and the yield on medium- and long-dated stocks fell from a high of 16.5 per cent at the end of October 1976 to 13.5 per cent at the end of January 1977.

Nor were these developments temporary phenomena. Sterling remained above $1.70 throughout 1977, and for the first ten months the Bank of England had to intervene, at times heavily, to prevent the rate from rising, as indeed it was committed to under the agreement with the Fund on intervention policy. The official foreign exchange reserves which had fallen to £2,426 million (just over $4 billion) at the end of 1976 rose to £5,592 million at the end of the first quarter of 1977, to £6,727 million at the end of the second, to £9,826 million at the end of the third and to £10,715 million (over $20 million) at the end of the year. This was a great deal more than the mere unwinding of the reserves loss experienced in 1976. The official sterling balance holders, who had been massive sellers of sterling in 1976, did not in fact reconstitute their depleted sterling holdings. The Basle agreement on the sterling balances implicitly discouraged them from doing this, and some took advantage, to the tune of nearly £400 million, of the foreign currency bond option to exchange, in April 1977, their sterling balances for dollar and other foreign currency obligations of the British Government. The net demand for sterling arose for a variety of reasons and the buyers were all in the private sector.

The most important factor was that the current balance of payments improved much faster than almost everyone expected. The NIF of October 1976 had predicted that the improvement would not lead to the closing of the deficit until the middle of 1978, when North Sea Oil would be flowing in volume. In fact balance was achieved in the middle of 1977 and in the second half of the year a surplus of nearly £1 billion on current account was realized. Indeed in that period *visible* trade was in surplus—a phenomenon that was exceedingly rare in Britain's post-war experience. The capital account too performed extraordinarily well. Whereas capital outflows had exceeded £2,800 million in 1976, they were mirrored by inflows of over £4,800 million in 1977. Nearly one half of this was private investment in the public sector of which again about one half (£1 billion) was in gilt-edged stock. Some of the improvement on capital account came from the Government's own foreign currency borrowing, notably the Fund drawing and the $1.5 billion commercial bank loan negotiated in January, and the overseas borrowing by public sector bodies both under the exchange cover scheme and outside it. But a large element of the capital inflow was unsought, and represented a sharp change in the attitude of investors and speculators to the prospects of the British economy in general, and sterling in particular.

Almost all of these developments had begun to take place before any of the measures agreed with the Fund, notably the public expenditure cuts and the commitments to containment of the PSBR and of the growth of the monetary variables for 1977–78 and 1978–79, took effect. It must be inferred, therefore, that the market developments were due either to expectations that the commitments would be honoured or that the fact that the IMF had blessed the Government's economic programme gave it some sort of legitimacy which merited the support of overseas investors. No doubt both factors played an important part. But whichever it was, the turnaround in the behaviour of both the international and the domestic financial markets was essentially a matter of confidence, justified or not. In large measure, therefore, the events of 1977 bore out the views of those in the British Government—and certainly the Treasury—who had seen the problem of 1976, certainly the problem of late 1976, as primarily one of confidence, not a 'real' issue. As we shall see, the prospective behaviour of the PSBR, of the profile of public expenditure and of the monetary variables even before the implementation of the expenditure cuts of December 1976 ware all pretty well in line with what the Letter of Intent committed the Government to. In no sense could the economy in 1977 be said to be overheated, with exports constrained by an excess of domestic demand, with public expenditure out of control, and with monetary growth accelerating. In one respect only was 1977 worrying so far as the trend of the economy was concerned and this was in the field of inflation. We come to this in a moment. But first it is necessary to look at how, in 1977, in the British economy developed in terms of activity and output and the allocation of resources and how the development corresponded to what had been predicted—by the Fund and by the Treasury.

Visible exports improved well under the influence of a more competitive exchange rate although they were not greatly helped by a pause in the growth of world activity which occurred in 1977—export volumes were up about 9 per cent, whereas imports were virtually flat. But most other sectors of the economy were very sluggish. GDP rose by about 2 per cent but the only positive factors were exports and stockbuilding. Consumers' expenditure, clearly affected by the pay policy, which was still being respected, continued to decline and gross fixed investment was also lower in 1977 than 1976 (which in turn was lower than 1975). Unemployment, which at the beginning of 1977 was over 1.3 million, increased by nearly 100,000 during the year. None of these developments dented the confidence of the financial markets that the UK was now a good risk. Indeed, insofar as the markets looked at the financial indicators, the outlook was better than expected. The money supply (£M3) grew by about 9.5 per cent in 1977 (well below the rate predicted by the post-agreement forecast) and DCE, for which the growth limit for the financial year was £7.7 billion, grew by scarcely more than £1 billion in the calendar year. The cause of such a huge discrepancy between forecast and out-turn for this variable was of course the enormous inflow of overseas credit which obviated the need for domestic borrowers, particularly local authorities and the central government, to seek credit from the UK banks.

What is more, the public finances in 1977 turned out to be in much better shape than had been expected. The PSBR for 1976–77, which had been forecast to be nearly £12 billion, proved to be only about £8.5 billion. The improvement in the out-turn for public expenditure, compared with plans, began in 1975–76 and continued in the following year with the introduction of cash limits and a rigorous enforcement of the contingency reserve as a control mechanism. At out-turn prices, total public expenditure in 1976–77 was £55.5 billion, nearly 11 per cent more than the previous year, but in volume terms the total of programmes excluding debt interest was *less* than in 1975–76 by nearly 3.5 per cent. This fall admittedly owed much to a reduction in net government lending to the nationalized industries, as the latter borrowed heavily in foreign currency. Including debt interest, the fall in public expenditure was somewhat less. So far as 1977–78 was concerned the White Paper published immediately after the Fund agreement provided for a fall in expenditure compared with the previous year (due mainly to the cuts for that year agreed with the Fund) but the actual fall was greater because of another large shortfall in nationalized industry borrowing, and a saving in the refinancing of export and shipbuilding credit. Expenditure was in fact about 7 per cent— roughly £3 billion—below the plans incorporated in the January 1977 White Paper. The drop exceeded by a factor of two the cuts which had been agreed with the Fund.

The one area where there could be concern that the improvements taking place might be undermined was that of wage settlements. Stage 2 of the TUC's pay guidance was just as successful as stage 1 had been. There were no recorded departures by individual unions from the guidelines negotiated with the

Government in May 1976, and the one threat to it—the seamen's ballot of September—was contained. By the middle of 1977 the policy had achieved everything that its architects had planned for. There were, however, darkening clouds. The year-on-year increase in retail prices in July 1977 was 17.7 per cent compared with 12.9 per cent a year earlier, in spite of the unions' adherence to the guidelines. This acceleration was largely due to the rise in import costs as a result of the depreciation of sterling in the course of 1976. But it was also caused by the inflation of domestic food prices which followed the severe drought of the summer of 1976. This deterioration led the TUC to conclude that it could not, for a third year, give formal guidance to its constituent unions on the level of pay settlements to reach in the wage round beginning August 1977. The Government had to accept this and on 15 July the Chancellor made a statement to Parliament urging all concerned to settle their pay claims at a level which would ensure that national earnings as a whole would not exceed 10 per cent.

The wage round of 1977–78 began, therefore, with much less certainty than had been the case with the two previous rounds. The result, in terms of a deceleration in the level of settlements, was disappointing. The seeds were sown for the breakdown in the whole pay policy which eventually took place in the winter of 1978–79. But that lies outside the scope of this study.

As the year 1977 passed it became increasingly clear that, whatever might be the advantages of the Fund's blessing of the (amended) UK economic programme, the actual Fund drawing was superfluous and indeed the Treasury's anxiety during the negotiations about the adequacy of the initial drawing proved to have been groundless. The Government nevertheless took the second and third drawings in May and August respectively, but decided thereafter not to borrow further and began the process of repaying the drawings that had been made (as well as those under the 1975 Fund agreement). However, for confidence reasons the Chancellor decided to abide by the commitments made on the PSBR for 1978–79[1] and he reiterated these in both of his Budgets of 1977 and 1978.

But if the Government kept its undertakings on the PSBR and on the monetary variables for the two financial years covered by the agreement with the Fund, it certainly did not on the public expenditure cuts which had formed the basis of the negotiation and had engendered such political heat with the Cabinet. As 1977 progressed and the economy stagnated, the Government came to the conclusion that some measure of reflation was called for. As a first instalment substantial increases in child benefits were announced in May together with an extension of the free school meals scheme and extra spending on training. These were augmented in October with further help for

---

[1] The memorandum of understanding with the Fund laid down a commitment to a path for DCE only until July 1977.

the construction industry which had been in particular difficulty, thanks in no small measure to the way that the public expenditure cuts of 1976 had fallen on building and civil engineering programmes like housing and road construction. In 1977 as a whole the level of activity in this industry was stagnant—it was in fact nearly 20 per cent below that of five years earlier and the October measures gave it an extra £400 million worth of work in the immediate future. The combination of the May and October measures was to increase spending by £1 billion in the current year (1977–78) and £2.5 billion in the following year.

The extra expenditure for 1978–79 avoided breaching the limits set in the 1977 White Paper but only by the device of charging them to the contingency reserve for that year. This had been set at £1,025 million, but the new measures reduced this to a little under £200 million. This was patently too small to accommodate what were bound to be unexpected claims in due course, but it enabled Ministers to argue, if pressed, that they were not in breach of their determination to make the White Paper figures a ceiling and not just an aspiration.

It is not an unreasonable assertion, therefore, to state that the decisions taken in the course of 1977 were a virtual cancellation of the cuts of December 1976 and they were made without damage to the commitments on PSBR and the monetary variables. In the light of what had become apparent the measures to cut public expenditure must have seemed to be unnecessary except perhaps as totemic gestures to a market which was hypnotized by the assumed effect of public expenditure on economic efficiency and made anxious by the monetary outlook, as it then appeared. The most effective containment measures of public expenditure which took place in 1976 were three-fold:

1 the introduction of cash limits;
2 the making of the contingency reserve as a control mechanism;
3 the expenditure cuts of July 1976 and the making of the medium-term commitments in the White Paper of February 1976 a firm ceiling that was not to be breached in the 1976 PESC.

It is fair to say that the market could be excused for not having given credit—or at any rate much credit—to these factors. The Treasury and the Government did not lay very great claim to their effectiveness in containing expenditure and they certainly did not know how to convey to the outside world such a degree of confidence as they had that expenditure was under firm control. In the negotiations of November–December 1976 the Expenditure Division sought to persuade the Fund team that the administrative measures taken in the course of that year would lead to significant improvement in the out-turn of spending plans. But they were plainly not successful and the Fund—the Managing Director in particular who made an impassioned case for cuts of

£1.5 billion in 1977–78 on the occasion of his 'crisis' visit to London on 1 December—clearly thought that without the cuts they were seeking the achievement of their targets for the PSBR and DCE would not be possible. The Treasury did little to disabuse them of this view. Indeed the NIF and the associated financial forecast of October 1976, as well as the post-agreement forecast, described in the previous chapter, both implied that the targets the Fund were seeking to impose could not be achieved without a fiscal adjustment of the size eventually agreed. The Fund can hardly be blamed for having made their demands (given their objectives) when the Treasury did not see any element of 'overkill' such as was, in the event, incorporated in the programme.

Whether, if the parties had appreciated and accepted that the administrative changes made to the system of expenditure control would lead to a situation where the Fund's targets for public borrowing and DCE growth would be met without any fiscal adjustment for either of the two years in question, the Fund could have granted the stand-by broadly on the basis of existing policies must however be doubted. If the NIF forecast in October had not been so pessimistic about the level of the PSBR in 1977–78 and had, for illustration, shown the same figure as the July NIF (£9 billion)—or perhaps even less with a more confident assumption about the success of the Treasury's control measures—there must be considerable doubt whether the Fund would have found the programme one it could support with financial assistance running to the whole of the UK's quota. The Fund team in Manila had already argued for a fiscal adjustment even though at that stage the forecast PSBR for 1977–78 was only £9 billion and this could have been achieved by the largely cosmetic cut of £0.5 billion achieved by the sale of the BP shares. Moreover, when they presented their proposals for a fiscal adjustment in their memorandum of 21 November (which involved a PSBR of £7.5 billion for 1977–78 and of £6.5 billion for 1978–79) these would have involved some retrenchment, even with the more realistic and acceptable profile of public borrowing which subsequent events would have justified. The fact that the Fund scaled back their demands for the profile of the PSBR for the two years from their original proposal does not mean that they would eventually have accepted an unamended fiscal programme as an acceptable outcome of the bargaining process. It is difficult to see how they could have sold such an outcome to their own Board even if they had been convinced. The Americans, and to a lesser extent the Germans, had come to the firm conclusion that some reduction in public borrowing and public expenditure was necessary, even though neither of them had the detailed knowledge of the British situation which would have justified such a firm view. Moreover the market would almost have certainly have been unimpressed with an outcome to the British application which largely confirmed existing policies, even with the Fund's *imprimatur*. Most of those engaged in the events of 1976, certainly including the author of this study, would not have expected the market to be satisfied with the *status quo*, even backed up with firm commitments on the level of public borrowing and the growth of the monetary variables, however rational in terms of formal economic analysis this might have been. Some symbolic gesture had to be made and the only one the market wanted was that of sizeable expenditure cuts.

It was not only in the field of public expenditure where, under pressure of events, the Government departed from the line agreed with the Fund. The reversal of the public expenditure cuts could perhaps be defended on the grounds that the ultimate objectives of the Fund, notably the level of public borrowing and the growth of domestic credit, were being respected. But the Government was in much more serious breach of its stated intentions in the field of the exchange rate. At his meeting with the Fund mission on 10 December 1976 the Chancellor had agreed that a necessary condition for improving the growth of exports to which the Fund attached so much importance was an exchange rate which maintained the UK's competitiveness and had added that a rate in the region of $1.60–1.65 was appropriate. He said he thought that it would be 'inappropriate for the rate to appreciate'. None of this was a formal commitment, but it was the statement of an intention to which the Fund attached the highest importance. A competitive exchange rate was as integral to their prescription for the British economy as was fiscal discipline.

The exchange rate in fact never fell within the 'target' range $1.60–$1.65 throughout 1977 and by early 1978 it was over $1.90. At the end of October 1977 the Bank, with the approval of the Prime Minister and the Chancellor, gave up the effort to cap the rate at about $1.75. They were becoming increasingly worried about the expansion of the money supply which they thought was threatened by the huge inflow and which they believed would go into bank deposits of one form or another. The justification for this view and the merits of the decision to uncap the rate lie outside the scope of this study. It suffices here to say that the events of late 1977 in the foreign exchange market led to some undermining of the Fund's programme, and indeed of the Treasury's own strategy of promoting growth through an improvement in the trade balance. At the time of the Article VIII consultations with the Fund in November 1977 Whittome told the Treasury that he was 'deeply worried about the loss of competitiveness'[2] as indeed was the Treasury itself at the time.

Given that, by late 1977, it was clear that the UK was not likely to draw the remainder of the stand-by—and indeed that it would probably be repaying before very long the three drawings made—the question of whether it was in default of any fundamental part of the agreement is perhaps academic. A creditor is primarily concerned with the ability of his debtor to repay the debt, not with strict observance of the conditions of the credit. The Fund was scarcely in any doubt about the security of its loan; it could moreover

---

[2] IM 38/268/06, 29 November 1977.

look on the UK as having turned its economy round to its own satisfaction whether or not the precise terms of the agreement were observed.

But whether the terms of the agreement were met to the letter, it has to be asked whether the intellectual position taken up by the Fund during the negotiations was confirmed by subsequent developments. Any *post hoc* appraisal of whether what actually happened in any circumstances was as predicted is open to a number of objections, not least that extraneous circumstances affecting the outcome may well have differed significantly from what it had been reasonable to expect beforehand. Nevertheless it is instructive to examine the propositions the Fund made during the negotiations about the likely course of the UK economy if its prescriptions were accepted and what actually occurred, for the Fund made much of the beneficial effects of their remedy, not just on external confidence (about which there can be no dispute), but on British economic performance (about which there can).

In their seminal document of 21 November, in which they set out their objectives for the two-year programme, the Fund started from the proposition that there should be a target for the growth of DCE of £5 billion in 1978–79 representing a decline from what was then expected of £10.1 billion in 1976–77, with £6.7 billion for the intermediate year. (We re-examine later why the Fund began their calculations, and indeed their prescription, with DCE rather than some other objective of policy.) The target of £5 billion was argued to be achievable only with a PSBR for that year (1978–79) of £6.5 billion. These targets were associated with an exchange rate objective of at least maintaining competitiveness. On that basis the Fund argued that economic growth would rise from about 1.5 per cent in 1977 to 4 per cent in 1978. The mainsprings of growth would be net exports and industrial investment, which they expected to rise strongly as credit for the private sector became readily available following the reduced credit demands of the public sector.

What eventuated after the agreement of December 1976 hardly bore out these prognostications, as indeed the Treasury expected and argued at the time. It is true that the measures finally agreed with the Fund, and the targets for both DCE growth and the PSBR, were a good deal less demanding than those set out in the Fund's memorandum. But it is not unfair to say that had the full programme of the Fund been adopted (with expenditure cuts in 1978–79 very much greater than those eventually agreed) the lack-lustre performance of the economy would have been worse. It also has to be granted that the Fund's *desideratum* of a competitive exchange rate was not satisfied either. So on two grounds it could be held that the events that followed the agreement would have been different had the UK adopted the full programme proposed by the Fund.

But even if full allowance is made for these 'counterfactual' differences, the Fund's confidence in their programme as a prescription for renewed economic growth was hardly borne out in any area. Economic growth in 1977 was under

2 per cent and in 1978 it was about 3 per cent. The Fund's confidence, which they expressed in the conditional clause in the stand-by about further fiscal action being taken in 1978 if the outlook for growth in the two years 1978 and 1979 exceeded 3.5 per cent per annum, proved to be significantly misplaced. The annual rate of growth over this period turned out to be 1.95 per cent. Indeed in the three years from the end of 1976, when the agreement was reached, to the end of 1979 the economy grew by only 6.5 per cent—an annual rate of 2.1 per cent—and this was partly under the influence of stimulatory measures taken in 1977 and in the Budget of 1978. It is, to put it no higher, difficult to find in the events of the two or three years following the Fund agreement much evidence for the underlying improvement in the UK's economic performance which the Fund were confident would take place. The areas of success were in establishing control of public expenditure, of convincing the markets that the monetary variables were growing only moderately, and of the balance of payments on current account. The latter was largely due to the flow of North Sea Oil from 1978 onwards, but the sluggishness of home demand also helped. Exports were not, however, helped by the erosion of competitiveness caused by the uncapping of sterling in 1977 and by the rise in wage costs after the ending of the TUC's commitment to specific wage targets in July of that year. By 1979, excluding trade in oil, the account in goods and services with the rest of the world was again in deficit. The anxieties which the Treasury had expressed in February 1976 about the employment consequences of failing to maintain a competitive exchange rate were being realized in full and they continued to be a source of concern in the early 1980s for the Conservative government which took office in May 1979.

The other area of disappointment following the Fund agreement was in the field of wages. It was perhaps inevitable that following two successful years of pay restraint, which involved substantial falls in 'real' income for wage earners, there should have been something of a reaction. The TUC, although sceptical about some of the arguments for the fiscal adjustment incorporated in the Fund agreement, remained supportive of the government's economic policy and did not themselves do anything to undermine the government's wage policy. But some of the constituent unions did not feel able to resist shop-floor pressure for larger wage increases and industrial action to secure these became frequent in the course of 1978 and led inexorably to the industrial unrest of the winter of 1978–79.

If, as has been argued above, the Fund's expectation of the effects of 'their' programme were not realized, what grounds had they for supposing that the effects would be as beneficial as they argued? A full answer to this question can only be given by the Fund itself, but there are keys to the Fund's thinking in the research work they conducted—and published—over a long period about their approach to the balance of payments corrective measures they pressed on member countries in payments difficulties. At the heart of this approach was the desire to devise some system of universal applicability given the need for the institution to be even-handed in its dealings with member countries. A second need was for simplicity for, as the Fund publications show, a system was needed which could be operated in 'the field' by Fund missions with slender resources to hand for conducting simulations of possible measures.

In the early days of the Fund's operations the main applicants were low- to medium-income countries, many of them in Latin America, with rudimentary systems of national accounts. It was virtually impossible for them, or for the Fund in conducting a review of their economic performance, to carry out a full national income appraisal with simulations of possible economic policy changes, for the requisite statistics were not available. The one area where statistics were available and were reasonably reliable was in banking. The banks could say how much credit they made available to residents and they could say how much foreign exchange was taken in or owed to non-residents. The Fund decided as early as the 1950s to devise a model which used banking statistics as the basis for policy prescriptions. At the same time they developed a theory of balance of payments adjustment which they entitled 'The Monetary Approach to the Balance of Payments'. Over the years this theory was refined and endorsed not only by the Fund staff, but also by academic economists, notably those at the University of Chicago. In the mid-1970s a respectable literature had developed. It is probably fair to say however that as an approach to balance of payments adjustment it had few supporters in national governments or in international institutions such as the OECD.

The essence of the approach was to regard the balance of payments, by which was variously meant the current balance and the total balance (current and long-term capital), as determined by the *absorption* by the country concerned of goods and services, that is the excess of goods and services consumed over the same net quantity of items produced. This net absorption factor was, as an accounting identity, exactly equal to the net bank credit created for the domestic sector. Thus, putting the theory very simply, the key to any correction of the balance of payments lay in containing the creation of domestic credit (DCE). In this way was born the preoccupation of the Fund with DCE growth whenever a member country was in balance of payments difficulties and needed to have access to the Fund's resources. The next step in the conventional Fund approach was to regard the fiscal balance as the main way of reducing DCE growth (and if need be for allowing the private sector access to bank credit which otherwise it would be denied). Moreover, in most of the low- to medium-income countries to which this approach was applied, any increment to the fiscal deficit had to be met by the banks, given the absence of a developed market in government securities. Hence a change in the fiscal balance had an immediate and consequential effect on the growth of DCE.

It was this simple model which led the Fund to see the fiscal deficit as having an almost 1:1 relationship with the balance of payments.

So much for the intellectual foundations for the Fund's approach and in particular its approach to the UK's problem in 1976. There were a number of objections to it, although none of these were explored during the negotiations, perhaps because they were considered too academic at a time when immediate and practical solutions were wanted. The first was that the UK was far from the sort of economy that was amenable to the Fund's appraisal. The Fund staff's concern that the Corset could 'distort' the figures for bank credit expansion showed some recognition of this. The UK was an open economy with many sources of credit besides the domestic banking system. It was also the case that the financing of the fiscal deficit could variously be achieved by selling debt to the non-bank sector, by borrowing abroad or by bank borrowing in one form or another. The 'mix' of financing varied considerably often for reasons which were difficult to explain *ex ante* and the Government had little control of the 'mix'. Broadly, therefore, any level of DCE growth was consistent with a variety of fiscal deficits; and to argue, as the Fund did in effect, that their objective of a particular figure for DCE implied a unique PSBR was intellectually flawed as indeed the Treasury argued at the time. Subsequent events bore this out. DCE growth was reduced to about £1 billion in 1977 when the fiscal deficit was many times larger. The plain fact was that there was a vast increase in overseas credit and a considerable fall in the public sector's need for bank finance at home. The benefits to DCE were due almost entirely to confidence factors, not to underlying domestic monetary conditions.

But if the Fund's 'monetary' approach to the UK problem was inappropriate, the Treasury cannot claim that its own forecasting and simulatory methods were all that much better. The October NIF was a particularly bad one in terms of appraising the way the economy was going. This is not to criticize the model nor those who made the forecast. The whole exercise was artificial in the sense that without a return of confidence in the overseas, and to some extent in the domestic, financial markets it was inherently implausible that the overall balance of payments deficit could be financed and hence that the exchange rate would behave in the rather formal way that, treated as an exogenous variable, was implied. The financial forecast made at the same time suffered from similar shortcomings and so the predictions for the growth of the monetary variables were unreliable. But even without these problems the forecast was faulty. It drew too heavily on the poor immediate response of the balance of payments to what was happening to the exchange rate and of course it got the fiscal deficit for the current year (1976–77) badly wrong—partly because the Treasury were taken by surprise at the success of cash limits in controlling expenditure. It is perhaps idle to speculate what might have happened if the forecast had been more accurate, particularly in the field of the PSBR.

In his own memoir the Chancellor argues that, if the forecast had been more accurate, there would have been no need to seek the Fund's assistance. This is doubtful. There was a huge external financing requirement revealed in the appraisal made in September 1976 and in any case market confidence still remained a problem. It was on the basis of the Treasury appraisal of the need for more external finance than conventional funding could provide that the Chancellor and his Cabinet colleagues decided in September to apply for a Fund drawing. This was a month before the October forecast, with its pessimistic and flawed prediction for the PSBR, was delivered. Such confidence as did return in October was inspired, no doubt, more by the news that the Fund would be giving their verdict on the economy than by any reappraisal of the adequacy, in the market's view, of British economic policy. It is perhaps the case that if the forecast had been more accurate the Fund would have been satisfied with a rather smaller package of expenditure cuts. But the Fund—and the Managing Director in particular—clearly regarded something in the region of £1–1.5 billion of cuts for 1977–78 as an irreducible minimum, and it is difficult to conceive of their having settled for something less. The US Treasury and Federal Reserve also had their own views, justified or not, on what needed to be done on the fiscal front and these were more or less independent of the forecast. It is not unreasonable to argue therefore that although the forecast was a poor one the difference it made to the outcome was negligible.

But the Treasury has other questions to answer, not just about how it handled the crisis of 1976 including the negotiations with the Fund, but, over a longer period, about how it sought to re-establish stability in the economy after the assumption of office of the new Government in 1974. A full charge-sheet against the Treasury would perhaps be a rather long one, and the list posed in this chapter is to some extent arbitrary, reflecting, as it inevitably does, the biases, the prejudices and the intellectual baggage of the author. As an excursion of self-criticism it suffers from the drawbacks of all self-criticism. Other observers, and indeed participants of the events of that time, would have a different scale of values and objectives; and their questions and their criticism would be different. But perhaps there would be reasonable unanimity that as a minimum the objective historian, if there is such a being, would focus on a small number of critical issues, where there was a choice and where it is far from obvious that the right choice was made. The questions we seek to address in this chapter are summarily the following, taken very broadly in time-sequential order:

- *The Treasury's position in 1974*
  Was the Treasury's posture in 1974 towards the incoming Government's economic policies a defensible one, given the nature of the emerging crisis and the palpable inadequacy of those policies to deal with it?

- *The Treasury's remedies in 1975*
  Once the Treasury had embarked, in early 1975, on a course of persuading the Government to change its declared policies, did it do so in a sufficiently vigorous and determined manner, and were the changes recommended the 'right' ones?

- *The Treasury and public expenditure*
  Were the Treasury's attempts to improve the effectiveness of expenditure control adequate and timely, and were its efforts to bring the projected path of expenditure down and realistically in line with likely growth of the economy after the rapid rise in 1974 adequate and appropriate?

- *The Treasury's position on the exchange rate*
  Was the Treasury's preferred option, throughout the period covered by this study, of seeking a depreciation in the 'real' exchange rate to restore equilibrium in the balance of payments both necessary and achievable?

- *The Treasury and the sterling crisis*
  Once the financial crisis had broken in early 1976, were the Treasury's responses the 'right' ones, in the sense that they were conducive at one and the same time to the stabilizing of the situation without inflicting too much damage to the Government's medium-term objectives?

- *The Treasury and the official sterling balances*
  Did the Treasury adequately foresee the vulnerability of sterling to the decisions of the official holders to sell their holdings when sterling came under pressure? Could anything have been done before the crisis broke to neutralize these balances?

- *The Treasury and the fund negotiations*
  Were the Treasury tactics during the Fund negotiations of leaving the running to the Fund and seeking to minimize the policy changes, in particular the expenditure cuts the Fund were seeking to secure, best suited to the situation?

The Treasury's Position in 1974

The first General Election of 1974 was fought on the issue of getting Britain back to full-time work after the three-day week and founding economic policy on the Social Contract which had been agreed a year earlier between the Labour Party and the TUC. The new Government had committed itself to the repeal of the statutory incomes (but not the statutory prices) policy introduced in the Autumn of 1972 and its replacement by a voluntary policy whereby the unions affiliated to the TUC would seek in their pay negotiations only to maintain living standards, not to improve them. It had also committed itself, as part of the Social Contract, to some substantial improvements in publicly provided services and subsidies at considerable cost to the public purse.

Whatever reservations the Treasury may have had about the 'appropriateness' of those policies in the domestic and international environment developing in 1974, it did nothing to dissuade Ministers from following them. The documentary evidence of the time does not suggest that the Treasury was seriously worried—at any rate immediately. The public expenditure increases introduced in the March budget were sharply at variance with the programme of cuts which the Treasury had pressed on the previous Government in December 1973, but these were in part a response to the miners' industrial action and the latter had been called off in March 1974 on the assumption of office by the Labour Party. The UK economy was already slowing down, and in any case the expenditure increases in the Budget were matched by income tax increases, and the totality of the action was presented as a broadly neutral measure— indeed in financial terms it saw a fall in public sector borrowing. The agreement with the TUC concerning pay claims was not inherently an inflationary measure. If it had been strictly carried out, and pay deals had been made throughout the economy which ensured that earnings only matched price increases, there would have been something of a slow deceleration in inflation, particularly as, by early 1974, the worst of the price increases of imports, notably oil but also to some extent other raw materials, was past. The deceleration would probably have been less than that achieved by the UK's main overseas competitors, who were deflating sharply in order to curb wage increases, but it would not have led to the wide divergence between the UK's price performance and that of others which eventually emerged.

But whether the Treasury expected this to be the consequence of the Social Contract or not, it is clear that officials did not think that it lay within their constitutional duty or power to recommend Ministers to default on the undertakings they gave to the electorate in the course of the first 1974 Election campaign. The question this attitude invites is of course a very big one, and there can be differing views about the 'right' answer. One particular Ministerial participant[3] in the events of 1974 believes that the Treasury was in default that year of its duty to advise Ministers what was 'right' by not urging them to be more deflationary and more interventionist in the wage arena. This is a legitimate point of view, but it was not one shared at official level in Whitehall. Indeed, as our narrative has brought out, the consensual view among permanent secretaries even in the Autumn of 1974, when the letter of the Social

---

[3] Dell.

Contract was plainly not being respected, was that it would at that time have been pointless to press on Ministers an alternative pay policy.

A chance did present itself to the Treasury to consider a more restrictive policy when Ministers decided to introduce a mini-Budget in July 1974; but the explicit purpose of that measure was to use expenditure subsidies and a reduction in VAT to reduce prices with the aim of getting the unions to moderate their pay claims (as should have been the case under the Social Contract). Moreover it is evident that in the minds of some ministers the measure was a precursor to the General Election which was generally expected to be called later in the year to resolve the deadlock in the House of Commons, where no party had an overall majority. Both the Treasury and the Bank urged Ministers to be moderate in the actions they were proposing to take, but that was about as far as they deemed it possible to go. Again a case can be made that the Treasury should have been more robust in its attitude by, for instance, arguing against the cut in VAT on the grounds that it probably would not have much effect in moderating wage demands and would create in the minds of overseas commentators the impression that the UK was not serious about reducing the pressure of demand as a means to combat inflation. This point was made to the Chancellor, but perhaps not forcibly enough and to little effect. It is hard to see that a much stronger message from the Treasury and the Bank would have resulted in a different outcome, given the importance of the political factor, which must have been uppermost in Ministers' minds. In the event a second General Election was called in September and was held in early October. This was perhaps the moment when the Treasury should have come out of its corner and proposed a restrictive budget. It was plainly out of the question to contemplate any economic action until the Election had been held, but when this was out of the way, and the Labour Party had secured a narrow overall majority might this not have been the occasion to propose a change of course? After all the Chancellor had committed himself to a second Budget in his first days in office in order to bring to the Statute Book the structural tax reforms (notably a Capital Transfer Tax) his party had committed itself to in its Manifesto of February 1974. It is evident from the papers of the time that the Chancellor did not see the Budget as a conjunctural measure and there was little in it (apart from the increase in fuel duties and the help to companies' finance) which was specifically aimed at the current economic situation. The Treasury certainly made a very full submission about the various aspects of the economy which it thought the Budget should address. But there was not much in this which smacked of retrenchment. As the autumn passed the Treasury did become more worried about the economic situation—the narrative has shown how the rather permissive line taken in September had hardened by late October. But at no point in the run-up to the budget of 12 November did the Treasury express the anxieties which surfaced in December. In part this was because there was, in fact, a quite serious deterioration in the economic outlook in the last two months of the year. December saw a very sharp decline in overseas confidence, which thoroughly alarmed both the Bank and the Treasury. But even without this, it would have been perfectly possible for officials to have seized the occasion of a budget to press for a more restrictive fiscal policy. This would, however, have presented quite serious difficulties. By October the PESC round had almost been completed and it would have been virtually impossible within the allotted timetable to have gone back to Ministers, who had spent an agonizing six months on the Survey, and told them that a completely new approach was required, involving expenditure cuts in the November Budget. Any fiscal action in November would have had to be in the field of taxation and would have to have been justified on the grounds that the PSBR was running ahead of the March forecast. This would have been a perfectly reasonable justification, but the Chancellor would have had to explain to the House of Commons why he was raising taxation in November after having given no inkling of this intention in the Election campaign of only one month previously. Although the thought was unspoken, Treasury officials were well aware of the impossibility this factor posed of using the November Budget for a significant shift in policy.

And so it came about that the first attempt to change the direction of government policy did not take place until the memorandum of 19 December, which perhaps marked the beginning of a new approach to macro-economic policy. Nine months had passed without any very determined effort to change course. A great deal of damage had been done in the pay field by the irresponsibility of the trade unions in their observance of the terms of the Social Contract. And a great deal of damage had also been done to the cause of containing public expenditure as the increases provided in the March Budget were augmented by other measures introduced during the year. But at least the tone and content of the December memorandum provided the basis for a new approach in the New Year and this indeed occurred. A lot of valuable time had however been lost.

There is another respect in which the Treasury can be faulted for its stance in 1974 and this relates to the conduct of the PESC round, but this is something better discussed below when the whole approach to public expenditure is examined.

The Treasury's remedies in 1975

The starting point of a review of the position and stance of the Treasury in 1975 has to be the memorandum of December 1974, for that laid out the main heads of policy it thought the Government should adopt. It had three main elements:

1 An attempt should be made to break into the wage/price spiral by laying down a norm for pay increases.
2 There should be a deflation of domestic demand as a means of reducing the large balance of payments deficit.
3 There should be a re-examination of the medium-term target for the growth of public expenditure.

The memorandum did not raise again the question of whether the exchange rate needed to be adjusted as part of the programme of reducing the external deficit. That issue had been inconclusively examined in the middle and later part of 1974 and it was not brought back into the policy debate until the end of 1975. Much of 1975 was taken up with discussion of more direct ways of reducing imports and promoting exports and, although none of these was favoured by the Treasury, their examination tended to drive out further discussion of a more 'interventionist' exchange rate policy to reduce the deficit.

The issue of inflation was by far the most urgent of the problems faced. Both wage and price rises accelerated sharply in the first half of 1975 and it became abundantly clear that the Government's policy of leaving the unions free to interpret the Social Contract as they wished was a failure. Ministers did seek to persuade the TUC to be more assertive with the constituent unions in observing the spirit of the concordat and they did try, by public speeches, to condition public opinion to the need for pay restraint. But the focus of collective ministerial attention in the early part of 1975 was either on a policy of influencing prices through subsidies and indirect tax cuts or by adopting some form of tax-based Incomes Policy, for example of taxing individual excessive pay increases.

The Treasury had little sympathy with either of these approaches. In the many submissions made to the Chancellor in the course of the spring of 1975 the choices identified were, in effect, either an Incomes Policy, statutory or otherwise, with a norm laid down by the government, or substantial deflation. Some strengthening of the existing policy of leaving implementation of the Social Contract to the TUC was examined, in effect only to be dismissed as likely to be ineffectual.

The examination of a substantial deflation of demand was also somewhat perfunctory. The prevailing view of officials, not only in the Treasury but in Whitehall generally, was that the Phillips curve was a non-existent figment of the imagination of some academic economists. At best it was a horizontal straight line. The concept of a 'non-accelerating inflation rate of unemployment' had not by then gained any adherents either inside or outside the Treasury. If, perhaps, inflation might be reduced by a general slackening of demand, it was at best conceded that this would take a very long time and would require very substantial unemployment and reduced economic activity.

This left the Treasury with only an Incomes Policy as the way out—the position it had taken with every acceleration of inflation since the early 1960s.

The narrative of the preceding chapters has shown that, although the Treasury had only limited success for some time in persuading Ministers of the need for a government-administered Incomes Policy, eventually, at the end of June, largely as a result of a spectacular attack on sterling in the exchange markets, the Chancellor, if not all his colleagues, did accept that there was no alternative to an immediate statutory policy. But of course there was an alternative, as the Cabinet—and the Prime Minister in particular—were able to demonstrate by reaching an understanding with senior trade unionists at the very moment that a formal Incomes Policy was being pressed on his colleagues by the Chancellor. It was perhaps something of a 'shotgun' understanding but it was an understanding nonetheless, and as such it was a spectacular triumph of the political over the administrative sides of government. It led to the most astonishing success in the containment of inflation over a period of two years—something that a statutory policy might well not have achieved. The Treasury had never envisaged that a political deal of the sort concluded informally between Ministers and the TUC could be effective and had only half-heartedly suggested such a route as a way of reducing inflation. The success of the deal clearly lay in the way that Ministers were able to deploy the argument, which the TUC accepted, that a failure to implement an effective Incomes Policy of their own, would lead to a government-administered one or to massive deflation. Officials simply did not believe that the argument would carry conviction—a TUC administered policy would be ineffective, as the Social Contract policy up to June 1975 had been ineffective.

Perhaps officials had every reason for their scepticism. A voluntary Incomes Policy had been tried in 1964 and 1965 with the advent of a previous Labour Government and had been quite unsuccessful, requiring its replacement by more formal, government-administered rules. It was simply assumed that the authority of the TUC over its constituent unions was too weak to enforce what was bound to be a stringent policy. But officials were wrong—and the politicians were right. The Treasury cannot escape the verdict that it was too confident of its own appraisal of the possibilities.

Whether a formal and unilateral government-based (and statutorily backed) policy would have been as effective as the TUC based policy was, at least for two years and indeed in some senses for even longer, cannot be assessed. The Conservative government's policy of 1972 was effective for little over one year and led to a disastrous breakdown. Treasury officials themselves did not expect the policy to have a long life and a good deal of attention was paid in the early months of 1975 to the problem of 're-entry', that is the resumption of normal wage bargaining after the expiry of the proposed statutory policy. It is difficult to avoid the conclusion that the agreement Ministers reached with the TUC following the Cabinet of 1 July was greatly to be preferred to the Treasury's solution.

But if the Treasury 'got it wrong' in judging how effective a voluntary wage policy could be, how right was it in the recommendations it made for macroeconomic policy generally in 1975? The narrative has shown that in the early months of the year it was convinced that a substantial measure of deflation was called for and it recommended very strong fiscal action in the Budget of that year. The motive for this move, in sharp contrast to the conventional post-war approach of seeking to balance aggregate demand to aggregate supply potential, was three-fold. First was the confidence factor. The UK was, at the time, heavily dependent on foreign finance to cover its massive external deficit and a move of fiscal prudence was judged to be essential to reassure external opinion. Secondly the fiscal deficit had reached very large proportions and there was a fear, perhaps not very clearly articulated, that the financing of it could lead to an explosion of the money supply with possible consequences for prices, including asset prices. Thirdly some slackening of demand would help to curb the alarming rate of growth of pay claims, and also reduce the import bill, thereby reducing the external deficit.

Of these arguments, the first and third were the most important in the Treasury's view, although opinion in the department was not unanimous. The economists tended to be sceptical about the efficacy of deflation in conditions of already weak demand except possibly in improving the external balance. On the other side, OF Division, conscious of overseas opinion and the need for the UK to be seen to be prudent, were strong supporters of a restrictive Budget.

In the event the restrictive Budget seems to have been amply justified. The external balance improved substantially and once the pay policy had been put in place at the beginning of July, overseas opinion seemed to be greatly reassured and sterling stabilized. The exchange rate moved from $2.38 in January to $2.03 at the end of the year—a much smaller fall than was justified on the basis of comparative costs. When the UK came to apply for a Fund drawing at the end of the year, the Fund staff were critical about the future of the fiscal deficit, the growth of public expenditure and the strength of the exchange rate. But there was little concern about the pressure of demand as such. Indeed the Fund's anxieties were not so different from those of the Treasury itself, which was seeking strongly to improve the methods of controlling expenditure and in reducing its rate of growth over the PESC period.

No doubt the 1975 Budget could have been more restrictive. The original Treasury recommendation was for a reduction in the fiscal deficit in 1975–76 of £2 billion. But this figure was not translated into specific tax and expenditure recommendations. Had it been done so, it would have been seen to have involved huge tax increases and/or big cuts of a crisis nature in expenditure programmes. The Chancellor did achieve very big reductions in the programmes for 1976–77 with some, but not too much, opposition from his Cabinet colleagues, and it is tempting to think that he could have obtained more if he had been more ambitious. But he was not himself persuaded that more needed to be done than in fact he did; and it is the case that when he did canvass the idea of big cuts in June—to meet a situation when pay claims were getting out of control—he met with fierce opposition from his colleagues.

What has to be asked seems to be not whether the Treasury's macro-economic position in 1975 was defensible but whether it had a credible plan that year for getting the economy back into some sort of balance in the medium term, that is by the later years of the decade and that question takes us immediately to the issue of the profile of public expenditure, to the systemic methods of keeping it under control and how realistic were its proposals for getting the external payments situation into balance.

The Treasury and public expenditure

The Treasury received a lot of criticism from outsiders in the period 1974–76 about its failure to control public expenditure and to produce the cuts, particularly in 1976, that opinion generally thought were necessary to restore equilibrium. We deal with the specific criticism of the 'inadequacy' of the cuts made in 1976 in the section dealing with that episode. Here we are concerned with the system and how it operated in the whole three-year period and whether the Treasury was sufficiently robust in its advocacy of less public expenditure.

There can be little quarrel with the proposition that the system of expenditure control which was in operation at the beginning of the 1970s was ill-suited to handle the problems which rapidly escalating inflation brought about. The Plowden approach of planning expenditure over a four-year time horizon in purely volume (i.e. resource) terms might have been workable in a situation of reasonably stable prices, but when pay and prices began to escalate—and escalate at differential rates—the volume approach made *financial* control almost unworkable. It made the financial requirements of departments extremely difficult to calculate, and *a fortiori* it made central forecasting of the financial variables by the Treasury economists virtually impossible. It also made the business of audit hopelessly complex, if not indeed unworkable. It was possible for the Treasury to make a judgement, based on what departments were able to tell it, about whether the volume of spending approved had broadly been carried out. But as there was very little, except for those programmes covered by Parliamentary Estimates, laid down about the cash provision required, it was almost impossible to determine *ex post* for much of public expenditure whether there had been an over-spend in a particular programme.

The weaknesses of the system, certainly in the inflationary environment of the 1970s, were not lost on the Treasury, and, if they had been, Professor Godley made sure that they were brought to light. His particular criticisms and proposals, in particular that there should be cash planning over the full PESC period, did not find much favour with his former colleagues, although there was grudging acceptance that his general thesis was valid.

The Treasury saw the failings of the system as having four components:

1 There needed to be some sort of cash description of the programmes which departments obtained, at any rate in the first year of the period covered.
2 The problem of dealing with expenditure claims which arose during the course of the cycle, in particular in the first year, needed to be addressed by making the contingency reserve an effective instrument of control.
3 There needed to be an improved reporting system of what departments had actually spent. In the early days of the period we have studied a detailed breakdown from departments of their expenditure was given only once a quarter—and several weeks after the end of the quarter.
4 Treasury Ministers were seen to be effectively in commission, as alone of economic instruments public expenditure was subject to collective agreement by the whole Cabinet. All the other instruments, notably taxation and monetary policy (external as well as internal), were under the sole control of Treasury ministers, including of course the Prime Minister as First Lord of the Treasury.

The narrative of previous chapters has shown how the system of cash limits, of the monitoring requirements that went with it and of the enforcement of the contingency reserve were introduced in the early months of 1976, after a planning process which lasted nearly a year. The experience of the first year of these systemic changes, which came to light only after the first full year of operation in 1977, showed how powerful they had been in restoring control to a situation which had until then become almost impossible to operate. In late 1975 the Treasury made a considerable improvement in the reporting system. Departments were required to submit monthly returns of expenditure incurred and these had to be delivered within ten days of the end of the month.

The fourth weakness was perhaps endemic in a system of collective Cabinet responsibility. Since spending Ministers were responsible to Parliament for the efficacy of the programmes with which they were charged it was out of the question to deny them a voice in the determination of those programmes. The doctrine of collective responsibility for both individual programmes and, by extension, to the totality of public expenditure certainly made life much harder for the Expenditure Divisions of the Treasury than, for instance, it was for the Finance Divisions whose recommendations for policy had only to be approved by the Chancellor or at most by the Prime Minister. This collective responsibility certainly made for a long and tortuous process of decision taking. But it also led to a system where the pure milk of Treasury orthodoxy was often, if not indeed usually, diluted by the 'watery' requirements of spending departments. The system, therefore, usually required the Expenditure divisions to make a good deal of allowance for what, in their view, was 'politically acceptable'. The papers reveal a pervasive feeling of exasperation on the part of officials at this political reality and indeed the Managing Director of the IMF told the Chancellor in the autumn of 1976 how unsatisfactory the UK practice was (compared with that in other countries where the voice of the Finance Minister over expenditure totals was final) when it came to making spending cuts. It was impossible to deal with this fact of life in a systemic way. In the last analysis the Treasury and the Chancellor could only get their way in the face of a hostile Cabinet if the Prime Minister threw his weight behind the Chancellor as he did on several occasions, most notably in December, in 1976. This was not, however, a systemic change—only a political one.

By the end of 1976 the system of control had been enormously improved and although the Treasury should not be too self-complimentary about the achievements of the previous two years, it can claim to have satisfied most of the critics of the system if not those who criticized the quantum of expenditure the system permitted. But, leaving aside the systemic changes, it may fairly be asked whether the Treasury was sufficiently ambitious—in all three years covered by this survey—in the targets it set for the containment of the programmes which it proposed in the Surveys of those years and in the periodic interim reviews of those programmes.

This question is implicitly founded on the presumption that public expenditure is in some sense inimical to economic efficiency and that a reduction in expenditure is *ipso facto* desirable. This thought was expressly stated in the opening paragraph of the first of the Thatcher Government's Public Expenditure White Papers.[4] It has to be understood that this was a political statement expressly drafted by Ministers at the time. It hardly represented official Treasury thinking.

The case that public expenditure is inimical to economic efficiency rests on the argument that, as a rule, any good or service provided free, or at a price below economic cost, and paid for, in part at least, out of taxation, diminishes the role of the market and therefore leads to a sub-optimal allocation of resources. The qualification 'as a rule' has to be made for a certain amount of public expenditure, for example the financing of the nationalized industries by the government did not involve, in principle, much of a departure from market principles. Some public expenditure, for instance on the economic infrastructure or on education, served the purpose of correcting market inefficiencies or

---

[4] 'Public Expenditure is at the heart of Britain's present economic difficulties' Cmnd 7746.

imperfections or of bringing economic 'externalities' into the reckoning, and this probably increased rather than diminished the efficacy of the market. A great deal of public expenditure, on law and order and on defence for instance, is essential to the effective functioning of society and, although in theory it is possible to conceive, as some American economists have proposed, of these services being provided through some form of market, most would accept that this category of expenditure, while not showing a measurable market return, is not intrinsically inefficient. Nevertheless it must be conceded that some social expenditure is designed not to produce a measurable economic return but to eliminate or reduce hardship and promote welfare, and it may well be the case that this reduces economic efficiency—although even in this area there may be hidden economic gains from such expenditure by, for instance, enabling the temporarily unemployed to spend more time searching for a suitable job and not taking the first on offer. The argument that public expenditure is intrinsically inefficient and should therefore be opposed by those, such as the Treasury, whose concern is to promote economic efficiency, is a doubtful one. This argument is of course quite different from the argument that public expenditure should secure 'value for money' and should be incurred with great circumspection, with adequate tests of efficiency, relevance, and propriety. These objectives lie at the heart of Treasury control and form the very basis of the Treasury's historic purpose.

In the 1970s, however, a thesis was developed that it was the *rate of growth* of public expenditure which was the cause of the UK's economic problems. Its most notable proponents were Bacon and Eltis who in 1976, after canvassing this proposition in the press, published a book *Britain's Economic Problem: Too Few Producers*. The burden of their argument was that, when public expenditure in aggregate grew at a faster rate than the economy as a whole, the burden of taxation on either wage earners or businesses (or both) had to rise. The former gave rise to inflationary wage claims as the workers sought to compensate for the income loss they sustained through rising personal taxes and the latter, by depriving them of the finance they needed for investment, led them to cut back capital formation. The case was developed in a rather simplistic way and was buttressed by a formal, and very theoretical, model. The empirical evidence, as is usually the case with generalized arguments, was to say the least ambiguous.

Although the argument was put forward in a way which was open to a fair amount of intellectual criticism, it was not one with which the Treasury would have had—or indeed had—much difficulty. Indeed much of the case put forward by officials for containing the growth of public expenditure over the PESC cycle rested on the need to provide resources for investment and exports (and to avoid having to raise personal taxation). The Treasury might not have accepted the detailed analysis of Bacon and Eltis, but it did not quarrel with the general thrust of the argument—that it was the rate of growth of expenditure which had to be watched rather than its absolute level.

But the political reception to Bacon and Eltis was much less about the precise argument they made and focused on the *totality* of expenditure, not its rate of growth. To some extent the Government itself fostered this adaptation of the argument by emphasizing the proportion of GDP which was devoted to public spending, without regard to whether it consumed resources or was a financing item. Indeed in the Public Expenditure White Paper of February 1976 (Cmnd 6393) it specifically stated, with evident disapproval, that this ratio had risen from 42 per cent in 1961, to 50 per cent in 1973 and now to 60 per cent. With the Government itself feeding the concern, it was not surprising that outsiders, whether the political opposition or the financial markets, should themselves focus on the totality of expenditure, rather than, as Bacon and Eltis and the Treasury were arguing, its rate of growth. In fact the international empirical evidence that it was the totality of expenditure which was inimical to economic efficiency was very slender. Some low expenditure economies like Japan performed well, but so did some high expenditure economies, notably the Scandinavian countries.

It is fair to say that in the 1970s the Treasury as a whole did not subscribe to the simple view that public expenditure was intrinsically undesirable. Many initiatives to promote economic growth, for example the expansion of programmes to diminish the economic inequalities between the different regions of the UK (and implicitly improve national efficiency) and the introduction of investment grants, were viewed with favour by the Treasury—certainly by the economists who often played a large part in devising the schemes.

On its own terms the Treasury has to be judged whether in adopting this approach it was, certainly in the early years covered by this review, much too optimistic about the likely availability of resources over the medium-term and therefore too indulgent in what it thought might be devoted to public ends. The 1974 Survey, which led to the White Paper of February 1975, took as its *central* case a scenario in which GDP grew between 1973 and 1979 by 3 per cent per annum.[5] In retrospect this was an absurdly high *central* assumption. Indeed output was flat for the whole four years, 1973 to 1977, and picked up only slightly in the following two years. It is small wonder that so much effort had to be applied in 1975 and 1976 to reining back the plans made in 1974. In 1975 and even more so in 1976 the Treasury were making a much more sober assessment of what economic growth (and its potential) would be, but even these revisions did not accept the harsh reality that the economic growth on which the public expenditure plans were devised was not going to occur. The Treasury can fairly be charged with excessive optimism—or perhaps more reasonably with a failure to foresee what would be the debilitating effects of

[5] This was based on the MTA Assessment in mid-1974 which estimated that productive potential would grow at 3.5 per cent per annum and GDP at 3 per cent over the quadrennium (SCE(74)18).

the global recession of 1974 and 1975, of the restrictive budget of 1975 and of the fall in consumer spending caused by the attack on inflation on the UK's economic performance. Recorded output per head in the UK increased by 0.75 per cent per annum between 1974 and 1977, compared with a potential estimated to be 1.5 per cent. The Treasury relied far too much on the concept of 'potential', and too little on what was likely to happen. Its defence would be that it had no experience comparable to the recession of the 1970s on which to judge the effect of deflation on economic potential. This is true. But a critic could well say that a bigger margin of error ought to have been incorporated in the medium-term projections and that Ministers should have been advised to go for even more severely restrictive growth targets in 1975 and 1976 than they did.

On the other hand the depth of the recession in 1975 was such that it was difficult for the Treasury to argue, at any rate for the Surveys in that year and 1976, that the public expenditure plans pre-empted resources that should have gone on other ends. Indeed it was the absence of a compelling resource argument in 1976 for the cuts proposed in July and December that year for the following year that made the Chancellor's case so difficult to put across to his colleagues in Cabinet most of whom were either Keynesian in outlook or inclined to a *dirigiste* approach to policy. The argument that the Treasury was too optimistic was essentially a medium-term argument, not a conjunctural one. And on this, although the Treasury were still, in 1976, postulating a more favourable medium-term outlook than occurred, they did at least argue for a much lower rate of increase of public expenditure than in the past; and the out-turn of public spending over the second half of the decade was in fact remarkably modest as the figures given in Table 6.1 show.

Not too much should be made of these figures, for the large fall in 1977–78 was due in part to the increase in nationalized industry borrowing in foreign currency and to the fall in the refinancing of export credit—neither of which had much effect on the pre-emption of resources by the public sector. But even allowing for this, the profile does not seem to be an unreasonable one. The ratio of public expenditure on resources to GDP, a statistic many critics of the government's attitude to public spending were inclined to quote, declined from 46 per cent in 1974–75 to 41 per cent in 1978–79. The Conservative

Table 6.1 Percentage increase over previous year in public expenditure programmes including the contingency reserve and excluding debt interest but including lending to the nationalized industries (1978 survey prices)

1974–75	1975–76	1976–77	1977–78	1978–79
9.5%	1.0%	–3.2%	–5.7%	8.9%

Government which took office in 1979, committed as they were by their White Paper in November 1979 to the reduction of public expenditure, saw this ratio rise to 44 per cent in 1982–83.

The Treasury and the exchange rate

The narrative has shown how persistently throughout the period covered the Treasury argued that the sterling exchange rate was too high for the achievement of equilibrium in the current account of the balance of payments at anything approaching full employment—an objective it took almost as an article of faith. From early 1974 when virtually all form of pay restraint was abandoned until the second quarter of 1976 UK exports were judged to be at a significant price disadvantage with the competition, and the only practical remedy seriously put forward was that somehow or other a depreciation of sterling had to be engineered. This advice was not accepted by Treasury Ministers—except rather grudgingly in March 1976 when, fortuitously, the policy was no longer required; and for most of the period reviewed in this history British manufactured goods were at a price disadvantage with their overseas competitors and the balance of payments (certainly the 'full employment' balance of payments) was seriously in deficit. A good part of this deficit was of course due to the sharp increase in the price of oil, which imposed deficits on most of the industrialized countries of Europe, North America and Japan. But the UK also had a non-oil deficit throughout 1974, whereas most other advanced countries avoided this by deflating their economies that year—not primarily to redress their new balance of payments deficits but to discourage cost inflation in their domestic economies. The UK at first called on them not to do this as it aggravated its own balance of payments problem, but in the end it was forced to adopt such a policy in 1975. But deflation by itself was not seen by the Treasury as the optimum policy for rectifying the balance of payments, although in the absence of alternatives it was the only one available. The Treasury throughout argued that, rather than seek to correct the balance of payments deficit by contracting the economy, the authorities should somehow or other contrive a devaluation of the currency.

To understand why this was such a strongly held view we have to go back a few years to the origin of the decision to float the pound in 1972. The starting point for that decision may be taken as the decision of the US Treasury in August 1971 to end the guarantee of the convertibility of the dollar at $35 per fine ounce. This led immediately to very uncertain and unstable conditions in the foreign exchange markets which were only dispelled—and then not completely—by the multilateral agreement reached at the IMF meeting in the Smithsonian Institution in Washington in December 1971 when the system of currency parities was revised to take account of the Americans' change of policy. This agreement sought to re-establish a system of par values and fixed exchange rates on the lines of the original Bretton Woods agreement. It was however a short-lived system, for six months later the UK abandoned it and allowed sterling to float, that is to find its market value without any commitment by the Bank of England to buy or sell sterling so as to keep its international value at the 'Smithsonian' level. The move was an explicit attempt to remove what was described as the balance of payments constraint on economic growth. At the time it is fair to say that neither the Treasury nor the Bank knew how floating would work. The response to any movement in the exchange rate as a result of market pressures was not worked out, still less laid down in operational terms; indeed there may not have been even the elements of a strategy to deal with such contingencies. The main thought was that if the UK got into balance of payments difficulties, either on capital or current account, the market would depreciate sterling and the difficulties would thereby be corrected by a market mechanism. What was not envisaged was that a balance of payments problem might occur and that the exchange rate would not respond *pro tanto*. The market would not in fact 'clear'. This is what happened in 1974 and continued to happen for two years thereafter. The Treasury had no prior strategy to deal with this situation.

The prevailing mood in the Treasury certainly at the beginning of 1974 therefore was that, although the exchange rate might have to be smoothed on a short-term basis, it would over time move, under market pressures, so as to ensure that any misalignment with international cost movements would be compensated by a fall in the sterling rate. It was no part of the Treasury's thinking that an appropriate way of meeting any loss of competitiveness would be to deflate the economy. Any external deficit which might temporarily arise through the application of the policy would be met by foreign borrowing. The onset of the flow of North Sea Oil in the late 1970s provided both the justification for this policy and the security for the loans which were required. It was all rather a neat solution, but there were serious internal inconsistencies in the approach. For one thing, to the extent that the UK was successful in mobilizing foreign credit the overall balance would be less than the current balance and the fall in the exchange rate would be moderated. This indeed is exactly what happened. In 1974 the Treasury and the Bank were hugely successful in securing foreign lending and in persuading the large official sterling holders to increase their reserves in sterling. At the time this seemed to be desirable from every point of view. It gave the UK a breathing space in which to adjust to the situation created by the huge oil price increase. But it also permitted it not to deal with the problem of inflation and not to remedy the worsening current account. It also led to the accumulation of large sterling balances in the hands of a few official holders who proved to be very mercurial creditors when in 1976 the future value of sterling became uncertain. We examine the Treasury's attitude to the official balances in the next section. Here it suffices to say that the success in the overseas borrowing programme was instrumental in allowing the Treasury to be too relaxed about the need for some active management of the exchange rate when, in the course of 1974, it became apparent that the rate was not adjusting (as had been expected) and inflation in the UK, certainly in comparison with its competitors, was accelerating.

It was not however a case of the Treasury's not perceiving what was happening. The narrative has brought out the repeated attempts by the Treasury to alert Ministers to the problem, first in the early summer of 1974 and more emphatically in the run-up to the autumn budget of that year. The Chancellor was not impressed with the Treasury's worries, and he was able to take refuge in the fact that neither the Bank nor the Treasury had a clear policy prescription for achieving the end that they both, initially at any rate, thought was desirable. The most that they could agree on, and persuade Ministers to accept, was that when any downward market pressure on sterling emerged it should not be resisted. But even this prescription was not acted on, or at least not acted on with any determination. When sterling came under market pressure in December 1974, the Bank spent about \$1 billion of the foreign exchange reserves countering it. Sterling continued to be above the 'equilibrium' rate, not only in 1974 but throughout 1975.

The Treasury wanted to make the necessary adjustment and repeatedly argued with Ministers that the policy, effectively of *laisser faire* (that is to say doing nothing), to promote a fall in the exchange rate but equally of not fiercely resisting an attack, was not achieving the desired end of an adequate decline. The Bank, by contrast, although accepting the case made by the Treasury, were particularly hesitant about the wisdom of doing anything to sow doubt in the minds of sterling holders about the value of their holdings. In part this was the natural, and indeed laudable, attitude of a banker to his customers. The fiduciary duty is a strong one and the Bank had, throughout the post-war period, felt that this duty placed limits on what could properly be done administratively to devalue the sterling assets of overseas holders— particularly the Central Banks and Monetary Authorities.[6] But the Bank also had in mind that the value of sterling was an important ingredient in the mix of services that the City of London offered as a financial centre and that any diminution of sterling's international role might well damage the business standing of British banks, insurance businesses and the many financial markets which operated in London.

These concerns of the Bank were entirely legitimate, but they were not concerns which were at the forefront of the Treasury's thinking and this

[6] As far back as 1952 the Bank, at Governor level, were arguing strongly about their duty to safeguard the assets of sterling area countries—particularly the colonies to whom the UK had a duty of care—see Lord Cobbold's minute of 15 February 1952, Bank of England FOI release. See also Fforde p. 431.

difference did contribute to some sharp distinctions—not only of attitude but also of policy—between the two institutions during the course of 1975 and 1976. These distinctions were mainly about the practicability of achieving by administrative action the depreciation the Treasury wanted, but they were also to some extent about the analysis on which the Treasury based its policy recommendation. The Bank had increasing doubts about the desirability of a devaluation designed to improve competitiveness. These doubts surfaced at the meeting between the two institutions in December 1975 when the Bank expressed its scepticism about the *efficacy* of a contrived depreciation. They feared the effects on the domestic price level and the impact on the pay policy. But they also showed some lack of conviction about the elasticities the Treasury used for both exports and imports in response to a relative price change. They also thought that the competitive advantage of a depreciation might easily be eroded in higher domestic costs. These concerns and doubts were expressed most coherently in a paper which the Bank's research department produced on the eve of the Fund's arrival in October 1976.[7] This looked at a variety of evidence about the effects of a devaluation and at the extent to which the financial advantage which it would have on exporters would be taken in higher profit margins or higher volumes of sales.

For the most part the Treasury did not share the Bank's doubts about the efficacy of a devaluation. Their model certainly made a good deal of allowance for an erosion of the initial gain from such a move as domestic prices rose. More importantly the Treasury view was backed by most empirical research and was strongly supported by the Fund whose practical experience, as they argued during the 1976 negotiations, showed that devaluation 'worked', although not in any mechanistic sense. The Treasury also regarded the experience of the 1967 devaluation as convincing evidence that positive balance of payments gains could be secured by a depreciation if accompanied by appropriate domestic policies.

There was, therefore, something of a division of opinion between the two main institutions about the optimum approach and this division manifested itself from time to time when specific action had to be taken, for instance in response to a bear attack on sterling. But there was also something of a difference of opinion in the Treasury—between the Chancellor on the one hand and his advisers on the other. This division was never clearly articulated but, whenever the issue of a contrived devaluation was broached by officials, the Chancellor found reasons either to resist the advice or to delay taking a decision. He clearly had the greatest reservations about the effect on domestic prices and hence on the damage it could do to the TUC's pay policy. He also feared the effect on sterling holders of a fall in their assets and of their willingness to go on keeping their assets in London. But, in addition, he

[7] IM 1/33/02.

seemed to share some of the Bank's doubts about the efficacy of devaluation to secure the end in view.

It was this confusion of attitudes—in the Treasury and between the Treasury and the Bank—which led to a decision on positive action being delayed and postponed over a period of nearly two years and, when the depreciation which the Treasury wanted came, it came fortuitously, not as a result of a policy decision. But when it came, it did seem to have a favourable effect on the balance of payments (before it was eroded by the appreciation of sterling in 1977 and thereafter). The depreciation which occurred in 1976 was also something that the Fund welcomed—they wanted still more—and if it had not occurred it has to be reckoned that the Fund would have wanted some firm commitment of action to make it happen.

The author of this study thought at the time that a deliberate devaluation was, in the circumstances, both necessary and desirable, and continues to think so. But it has to be conceded that the instruments put forward by the Treasury to achieve it were untested and might well have had serious side effects to which the Treasury did not at the time give sufficient weight. What the Treasury proposed was that a weakening of sterling should be contrived by deliberately reducing interest rates and by not supporting sterling in the market when it came under pressure. The alternative of a step-devaluation, under which the Bank would announce a new, and low, level of the exchange rate at which it would *sell* sterling but would not commit itself to *buy* sterling, was briefly considered but never subjected to any serious analysis. The Bank memorandum of 5 February 1976 was the nearest thing to a scrutiny of the idea, and even this was somewhat perfunctory. A step-change in a floating environment would have been a policy without precedent and what discussion there was of it was highly speculative and without empirical evidence one way or another.

The preferred policy of using interests rates and less support for sterling was also without precedent and its effectiveness was admitted at the time to be uncertain and indeed potentially dangerous. When sterling came under attack during 1974 and 1975, it was usually because of market anxieties about the effectiveness of UK macro-economic policy and/or of worries about the future of sterling. Perhaps the most important of these attacks was that of 30 June 1975 when anxiety about the outlook for inflation was most acute. This attack, and indeed other attacks, on sterling during the period under review, came largely from official holders of sterling and it is easy to see why they were the main source of the selling which took place. They, or at least the four main holders, had a very heavy investment in sterling and it was only common prudence for them to reduce their exposure to any weakness, real or supposed, in the value of their assets. By contrast the non-official holders were widely dispersed, consisting of a myriad of commercial banks and business enterprises throughout the world who held sterling in individually small amounts and did so for commercial, not investment, reasons. Their exposure to sterling, measured as a proportion of their total credit risk, was relatively small. They had no particular reason to reduce their sterling assets, which they needed for business reasons and were in the nature of 'working balances', when sterling weakened by a few points. The other point of potential weakness was that of UK importers and exporters speculating against sterling at times of uncertainty by 'leading and lagging' their payments and receipts. The extent to which they did this at times of uncertainty was not known, but both the Treasury and the Bank suspected that this could add to any problem which arose for other reasons. However, traders who indulged in 'leading and lagging' had to do so on credit and for them the cost of money was a factor in determining whether they would speculate against sterling. Although 'leading and lagging' was often said to be part of the problem, no evidence was produced to demonstrate that this was indeed the case. The author's experience of business decision taking after his retirement suggests that currency uncertainty does not greatly affect the speed at which exports are invoiced or imports are ordered and paid for.

This analysis was amply confirmed empirically during the course of 1976 when the main selling came from official holders, and non-official holders scarcely moved their holdings even during periods of intense uncertainty. Leading and lagging may have become something of a problem, but its extent was largely unknown. As a factor it was probably vastly less important than the movement of the official balances. The American pre-occupation with monetary measures to combat the crisis does not seem to have been justified.

The question that has to be asked, if it was the case that the main source of weakness was the group of about four official holders, is how they would have reacted if the Treasury's preferred policy had been followed: engineering a fall in the rate by reducing interest rates and by reducing intervention by the Bank when sterling was weak if this had been adopted in (say) 1974 or 1975. Here again, 1976 provided some real evidence, for what happened on 4 and 5 March that year was, if not by design at least in practice, an experiment in that policy. And indeed the relatively relaxed attitude of the authorities to the fall in the early stages was again the sort of response that the Treasury would have proposed if their recommendations had been adopted. What 1976 showed was that once the official holders began to have anxieties about the capital value of their sterling investments they became aggressive sellers—and they had a lot to sell. They continued to sell, moreover, even when the British Government insisted that it did not want sterling to fall and was prepared to adopt restrictive policies (as in July of that year) to reassure investors.

One experiment does not provide conclusive evidence, but what happened in 1976 does suggest that the Treasury's preferred course would have created very large problems of management and that the controlled, and fairly modest, devaluation it was intended to bring about might well have escalated out of control. This possibility was not overlooked, but there was no way, *a priori*, of determining how serious it was. But if that had been the outcome the effect on domestic prices, and hence the viability of the compact with the TUC, might have been disastrous. Some form of hyperinflation might have ensued. But throughout 1974 and 1975 there was no serious examination of what might happen and what the response should be to a given contingency. It is probably fair to say that the Treasury and Bank analysis did not foresee that it was only the official holders that were the problem and they did not become aware of this fact until late June 1976—some three months after the slide in the value of sterling began. The discussion was always about 'market pressures or market sentiment' when, as events showed, it was only the overseas central banks and monetary authorities that were the problem. Whether it would have been possible to deal with them by some special arrangement *well in advance* of the emergence of the case for a devaluation and so reduce the size of the management of the devaluation is something we examine in the next section where the question of the safety net is reviewed. But it was certainly not examined as a practical issue during the period 1974–76 when the prevailing mood in London was almost relief that the sterling balance holders were no longer guaranteed any special treatment.

Nor, as we argued above, was the viability of a step-devaluation by means of a stated and explicit intervention policy ever seriously examined. It was baldly assumed that such an action would have such a disastrous effect on the official holders that it would shatter their confidence in holding any assets in sterling and so make any stabilization of the rate virtually impossible. This too seems, in retrospect, to have been a simplistic view. Whether a full-blooded appraisal jointly by both institutions and a serious examination of the likely behaviour of the four main monetary authorities would have led to a different conclusion is open to question. But in view of the crucial importance of a depreciation to the whole of the Treasury's strategy it does seem surprising that the question of dealing with the official selling of sterling was not examined with some care. The possibility of dealing with the anxieties of the official holders might have been handled by some special treatment, such as a guarantee or by *post factum* compensation and such a course was briefly, but rather casually, considered. But it was clear that neither the Bank nor the Treasury had any wish to engage in a repeat of the lengthy negotiations with all the official holders that took place in 1968 when the system of guarantees was introduced as part of the safety-net operations. Moreover, any such negotiations would have been thought of as preceding a step-change in order to mitigate any surge of selling; and it was out of the question for the British Government to give advance notice of a devaluation to a host of overseas institutions.

The criticism is perhaps less that the conclusion reached was wrong than that it was based on flimsy evidence and only a modicum of serious analysis. The effects of such a step, not preceded by any special arrangements with overseas official holders, would have been very uncertain, perhaps even more uncertain than the Treasury's preferred course. Certainly no one in the Treasury, and *a fortiori* no one in the Bank, was a serious advocate of it as a policy option. Given the amount of thought that was devoted to the question of the exchange rate, it has to be concluded that the instinctive dislike of most experts for this particular course was, in all the circumstances, justified.

The only other option which might have been exercised was to allow sterling to fall when it was attacked and to rely on the market to establish a new equilibrium rate—something known as a 'free float'. This was precisely the policy followed by the US Treasury in the 1980s when it was dubbed 'benign neglect'. This was only put forward as a suggestion within the Treasury late in 1976—significantly by the economists, not by OF. The fear of the Bank, and to some extent of the Treasury itself, was that, if the official overseas holders saw that their assets were not being defended by the Bank, they would rapidly become sellers and, in the absence of offsetting buying by the Bank, a 'one way' market would develop with catastrophic effects on the rate. It would be impossible to predict where the new equilibrium would be. It might be at a level where the effect on import prices (raw materials and some basic foodstuffs) would fuel inflation so much that the Incomes Policy would collapse under the strain. This was the nightmare that led the Treasury to dismiss the idea out of hand. But was it right to rule out any serious appraisal of the course? It seems implausible that a sharp fall in sterling—say of 20 per cent—would not have provoked an immediate response from the UK's competitors. Several of them had expressed concern at the 10 per cent gain in competitiveness brought about by the 1976 depreciation. If this had increased to 20 per cent or 25 per cent, there would have been widespread dismay, not only at the competitive advantage this gave the UK but at the possibility that the stability of other currencies was now at risk. The whole international community had an interest in the preservation of reasonable monetary stability and it seems unlikely that it would calmly have allowed sterling to fall through the floor. The damage to the global monetary system would have been catastrophic. It seems never to have occurred to the Treasury (or the Bank) that the UK's apparent weakness could have been turned into a strength. It is often forgotten, particularly by civil servants, who by their nature are inclined to avoid risk, that a debtor (particularly a big debtor) is frequently in a much stronger position in a negotiation than his creditors. The fact that at the end of 1976 the leading industrial nations all came together to protect sterling via the 'safety net' provides some evidence that they perceived this action as in their own interests, or at least in the interests of the whole international community, and not just the UK's.

This said, to have been 'benignly neglectful' in the sense described above would have been a high-risk policy, and no one in a senior position in White-hall or the City was prepared to take the risk or to recommend it to Ministers. No doubt they were right. But it can at least be argued that the risk ought to have been subjected to some critical analysis, and it was not.

The line taken by the Treasury towards the exchange rate thus emerges as both an imprecise one and one which was not based on a great deal of prior experience or even of very serious analysis. The case for some sort of devaluation over and above that which was taking place of its own accord was well argued and, although it was contested in some quarters, it was not by any means a faulty one. The modalities of securing it, however, were treated rather superficially, and that is perhaps a serious statement even though, as the policy was not formally adopted, it did not lead to any serious consequences. This criticism has to apply both to those who advocated a devaluation and to those who did not. For the opponents of the preferred course did not base their opposition on a hard and detailed examination of the consequences, but on a general expression of doubt and anxiety.

The Treasury and the official sterling balances

In his television interview on 25 October 1976 the Prime Minister expressed in public his strong desire to 'get rid of (sterling as a) reserve currency' by which he clearly meant the holding by overseas central banks of at least a significant proportion of their reserves in sterling; and he added 'I am not sure that everybody in the Treasury would, or maybe in the Bank'. These were very important statements and what we have said above provides ample justification for them. But at the time they not unnaturally caused some concern among officials responsible for overseas financial policy. They were followed by intense activity at all levels of government and central banking to obtain some 'neutralization', if not elimination, of these balances, and eventually to the Basle agreement of 10 January 1977 which put in place the safety net and the scheme for the voluntary exchange of the balances for non-sterling denominated UK government debt.

The relevance of the safety net to the urgent problems the UK faced in the autumn of 1976 is not very clear. There was a major crisis of confidence in its economic policy, but when this was resolved by the agreement with the Fund the problems disappeared, almost overnight—indeed well before the safety net arrangements were agreed and announced. To many in Whitehall it seemed that the Prime Minister's concerns were misplaced and that, although the safety net was a useful back-up to the policy changes and the Fund stand-by announced, it was not a central issue. Certainly the US Treasury and the Federal Reserve thought so and said so in no uncertain terms in the course of 1976. Some of the official sterling holders converted a part of their balances into the dollar bonds, but for the most part they did not and continued to hold sterling, although on a much reduced scale thanks to the large disposals they had made during 1976. So was the whole sterling balance problem a figment of the Prime Minister's imagination and was the safety net unnecessary?

The safety net may well have been unnecessary as a remedial measure for the difficulties of the autumn of 1976, but that does not mean that the Prime Minister's concern about the general problem created by sterling's reserve currency status was misplaced. We saw in the previous section that it was the *official* sterling holders who led the exodus from sterling in the course of 1976 (and to some extent in the previous year too) and it was argued that if they had not done so the weakness of sterling deriving from the selling of the private balance holders and from 'leading and lagging' (if indeed it was occurring) might have been susceptible to some sort of control by monetary measures. It is at least an arguable proposition that, if the official sterling balance problem had been disposed of *before* the onset of the crisis, the whole episode involving a drawing from the Fund and the acceptance of the Fund's prescription would have been unnecessary. That is not a proposition capable of much serious analysis, but it is at least a plausible one. The question has to be asked, therefore, in reviewing the actions and recommendations of the Treasury in the period 1974–76, whether as much was done, particularly before the development of the financial crisis, to neutralize the balances.

The Treasury and Bank attitudes to this question were heavily influenced by the experience of 1968 when the previous safety net had been put in place. It had involved detailed negotiations with all the overseas holders, including the former British colonies, many of whom had relatively small sterling balances but for whom sterling was still the principal reserve currency. They were given exchange guarantees and for their part agreed to hold minimum balances in sterling. The whole system was underpinned by a safety net supported by the BIS. The arrangements proved to be mainly an insurance which scarcely had to be resorted to, and when they came to an end in 1973 there was no attempt to renew them, although unilateral guarantees were given for a limited time. At the end of 1974 the Treasury and the Bank were at one in recommending that the guarantees should not be extended further and that the position of the official holders should revert to what it had been prior to 1968. Thereafter, certainly until the middle of 1976, the question of some systemic change in the position of the balances was, with one episodic exception, given little consideration and the idea of giving holders some form of guarantee to deter them from liquidating their sterling assets—an idea put forward from outside the two institutions including one from the Prime Minister in June 1975 (Wilson), backed up by other Ministers, received short shrift from officials.

The case against a unilateral guarantee was a strong one. It would, so the Treasury and Bank thought, trigger the very doubts it was intended to allay. It would, moreover, give an uncovenanted benefit to the holders by effectively providing them with sterling rates of interest on assets which were, in all but name, dollar-based. But the Bank also probably felt that the public expression of doubt about the value of a sterling asset would be damaging to the standing of the City of London and possibly to the longer-term role of the City in international finance. However the idea of a system of guarantees would not go away and it did implicitly reappear in the arrangements agreed in January 1977—although of course they were then unilateral. So the objections of principle which the Treasury and Bank saw could not have been quite as great as then set out.

The idea of some 'solution' to the official sterling balance problem was not left completely unconsidered after the expiry of the 1968 arrangements. It was placed on the agenda of the Committee of Twenty—the IMF body set up in 1972 to review the case for some amendment in the Fund's constitution and its practices to take account of generalized floating—but the consideration did not lead to any conclusion, perhaps understandably given the difficulties of doing anything except in a crisis situation. But the issue came up again in the context of the UK's accession to the Treaty of Rome when the Six Founder members, fearful perhaps that the sterling balances would be some sort of 'Trojan Horse' threat to the stability of the Community as a whole, sought assurances from the UK that it would deal with this 'problem'. Such assurances were given in a letter which the responsible Minister sent to the representatives of the Six in 1972. Nothing seems to have been done to give effect to those assurances and they were not a live issue when the UK became a full member of the Community in January 1973. It is hard to avoid the suspicion that neither the Bank nor the Treasury took the commitment to the Six very seriously—there is no evidence that it led to any discussion as to how it would be implemented. It suited both institutions to continue to advocate the benefits of sterling and the resources of the City of London in the hope that this would be conducive to stability in the balances; and when the oil crisis broke they both congratulated themselves on the fact that the official balances actually increased. No doubt it would have been very difficult for the Bank to have advised its customers in the sterling area (as well as those on the periphery) to convert their sterling balances into another currency. When the Basle settlement of the balances was finally agreed in early 1977 and the Bank had the job of selling the idea of such a conversion to its old friends overseas it did so with not a little regret.

The problem of dealing with the official sterling balances in a situation not of a critical nature, which was broadly the case from 1969 until 1974, should not be underestimated. Any move by the UK authorities *vis-à-vis* the holders would almost certainly have aroused anxieties in their breasts which, in the period covered, were simply not there. What steps the UK could have taken to deal with the problem short of an understanding with the holders is by no means obvious. The one unilateral act the UK could have taken would have been to raise substantial long-term loans in dollars on the world capital markets to form a counterpart to the sterling liabilities and so provide the means for dealing with any future run on sterling by the official holders. The maturities of those liabilities would have to have been long—or at least medium-term on a renewable basis—and the amounts would have had to run into several billions of dollars. It must be a matter of considerable doubt whether the Government could have achieved this in the state and strength of the international capital markets between 1969 and 1973. The huge oil surpluses which developed in 1974 and became a source of funds for the international capital markets thereafter had not emerged. The eurodollar market existed, but it was not then much of a market in long-term funds. The British Government was able to raise a medium-term commercial bank (i.e. non-market) dollar loan in early 1974 of $2.5 billion, but this was in effect a recycling of the emerging oil surpluses and would probably not have been an option a year earlier. The Government did reinstate a programme of overseas borrowing by the nationalized industries and local authorities in early 1973, but, because of the timing, the proceeds went simply to cover the emerging balance of payments deficit and not to form a counterpart to the sterling balance liabilities. One possibility thought to have the potential to tie-in the official balances was to invite the main oil-surplus countries which were building up large sterling balances from the beginning of 1974 to invest their assets at long-term or to make a dollar—or SDR denominated—loan to the UK, as indeed the Iranian government did in July of that year. This idea was tried out on Saudi Arabia several times, but the Saudis were not really interested. They made a comparatively small dollar investment in the UK public sector, and they talked vaguely of investing in British equities. But they evidently did not want to tie up their financial assets in potentially illiquid assets. This was not the function of a monetary authority. The failure seriously to interest the Saudis in this idea no doubt led the Treasury and the Bank to see little prospect of a wholesale conversion of the official balances into longer-term securities. In the course of 1975 the two institutions did look seriously at the idea of an SDR denominated bond to be issued in exchange for sterling held by official institutions, but the timing was always found to be awkward and anyway it would have involved asking monetary institutions to 'go long'. In retrospect this objection may perhaps seem a little contrived, but at the time there was no dissent from the recommendation that other options should be pursued.

A full study of the options which might in fact have been pursued before the matter became critical in 1976 would take us outside the scope of the present work. But although the relative inactivity of the Treasury in pursuing the sterling balance issue when it was not critical cannot easily be put down to neglect, it has to be asked whether the issue was put high enough on officials' agendas in the Treasury and the Bank. There was no obvious solution at that time. The international community were not greatly interested in joining the UK in some multilateral solution, and the events of 1976 showed that the situation had to assume crisis proportions before, as a matter of self-interest, they were prepared to collaborate; the scope for some purely UK solution was clearly very limited, if it existed at all.

The final question that has to be asked is whether, when the oil crisis developed and the UK's current account problems became acute in 1974, some re-examination of the sterling balance issue should have been undertaken. Such action would probably have had to be unilateral for the IMF Committee of Twenty examination had shown that the scope for a multilateral solution was limited. From early 1974 the UK did not have the luxury of being able to consider reducing its liabilities in sterling and increasing those in dollars although this was a course which was repeatedly canvassed by Lever,[8] who had what officials considered to be an unrealistic assessment of the scope for overseas borrowing by the Government. It was stretched to the limit in finding sufficient finance in any form and, when the official sterling holders began to *increase* their balances in the course of that year,[9] this was less a cause for concern than for rejoicing. At least the rise in the oil-surplus countries balances reduced the need for foreign currency borrowing, which was being undertaken to the maximum extent thought possible. Where perhaps the Treasury and the Bank were at fault was in not perceiving where the strong rise in the official balances was taking the UK, given that both institutions recognized, from the middle of 1974, that some real depreciation of sterling would be necessary and that the existence of a large new accumulation of overseas balances would make that course hazardous. As we saw in the previous section, neither the Treasury nor the Bank seem to have perceived that it would be the official holders that would be the problem, not the market in general. But it is fair to ask whether, even if that had been the perception, very much could have been done about it prior to 1976. The most that can be said is that neither institution gave any warning of the problems that the balances would present to the management of the exchange rate, and that they did not do so owes as much as anything to the fact that they were not conscious of them.

Finally it must always be borne in mind that the Bank had serious reservations about the whole exercise of reducing the operational role of sterling in the international financial system. They were after all the 'Bank of Issue', and it would be straining credulity to suppose that they would have been keen to see their fiat money, which had once financed one-third of all international trade, reduced to the role of a purely national currency. It was really only in June 1976, when the Chancellor and the Prime Minister began to show a keen interest in disposing of the sterling balance problem that the Bank came up with a proposal, and even this was only a recycling of the 1968 arrangements.

With this perspective, it is not difficult to see why the Prime Minister made his television remarks as he did. It may not have been the best of constitutional form for the occupant of No 10 Downing Street to make a public

---

[8] BP 32/100/32, 12 March 1975 and DW 036, 9 October 1975.
[9] The official sterling balances rose in 1974 by almost £1 billion, or over 30 per cent.

criticism of the commitment of his advisers for the policy he wanted to pursue, but it is easy to understand, particularly as he had been an active participant in the arrangements in the 1960s to reduce the role of sterling, why he made his statement and indeed why thereafter he was such an enthusiastic champion of the 'safety net'.

The Treasury and the financial crisis

Perhaps the most serious charge that can be made against the Treasury over its conduct of macro-economic policy in the three years we have studied is that it did not handle with very professional skill the whole sterling crisis, from March 1976, when it broke, until December when it finally came to an end.

We break this charge down into a number of elements:

- There was no articulated contingency plan for action to counter a major and sustained attack on sterling.
- There was too slow a response to the attack when it was made, and the delay in putting remedial measures in place made the problem even more intractable than it was anyway.
- When the remedial measures were proposed, they were insufficient to do duty to their purpose.
- There was no clear and consistent policy on exchange rate intervention—policy was made 'on the hoof'.
- The seeking and obtaining of the central bank credit of June was a tactical mistake and indeed speeded the development of the crisis rather than helped to resolve it.
- There was no clear strategy for dealing with the Fund negotiations and the running was left to the Fund to lay down its own conditions.

That there was no specific contingency plan for the events of 1976 is clear from the documents. The British Civil Service prides itself on its capacity to prepare for almost every conceivable eventuality. But in 1976, beyond a simple statement that there would have to be unspecified 'crash' measures—public expenditure cuts, interest rate increases, etc.—there was no plan to deal with a situation where the major official sterling holders decided, almost *en masse*, to sell a significant part of their holdings. We have looked at some of the reasons why so little was done before 1976 to prevent this occurrence happening or at least to handle it. That account provides some clues as to why there was no plan to deal with its actually coming about. The answer must be that the Treasury and the Bank did not expect that the main problem of confidence in sterling would come only from the official holders. Of course they were seen to be potential sellers of sterling in a crisis and indeed had had that role in the middle of 1975 when anxiety was acute over the acceleration of inflation. But the supposition was that the private holders would be just as nervous and would reduce their exposure. In such a situation any solution to the problem of confidence had to be a general one, to be dealt with by the sort of economic and financial measures which had always been resorted to in a crisis, that is retraction of demand, cuts in public expenditure, increases in interest rates and, where available, the strengthening of administrative controls. At the back of the Treasury's and the Bank's minds was the thought, never explicitly stated, that, if sterling were attacked over a period, such measures would be the remedy. Of course in a situation of a short, possibly sharp, attack, a spirited defence of the exchange rate by vigorous intervention would be the weapon, but when this was seen to be insufficient longer-term measures would be applied. So in a sense there was a contingency plan, although it was never articulated in the terms set out above; and as our narrative has shown it was not long into the crisis period before Treasury officials were talking of the need to produce public expenditure cuts to restore confidence. The Governor of the Bank had been talking in such terms over a much longer period, but his ideas were less a response to a critical situation than one derived from a more deep-seated doubt—based on market observation—about the course of economic policy.

What then is to be made of the charge that officials were too slow to respond to the crisis when it emerged? To examine this case, it has to be remembered that it was the Treasury's policy to seek a real reduction in the exchange value of sterling—and the Chancellor had eventually accepted this policy on 1 March. Therefore, when events, unaided, provided this reduction, it was not something that the Treasury wanted to reverse. The value of sterling on 4 March was $2.0149. The Treasury wanted a devaluation of perhaps 10 per cent or 15 per cent which would have put the exchange rate at $1.70 or $1.80. The rate did not fall to $1.80 until the middle of May and to $1.70 until September. Certainly while the rate was above $1.80 there was no need in the Treasury's mind for action to reverse, or even halt, what had happened. It is perhaps not surprising therefore that no specific action was taken, other than in the field of intervention policy, to moderate the selling of sterling which was taking place. Interest rates were raised on 26 April when sterling was at $1.82 but this move was only to reverse the rather anomalous fall in short-term rates that had taken place since the beginning of the year. It was only on 21 May that a specific move was made—a rise of 1 per cent in MLR—designed specifically to restore confidence. Even this move was opposed by the official Treasury who could see no domestic reason for an increase of such a size and who still believed that the exchange rate was not too high.

But if there seemed a valid justification at the time for the relative inactivity of the authorities to moderate the fall, there can be little doubt that 'benign neglect', was having its effect on the official sterling holders who had, by the end of May, substantially reduced their holdings in response to the capital loss they had sustained. They were to make further reductions but these were less a reaction to further falls in sterling—the rate declined scarcely at all in the three months following the May measures—than to what must have been a perception that sterling could well fall further and that the economic measures of July were insufficient to guarantee continuing stability.

The charge of an inadequate initial response is therefore not an easy one to sustain, given the priorities the Treasury had. A more serious charge is that when the crisis of confidence had plainly not been resolved by the limited monetary measures of May—and by the central bank credit of June—the Treasury did not act more strongly in July when it recommended Ministers to make cuts of £1 billion in the expenditure programmes for 1977–78 and did so on the stated case that only this would restore the confidence that had ebbed away. The Treasury did, after all, base its recommendations primarily on the issue of confidence and the resource and financial cases were adduced very much as something the Chancellor felt he had to have to persuade his colleagues.

The only issue in the mind of Treasury officials in June and July was how big the expenditure cuts should be. It had become clear that nothing but expenditure cuts would be required. Most outside commentators, including the IMF (although the Fund was more concerned to reduce the fiscal deficit than in the precise means by which this was achieved), and market participants subscribed to this view. Public expenditure had assumed an almost totemic character, for reasons that were analysed earlier. The Treasury had to accept this as a fact of life and the only question was how big the cuts should be to satisfy the critics. This was an issue which was hardly capable of rigorous analysis and the judgement officials made was inevitably qualitative and subjective. The Fund had talked rather vaguely of £3 billion of cuts, but it was not clear which year they referred to. Perhaps the best guide the Treasury could have was contained in the short-term and medium-term analyses which were carried out in June. These suggested that the PSBR for 1977–78, unconstrained, would probably be of the order of £12 billion (with continuing deficits of the order of £10 billion for a further two years) and, although as a proportion of GDP it promised to be a good deal less than in the current year, it was thought that to publish such a figure would further undermine confidence. In the event, the Treasury was split between those who wanted cuts of £2 billion and thought that the Chancellor should be pressed to seek this from his colleagues and those, primarily on the expenditure side, who thought on the basis of the PESC exercise which was then in progress, that the Chancellor would simply not be able to persuade his colleagues to accept a cut of this size. The Treasury recommendation was for £1 billion on the grounds of realism, although this was supplemented by the increase in the national insurance contribution surcharge worth about £1 billion. Subsequent events showed that this combination failed to persuade the market. Whether cuts of £2 billion would have succeeded cannot be known. Had they not succeeded and the Government had had to go to the Fund anyway—as it probably would given the size of the financing requirement—the room for further cuts, which the Fund would certainly have insisted on, would have been very small given the enormous resistance the Cabinet showed both in July and in December to what were not by any means excessive reductions. The author of this study had, and still has, the gravest doubts about whether the Chancellor could have been persuaded to seek £2 billion of cuts in July and equally grave doubts about whether if he had he would have been able to secure them from his Cabinet colleagues. This is the sort of political judgement which officials are required to make from time to time and calls for an understanding of the nature of raw politics which goes beyond the ordinary experience and training of civil servants. It has to be a matter of pure speculation whether, when all the dust had settled in December, the outcome would have been better both in political and economic terms if the Treasury had, with one voice, both urged the Chancellor to seek £2 billion of cuts and actually persuaded him to do so. It is at least arguable that the end result would have been even larger aggregate cuts and a greater political trauma, with no discernible improvement in the ultimate outcome.

There was one feature of the July measures which is perhaps less open to dispute. This was the decision to announce what was taken to be a monetary growth target—of 12 per cent over the financial year. This again was seen primarily as a confidence-raising measure, but, although the market was inclined to give weight to monetarist arguments, the statement had little positive effect. It has to be doubted whether, against the overriding importance it showed to actual cuts in expenditure, the existence of a declared monetary objective carried much conviction. It is perhaps worth asking whether, instead of adopting a monetary target, the Government had actually increased interest rates the effect would have been more positive. The prevailing view in the Treasury and the Bank at the time was that interest rate increases, or indeed monetary tightening of any other kind, would do little to strengthen sterling or improve confidence. The market's expectations about the future of sterling were not likely to be allayed by the knowledge that an extra 1 per cent (for instance) could be obtained on short-term deposits in London. No one advocated this and indeed, when the Bank briefly contemplated an increase in June, it had second thoughts about the idea and did not pursue it. The Treasury did briefly consider the introduction of import deposits as a credit-reducing measure in September but there were many in the Bank as well as those on the home finance side of the Treasury who thought it a bad idea. Interest rates were raised sharply in October and seemed to have a beneficial effect on market sentiment and they were reinforced by a call for Special Deposits at about the same time. But this was quickly seen to be of limited use and the second part of the call was postponed when the time for payment came. The reintroduction of the Corset in November was intended primarily to ensure that the Chancellor's monetary objectives were met: it came too late to have any real effect on the exchange rate which by then had recovered considerably.

The neglect, if so it can be termed, of the monetary weapon by the Treasury and the Bank contrasts sharply with the keenness of the US Under Secretary (Yeo) for the UK to engineer a bear squeeze on the speculators. He raised this as an issue in a telephone conversation with the Chancellor at the end of September, and the Chancellor was sufficiently interested to ask him to call in on London on his way to the IMF meeting in Manila to develop his case. Meetings took place with the Treasury and the Bank but neither institution was taken by Yeo's arguments. One fear was that a credit squeeze would damage gilt sales, but the prevailing mood was that it would do little to help. The Fund too did not seem to want very much of a contribution to the solution to the British problem from purely monetary measures. They wanted to contain the growth of DCE and the money supply, but this was to be achieved by expenditure cuts, not by interest rate increases or by a credit squeeze. The official holders, who were the main problem, would not have been affected by the sharpening of the credit market, and any reflow of private credit would probably not have had much effect on the exchange rate. To sum up therefore, while it is certainly the case that the July measures failed in their objective, it is far from certain that anything more substantial could be agreed by Ministers, who of course were the collective custodians of public expenditure; and the Treasury's judgement on this, in the light of the enormous political difficulty that was encountered in December, was probably right. But the Treasury and Bank could perhaps have been more vigorous in searching for supplementary measures in the field of direct controls and a squeezing of credit at an earlier stage than they did, although they would probably have had little impact on the official sterling balance holders, who were the main problem, and they would probably have done little to resolve the basic issue.

The charge that during the whole of the crisis there was no clear policy on intervention in the exchange markets is difficult to refute. The record is punctuated with the minutes of meetings and telephone conversations in which the Bank sought authority to spend foreign exchange to meet a bear attack on sterling and the Treasury, sometimes at ministerial level, grudgingly agreed, although with limits that had time and again to be revised. The plain fact of the matter is that there were two conflicting objectives—to prevent the exchange rate from deteriorating out of hand and to conserve the dwindling stock of the reserves. The agreement reached with the Bank on each occasion that the issue came up was a compromise which sometimes leaned in the direction of strong intervention and at others of a reluctant presence. The complete withdrawal of the Bank from the market in early September was an attempt to define, in rather strong terms, an explicit policy, but the results of that move were more than was bargained for and the practice of intervention soon reverted to what it had been beforehand.

The situation developed in 1976 in many ways in an unexpected fashion and it is difficult to envisage what might have been laid down at the outset, or indeed at any stage of the crisis, which would have given the Bank clear operational guidelines. There were conflicting views as to what were the main objectives of policy and those views changed over the course of the crisis. Simple rules of thumb would have been quite inappropriate and there was probably no alternative to the 'spatchcocking' that proved to be the operational mode.

We have already examined the charge that the Treasury did not give sufficiently serious study to the consequences of a 'free float' either in the period before 1976 or during the crisis itself. The charge of inadequate study can also be made against the decision in early June to seek the central bank short-term credit of $5.3 billion. The narrative has brought out that this was an initiative of the Chancellor of the Duchy of Lancaster (Harold Lever), who had throughout the period under review been an advocate of seeking a way out of the difficulty which the fall in sterling presented by way of more external credit. The circumstances of the seeking of this credit were that there was very little involvement by the official Treasury or by the Bank at working level. The experts in those institutions had, throughout the period 1974–76, insisted that the only worthwhile credit the UK should seek should be medium- or long-term. They did not want to face the refinancing problem which short-term credit presented and they had specifically rejected opportunities for foreign borrowing at less than five years maturity. They would certainly never have seen the network of credit swaps between the G10 central banks as relevant to the problem of 1976. This was a view based on the virtual certainty that the UK would not be able to repay debt until its balance of payments had improved and North Sea Oil was flowing in quantity. These officials scarcely had a 'look in' over the weekend of 5–6 June when the credit was hastily put together. The entire negotiation was conducted at Ministerial/Gubernatorial level—and much of it on the telephone without serious analysis.

Lever convinced the Chancellor that the *masse de manoeuvre* which the credit[10] could provide would both reassure the market and provide the Bank with the foreign exchange resources to meet the selling pressure. Senior Treasury officials who were present at the high level meetings which led to the credit did express some doubt about the value of the credit, but not to the extent that it was seriously questioned. The Chancellor clearly saw it as a life-line in a situation where he was rapidly finding himself, so to speak, out of his depth.

The consequences of the credit were chiefly that from then on the UK was more or less bound to have to apply to the Fund and to accept whatever terms could be negotiated. The credit had no confidence or indeed operational

[10] The credit was at first seen as one provided by the USA, and it only later developed into a multilateral facility.

350

value at all, and, because of the problem of repayment, after six months only a quarter of it was drawn. But it did firmly place in the mind of market operators and indeed of overseas governments the fact that the UK would have to make a Fund drawing and this—perhaps perversely—was not conducive to confidence.

Not to have negotiated the credit would have obliged the UK to be more sparing in its use of foreign exchange in the period from June onwards and might have led to a faster fall in the exchange rate. But it might have made it clearer to Ministers that the only remedy to the confidence problem was a policy change in which public expenditure cuts had to play a crucial role. Again this is a counterfactual statement which is not capable of proof. What can be said without question, however, is that the credit did very little, if anything, to resolve the crisis and indeed it probably made it worse rather than better. Whether, if Treasury officials had argued for more time to consider the proposition when it was being rushed through, this would have led to a different outcome is hard to say. But the important principle of civil service life, that is that policy propositions should be properly and seriously considered before being implemented, was not followed in this case, and this cannot have been a good thing.

The Treasury and the Fund negotiations

The final question that we pose in this review is whether the Treasury adopted the 'right' posture in its negotiations with the Fund when they began in November. In one sense this is an easy charge to rebut. Even before discussions with the Fund began, the Ministerial Committee on Economic Strategy (EY) had decided that officials should not discuss possible policy changes with them and this embargo was not lifted for two weeks, in the course of which the Fund had, in effect, taken the initiative and put forward their own proposals. Even the limited suggestion made by the Treasury on 18 November was a Ministerially-authorized proposal and was very limited in its scope. It was therefore left to the Fund to make the running and the Treasury's role thereafter was defensive—as was that of the Ministers. Counterproposals were put forward and criticisms made of the Fund's ideas but the home side were on the back foot throughout and the eventual agreement was structured on lines that the Fund wanted, with performance targets for the PSBR and the growth of DCE and specific expenditure cuts of an agreed size over two financial years.

Although these tactics were the corollary of Ministers' instructions, they were not necessarily at variance with what the Treasury would have proposed. It is true that before the Fund team arrived and before Ministers had issued their interdiction on the making of policy proposals, senior officials did discuss whether the Treasury should put forward its own proposals for a stand-by, and a number of variants were examined. But although some in the Treasury favoured a pro-active position, the majority view was that it was better to see what the Fund's terms were and then negotiate for an adjustment to suit the UK's purposes. This approach, which is what in the event Ministers decided was the best course, turned the application for a stand-by into a negotiation—something the leader of the Fund Mission deplored. He wanted the UK to see the error of its ways and propose a solution which he expected to be close to what the Fund wanted. But the tactics adopted probably resulted in a better outcome than one in which the Fund's ideas were accepted uncritically and in effect put forward as the UK's own proposals.

The first ideas of the Fund were certainly very severe. They wanted a very low DCE objective for the second year and a correspondingly low PSBR. The expenditure cuts they had in mind ran to £3–4 billion by the second year. The process of negotiation and attrition, in which officials and ministers both played their parts, led to a considerable softening of these terms. Indeed, in the end, the Fund accepted a PSBR for the first year which, allowing for the largely cosmetic expenditure saving represented by the BP sale, was actually about the same as the forecast made after the July measures, which the Fund had regarded as quite inadequate. The outcome was in many ways a triumph for the Chancellor and the Prime Minister, for their tactics with the Managing Director, following the outline understanding reached with officials, involved only minimal reductions in expenditure and these were largely offset by new expenditure measures announced in May and in October 1977. It is possible to argue of course that the easing of the terms obtained in negotiation was not something to be desired, that an enforced cut in public expenditure (perhaps offset later on by tax reductions) would have been a better outcome for the British economy. The demand and resource picture would have been little different, but the balance between the public and private sector would have been more favourable to the latter. This may well be so, although it is an arguable proposition, but it was not what was in the minds of Ministers. Although by 1976 they had come to see tax reductions as having considerable merit in helping to ease the squeeze on real incomes generated by the pay policy, they were still noticeably biased towards the protection of public expenditure—as the protracted discussions in Cabinet in December, not to mention July, showed. In terms of Ministerial priorities, the achieving of a mitigation of the Fund's expenditure ideas was a success not a failure: and the tactics employed, although at times rather fierce and hectoring, were, in the event justified.

It is significant that the feeling of the negotiations having been successful was not confined to the British side. The official historian of the Fund for the 1970s records that both the Fund management and the Executive Board regarded the outcome as one of the most successful of all the Fund's excursions into rescue operations. Significantly it was the last of the big stand-bys to be arranged. After 1976 the Fund's role was confined to helping countries from the developing world either by balance of payments support or, in effect, by development aid. And on the UK side the need to go to the Fund for help did not arise again and was not even remotely contemplated in the period that followed. The episode was therefore something of a watershed for both parties. The world they lived in was changed seismically after 1976.

Alternative solutions

The account of what happened in the three years prior to the Fund drawing has referred frequently to the idea of an Alternative Strategy, the protagonists of which argued that rather than tinker with the mechanism for 'managing the economy' a completely different approach was called for. The main champion of this course was Benn and the narrative has brought out how persistently he argued his case, although it has not gone into a rigorous exposition and critique of what would have been involved. In part this is because it attracted very little support from fellow members of the Cabinet, and it had no support whatsoever among officials either in Whitehall or the Bank of England. But a serious student of economic thinking ought perhaps to reflect on what would have been involved and whether the outcome would have been 'better' than the rather messy solution which finally emerged in December 1976.

The elements of the Alternative Strategy were that the Government should take a much more interventionist line on the way British business functioned, directing resources to where they could best serve national ends and involving the trade unions much more intimately in the way business decisions were taken. At the same time, some form of control should be exercised over the volume of goods and services that were imported. In short there would be a degree of centralized planning of a kind that had been resorted to in the Second World War. Benn argued that this had been implicitly accepted by the Labour Party when it concluded the Social Contract in February 1973 and that what the Chancellor was recommending to his colleagues was a departure from that policy.

The supporters of the Alternative Strategy argued that economic policy, as it was conceived in the 1970s, took no account of the tendency of the UK economy to 'underperform' in relation to those of its principal competitors in such areas as productivity growth, net capital formation, import penetration, export performance, innovation, and so on. Moreover an undue proportion of the country's investment was overseas, where the benefits, in terms of employment and income, largely accrued to foreigners. There was some substance, indeed one might say a good deal of substance, in what the critics said by way of appraisal. And it was an undoubted fact that in the fifteen or so years before the events described in this book took place governments of all colours had spent a great deal of time and effort reflecting about the country's poor industrial performance and had introduced a number of measures to remedy some of these perceived shortcomings. Benn and others argued that the measures in place, ranging from investment grants, regional incentives, export credit facilities, etc., all of which were designed not to direct business or to intervene directly in business decision taking but to harness the market to secure what were national priorities, had proved to be ineffective. An additional dimension to a more 'interventionist' policy would be greater involvement of the relevant trade unions in the way businesses were run.

The ideas behind the Alternative Strategy were by no means confined to what might be called the 'Labour Left'. A quite respectable number of economists, as the contemporary correspondence columns of *The Times* bear out, believed both that there was a fundamental weakness in the British manufacturing sector and that some form of protection from import penetration was not only feasible but actually desirable, at any rate for some considerable period during which industry would re-equip itself and become capable of facing foreign competition. The Treasury and indeed the rest of Whitehall, and certainly the Bank, did not share this view and they had little difficulty in persuading their political chiefs that intervention and protection were not the cure for the British disease. Their case rested on three legs:

1 the politico-legal aspect;
2 the damage that protection would do to the long-term efficiency of UK industry;
3 the likelihood of retaliation and hence to the vitiation of any short-term advantages.

The first argument rested on the commitments the UK had entered into under the GATT, the IMF Articles of Agreement, and the Treaty of Accession to the EEC. There was also the OECD Trade Pledge, freely entered into in May 1974. None of these commitments prevented a contracting party from placing restriction on imports for a limited period in response to specific problems, for example a balance of payments crisis, or the desirability of protection for a time to help a particular industry in difficulties. What all the commitments denied was the right to indulge in protection as a deliberate act of general policy for an indefinite period. There was little doubt in the minds of most of the policy makers that there would have been the most enormous difficulty in persuading the UK's Treaty Partners that it had a special case for indefinite protection. In fact the expectation was that resort to generalized controls would have obliged the UK to withdraw, perhaps indefinitely, from the EEC. To Benn, who had campaigned in the 1975 Referendum for withdrawal from the EEC, this would perhaps have been a bonus. But to Whitehall generally and to the leaders of British industry it would have been a disaster.

The second argument rested on the classical economic argument that competition on the widest possible scale was on the whole more likely to lead to improved, not worsened, economic performance. To withdraw from the liberal international trade system which had been steadily developed over the whole post-war period would actually worsen British market competitiveness. Parallels were drawn with the state of industry in countries like North Korea and Albania which had shut themselves away from international competition. This argument was less compelling than the first, for the proponents of protection were able to point to specific cases—that of Germany under Bismarck for example—where protection for a lengthy period had enabled new industries to catch up with the international competition. Most of Whitehall believed that the empirical evidence did not support the case on industrial efficiency grounds for resorting to protection and, as we saw in the narrative, when the possibility of generalized protective measures were put on the table, the argument of efficiency was always deployed against them.

Finally there was the argument that although protection might save imports it would almost certainly lead to a loss of exports as our trading partners retaliated. The end result might be worse than the beginning. This was an argument that was difficult to establish beyond all doubt. But in the world of the 1970s when all the industrialized countries of the world were experiencing both a deep recession and a balance of payments problem it was inconceivable to most policy makers that retaliation would not have been inevitable had the UK resorted to generalized controls on imports.

These arguments were never effectively answered by the proponents of the Alternative Strategy and it is small wonder that whenever the issue came before Ministers, as it did on several occasions in the 1970s, the majority decided against it. When the possibility of a breakdown in the negotiations with the IMF emerged in December 1976, the case for some limited protection during a period of adjustment became a possibility and was offered to Ministers, but it was always envisaged that the measures would be temporary and that the aim would be to revert to the open trade system which had been the aim of British overseas economic policy since the Second World War.

One policy option never seriously considered during the period of our review was that of moving not in the direction of greater control of industry, but of less, in other words of adopting something like the policies of the first days of the Heath Government and those eventually embraced and implemented by the Thatcher Government. It almost goes without saying that the political complexion of the Wilson/Callaghan administration was such that it would have been out of the question for officials to have recommended such a course. Indeed even when options like the pursuit of strict deflationary policies as a means of bringing inflation down were considered by officials, they were quickly dismissed as unacceptable to a government which depended heavily on trade union cooperation. Whitehall was, of course, well aware that there was a substantial body of political and economic opinion that did favour a return to 'free market' principles. The Institute of Economic Affairs, and from the 1970s the Centre for Policy Studies, were actively canvassing policies not unlike those eventually embraced by the Thatcher Government and the Treasury were well aware of the case for such a course. But leaving aside the political impossibility of proposing such a route for a government that was committed to cooperating with the trade union movement, it is undoubtedly the case that a policy of what might be called economic liberalism would only have borne fruit after many years. In the 1970s the UK was confronted with short-term problems—those of getting inflation down quickly, of restoring balance in the external accounts and financing the deficit. The adoption of liberal market policies, even if they could have been introduced overnight, would have done little immediately to deal with these issues. It can reasonably be argued that the fruits of the reforms made by the Thatcher government— lower inflation principally—did not emerge for some fifteen years after they were made. Changing the whole structure of the economy is a long-term business, and in the 1970s the problems confronting the UK would not have been lessened by an overnight switch to a free-market system.

Could it happen again?

What happened in 1976, and indeed in the two previous years, must seem almost incomprehensible to a present-day student of economic policy who accepts the prevailing consensus on economic policy. The Treasury seems now to have no interest in balancing the UK's external current account, even though it is in deficit by an amount as a proportion of GDP which bears comparison with that of the mid-1970s. There are many reasons why the balance of payments has ceased to be a problem for policy makers. One is that the freeing of virtually all restrictions on capital movements has made it much easier for debtor countries to finance their deficits. Another is the elimination of inflation—and certainly differential inflation between major countries—which has had the effect of giving investors confidence to move capital freely in response to investment opportunities and to interest rate differentials. Moreover they now move capital to acquire equity assets in different countries in a way that was not open to them on any scale (except in the United States) in the 1970s. A country's current account deficit does not weigh heavily in their scheme of things, and if a country has a deficit it tends to become financed of its own accord by virtue of free capital movements (assisted by appropriate interest rate changes) or by the willingness of central banks to hold almost limitless amounts of dollar assets. Nor do debtor countries—principally the United States and the United Kingdom—see current account deficits as having a negative or damaging effect. The Bank of England regularly publishes assessments of the UK's aggregate overseas balance sheet[11] and these draw attention to the fact that, although the country is habitually in current account deficit and is therefore driven overall to borrow, the overseas assets of UK residents tend to grow more swiftly than the overseas liabilities, and the extra financial indebtedness is financed by, in effect, equity growth. The 'net worth' of the UK does not seem to be diminishing.[12] Of course another factor which is different at the time of writing (2007) is the absence of large overseas holdings of sterling by monetary authorities. Sterling assets tend now to be held widely among a vast number of primarily private investors, businesses, traders and, to some extent, institutional funds. These are less likely to behave in the way that the 1976 official holders did when they saw the value of their reserves falling. When a currency depreciates today, there tends to be a fairly automatic correction brought about sooner or later as speculators take precautionary action or the monetary authorities make small changes in domestic interest rates. Of course, if there is some perceived 'fundamental disequilibrium' in the sense that a particular matrix of currency valuations is unsustainable (whatever that may mean), the cross-rates will eventually adjust. In such conditions the authorities do not seem to take any vigorous action to counter the movement—and leave it to the market to find its own equilibrium. Finally the UK now has considerably more foreign exchange reserves to handle any intervention it might want to make. All in all the balance of payments is simply not a factor which greatly concerns policy makers anywhere.

There are other economic variables which today count for very little in policy makers' minds, but which were of major concern to those of thirty years ago. The principal is perhaps the level of unemployment. Here the prevailing mood, unlike that of the 1970s, is that governments can do very little of a macro-economic kind to promote employment. The only measures which are relevant are those which improve the effective functioning of markets, particularly the labour market, for example removing restrictions on employers in the way they recruit and treat their workforce and removing legislative barriers to the freedom of that market. This is not the place to debate the effectiveness of such measures to promote employment nor to raise the social questions surrounding such a policy. What is important is that the policy maker of the twenty-first century does not see macro-economic policy (if indeed there is such a thing in the intellectual climate today) as having any direct employment—or indeed economic activity—function. Fiscal policy is not seen as

---

[11] See for instance the article by Stephen Nickell in the *Bank of England Bulletin* Vol 46 Number 2, Summer 2006 and that by John Elliott and Erica Wong Min in Vol 44 Number 4, Winter 2004.

[12] This is true if the assets are valued at market prices, but if book value is the basis the net worth of the UK is significantly negative—see *Bank of England Quarterly Bulletin* Vol 47 No 2 p. 248.

having an equilibrating function. This effectively removes one major constraint his or her predecessor of the 1970s had to cope with. The government's employment objectives and the prevailing 'Keynesian' ethos placed a huge restriction on the choice of instruments which could be used to achieve any desired aim: low inflation, a balance of payments surplus, etc. And in the 1970s policy, to some extent under a Conservative as well as a Labour Government, was constrained by the existence and strength of the trade union movement. Again no value judgement is made here about this factor. But it did act as a powerful influence on economic policy making in a way that is utterly unlike its role today. Many of the rigidities which lay in the economic framework of the 1970s have disappeared, perhaps in the UK more than elsewhere, but the movement has been spread throughout the developed world. To the classical economist these developments can only be welcomed—and they have certainly led to policy makers having a quieter life than their predecessors of three decades ago. Whether that is the end of the argument, however, is a different matter. It is not one which this book is intended to address. The question whether in the long run economic welfare in its widest sense generally—and globally—is enhanced by the minimizing of government interference with the working of the free market can be debated, as can even more controversially the question of whether the social costs of the free market are sufficiently brought into the aggregate balance sheet of reckoning. The 1970s does not offer much guidance on this question, for they presented an environment which subjected the 'managed economy' to enormous strains of a kind not seen since. It will be interesting to see how, when they come, as they undoubtedly will, the world of the twenty-first century responds to the sort of shocks and strains that were inflicted on the world of thirty years ago and whether the response will be seen to be adequate.

Sources and Bibliography

My principal sources have been Treasury, Cabinet Office, Prime Ministerial, Bank of England, Department of Employment, and IMF files of the period 1973 to 1977. Some of these are now in the National Archives (NA), and for those which have been transferred I have given the NA prefix and reference according to the following code:

Treasury	T
Cabinet Office	CAB
Prime Minister's Office	PREM
Department of Employment	LAB

I have in general given in the footnotes the National Archives reference to the document referred to, but here and there, because at the time of writing the documents had not yet been released and numbered, I have given the Departmental file reference number. I have therefore included in the list of sources several Departmental file reference titles and numbers. Anyone wishing to consult such files when they have been transferred to the National Archives will be able to do so by referring to the reference I have given in the 'Browser' page of the NA website. I have, where I have been able to do so, given a translation of the two references in a table below. This is not however an exhaustive list.

For the Bank of England and IMF references I have simply given the file number and title.

I National Archive Files

The main NA files consulted are as follows:

Treasury files

T 171—Chancellor of the Exchequer files
/1067	The Budget Judgement 1974
/1148	The mini-Budget and the Autumn Budget 1974
/1151–52	The mini-Budget 1974
/1166	Chancellor's Meetings 1974
/1181	The External Side
/1182	Economic Strategy
/1228–31	Import Controls—DELVE

| /1237 | Chancellor's Meetings 1975 |

T 233—Home Finance Division files

/2658	Financial forecast—Autumn Budget 1974
/2692–95	Foreign currency borrowing by local authorities and nationalized industries
/2722–23	Building Societies financial crisis
/2837–38	Monetary Policy Group 1974 and 1975
/2842	Bank of England support operations for secondary banks
/2857–60	Financial forecast November 1974–July 1975
/2872	Building Societies £500 million Loan 1974
/2992	Management of the Exchange Rate
/3018	Support Operations in the Property Market
/3021	Control of DCE

T 267—Treasury Historical Memoranda

/8–10	The Government and Wages—1945–60
/33	The Sterling Agreements. 1968
/36	The Collapse of the Bretton Woods System, 1968–73

T 277—Committee Section files

/2859–60	Sterling Agreements Review Committee
/2880–81	Chancellor of the Exchequer's visit to Saudi Arabia—December 1974
/2866	Committee on Vast Surpluses of Oil Producers
/2949–52	Public Expenditure Survey Committee (PESC) 1974
/2920–22	Working Party on International Monetary Reform
/2904–05	Review of Fixed Rate export and shipbuilding credit
/2928–29	Medium-term Assessment Committee (MTAC) papers 1974
/2960–61	Sterling Agreements Review Committee
/2962–63	Monetary Policy Group (MPG) papers—1974
/2984–85	Chancellor's visit to Iran 1975
/2959	Short-term Economic Policy Committee (STEP) papers—1974
/3053–59	Policy Coordinating Committee (PCC) Memoranda 1975
/3061–65	PESC—1975
/3034–35	MPG papers—1975
/3029	MTAC papers 1975
/3075	STEP—1975
/3175–79	PCC papers and minutes—1976
/3189–92	PESC memoranda—1976
/3136	Working Party on Import Restraints 1976
/3204–05	STEP—1976
/3214–15	MPG—1976

T 331—Supply Divisions

/853	Mini-Budget July 1974
/945	Claims on the contingency reserve
/947	Goldman study of expenditure management and control

/959   Planning for the 1974 Expenditure Survey
/961–971   Planning for the 1975 Expenditure Survey
/976–983   Expenditure Savings for the 1975 Budget
/991   Public Expenditure Survey—nationalized industries policy

T 338—Economic Planning
/189   Counter-inflation policy 1970–73
/247–48   NIF 1974
/269   Treasury Unified Model
/292   Improvements in the linkages between the MTA and the PESC
/296   Exchange rate and sterling balances
/305–06   NIF 1975
/319   Unified Model Development Group

T 354—Overseas Finance Divisions—IM files
/227–223   IMF Article VIII Consultations 1974
/288   IMF Article VIII Consultations 1975
/380   Working Party on International Monetary Reform
/439   OECD Trade Pledge

T 357—Prices and Incomes
/316–317   Threshold agreements—General policy
/389   Payroll tax and subsidy
/424–426   Contingency planning on pay
/427   Contingency planning on pay—the Elkan scheme
/428   Contingency planning on pay—tax schemes
/431–435   Pay policy July 1974 onwards
/486   Prime Minister's meetings with TUC and CBI

T 358—Overseas Finance Divisions—RMSA, BP, and OF files
/57–60   Foreign currency borrowing by the public sector
/80–82   Unilateral declaration of sterling guarantees
/83   Sterling balances after March 1974
/105   £ exchange rate and balance of payments in the medium term
/120–133   UK interest rates and management of the exchange rate in the medium term
/140   Financing the oil deficit
/163   £ guarantees after December 1974
/176   HMG loan of $2.5 billion in March 1974
/187   Loans from Saudi Arabia
/188   Visit of Chancellor to Saudi Arabia—December 1974
/189–190   Iranian loan to the UK—July 1974
/195–201   External Financing Strategy 1974 and 1975

T 364—Permanent Secretary's Personal Files

Treasury reference	NA reference	Subject
DW 012	/13	Second Secretaries Meetings 1974
DW 013	/14	Second Secretaries Meetings 1975

DW 014	/15	Second Secretaries Meetings 1976
DW 015	/16–17	Economic Strategy
DW 033	/23–25	Import Controls
DW 036	/30–33	Sterling
DW 039	/35	Strategy Options
DW 047	/40	Reflation and the Balance of Payments
DW 056	/45–48	Public Expenditure—1976
DW 062	/50–52	IMF Application
DW 080	/68	Burmah v Bank of England
DW 085	/56	Contingency Planning
DW 098		Steering Committee on Economic Policy (misc Correspondence)
DW 100		Monetary Policy Group
DW 102	/61	Management of the Exchange Rate
DW 128		Economic Strategy and the Exchange Rate
DW 136		Foreign Exchange
DW 146		The NIF
DW 172		Economic Strategy and Forecasting
DW 198		
DW 433	/70	Spring Budget 1975
DW 442		Budget 1975

T 371—General Expenditure Division
/20–23   Measures to alleviate unemployment—1975

T 381—Overseas Finance (RSMA, BP, and OF files continued)
/1–4   External Financing Strategy
/5–9   The Safety Net
/10–11   Central Bank credit $5.3 billion
/12–19   IMF Drawing 1975 and 1976

Cabinet Office Files

CAB 128/54–60   Cabinet Minutes 1974–76
CAB 129/175–193   Cabinet Memoranda 1974–76
CAB 130/819   MISC 91
CAB 134/3789–09   MES papers and minutes 1974
CAB 134/3738–40   Ministerial Committee on Economic Policy—1974
CAB 134/3838–40   Steering Committee on Economic Policy (SCE)—1974
CAB 134/3929–30   MES Papers and minutes 1975

CAB 134/4025–27	EY Papers and minutes 1976
CAB 134/4048	MES Papers and minutes 1976

Prime Minister's Files

PREM 16/343	Counter-Inflation Policy June 1975
PREM 16/368	Prime Minister's Meetings with Governor of Bank of England
PREM 16/371	Removal of £ guarantees
PREM 16/500	Chrysler Corporation
PREM 16/799–808	Safety Net and IMF negotiations
PREM 16/805	Prime Minister's discussions with German Chancellor

Department of Employment Files

LAB 77/22	Secretary of State's diary
LAB 77/49	TUC and the Social Contract

II Institutional Files

The following are departmental files of the various institutions referred to.

A. Treasury files

1. COMMITTEE SECTION

STEP (74), (75) and (76) Short-Term Economic Policy Committee
MPG (75) and (76) Treasury/Bank Monetary Policy Group
PESC (74), (75) and (76) Public Expenditure Survey Committee
IGCC (75) Interdepartmental Group on Cash Control
PCC (75) and (76) Policy Coordinating Committee

2. GEP DIVISION

GEP 8/01	Select Committee on Public Expenditure
GEP 8/9/01	'Financing of Public Expenditure 1976'
GEP 8/9/03	'The July 1976' cuts
GEP 8/78/01	'Cmnd 6393'
GEP 8/159/01	'Announced Changes to Cmnd 6393'
GEP 9/11/01	Godley report on public expenditure
GEP 9/26/01	Measures to alleviate unemployment 1975
GEP 9/29/01	IMF Consultations 1975
GEP 9/29/02	Public Expenditure and the IMF 1976

3. HF DIVISION

HF 9/01	Two-tier interest rates
HF 9/02	Interest rate policy
HF 12/2/02	A variable rate bond
HF 27/34/01	Tap stocks and gilt-edged
HF 27/386/01	Tax relief on dividends for non-residents
HF 33/04	Economic Packages December 1976
HF 35/04	Monetary Targets

4. OF DIVISION (IM PAPERS)

IM 1/33/02	Implications of IMF exchange rate policy for UK
IM 1/145/01	US Proposal for a super-credit tranche
IM 34/5/01	Visits of US officials to UK
IM 38/268/04	IMF Consultations November 1976
IM 38/268/06	IMF Consultations November 1977
IM 119/97/01	Safety Net for the Sterling Balances
IM 198/01	IMF Consultations May 1976

5. OF DIVISION (RESERVES MANAGEMENT AND STERLING AREA PAPERS)

2F(RMSA) 8/9/01	UK Official Reserves
2F(RMSA)12/35/02	Future of Sterling Area Agreements
2F(RMSA)22/24/01	A Gold-indexed Bond
2F(RMSA)32/100/01	Exchange rate and medium-term policy (T358/105)
2F(RMSA)32/100/02	Review of External Financing (pre 1976) (T358/195–201)
2F(RMSA)33/65/01	Public Sector Borrowing overseas
2F(RMSA)33/65/04	UK borrowing in Iran
2F(RMSA)33/65/05	UK borrowing in Saudi Arabia
2F(RMSA)33/65/06	Public Sector borrowing
2F(RMSA) 98/33/03	UK Interest Rates and Reserves Management (pre 1976)
BP32/100/02	Review of External Financing (1976) (T381/1–4)
BP62/24/02	Swap facility with NYFRB
BP98/16/02	Safety Net facility
BP98/33/01	UK Interest Rates and Management of the Exchange Rate
BP98/33/02	Central Bank Credit $5.3 billion
BP98/33/03	UK Interest Rates and Reserves Management (1976)
BP122/24/01	IMF Drawings 1975 and 1976
BP138/24/01	HMG loan of $2.5 billion March 1974
BP161 /38/01	Visit by officials to Saudi Arabia

B. *Bank of England files*

2A 77/1	The Central Bank Credit of June 1976
4A 100/7	Official Sterling Holdings
4A 115/1	Movements in Sterling Balances

5A 175/8	The Definition of DCE
6A 399/1	Article VIII Consultations with IMF May 1976
C 43/779	Exchange Rate Strategy
G 3/285	IMF Drawing 1976

C. *International Monetary Fund files*

SM/75/137	Staff Report on Art VIII Consultations with the UK June 1975
SM/76/153	Staff Report on Art VIII Consultations with the UK July 1976
SM/74/249	1975 Oil Facility
SM/76/88	Policy on the Exchange Rate
SM/76/106	Policy on the Exchange Rate
EBS/76/519	UK Request for a Standby—Dec 1976
EBS/76/521	General Arrangements to Borrow (1976)

III Parliamentary Papers

I have consulted and quoted from the following Parliamentary Papers.

Parliamentary Debates and Questions: The reference is simply to *Hansard* with the relevant date

Public Expenditure White Papers

December 1973	Cmnd 5519—Parly Papers Session 1973–74 Vol V p 857
February 1975	Cmnd 5879—Parly Papers Session 1974–75 Vol XX p 705
February 1976	Cmnd 6393—Parly Papers Session 1975–76 Vol XXV p 603
February 1977	Cmnd 6721—Parly Papers Session 1976–77 Vol XXIII
February 1978	Cmnd 7049—Parly Papers Session 1977–78 Vol XXVII p 797
February 1979	Cmnd 7439—Parly Papers Session 1978–79 Vol XVIII
November 1979	Cmnd 7746

Financial Statements and Budget Report

March 1974	Parly Papers Session 1974 Vol VIII
November 1974	Parly Papers Session 1974–75 Vol XIX
April 1975	Parly Papers Session 1974–75 Vol XX
April 1976	Parly Papers Session 1975–76 Vol XXV
April 1977	Parly Papers Session 1976–77 Vol XXIII
April 1978	Parly Papers Session 1977–78 Vol XXVII

Miscellaneous Command Papers

Beveridge Report	Cmd 6404
Employment Policy Report	Cmd 6527
Radcliffe Report	Cmnd 827

Plowden Report	Cmnd 1432
Public Expenditure—A New Approach	Cmnd 4017
The Attack on Inflation October 1973	Cmnd 5446
The Attack on Inflation July 1975	Cmnd 6151
Approach to an Industrial Strategy	Cmnd 6315
Cash Limits	Cmnd 6440
Monetary Control	Cmnd 7858

Other Parliamentary Papers
Select Committee on Expenditure   13th Report Parliamentary
                                                   Papers 1975–76 Vol XXXI

IV Other Published Sources

Various Newspapers—references made in text.

Books and Journals

Bacon, R. and Eltis, W. *Britain's Economic Problem* (London, Macmillan 1976)

Barnett, Joel *Inside the Treasury* (London, Andre Deutsch 1982)

Benn, Tony *Against the Tide—Diaries 1973–76* (London, Hutchinson 1990)

Bernstein, Karen 'The IMF and Deficit Countries: The Case of Great Britain 1974–77' (Typescript available from University Microfilms, UMI, Reference no 8329691)

Blackaby, Frank *British Economic Policy 1960–74* (Cambridge, Cambridge University Press 1978)

Buira, Ariel 'An Analysis of IMF Conditionality' (Oxford University, Dept of Economics 2002)

Burch, Martin *British Cabinet Politics: Public Expenditure and the IMF* (Ormskirk, Hesketh 1980)

Burk, Kathleen and Cairncross, Alec *Goodbye Great Britain* (London, Yale University Press 1992)

Callaghan, James *Time and Chance* (London, Collins 1987)

Castle, Barbara *The Castle Diaries 1964–76* (London, Weidenfeld and Nicolson 1980)

Contemporary Record Vol 3 No 2 'Symposium: 1976—IMF Crisis'

Crosland, Anthony *The Future of Socialism* (London, Jonathan Cape 1956)

Crosland, Susan *Tony Crosland* (London, Jonathan Cape 1982)

De Vries, Margaret Garritsen *The International Monetary Fund 1972–1978* (Washington, IMF 1985)

Dell, Edmund *A Hard Pounding: Political and Economic Crisis 1974–76* (Oxford, Oxford University Press 1991)

Donoughue, Bernard *Prime Ministers: The Conduct of Policy under Harold Wilson and James Callaghan* (London, Jonathan Cape 1987)

Fay, Stephen and Young, Hugo "The Day the £ Nearly Died" (*The Sunday Times* 14, 21, and 28 May 1978)

Fforde, John *The Bank of England and Public Policy 1941–58* (Cambridge, Cambridge University Press 1992)

Frenkel, Jacob and Johnson, Harry (eds) *The Monetary Approach to the Balance of Payments* (London, Allen & Unwin 1976)

Friedman, Milton *A Monetary History of the United States 1867–1960* (Princeton, Princeton University Press 1963)

Friedman, Milton 'The Role of Monetary Policy' (*American Economic Review* March 1968)

Harmon, Mark *The British Labour Government and the 1976 IMF Crisis* (London, Macmillan 1997)

Healey, Denis *The Time of My Life* (London, Michael Joseph 1989)

Hickson, Kevin 'The IMF Crisis and British Politics' (British Library DX No 57064 DSC)

International Monetary Fund *The Monetary Approach to the Balance of Payments* (Washington, IMF 1977)

International Monetary Fund 'Theoretical Aspects of the Design of Fund-Supported Adjustment Programs' (Washington, IMF Occasional Paper No 55 1987)

Keegan, William and Pennant-Rea, Rupert *Who Runs the Economy* (London, Maurice Temple Smith 1978)

Middlemas, Keith *Power, Competition and The State* (Basingstoke, Macmillan 1986)

OECD *The Problem of Rising Prices* (Paris, OECD 1961)

Pliatzky, Leo *Getting and Spending* (Oxford, Basil Blackwell 1982)

Polak, Jacques 'The Changing Nature of IMF Conditionality' (*Essays in International Finance* No 184 Princeton University 1991)

Reid, Margaret *The Secondary Banking Crisis 1973–75* (Macmillan 1992)

Sayers, R. S. *The Bank of England 1891–1944* (Cambridge, Cambridge University Press 1976)

Whitehead, Philip *The Writing on the Wall* (London, Michael Joseph 1985)

Zawadzki, K. K. F. *Competition and Credit Control* (Oxford, Basil Blackwell 1981)

V Statistics

Most of the statistics quoted are derived from the following publications for the relevant period and can be verified from them. Where I have quoted from contemporary publications it is possible that subsequent corrections to the series may have changed the figures, but where I have been able to check these corrections they have proved to be small. Some statistics (e.g. the scale of intervention by the Bank of England in the currency markets) are no longer verifiable as they are derived from unpublished material and where these are quoted the source is given.

Bank of England Quarterly Bulletin 1974–77
Economic Trends 1974–77
Financial Statistics 1974–77
Statistical Digest 1974–77

International statistics, where quoted, are derived from the *UN Statistics Yearbook* 1979–80 or from the website of the BIS.

The only other sources of statistical material published as such have been the websites of the Office of National Statistics and the Bank of England.

Where figures have been quoted from non-statistical official publications, for example the Public Expenditure White Papers, these have been identified in the footnotes.

In some places in the narrative I have given a rate of growth of a particular variable over a time-period, for example the rate of increase of public expenditure over a four-year time span. The method I have used was simply to calculate the annualized compound rate of increase by taking the nth root of the quotient of the two terminal figures where n is the number of years covered.

Index

Index